Evidence

Evidence

Inns of Court School of Law
Institute of Law, City University, London

OXFORD
UNIVERSITY PRESS

OXFORD

UNIVERSITY PRESS

Great Clarendon Street, Oxford OX2 6DP

Oxford University Press is a department of the University of Oxford.
It furthers the University's objective of excellence in research, scholarship,
and education by publishing worldwide in

Oxford New York

Auckland Cape Town Dar es Salaam Hong Kong Karachi
Kuala Lumpur Madrid Melbourne Mexico City Nairobi
New Delhi Shanghai Taipei Toronto

With offices in

Argentina Austria Brazil Chile Czech Republic France Greece
Guatemala Hungary Italy Japan Poland Portugal Singapore
South Korea Switzerland Thailand Turkey Ukraine Vietnam

Oxford is a registered trade mark of Oxford University Press
in the UK and in certain other countries

Published in the United States
by Oxford University Press Inc., New York

© Inns of Court School of Law, 2005

British Library Cataloguing in Publication Data
Data available

Library of Congress Cataloging in Publication Data
Data available

Typeset by Newgen Imaging Systems (P) Ltd., Chennai, India
Printed in Great Britain
on acid-free paper by
Ashford Colour Press, Gosport, Hampshire

ISBN 0-19-928153-X 978-0-19-928153-4

1 3 5 7 9 10 8 6 4 2

FOREWORD

It is a privilege to write this Foreword, following the tradition set by my predecessor, the Hon. Mr Justice Elias.

The Bar Vocational Course (BVC) bridges the gap between completion of a university degree and the start of a professional working life, whether by way of pupillage preliminary to a career at the Bar, or otherwise. These Manuals are geared to the practical and professional approach that is central to the BVC. Updated and revised, the Manuals form an integral part of the student's vocational training; as such, they are an important ingredient in the constant drive to raise standards in the public interest.

The Manuals are written by staff at the Inns of Court School of Law (ICSL). The range and coverage of the Manuals have grown steadily. They are intended to provide a useful resource for all concerned in the training of legal skills, hopefully at whichever validated institution such training takes place.

Legal vocational training does not stand still; the ICSL and authors would welcome feedback from any source, which may assist to improve the Manuals in the future. Any such comments should be addressed to the BVC Course Director at the ICSL.

Finally a word of thanks is appropriate to the publishers for their enthusiasm and efficiency in arranging production and publication of the Manuals.

The Hon. Mr Justice Gross
Chairman, Advisory Board of the Institute of Law
City University, London
October 2004

OUTLINE CONTENTS

DETAILED CONTENTS

PREFACE

The law of evidence regulates the means by which facts may be proved in courts of law. It is for this reason that mastery of its basic principles and rules is essential to the practitioner. All too often, both before a trial and during its conduct in court, the rules of evidence must be applied on the spur of the moment, without the opportunity to consult books or articles. Perhaps instructions have been belatedly received. Perhaps a problem arises at the trial itself: during examination in chief, cross-examination or re-examination; when the admissibility of an item of evidence is suddenly questioned; or when it becomes necessary to deal with a judicial intervention or to make submissions about the contents of a summing-up.

This Manual, by its combination of text, materials, examples and problems, aims to develop not only a knowledge of evidence law, but also understanding of the ways in which it is applied in practice.

The law is stated on the basis that all the provisions of the Criminal Justice Act 2003 are fully in force.

TABLE OF CASES

TABLE OF STATUTES

International legislation

TABLE OF SECONDARY LEGISLATION

Fundamentals of evidence

1.1 What is evidence?

Before looking at the rules of evidence (ie, the law governing what evidence will or will not be allowed into court) it is useful to be clear about some of the matters of fundamental importance in understanding how evidence works. The subject matter of this chapter is therefore of considerable importance. You will find that the key terms that are being referred to in this chapter are used throughout this book.

1.1.1 Facts and law

The legal sanctions that the court can impose depend upon the proven facts of the case. Therefore, before a judge in the Crown Court can impose a sentence on a defendant, the defendant must be proven to have committed an offence. Further, the type of sentence imposed on the defendant depends on which offence or offences that defendant is proven to have committed: in effect, which factual allegations the court has accepted. Likewise a civil court could not award damages to a claimant for three breaches of contract if the claimant had only proven a single breach. Furthermore, the amount of any damages awarded would depend on how much loss the claimant could prove flowed from that breach.

It will be seen therefore that the court's power to exercise legal sanctions and to apply legal rules depends on *proof* of particular facts. The function of the law is to establish which facts have to be proven in any given case.

1.1.2 Proof

The word 'proof' is used commonly in evidential discussion. Later, in this and the next chapter, you will be introduced to concepts such as 'burden of proof', 'standard or proof' and 'probative value'. Before defining these terms, it is worth attempting a working definition of the key word 'proof'.

The legal meaning of proof is not so different from its ordinary meaning. In ordinary speech 'proof' is most commonly used to mean *either* the process of convincing a person of a particular conclusion by the use of facts and logic *or* successfully convincing a person of a particular conclusion in that way. Therefore if A says to B, 'Prove it', A means that B should produce facts and make arguments on the point in question and that the facts and arguments produced should be such as will convince A. It is worth noting the following points:

(a) Proof is achieved by combining facts and arguments.

(b) There is an implicit standard below which a conclusion would be 'unproven'. Some things are more difficult to prove than others. The more improbable the desired conclusion the harder it will be to prove it. By 'harder' we mean that more facts and better arguments will be required to convince the person to reach the conclusion in question.

(c) Facts and arguments are not all equally valuable in proving conclusions. We expect anyone deciding whether something is proven to treat facts and arguments differently for a variety of reasons. Some have less relevance or bearing on the matter in question. Some facts relied upon may be less reliable than others whether because the source of the fact is suspect or because there is an impression that the fact does not give the whole picture.

(d) There is always someone who has to decide whether something has been proven. Proof requires a tribunal to determine whether something is proven.

The approach of the courts to proof is essentially the same as that set out above. However, as one might expect from the formal nature of courts, proof is subject to a system of rules and practices. These rules and practices are at the heart of the rules of evidence and most of this Manual will examine how the formal process of proof is based on these rules and practices. It is therefore worth considering some of the ways in which the points noted above are applied in a formal, legal setting.

1.1.2.1   Facts and arguments

The legal process of proof in court also requires a combination of facts and arguments to prove cases. The rules of evidence and of court procedure draw a distinction between facts, which are proven by the evidence (usually the calling of witnesses) and arguments, which are advanced later on by the advocates in the case. For example, an advocate in a Crown Court trial should not comment on the evidence given by a witness while conducting cross-examination (see the *Advocacy Manual*). Rather he or she will make comments upon that evidence (ie, make arguments about it) during a closing speech after all of the facts have been put before the jury (see the *Civil Litigation* and *Criminal Litigation Manuals*).

1.1.2.2   Standards of proof

Every allegation in a case must be established to a particular 'standard of proof'. The standard for any particular allegation is set by the law. It is in this context that phrases you may have heard before like 'beyond reasonable doubt' and 'on the balance of probabilities' are used. The law has also regulated who must prove facts. The 'prove it' demand is generally but not always imposed upon the party bringing the case (ie, the claimant in civil cases and the prosecution in criminal cases) but, given the complexity of the litigation process, this is not always so. The requirement that a party prove a particular conclusion is called the 'burden of proof'. We shall examine the burden and standard of proof more closely in **Chapter 2**.

1.1.2.3   Facts and arguments are variable

The rules of evidence recognise that facts are equally useful in proving conclusions. While the rules of evidence generally seek to admit all facts that might prove a conclusion ('relevant facts') there are numerous safeguards that aim to prevent the trial process being undermined by the reception of weak evidence.

The formalised trial process has rules for how facts are proven (see **1.8** below) and there are also rules preventing some facts from being proven if the source of the fact in question is in some way potentially unreliable (for example, 'hearsay' evidence **Chapters 10** and **11** and the requirement that an expert is proven to be an expert witness before expert opinion evidence can be given: see **Chapter 15**).

We shall see that some of these rules aim to prevent parties from wasting the time and resources of the court with facts that have little value in deciding the issues of the case (for example, rules that limit the extent to which parties can prove that witnesses are of bad character: see **Chapter 8 and 9**). Other rules seek to prevent the court from being distracted from deciding the real issues of the case. There is therefore a process of filtering out some facts from cases. This is more frequently the case in criminal trials than in civil trials.

At the heart of this filtering process is the concept of 'weight' (see **1.3.2** below), which is simply a way of evaluating the capacity of some facts, or combinations of facts and arguments, to prove conclusions. The weight to be attached to any fact (or facts) is significant in two ways. First, it often determines whether the court will admit evidence of the fact at all (for example, where the fact seeks to prove the bad character of a criminal defendant: see **Chapter 8**). Secondly, it is used to decide whether the fact or facts are sufficient to reach a particular standard of proof (as noted above and see **Chapter 2**).

1.1.2.4   The tribunal of fact

A general term for the person or persons who must decide whether the facts in question are proven is 'the tribunal of fact' or the 'fact-finder'. Quite who this is depends on which court a party is appearing in. The tribunal of fact in a Crown Court trial is the jury. In the Crown Court the jury is responsible for reaching factual decisions and the judge for deciding legal issues. This raises an important distinction that we will return to later (**1.8**). The 'law-decider' is generally referred to as the 'tribunal of law'. The legal decisions include matters such as the appropriate sentence for a person who has been found guilty of an offence or the effect of the frustration of a contract. However, legal decisions also include decisions such as whether particular facts (ie, evidence) should be put in front of a tribunal of fact at all. Therefore the tribunal of law may occasionally have to examine the facts (and particularly the weight to be attached to the facts) to decide legal issues. For example, a judge deciding whether a confession was obtained unlawfully would have to decide the *factual* questions surrounding the curcumstances in which it was obtained in order to reach a *legal* conclusion as to the admissibility of the confessions.

The tribunal of fact and the tribunal of law are often the same person or group of people. Most civil cases are heard by a single judge who determines both the facts of the case and the legal issues. This is also so with criminal cases heard in the magistrates' court. Although the fact-finder and the tribunal of law are the same in many cases the distinction between tribunals of fact and law is important.

1.1.3   Evidence

Facts and arguments combine to prove conclusions and this is so in cases brought before the courts as much as anywhere else. However, not all things asserted as 'facts' are accepted as such by other people. The term 'fact' is slightly misleading. The meaning given to the word by the *Oxford English Dictionary* is, '*Something that has really occurred or is actually the case; . . . hence, a particular truth known by actual observation or authentic testimony, as opposed to what is merely inferred*'. Although there is no formal definition of the term in law the word is most correctly used to illustrate matters that are accepted to have occurred by the tribunal of fact. The tribunal of fact will consider various matters put before it and decide whether the alleged thing is true or not (ie, whether the alleged thing is a 'fact'). The matters it receives to reach that decision are 'evidence of that facts'. Looking again at the definition given above, a tribunal of fact will not be relying on 'actual observation' and so will have to rely on 'authentic testimony' to reach its conclusions.

We shall see that testimony is given a particular meaning at law but for the time being we can take testimony to mean evidence and note that evidence establishes facts.

It is worth noting at this point that evidence will not only prove a fact but that a proven fact may combine with other evidence (or proven facts) to prove some other fact. In other words a fact may be evidence of another fact.

In essence, evidence is that which proves facts and the 'proof' is the process of converting evidence into facts.

1.2 Facts in issue

It was noted above that all issues in a case must be proven. These are often termed the 'facts in issue'. Identifying the facts in issue is not as straightforward as it might first appear. First, what the facts in issue are in a particular case depends on the relevant law. Secondly, because of the adversarial nature of litigation in England and Wales, the parties to a case will make allegations and counter-allegations. A defendant may either challenge the allegations of the prosecution (in criminal cases) or claimant (in civil cases) or may raise some entirely different legal defence. Clearly, these counter-allegations have to be resolved. Finally, quite what the facts in issue are at trial is affected by rules of procedure (ie, rules dictating how the trial process will run). This means that there are differences between civil and criminal cases.

1.2.1 Criminal cases

1.2.1.1 General principle

In criminal cases, whether in the Crown Court or a magistrates' court, a trial starts with a process of arraignment or plea. The defendant is accused formally of the commission of an offence and asked to plead to it. If the plea is 'not guilty', *all* of the elements of the offence are put in issue (ie, the defendant has required the prosecution to prove them all). Furthermore the defendant may raise defences during trial which will also be put in issue.

Therefore every element of the offence for which a defendant is being tried must be established in criminal cases. In addition any defence alleged and for which some evidence is admitted (see the 'evidential burden' in **Chapter 2**) will become a fact in issue. In *R v Sims* [1946] KB 531, CCA, Lord Goddard CJ said (at p 539):

The prosecution has to prove the whole of their case including the identity of the accused, the nature of the act and the existence of any necessary knowledge or intent.

Therefore the facts in issue in a criminal case are:

- the identity of the culprit;
- the *actus reus* of the offence;
- the *mens rea* of the offence; and
- any defences raised at trial.

1.2.2 Civil cases

1.2.2.1 General principle

In civil cases, the process of making allegations begins much earlier and is more sophist-icated than in criminal cases. Cases are initiated by the 'statement of case' process (see *Civil*

Litigation Manual). The claimant will make detailed allegations of some particular civil wrong (such as a breach of contract) in his or her 'particulars of claim'. The defendant will respond by way of a defence (assuming the defendant does not fully admit liability at this point). The defence will respond to each particular allegation made by the claimant.

The Civil Procedure Rules 1998 (CPR), r 16.5(1), provides:

In his defence, the defendant must state—

(a) *which of the allegations . . . he denies;*

(b) *which allegations he is unable to admit or deny, but which he requires the claimant to prove; and*

(c) *which allegations he admits.*

Denial of an allegation puts the party denying under an obligation to state reasons for denial (CPR, r 16.5(2)). The requirement to prove in paragraph (b) recognises that there may be allegations made by a claimant that a defendant is simply not able to form a judgment or produce evidence upon (particularly matters such as loss and damage that may be within the personal knowledge of the claimant).

Insofar as a party admits an allegation made by another party it ceases to be a fact in issue. Otherwise the allegation remains a fact in issue.

In addition to responding to the case alleged by a claimant a defendant may raise new issues that would constitute a defence. For example, even if a defendant admits to having entered into a contract with the claimant, she might allege the existence of a frustrating event (ie, raise the defence of frustration). This would be done in her defence and would raise a new fact in issue.

There is therefore much more flexibility as to what may or not be a fact in issue in a civil case. First of all, the parties have far more control over what might be a fact in issue before trial. Secondly, there is a greater variety of subject matter being litigated in civil courts. While all criminal cases are composed of an *actus reus* and a *mens rea*, civil cases are not so strictly categorised. Each area of substantive civil law will have different potential facts in issue.

1.2.3 Significance of facts in issue

It might be wondered why a lawyer will bother to identify the facts in issue in a case. In fact many lawyers who have experience in particular areas probably identify the facts in issue by instinct. The phrase 'facts in issue' is in fact not used widely in the courts. However, it is useful in understanding how evidence proves cases. By identifying the facts in issue in a case, three things are achieved:

(a) A list of issues are identified so that it is possible to go on to determine *who* it is that must prove which issue. In other words identifying the facts in issue is the first step in determining who bears the various *burdens of proof* in a case. This is dealt with in more detail in **Chapter 2**.

(b) This list places limits on the evidence that should and can be admitted at trial. The courts will not entertain evidence that does not assist in resolving the matters in dispute (ie, the facts in issue). In other words the facts in issue determine the *relevance* of evidence. Relevance in turn is one of the factors that determines the *admissibility* of evidence: evidence that is not relevant to one or more fact in issue is inadmissible at trial.

(c) A lawyer is thereby better able to analyse the case, to identify evidence to be admitted and to formulate arguments about evidence.

1.3 Proof concepts

The rules of evidence are based on four very important concepts: relevance, weight, probative value and prejudicial effect. One or more of these concepts underpins every rule of evidence.

1.3.1 Relevance

As noted in **1.2.3** above, the concept of relevance is fundamental to all evidence. Evidence must be relevant for it to be admissible in both civil and criminal cases. Furthermore, a clear understanding of the relevance of a particular piece of evidence is necessary in applying other rules of admissibility such as the rule against hearsay.

1.3.1.1 Definition

There have been a number of attempts to define relevance. In *DPP v Kilbourne* [1973] AC 729, Lord Simon said (at p 756):

> Evidence is relevant if it is logically probative or disprobative of some matter which requires proof. It is sufficient to say . . . that relevant (ie logically probative or disprobative) evidence is evidence which makes the matter . . . more or less probable.

Note the stress upon logic in the above except. Relevance does not stem from intuition or feelings about a particular piece of evidence but from how one might rationalise and explain it. An advocate will often highlight the relevance of particular pieces of evidence in his or her closing speech in order to persuade them to reach a particular conclusion.

A slightly more complicated definition was given by Stephen in his *Digest of the Law of Evidence*, where it was said:

> Any two facts to which it was applied are so related to each other that according to the common course of events one either taken by itself or in connection with other facts proves or renders probable the . . . existence or non-existence of the other.

It follows that evidence does not have to *prove* a matter to be relevant. Rather, it has to *assist* in proving a matter. As Stephen makes clear, one fact (the item of evidence) has a relationship with another fact (the conclusion from the item of evidence) because it at least renders probable the conclusion.

In *R v Randall* [2004] 1 WLR 56 Lord Steyn noted that a judge in determining the issue of relevance 'has to decide whether the evidence is capable of increasing or decreasing the existence of a fact in issue'.

Lord Steyn also adopted the observation in Keane, *The Modern Law of Evidence*, 6th edn (2005) that the question of relevance 'is typically a matter of degree to be determined, for the most part by common sense and experience'. Relevance is therefore not a rule of law. There are no cases that set precedents for what will or will not be relevant in any particular situation.

1.3.1.2 Direct and circumstantial evidence

Relevant facts may tend to prove or disprove a fact in issue either directly or indirectly. Classic examples of direct evidence include:

(a) testimony by a witness about his or her own perception of a fact in issue, for example, that he saw the accused stab the deceased;

(b) the production to the court of some object, the existence of which is in issue, for example, a lease or a policy of insurance;

Circumstantial evidence does not involve the immediate perception of a fact in issue, but is evidence from which the existence from or non-existence of a fact in issue can be inferred. Examples include:

(a) evidence of opportunity, ie evidence of presence at the time and place of the act in question;

(b) certain types of evidence of identity, eg that DNA samples taken from the accused match those found at the scene of the crime; and

(c) evidence of facts providing a motive for a person to have done a particular act.

1.3.1.3   Sufficiency of relevance

It is sometimes said that a fact is 'not very relevant' or 'of marginal relevance' or that one fact is 'more' relevant than another. On the other hand, if relevance is determined by a strictly logical test of whether something makes a 'matter . . . more or less probable' (per Lord Simon in *DPP v Kilbourne* [1973] AC 729), then relevance is a quality a piece of evidence either does or does not have.

Consider an example in a civil case:

Arthur is being sued for negligence and breach of contract in respect of building works he has carried out for Amy. Amy wishes to show that he has been successfully sued in respect of a road accident in which he was alleged to have driven carelessly.

If we were to adopt a literal approach to Lord Simon's test we might say that the driving case is relevant to the building works case. Our argument would be that the previous case shows that Arthur has previously been less than careful. We would say that Arthur is therefore a relatively careless person and that this would show, to some small extent, that he may have been careless when carrying out week for Amy. By a very small degree it renders the conclusion that Arthur was negligent on this occasion more probable.

In fact, a court would probably be unwilling to accept this evidence and this would be on the grounds that it is not relevant. It would therefore appear that the courts have qualified the strictness of the test for relevance by introducing the concept of 'sufficiency of relevance', ie that evidence must display a sufficent degree of relevance before it will be admitted.

Consider the following examples:

- In *R v Whitehead* (1848) 3 Car & Kir 202, a doctor was tried for manslaughter of one patient. Evidence that the doctor had treated other patients skilfully was held to be irrelevant. Only evidence of the skill used in treating the patient who died was held to be relevant.

- In *Hart v Lancashire and Yorkshire Railway Co* (1869) 21 LT 261 the defendants were sued for negligently causing an accident. It was alleged that the accident had been caused by the changing of railway points. Evidence that the defendant company had altered its practice in changing railway points after an accident was held to be irrelevant.

- *Hollingham v Head* (1858) 27 LJ CP 241 was a breach of contract case in which the defendant sought to prove certain terms of the contract that would excuse him from liability. To prove those terms were incorporated into the contract with the defendant, he sought to adduce evidence that the plaintiff had entered into contracts with other persons on those same terms. The Court of Common Pleas held that evidence of contracting behaviour with other parties was irrelevant.

- *R v Blastland* [1986] AC 41 concerned the murder and buggery of a boy. The defendant wished to adduce evidence that showed that, before the victim's body had been found, another person, M, had spoken about the murder of a boy. The House of Lords held that evidence that showed that M knew of the murder was irrelevant to the issue in the case, namely whether the defendant was the murderer.

- In *R v Kearley* [1992] 2 AC 228, the House of Lords considered the relevance of statements made by third parties. In that case the police had raided a flat and, while they were searching it, they received repeated calls to the flat by people asking for the defendant and requesting drugs. In so far as the callers made statements that the defendant sold drugs, these statements would be inadmissible as hearsay evidence. However, the fact that the callers *believed* drugs were sold at the premises would make it an exception to the hearsay rule. The House of Lords recognised this but, as in *R v Blastland*, said that the state of mind of the maker of the statement was not relevant in this case.

Do you agree with these judgments? Do you think that the evidence was excluded because it did not render the conclusion more or less likely or because it was not sufficiently effective in doing so?

In these cases, the courts often justified the conclusion that there was no relevance to the evidence by identifying or describing a test that is slightly different to that identified in *Kilbourne*. In *Hollingham v Head* the court said that the previous contracting behaviour was not relevant because it supported no *reasonable* inference as to how the parties had contracted. The evidence does not simply have to be relevant, but it has to be sufficiently relevant to permit the tribunal of fact reasonably to draw an inference as to the existence of the term in the contract. In cases such as *Blastland* and *Kearley* it is not difficult to formulate arguments on the relevance of the evidence as follows:

Blastland:

- M said that the boy had been murdered before this was generally known.
- Therefore M had some peculiar knowledge of the death of the boy.
- Therefore M may have murdered the boy.
- Therefore the defendant may not have murdered the boy.

Kearley:

- Callers requested drugs at the defendant's flat.
- Therefore callers expected to receive drugs at the defendant's flat.
- Therefore the callers may have received drugs at the defendant's flat in the past.
- Therefore the defendant may have been selling drugs from his flat in the past.
- Therefore the defendant may still have been selling drugs from his flat.

Neither of these logical arguments is without its flaws but both of them are sustainable. Nonetheless the House of Lords on both occasions concluded that despite this sort of logical argument, the evidence represented by the first bullet point was not relevant to the conclusion in the final bullet point. This must be because the logic in each case is *insufficiently* strong or, in evidential terms, the evidence is *insufficiently* relevant.

The rationale for the restriction of evidence of marginal relevance is that it would increase the issues that have to be litigated with the resulting increase in cost and complexity of the trial process (see *R v Patel* [1951] 2 All ER 29).

Thus the test for relevance is not simply whether the evidence might tend to prove of disprove a fact in issue. Evidence must be capable of proving or disproving it to a sufficient degree. There is no clear statement of *how* relevant evidence has to be. In part this is because relevance is, as Lord Steyn affirmed in *R v Randall* [2004] 1 WLR 56, not an issue of law but a matter of logic, common sense or experience. This means that relevance cannot be assessed by reference to precedent but only on the basis of the facts of each one.

1.3.1.4 Conditional relevance

We have seen that some evidence does not have relevance on its own. Rather its relevance depends on its relationship to other evidence in the case. As a result, the court may admit evidence conditionally (or '*de bene esse*') upon the proof of such facts as render that evidence relevant. If the other evidence is not adduced, the judge will have to direct the jury to ignore the evidence that was conditionally admitted (or a civil judge or magistrate would have to disregard it). In extreme cases (where it will not be possible for the tribunal of fact to ignore it) the trial may have to be discontinued.

1.3.1.5 Importance of argument

To recap, the relevance of evidence is a matter of logic or of common sense. Relevance is a filter upon evidence; no evidence that is deemed irrelevant will be admitted. The test is whether it will increase or decrease the probability of a fact in issue being proved (or possibly whether it is sufficiently likely to do so or likely to do so to a sufficient extent). This will be a matter of argument or explanation. In many cases the relevance of direct evidence or circumstantial evidence will be so clear that the argument does not need to be stated. Generally, however, some argument will have to be made at some point during the carse of the trial. Given that relevance is not a matter of law but a matter of logic, it is not possible to lay down any rules about such arguments. However, the following points should be borne in mind:

(a) Evidence is not simply 'relevant'. Rather it is relevant to something. Identifying to which facts in issue evidence is relevant is necessary to constructing convincing arguments.

(b) Evidence need not be directy relevant to a fact in issue. Instead, the evidence may be relevant to a fact which, in turn, is relevant to a fact in issue.

(c) is not only necessary to identify *what* evidence is relevant to, it is necessary to identify *how* or *why* that evidence is relevant to that issue. This requires the drawing on logic or common sense to construct generalisations about human behaviour.

(d) Finally and most importantly, evidence is relevant if it is *capable* of leading to a particular conclusion not if it *will* lead to that conclusion.

1.3.2 Weight

We have seen in the preceding section that the *relevance* of evidence concerns what conclusions the evidence is capable of proving or disproving. The *weight* of the evidence concerns the extent to which the evidence does prove or disprove the conclusion. While it is still possible to disagree about what something is capable of proving, this is not likely in most cases and, even where it is, the disagreement is usually based on logical analysis. Weight is far more subjective. Among 12 jurors, some may be inclined to reach a particular conclusion from a particular piece of evidence, and others may not. There might be difficulty articulating why they do or do not do so. In so far as they can, they might draw on concepts like 'belief' or 'feelings' or 'instinct'. However, they may also draw on 'logic' and 'common sense'.

1.3.2.1 Importance of weight at trial

Weight is generally a matter for the tribunal of fact. Once the tribunal of law decides to admit evidence, it is a matter for the tribunal of fact to decide how much weight to attach to it.

There are a number of ways in which weight will influence what a lawyer does:

(a) A lawyer may seek to *influence* the weight to be attached to evidence by the tribunal of fact. An advocate cross-examining a witness is generally seeking to reduce the weight to be attached to the evidence of that witness. An advocate must therefore be aware of how particular evidence or questions might affect the weight that might be attached to other evidence in the case.

(b) Lawyers do not only fight cases at trial. Many cases are settled before trial. Defendants in criminal proceedings plead guilty in the face of strong evidence and civil litigants compromise their claims in the face of strong opposition. Therefore lawyers must be able to *assess* the weight of evidence for both parties so that they can give clear advice about the prospects of success.

(c) Lawyers will often have to *argue* about the weight to be attached to evidence. This arises in a number of different ways:

(i) In both civil and criminal cases advocates will make submissions or speeches to the tribunal of fact. In doing so they seek to persuade the tribunal to reach the desired conclusions by emphasising the weight of the favorable evidence, and attacking the apparent weight of the less favorable. This is only possible if the advocate understands the strengths and weaknesses of the evidence as presented.

(ii) As will be seen in later chapters of this Manual (such as **Chapter 8** on character evidence and later in this chapter), some evidence is excluded in part due to its lack of weight. To conduct arguments about the probative force of evidence, the weight of that evidence must be understood and explained.

(iii) The failure to call sufficient evidence (ie, evidence of sufficient weight) on a particular issue or as a whole has procedural consequences. The most dramatic is the submission of no case to answer (see the *Criminal Litigation and Sentencing Manual*). Furthermore, as will be seen in **Chapter 2**, a party is only required to disprove an issue once the opposing party has called evidence of sufficient weight to put the matter in issue.

1.3.2.2 Challenges to the weight of evidence

A distinction may be drawn between evidence that is relevant to the facts in issue and evidence that is relevant to the credibility of a witness. For example, where an eye-witness to a criminal offence is shown to have poor eyesight and a grudge against the defendant these would be matters going, not to the facts in issue, but to the credibility of the witness. Evidence affecting credibility is also known as collateral evidence.

(a) Challenges to the truthfulness of particular witnesses.

(b) Challenges to the ability of the particular witnesses to give an accurate account.

(c) Challenges to the strength or validity of the arguments or generalisations made about the evidence.

(d) Alternative explanations about the evidence.

Guidance on the weight to be attached to evidence is occasionally given in case law (eg, *R v Turnbull* [1977] QB 224 on identification, see **Chapter 14**) or by statute law (eg, Civil

Evidence Act 1995, **Chapter 10**) on what might influence the weight to be attached to the evidence.

1.3.2.3 Collateral evidence

Both civil and criminal courts seek to limit the extent to which collateral evidence will be admitted. While clearly of use to the tribunal of fact, to allow collateral facts to be admitted on all occasions could lead to a lot of evidence being admitted that does not directly bear on the issues in the case. This concern about keeping cases focused on the factual disputes has led to a general rule of limitation concerning collateral evidence, namely the rule of finality. This will be examined in detail in **Chapter 6**.

1.3.3 Probative value and prejudicial effect

Probative value and prejudicial effect are often balanced one against the other. As will be seen below (**1.5.2**) in a criminal case where the probative value of evidence is outweighed by its prejudicial effect, that evidence may be excluded (ie, it will never go before the jury). So what do these two concepts mean?

Probative value is a combination of relevance (what something might prove) and weight (whether it does prove it). Probative value is essentially an evaluation of the extent to which an item of evidence proves a case in a rational way.

Prejudicial effect is an evaluation of the *risk* that the evidence in question will be used by the tribunal in an inappropriate way, for example, becoming distracted from deciding the case to the requisite standard of proof (such as beyond reasonable doubt) or taking into consideration irrelevant or immaterial matters. Prejudicial effect includes an overwillingness on the part of the tribunal of fact to convict (or make some other adverse finding) contrary either to the relevance or the weight that ought to be attached to the evidence before it.

In so far as these concepts are to be compared and balanced, no real guidance has been provided on when one outweighs the other. As will be seen at **1.5.2**, the balance is exercised as a judicial discretion and therefore rules about how the test ought to be applied have been avoided.

1.4 Proof of facts without evidence

One party or another must prove each and every fact in issue. This is usually done by adducing evidence at court. Most of this Manual concerns the restrictions on the admissibility of that evidence. However, before examining such matters, it should be recognised that there are rules of practice and procedure that allow the court to reach conclusions on some facts in issue (or even on some very small details of a case) without calling evidence. Two of these will be examined: formal admissions and judicial notice. This section will also deal with the question of the extent to which a tribunal of fact or law can rely upon its own personal knowledge to evidential gaps in the case.

1.4.1 Formal admissions

Both the civil and criminal courts have rules of procedure that allow the parties to reduce the number of facts in issue in a case that have to proved by evidence. These rules allow a party formally to admit a fact in issue or a fact that might assist in proving a fact in issue.

Formal admission of this sort determines that particular matter: it is proved and no further evidence will be admitted to prove or disprove it.

Formal admissions are often made to enable cases to be disposed of more quickly and efficiently where there is no serious dispute on the matters admitted. Occasionally, however, a party might see a tactical advantage in admitting a particular fact rather than running extra risks in requiring the other side to call damaging evidence to prove it.

Note the distinction between formal and informal admissions.

(a) A *formal* admission is the result of a rule of procedure. The effect of the formal admission is that the particular issue is finally resolved: the admission is conclusive of that fact. Evidence that proves or disproves that issue alone is not relevant and will not be admitted.

(b) In contrast a party may make an *informal* admission, for example, by admitting to another person (including a police officer in a police station) particular relevant facts. This latter type of admission, commonly known as a confession, is only evidence on that particular fact. It is still possible for the tribunal of fact to disregard it. For detailed analysis of the rules of evidence concerning informal admissions see **Chapter 12**.

1.4.1.1   Criminal cases

Formal admissions are governed by the Criminal Justice Act 1967. Section 10(1) provides:

Subject to the provisions of this section, any fact of which oral evidence may be given . . . may be admitted . . ., and the admission by any party of any such fact under this section shall, as against that party, be conclusive evidence . . . of the fact admitted.

Section 10(2) sets out how such formal admissions are made. In essence the section provides that formal admissions:

- Can be made by the defendant (or the prosecutor if a private person) him or herself (s 10(1)).

- Can be made at trial or before trial (s 10(2)(a)).

- Can be made orally in court. If made on the behalf of the defendant they must be made by the defendant's solicitor or barrister (s 10(2)(b), (d)).

- Can be made in writing either in court or outside of court. The written formal admission must be signed either by the defendant (or prosecutor) in person or, if the party making the admission is a company, by an appropriate officer of that company (s 10(2)(c)).

A formal admission may be withdrawn with leave of the court (s 10(4)). *R v Kolton* [2000] Crim LR 761 suggests that this will only happen rarely. The court will expect evidence from both the party making the admission and their legal representatives that shows the admission to have been made by mistake or misunderstanding.

1.4.1.2   Civil cases

Statements of case may formally admit facts in issue. However the Civil Procedure Rules also provide for situations in which parties may wish to admit facts once the statement of case process has ended. CPR, r 14.1, states:

(1)   A party may admit the truth of the whole or any part of another party's case.

(2)   He may do this by giving notice in writing (such as in a statement of case or by letter).

(3)   The court may allow a party to amend or withdraw an admission.

Such admissions can be made voluntarily by a party, usually to save costs and time. Furthermore, there are various provisions of the CPR that allow one party to request or demand of another party admissions on particular points or issues such as the 'notice to admit facts' (r 32.18) and the rules relating to written requests or court orders to provide additional information (rr 18.1 and 26.5(3) respectively).

1.4.2 Judicial notice

In some cases a judge may take judicial notice of a fact. Where this happens there is no longer any requirement to prove the fact in question. The matter is accepted by the court without evidence being adduced.

1.4.2.1 Judicial notice without enquiry

There are some matters that are so obvious or so far beyond dispute that it would be a waste of court resources for them to have to be proved every time a case is litigated. In such situations it is possible for a judge to 'take notice' of the fact and to dispense with any requirement that it be proved.

Where a fact is so commonly agreed as to be beyond serious dispute, a judge may take notice of it without hearing any evidence. Famous examples include:

- *R v Luffe* (1807) 8 East 193 (two weeks is too short a period for human gestation).
- *Dennis v A J White and Co* [1916] 2 KB 1 (that the streets of London are full of traffic).
- *Nye v Niblett* [1918] 1 KB 23 (cats are ordinarily kept for domestic purposes).
- *Green v Bannister* [2003] EWCA Civ 1819 (the existence of a 'blind spot' that cannot be observed in a car's wing mirror).

Some matters are taken on judicial notice by virtue of legislation. For example:

- Acts of Parliament do not have to be proved by evidence. It is not necessary to prove an Act's content or that it was passed by both Houses of Parliament (Interpretation Act 1978, ss 3, 22(1)).
- European Community Treaties, the Official Journal of the Communities and decisions of the European Court are taken on judicial notice (European Communities Act 1972, s 3(2)).
- A judicial or official document that appears to have been signed and stamped by a judge of the Supreme Court shall be taken on judicial notice to have been signed or stamped by him or her (Evidence Act 1845, s 2).

1.4.2.2 Judicial notice after enquiry

Where a fact is not so notorious or widely known, it is still possible for judicial notice of that fact to be taken. However, in such cases, the judge confronted with the issue in question will conduct an investigation. This will happen when the matter is one that is easily resolved by reference to sources of great reliability (such as ministerial certificates, learned works, etc).

This enquiry is not a trial on the matter. The rules of evidence do not regulate what the judge may consult and it is not possible to call evidence to rebut the judge's findings. Furthermore, the conclusions of the judge in the particular case constitute a binding legal precedent on the point.

This form of judicial notice will take place in relation to the following types of information:

(a) Facts of a general nature that can be readily demonstrated by reference to authoritative extraneous sources such as diaries, atlases, encyclopaedia, etc. In *McQuaker v Goddard* [1940] 1 KB 687, a judge resolved that a camel was a domestic creature by consulting books and hearing expert evidence.

(b) Facts of a political nature. Judicial notice can be taken of these following enquiry of political sources. In *R v Bottrill, ex p Kuechenmeister* [1947] 1 KB 41, judicial notice was taken of the fact that the country was still at war with Germany after examining a certificate from the Foreign Secretary to that effect.

(c) Customs and professional practices following consultation of suitably qualified experts in that field or area. For example, in *Heather v P-E Consulting Group Ltd* [1973] Ch 189 judicial notice was taken of accountancy practices.

1.4.3 Personal knowledge

To what extent can a judge take judicial notice of something within his or her own personal knowledge? May a juror or a magistrate do so? The general rule is that neither the judge or juror may apply their personal knowledge of facts (*Palmer v Crone* [1927] 1 KB 804) and jurors should be warned not to take steps to acquire such knowledge during trial (for example, by visiting the scene of an alleged crime) (*R v Oliver* [1996] 2 Cr App R 514). In *Bowman v DPP* [1991] RTR 263, the use of personal knowledge was distinguished from judicial notice. It was also stated that any personal knowledge ought to be identified so as to allow comment by parties to the case.

However, the courts have allowed judges to use their general knowledge and magistrates may use their local knowledge in reaching decisions (for example, *Paul v DPP* (1989) 90 Cr App R 173). In *Wetherhall v Harrison* [1976] QB 773, the Divisional Court drew a distinction between judges, on the one hand, and jurors and magistrates, on the other. They said that the former ought not to use their personal knowledge but the latter could. The rationale was in part to facilitate the sharing of their personal experiences and local knowledge.

There are no clear rules on the extent to which personal knowledge of matters not established by evidence can be used to determine matters. In part, this is due to the difficulty of separating the personal knowledge of a judge from judicial notice in many cases. So far as personal knowledge of jurors and lay magistrates is concerned, as their deliberations take place away from the public gaze it will rarely be apparent that they have not resorted to personal knowledge or experience.

In *Hammington v Berker Sportcraft Ltd* [1980] ICR 248, it was stated that the tribunal of fact should only be able to rely on personal knowledge if the parties had been given the opportunity to deal with the evidence during the trial.

1.5 Admissibility

So far, we have considered how evidence proves cases. However, we shall see in the rest of this Manual that many of the rules of evidence are concerned with whether evidence that could prove a relevant fact will be admitted. The starting point is that any item of evidence if sufficiently relevant is admissible unless there is a specific rule that it is not admissible. In other words, the vast majority of the rules of evidence are about the *inadmissibility* of evidence: the rules of evidence are a series of filters keeping evidence out of court rather than a series of principles letting it in.

For example, an item of evidence might be relevant in a particular criminal case but because it is hearsay evidence it is *inadmissible*.

1.5.1   Preliminary facts

Some rules of evidence simply state that evidence of a particular class is admissible or inadmissible as a matter of law or logic. An example of this is hearsay evidence. It is not necessary to determine whether or not the evidence was obtained in any particular way. The court can determine the admissibility of this evidence without having to hear any evidence as to how it was obtained, for example.

However, some rules of evidence state that evidence will not be admissible if it was obtained in particular circumstances (such as the exclusion of confession evidence obtained by oppression under s 76(2)(b) of the Police and Criminal Evidence Act 1984) or that evidence will only be admitted if certain matters are proved (for example, a witness cannot give expert opinion evidence until he or she is proved to be an expert). Therefore, admissibility depends on proof of particular facts. The facts that lead to the admission or exclusion of evidence are not ordinary facts in the case. They do not go to prove the issues themselves. They are a necessary step for the admission of other evidence. They are called '*preliminary facts*' because they have to be proved before the evidence to which they relate can be admitted. The process of determining these factual disputes is called a 'trial within a trial' or a '*voir dire*'.

1.6   Exclusion

There is no general judicial discretion to *include* evidence that is rendered inadmissible by a rule of evidence (see *Sparks v R* [1964] AC 964, PC and *Myers v DPP* [1965] AC 1001, HL).

However, there is a power to exclude otherwise admissible evidence in both civil and criminal cases.

1.6.1   Civil cases

The general exclusionary discretion to exclude evidence is contained in CPR, r 32.1, which provides:

(1)   *The court may control the evidence by giving directions as to—*
    (a)   *the issues on which it requires evidence;*
    (b)   *the nature of the evidence which it requires to decide those issues; and*
    (c)   *the way in which the evidence is to be placed before the court*
(2)   *The court may use its power under this rule to exclude evidence that would otherwise be admissible.*
(3)   *The court may limit cross examination.*

This power should be exercised to give effect to the 'overriding objective' (see *Civil Litigation Manual*).

1.6.2   Criminal cases

There are important discretions to exclude evidence in criminal cases. There are two types of discretion that must be considered:

- discretion to exclude prejudicial evidence;
- discretion to exclude evidence obtained unfairly.

1.6.2.1   Discretion to exclude prejudicial evidence

In *R v Sang* [1980] AC 402, it was held that a trial judge had a discretion to exclude evidence tendered by the prosecution if its prejudicial effect outweighed its probative value. This discretion was an aspect of the judge's duty to regulate the trial process. It is important to be clear about the two important concepts.

Probative value. This has already been referred to above (**1.1.2** and **1.3**). Probative value is the likely effect of the evidence on the minds of a tribunal of fact that is acting rationally.

Prejudicial effect. This is the use of evidence in an irrational way. The prejudicial effect could either be the capacity of the evidence to tempt the tribunal of fact to convict on inadequate evidence (for example, because the evidence causes the jury to be disgusted with the defendant's alleged conduct), or to reach false conclusions on the evidence in question (for example, evidence that the defendant has committed offences in the past might be given too much weight in deciding his or her guilt for the present offence).

The discretion to exclude prejudicial evidence is aimed at situations in which evidence might have multiple uses by a tribunal of fact. On the one hand, it will have probative value but, on the other, it will have one or more prejudicial effects.

Note that this principle does not oblige the judge to exclude such evidence, it is a matter of judicial discretion. The judge would have to weigh up the probative value of the evidence and compare it to the risk of prejudice.

The exclusionary discretion only applies to evidence tendered by the prosecution not evidence tendered by a co-accused (*R v Lobban* [1995] 2 All ER 602). The discretion exists to protect the accused from wrongful conviction. Thus, where a defendant seeks to exclude evidence adduced by a co-defendant, the judge would not be able to act without potentially increasing the risk of the wrongful conviction of the co-defendant. Therefore, the judge has no discretion to intervene in such a situation.

This discretion applies to any evidence that may lead the jury to follow an impermissible line of reasoning. *R v Lobban*, for example, concerned prejudice deriving from the admissibility of statements made in confessions, whereas the common application is still likely to be for evidence of previous bad character by a defendant.

1.6.2.2   Discretion to exclude unfairly obtained evidence

There is a statutory discretion under s 78 of the Police and Criminal Evidence Act 1984 to exclude evidence as follows:

> *(1)   In any proceedings the court may refuse to allow evidence on which the prosecution proposes to rely to be given if it appears to the court that, having regard to all the circumstances, including the circumstances in which the evidence was obtained, the admission of the evidence would have such an adverse effect on the fairness of the proceedings that the court ought not to admit it.*

The detail of this discretion will be considered in **Chapter 10**. However, some preliminary points are worth noting.

   (a)   There is some overlap between this and the common law power noted above and it seems that the courts are increasingly advised to exercise the common law discretion under the authority of s 78 (*Attorney-General's Reference (No 1 of 2003)* [2003] EWCA Crim 1286). However, the main difference is that the common law discretion is limited to balancing the probative value of the evidence and the irrational ways in which a jury will evaluate that same evidence. In exercising its discretion under s 78, both the probative value and the way in which the evidence might be misused may be taken into consideration, but s 78 goes much further. The court is required to consider the effect on the fairness of the proceedings and to examine how the evidence was obtained. This means that potentially probative evidence that would not lead to prejudicial thinking on the part of the jury could be excluded if it would have an adverse effect on the fairness of proceedings for other reasons. Examples of such exclusion include tricks played on the accused and/or his legal advisers with a view to obtaining confessions (*R v Mason* [1988] 1 WLR 139); denial of the accused's right to legal advice (*R v Samuel* [1988] QB 615) and the improper use of undercover surveillance (*R v Loosely* [2001] 4 All ER 897).

(b) This discretion only applies before evidence is admitted. Once it has been admitted, the defence will have to rely on the common law discretion to exclude the evidence that is preserved by s 82(3) (see *R v Sat-Bhambra* (1989) 88 Cr App R 55).

1.6.2.3 Appealing a refusal to exercise a discretion to exclude

As the exclusion of the evidence in both of these situations is discretionary, it will be very difficult to overturn a judge's decision on such a matter on appeal. In such situations the court will not intervene unless the discretion was exercised perversely by either refusing to exercise a discretion or erring in principle: see *R v Cook* [1959] 2 QB 340 and *R v Uniacke* [2003] EWCA Crim 30. However, the failure by a judge to apply (or show the application of) the concepts of relevance and weight may lead to his or her exercise of discretion being overturned.

1.6.2.4 Other discretions

Various statutes have created discretions to exclude particular classes of otherwise admissible evidence. For example, the Criminal Justice Act 2003, s 101(3) allows the judge to exclude evidence of the defendant's bad character. Section 126 of the same Act provides the court with a discretion to exclude hearsay evidence.

1.7 Adducing evidence

An advocate can only advance arguments based on evidence that has been presented to court by legitimate means. The three bases of putting evidence before the court ('adducing evidence') are:

- testimony;
- documentary evidence;
- real evidence.

1.7.1 Testimony

This is evidence that is given by a witness. Usually the witness will attend court, swear an oath or affirm and stand in the witness box and give his or her evidence orally. Each statement of fact by the witness is evidence of that fact. Having been given by a witness, the evidence becomes 'testimony'.

There are rules of procedure that allow parties to rely on written witness statements in place of calling the witness. In criminal cases this is, for example, by virtue of s 9 of the

Criminal Justice Act 1967 (see **4.3.1.1**). In civil cases, CPR, r 35(2) permits a witness's statement to stand as his or her evidence in chief unless the court orders otherwise (see **4.3.2**).

1.7.2 Documentary evidence

Documentary evidence is evidence that is contained in a document. In contrast to the exceptional practices set out in **1.7.1** above, the contents of the documents are not treated as the testimony of the maker.

Documentary evidence must be 'proved' by a witness. This means that the origin and relevance of the document must be established. It does not mean that the author of the document must in all cases be established. An anonymous note found lying at the scene of a crime might be admissible to prove certain facts without actually establishing who wrote it (although such proof may often be necessary to establish the relevance of the document to the proceedings in question). What proof in this sense requires is that it is established that the document has some bearing on the case in question.

The admissibility of documentary evidence is governed by the rules regulating hearsay in **Chapter 10**.

1.7.3 Real evidence

Real evidence derives evidential value from the physical nature of an object. The item is produced in court (as an exhibit) or the court will visit the item, for example, when the court goes to the place where an incident took place (often referred to as the *locus in quo*) to view it. The significance of real evidence is that the tribunal of fact can reach conclusions based on the physical characteristics of the item or place rather than any words narrated. Therefore a book could be both documentary evidence (by reading and interpreting it) and real evidence (by examining its physical characteristics). Furthermore a witness in court would be giving testimonial evidence but the witness would also be real evidence him or herself in so far as the tribunal of fact evaluates him or her as a person while giving evidence to determine, for example, whether they appear to be telling the truth or whether (where relevant to an issue in the case) they have particular physical characteristics.

1.8 Tribunals of fact and law

1.8.1 General rule: distinction between tribunal of law and tribunal of fact

The general rule is that the tribunal of fact in any given case will decide the facts and that the tribunal of law will decide the law. In the Crown Court, this distinction is clear to see. The judge, as tribunal of law, deals with legal issues and will often do so in the absence of the jury. The jury deals with factual issues and the judge is under a duty to remind jurors that it is their function to decide factual issues not his (*R v Jackson* [1992] Crim LR 214). The direction is a follows:

It is my job to tell you what the law is and how to apply it to the issues of fact that you have to decide and to remind you of the important evidence on these issues. As to the law, you must accept what I tell you. As to the facts, you alone are the judges. It is for you to decide what evidence you accept and what evidence you reject or of which you are unsure. If I appear to have a view of the evidence or of the facts with which you do not agree, reject my view. If I mention or emphasise evidence that you regard as unimportant, disregard that evidence. If I do not mention what you regard as important, follow your own view and take that evidence into account.

1.8.2   Exceptions to the general rule

The tribunal of law will decide factual matters in the following cases.

1.8.2.1   Summing up to the jury

The judge is not completely barred from considering and commenting upon the evidence in a case. As noted in **1.8.1**, it was said in *R v Jackson* [1992] Crim LR 214 that the judge should direct the jury on their respective functions. However, you will see by referring back to the detail of the direction that the judge could (indeed should) remind the jury of the evidence and review it. Clearly, this will involve some evaluation and consideration of the evidence. It is probably true to say, however, that judge is not in fact *deciding* factual issues.

Where the judge strays too far in commenting or sifting the facts of a case, there may be a ground of appeal. See *Blackstone's Criminal Practice 2005* or *Archbold 2005*.

1.8.2.2   Preliminary facts and the *voir dire*

As noted at **1.6.1** some questions of the admissibility of evidence must be resolved by the proof of particular facts ('preliminary facts'). As the admissibility issue is an issue of law, the tribunal of law must determine it and will therefore have to decide facts which must be proved or disproved to determine admissibility. For example, by virtue of s 76(2)(a) of the Police and Criminal Evidence Act 1984, a confession is only admissible if the prosecution prove that it was not obtained by oppression. As the consequence of proving this issue is the admissibility or inadmissibility of a confession it must be resolved by the judge and it is therefore the judge who will have to decide whether there was in fact oppressive conduct that led to the confession.

Generally the process of establishing the admissibility of evidence should be something of which the jury is unaware as their awareness of the evidence could lead to prejudice against a party if it was subsequently excluded. Therefore the determination of admissibility is achieved by a 'trial within a trial' or *voir dire*, which takes place in the absence of the jury. As its name suggests, this is a trial to resolve a preliminary issue during or at the start of the main trial to which it relates. Both parties can call witnesses on the matter in question and make submissions. The judge will then decide the issue and give reasons for the conclusion reached. In this respect, the judge is clearly exercising the role of a fact-finder. For further details of the *voir dire* process see the **Criminal Litigation Manual**, *Blackstones Criminal Practice 2005* or *Archbold 2005*.

Not all determinations of preliminary issues take place in the absence of the jury. Many matters (such as whether a witness is qualified to give expert evidence) are conducted in the presence of the jury. This is generally the case where the matter would not take long to resolve and where the jury would not be likely to reach prejudicial conclusions from knowing of the existence of the evidence.

1.8.2.3   Sufficiency of evidence

As will be seen in **Chapter 2** one party or another must call sufficient evidence to put a matter in dispute at trial ('discharging the evidential burden'). This is a question of law that must be resolved by analysis of the evidence.

In criminal cases the prosecution have to prove that there is a case for the defence to meet on all of the elements of the offence. The test is that set out in *R v Galbraith* [1981] 1 WLR 1039, CA:

(1) If there is no evidence that the crime alleged has been committed by the defendant there is no difficulty — the judge will stop the case.

(2) The difficulty arises where there is some evidence but it is of a tenuous character, for example, because of inherent weakness or vagueness or because it is inconsistent with other evidence: . . . where the judge concludes that the prosecution evidence, taken at its highest is such that a jury properly directed could not properly convict on it, it is his duty on a submission being made to stop the case.

This is determined at the end of the prosecution case and in the absence of the jury. Furthermore, the jury should not be told that the submission took place (*R v Smith* (1987) 85 Cr App R 197, CA). For further details on submissions of no case to answer see the **Criminal Litigation and Sentencing Manual**.

In civil cases with a jury, the judge has a discretion to rule that a party has no case to answer without that party calling evidence (*Young v Rank* [1950] 2 KB 510). Again, this discretion is exercised having evaluated the evidence that has been called by the other party.

1.8.2.4 The meaning of words

In *Brutus v Cozens* [1973] AC 854, HL, it was stated that generally the meaning of words is a question of fact for the jury to determine. However, Lord Reid envisaged that words might require judicial interpretation if it is shown that they are being used in an unusual way in the statute in question or if there is an issue as to whether the jury reached a perverse interpretation of the word in question.

1.8.2.5 Other special cases

There are particular situations in which the law has given the judge the responsibility of determining questions of fact. For example:

(a) In libel cases it is for the judge to determine whether a document is *capable* of bearing a defamatory meaning. It is then a matter for the jury whether the document does bear the defamatory meaning (*Nevill v Fine Arts and General Insurance Co Ltd* [1897] AC 68 and *Jameel v Wall Street Journal Europe* [2003] EWCA Civ 1694).

(b) Under the Perjury Act 1911, s 1(1), a person commits perjury if he or she makes a false statement that is 'material' to a proceeding. It is a question of law whether a statement was in fact material (s 11(6)).

(c) Questions of foreign law are questions of fact to be determined after consideration of evidence. However, in criminal cases under s 15 of the Administration of Justice Act 1920 and in civil cases under s 69(5) of the Supreme Court Act 1981 and s 68 of the County Courts Act 1984, it is for the judge rather than the jury to decide this issue.

1.8.3 When the same person or persons are tribunal of law and tribunal of fact

In a magistrates' court and in civil courts where a jury is not used, the functions of the tribunal of law and the tribunal of fact are exercised by the same person or group of persons. Therefore, a county court judge or a magistrate will determine both legal and factual issues. This often makes the process much simpler and more efficient but it also poses two practical difficulties for a lawyer:

(a) It can be difficult to determine the basis upon which a decision has been reached. In jury trials, while the same difficulty can arise, the appellate courts will consider the way in which the jury were directed by the judge to determine how they might have reached their decisions and to decide whether there is a valid basis of appeal due to an error. Where the same person or group is both tribunal of law and tribunal of fact there is no practical requirement for the tribunal of law to tell the tribunal of fact how to apply legal concepts. Therefore there is nothing upon which to base an appeal. To solve this difficulty, the rules of procedure for various courts set rules requiring the court to give reasons for its answers. Quite how much reasoning is required varies by the type of court. See the *Criminal Litigation and Sentencing Manual* and the *Civil Litigation Manual* for detail on the giving of reasons.

(b) The same person or group of people will both determine that evidence is inadmissible and will, at some later point, decide the factual issues in the case. In jury trials, where evidence is to be excluded, the decision to exclude evidence will be made in the absence of the jury. If the application succeeds, the jury will not have heard the evidence and will not have to discount it. Where there is no jury this is not possible. Magistrates, for example, may decide to exclude a confession under the Police and Criminal Evidence Act 1984, s 78, and will then have to proceed on the assumption that they never heard it. Clearly there is a risk that the bench will not be able to disregard that evidence completely. However, it does appear to be an implicit feature of these court processes that the magistrates, or the judge in a civil court, will be able to ignore evidence in such circumstances.

2

Burden and standard of proof

This chapter considers which parties bear the burden of proving or disproving facts in issue, and to what standard.

2.1 Introduction

2.1.1 Burden of Proof

The law of evidence recognises two principal burdens:

- the legal burden; and
- the evidential burden

2.1.1.1 Legal burden

The legal burden is the obligation placed on a party to prove a fact in issue. Whether a party has discharged the legal burden is a question to be determined by the tribunal of fact at the end of the trial. The legal burden is also known as the 'persuasive burden' and the 'burden of proof'.

Prove a fact

2.1.1.2 Evidential burden

The evidential burden is the obligation on a party to adduce sufficient evidence to raise a fact in issue, ie make a particular issue a live issue at trial. Whether a party has discharged the evidential burden is a question of law for the judge. The judge will assess whether the amount and quality of the evidence adduced by a party is sufficient to raise a fact in issue. If the court decides it is not sufficient, then the fact in issue has not been raised and the judge will not let the fact in issue go before the tribunal of fact.

Raise a fact

A party bearing a legal burden also, by necessity, bears an evidential burden, since a party cannot discharge a legal burden without also discharging an evidential burden.

2.1.2 Standard of proof

The standard of proof is the degree of cogency or persuasiveness required of the evidence adduced by a party in order to discharge a burden borne by him or her.

2.2 Criminal proceedings

The presumption of innocence in criminal law means that the legal burden in criminal cases properly lies with the prosecution, and that a high standard of proof is required.

2.2.1 Incidence of the legal burden

2.2.1.1 General rule

The general rule is that the prosecution, who bring criminal proceedings against a defendant, bear the legal burden to prove all elements of the offence(s) on which the defendant is tried. It was held in *Woolmington v DPP* [1935] AC 462, HL, per Lord Sankey LC:

Throughout the web of the English criminal law one golden thread is always to be seen, that it is the duty of the prosecution to prove the prisoner's guilt subject to what I have already said as to the defence of insanity and subject also to any statutory exception... No matter what the charge or where the trial, the principle that the prosecution must prove the guilt of the prisoner is part of the common law of England and no attempt to whittle it down can be entertained.

2.2.1.2 Exceptions

Defence of insanity
The only common law exception to the general rule is the defence of insanity. Where this defence is raised the legal burden of proving that the defendant was suffering from insanity is borne by the defence: *M'Naghten's Case* (1843) 10 Cl & F 200, *R v Smith* (1910) 6 Cr App R 19, *Sodeman v The King* [1936] 2 All ER 1138. For all other common law defences only an evidential burden is borne by the defence (see **2.2.2** below).

Express statutory exceptions
A number of statutory defences purport to place a legal burden on the defence ('a reverse burden'). For example, the Homicide Act 1957, s 2 makes it a defence to murder for the defendant to prove that he was suffering from an abnormality of the mind, which substantially impaired his mental responsibility for acts or omissions in doing or being a party to the killing.

Implied statutory exceptions
Reverse burdens may also be implied by statute. The Magistrates' Courts Act 1980, s 101 provides:

Where the defendant... relies for his defence on any exception, exemption, proviso, excuse, or qualification, whether or not it accompanies the description of the offence or matter of complaint in the enactment creating the offence or on which the complaint is founded, the burden of proving the exception, exemption, proviso, excuse or qualification shall be on him: and this notwithstanding that the information or complaint contains an allegation negativing the exception, exemption, proviso, excuse, or qualification.

For example, in a trial for the offence of driving a vehicle without a licence, it is for the driver to prove that he was the holder of a current driving licence (*John v Humphreys* [1955] 1 WLR 325).

On its wording, s 101 of the 1980 Act is confined to summary trials. The position in trials on indictment was set out in *R v Edwards* [1975] QB 27, in which the Court of Appeal held that a similar principal existed at common law. The court stated that there was an exception to the fundamental rule of our criminal law that the prosecution must prove every element of the offence charged. The exception is limited to offences arising under enactments which prohibit the doing of an act save in specified circumstances or by persons of specified classes or with specified qualifications or with the licence or permission of specified authorities. Where the accused seeks to rely on such a proviso, exemption, excuse or qualification he or she will bear a legal burden.

Whether a statutory provision impliedly places the legal burden of proof on the accused is a question of statutory construction for the court. Such questions are not always easy to resolve. It is an offence under s 155(1) of the Factories Act 1961, not to comply with s 29(1) of the Act which requires that any workplace 'shall, so as far as is reasonably practicable be made and kept safe for any person working therein'. In *Nimmo v Alexander Cowan and Sons Ltd* [1968] AC 107, HL, the question arose as to whether the phrase 'so far as is reasonably practicable' placed a legal burden on the defendant or the plaintiff in the case of proceedings brought for a statutory tort under the Factories Act 1960, s 29(1). Their Lordships held, by a majority, that it was for the plaintiff to prove that the workplace was not safe and for the defendant to prove that it was not reasonably practicable for him to do more in keeping his workplace safe than he had done.

In *R v Hunt* [1987] AC 352, where the defendant was prosecuted for possession of morphine under the Misuse of Drugs Act 1971, s 5. The Misuse of Drugs Regulations 1973, Sch 1, para 3, provide that s 5 shall have no effect in relation to any preparation of morphine containing not more than 0.2% of morphine. The House of Lords held that on its proper construction the statute required the prosecution to prove that the substance in question contained more than 0.2% of morphine. Lord Griffiths gave the following general guidance:

> . . . if the linguistic construction of the statute did not clearly indicate on whom the burden should lie the court should look to other considerations to determine the intention of Parliament, such as the mischief at which the Act was aimed and practical considerations affecting the burden of proof and, in particular, the ease or difficulty that the respective parties would encounter in discharging the burden.

Presumption of innocence

The European Convention on Human Rights (ECHR), Article 6(2) provides that:

> *Everyone charged with a criminal offence shall be presumed innocent until proved guilty according to law.*

The compatibility of the imposition of a legal burden on the defence with the presumption of innocence under the ECHR, Article 6(2) has been the subject of a number of recent decisions by the House of Lords and the Court of Appeal. The leading authority is *Attorney-General's Reference (No 4 of 2002)* [2005] 1 AC 264. While the case law does not lend itself to a brief summary the following principles may be distilled:

  (a) The defendant has a right to a fair trial.

  (b) The presumption of innocence is an important, but not an absolute right and so derogations from the principle are permitted.

  (c) The ECHR requires a balance to be struck between the rights of the individual and the wider interests of the community.

  (d) There is an obligation on the state to justify any derogation from the presumption of innocence.

  (e) For a reverse burden of proof to be acceptable there must be a compelling reason why it is fair and reasonable to deny the accused person the protection normally guaranteed to everyone by the presumption of innocence.

(f) In determining the justifiability of the imposition of a reverse burden on the defendant regard ought to be had to:

    (i)   the seriousness of the punishment which may flow from conviction;

    (ii) the extent and nature of the factual matters required to be proved by the accused, and their importance relative to the matters required to be proved by the prosecution;

    (iii) the extent to which the burden on the accused relates to facts which, if they exist, are readily provable by him as matters within his own knowledge or to which he has ready access;

    (iv) the particular social problem or mischief which the measure has been enacted to address.

(g) Where an infringement of Article 6(2) cannot be justified, the courts are, where possible, to 'read down' the offending provision under the Human Rights Act 1998, s 3 so that it imposes only an evidential burden on the defendant. The interpretative obligation under s 3 of the 1998 Act is a strong one; it places a duty on the court to strive to find a possible interpretation compatible with the ECHR. It applies even if there is no ambiguity in the language of the provision and it will sometimes be necessary to adopt an interpretation which linguistically may appear strained.

(h) Where it is not possible to read down the provision the court should make a declaration of incompatibility. However, this is a measure of last resort.

The following is a brief survey of whether burdens imposed by statute are legal or evidential, in the light of decisions so far:

Statutes imposing a legal burden

(a) Road Traffic Act 1988, s 5(2): where the accused is charged with an offence of being in charge of a motor vehicle on a road or other public place under s 5(1)(b) of the Act, the statutory defence provided by s 5(2), that there was no likelihood of him or her driving (*Attorney-General's Reference (No 4 of 2002)* [2005] 1 AC 264).

(b) Criminal Justice Act 1988, s 139(4): where the accused is charged with possession of a bladed article in a public place under s 139, the defence provided by s 139(4), that he or she had a good reason or lawful authority for being in possession of the article (*L v DPP* [2003] QB 137; *R v Matthews* [2004] QB 690).

(c) Trademarks Act 1994, s 95(2): where the accused is charged with unauthorised use of a trademark under s 92, the statutory defence provided by s 95(2), that he or she believed on reasonable grounds that his use of a sign was not infringing trademark (*R v Johnston* [2003] 1 WLR 1736, HL).

(d) Insolvency Act 1986, s 352: where the accused is bankrupt and is charged under s 353(1) with failing to inform the official receiver that property belonging to his estate has been disposed, the statutory defence contained in s 352, that he had no intention to defraud or conceal the state of this affairs (*Attorney-General's Reference (No 1 of 2004)* [2004] 1 WLR 2111).

(e) Protection From Eviction Act 1977, s 1(2): where a defendant landlord is charged with unlawful eviction, the statutory defence provided by s 1(2), that he believed the occupier had ceased to reside at the premises (*Attorney-General's Reference (No 1 of 2004)* [2004] 1 WLR 2111).

(f) Homicide Act 1957, s 4(1): where a defendant is charged with murder, the defence provided by s 4(1) of the Homicide Act 1957, that he survived a suicide pact (*Attorney-General's reference (No 1 of 2004)* [2004] 1 WLR 2111).

(g) Criminal Justice and Public Order Act 1994, s 51(7): where a defendant charged with witness intimidation under s 51(1), the defence of proving that this was not done with the relevant intention (*Attorney-General's Reference (No 1 of 2004)* [2004] 1 WLR 2111).

Statutes imposing an evidential burden

(a) Misuse of Drugs Act 1971, s 5(3): where a defendant is charged with possession of drugs with intent to supply under s 5(3), the statutory defence under s 28(2) and (3), that he neither believed, suspected or had reason to suspect that substance he had was a controlled drug (*R v Lambert* [2001] 3 All ER 547).

(b) Terrorism Act 2000, s 11(1): where a defendant is charged with membership of a proscribed organisation under s 11(1), the statutory defence provided by s 11(2), that the organisation was not proscribed on the last time he was or professed to be a member and he had not taken part in any of its activities whilst it was proscribed (*Attorney-General's Reference (No 4 of 2002)*; [2005] 1 AC 264).

(c) Insolvency Act 1986, s 352: where a bankrupt defendant is charged under s 353(2) with making a gift, transfer or creating a charge on property before the expiry of a five year period from the start of the bankruptcy, the statutory defence contained in s 352 (*Attorney-General's Reference (No 1 of 2004)* [2004] 1 WLR 2111).

2.2.2   Incidence of the evidential burden

The general rule is that a party bearing the legal burden on a particular issue usually bears the evidential burden. However, certain common law and statutory criminal defences place only an evidential burden on the accused. Once the accused has adduced sufficient evidence to discharge the evidential burden, the legal burden of disproving the defence is on the prosecution.

Examples of such common law defences include:

- self-defence (*R v Lobell* [1957] 1 QB 547, CCA);
- duress (*R v Gill* (1963) 47 Cr App R 166, CCA);
- non-insane automatism (*Bratty v Attorney-General for Northern Ireland* [1963] AC 386, HL);
- intoxication (*R v Foote* [1964] Crim L R 405);
- provocation (*Mancini v DPP* [1942] AC 1, HL).

Examples of such statutory defences include:

- Criminal Law Act 1967, s 3, which permits the use of reasonable force to prevent the commission of a crime or effect or assist in the lawful arrest of offenders, suspected offenders or those lawfully at large;
- Sexual Offences Act 2003, s 75 (see 3.5.4);
- various terrorism offences: see Terrorism Act 2000, ss 118(1)–(5), 12(4), 39(5)(a), 54, 57, 77 and Northern Ireland (Emergency Provisions) Act 1996, ss 13, 32 and 33 (possession of information offences).

Even if the defence do not specifically raise one of these defences, if there is sufficient evidence of such a defence, whether adduced by the prosecution or the defence, then the judge must leave the issue to the jury (*Palmer v The Queen* [1971] AC 814) and legal burden to disprove the defence will be on the prosecution (*Bullard v R* [1957] AC 635, PC). This remains the case even if the defence in question has been expressly disclaimed by the defence (*R v Kachikwu* (1968) 52 Cr App R 538, CA) or is inconsistent with the defence which the accused has in fact raised (*R v Newell* [1989] Crim LR 906).

2.2.3   Standard of proof

2.2.3.1   Legal burden

Borne by the prosecution

The standard of proof to which the prosecution must prove its case has been variously described as 'beyond reasonable doubt' (*Woolmington v DPP* [1935] AC 462, HL), and 'making the jury sure' (*R v Kritz* [1950] 1 KB 82). It was described in *Miller v Minister of Pensions* [1947] 2 All ER 372 per Denning J in the following terms:

> It need not reach certainty, but it must carry a high degree of probability. Proof beyond reasonable doubt does not mean proof beyond the shadow of doubt. The law would fail to protect the community if it admitted fanciful possibilities to deflect the course of justice. If the evidence is so strong against a man as to leave only a remote possibility in his favour which can be dismissed with the sentence 'of course it is possible, but not in the least probable', the case is proved beyond reasonable doubt, but nothing short of that will suffice.

Thus, if there is a reasonable doubt about the defendant's guilt, the standard of proof has not been met and the defendant must be acquitted. Although judges are not required to slavishly follow a formula when directing juries on the standard of proof, they must make it clear that the prosecution must prove its case beyond reasonable doubt, or to the extent that the jury is sure. The Judicial Studies Board has provided the following specimen direction to assist judges:

> How does the prosecution succeed in proving the defendant's guilt? The answer is—by making you sure of it. Nothing less than that will do. If after considering all the evidence you are sure that the defendant is guilty, you must return a verdict of 'Guilty'. If you are not sure, your verdict must be 'Not Guilty'. (See www.jsboard.co.uk.)

Borne by the defence

Where the defence bear the legal burden in relation to a fact in issue in a criminal trial the standard of proof is the balance of probabilities (*R v Carr-Briant* [1943] KB 607).

2.2.3.2   Evidential burden

Where either the prosecution or the defence bear the legal burden on an issue, the evidential burden may be described as the obligation to adduce such evidence as would be sufficient, if believed and left uncontradicted, to justify as a possibility a finding by the jury in their favour (*Jayasena v R* [1970] AC 618).

Where the defendant bears the evidential burden alone, he must adduce such evidence as would, if believed and left uncontradicted, induce a reasonable doubt in the mind of the jury as to whether his version might not be true (*Bratty v Attorney-General for Northern Ireland* [1963] AC 386, HL).

2.2.4   Preliminary matters in criminal cases and the burden and standard of proof

The admissibility of certain types of evidence, such as a confession alleged to have been obtained by oppression, fall to be dealt with as preliminary matters in criminal proceedings. Generally, the party seeking to have such evidence admitted will have the burden of proving its admissibility in accordance with the standard imposed by the relevant rules of evidence (*R v Sartori* [1961] Crim LR 397; *R v Yacoob* (1981) 72 Cr App R 313). Thus, where the prosecution seek to adduce evidence of a confession challenged on the basis that it was obtained by oppression, then the Police and Criminal Evidence Act 1984, s 76(2) requires the prosecution to prove beyond reasonable doubt that it was not so obtained. Where a defendant seeks to adduce the confession of a co-defendant, and oppression is raised, then the defendant is required by the Police and Criminal Evidence Act 1984, s 76A to disprove oppression on the balance of probabilities. See **Chapter 12**.

2.3   Civil proceedings

2.3.1   Incidence of the legal burden

2.3.1.1   Common law

In civil cases, at common law, the general rule is that the legal burden on any fact in issue is borne by the party asserting and not denying: he who asserts must prove not he who denies (*Joseph Constantine Steamship Line Ltd v Imperial Smelting Corporation Ltd* [1942] AC 154; *Re H (Minors) (Sexual Abuse: Standard of Proof)* [1996] AC 563, HL). Accordingly, the claimant usually bears the legal burden (and by necessity an evidential burden) of proving all the elements of his claim. Similarly, the defendant bears the legal (and evidential) burden of proving any defence and /or counter claim against the claimant. This general rule includes negative assertions: 'if the assertion of a negative is an essential part of the plaintiff's case, the proof of the assertion still rests upon the plaintiff' (per Bowen LJ, *Abrath v North Eastern Railway Company* (1883) 11 QBD 440, CA, at 457). So, for example, where a builder alleges breach of contract because he has not been paid for building works, he must prove not only that there was a contract for building works which were performed (positive assertions), but also that he has not been paid (a negative assertion).

The incidence of the legal burden is usually apparent from the statements of case (*BHP Billiton Petroleum Ltd v Dalmine SpA* [2003] BLR 271). However, sometimes a party may try to avoid a legal burden by drafting his statement of case in such a way as to make assertions of his own look like assertions of his opponent. Consider *Soward v Leggatt* (1856) 7 C & P 613. A landlord claimed that his tenant 'did not repair' the premises. The tenant claimed that he 'did well and sufficiently repair'. It was held that the landlord could as easily have pleaded that the defendant tenant 'allowed the house to become dilapidated.' The reality was that the landlord was alleging breach of covenant and, therefore, it was for him to prove it, not for the defendant to prove that there had been no breach.

However, difficulties arise when it is unclear whether a particular fact in issue properly classified as a part of the claimant's cause in action or the defendant's defence. Where this situation arises, it is for the court to determine who bears the burden of proof. In such cases the courts will determine the issue by reference to policy considerations and, in particular, the ease or difficulty that the respective parties would encounter in discharging the burden. Thus, in *Joseph Constantine Steamship Line Ltd v Imperial Smelting Corporation Ltd* [1942] AC 154, HL, the plaintiffs were charterers of a ship who claimed damages from the owners for failure to load. However, the ship had exploded before it could be loaded and the defendant owners relied on the defence of frustration. The defence of frustration is not available where the frustrating event was the fault of the party seeking to rely on it. Therefore, the charterers argued that the defendant owners could not rely on frustration unless they proved that the explosion was not their fault. The House of Lords held that once the defence of frustration was raised, the burden of proving that the frustration was due to the negligence of the defendant owners was on the charterers.

In the bailment cases it was held that once the bailor has proved bailment, the bailee has the burden of proving that the goods were lost or damaged without fault on his or her part (*Coldman v Hill* [1919] 1 KB 443; *Levison v Patent Steam Carpet Cleaning Ltd* [1978] QB 69). The rationale for these decisions was that it would be too onerous for the bailor to prove fault on the part of the bailee.

2.3.1.2   Agreement

In contract cases, which party bears the legal burden on a certain issue may be fixed by the express terms of the contract. Where the terms of the contract are silent as to who bears the burden on a particular issue, it is a matter of construction for the courts. In *Munro, Brice and Co v War Risks Association Ltd* [1918] 2 KB 78, a marine insurance policy against loss by perils of the sea contained an exemption clause excepting loss by capture, seizure, and consequences of hostilities. The insured ship left port and was never heard of again. It was held that it was for the claimant to show the loss was by the perils of the sea and for the defendant underwriters to show that the loss came within an exception, ie was by capture, seizure, or consequences of hostilities.

However, contrast *Munro, Brice and Co.* with *Hurst v Evans* [1917] 1 KB 352 which concerned a policy of insurance insuring against loss of or damage to jewellery unless caused by breakage or by theft or dishonesty committed by any servant of the assured. A robbery occurred during which jewellery was taken and damaged. The plaintiff made an claim under the policy of insurance and, when this was refused, brought an action for damages. The defendant insurance company relied on the exemption clause arguing that the loss was caused by the theft or dishonesty of one of the plaintiff's employees. It was held that the plaintiff bore the legal burden of proving that they were not stolen or damaged by his servants or agents. This decision was clearly influenced by policy considerations, the judge stating that to hold that the burden was on the defendant, on the facts of the case, would 'produce absurd results'.

Where the claimant relies upon a proviso to an exemption clause, the courts have held that it is for the claimant to prove that the facts of the case bring it within proviso. In *The Glendarroch* [1894] P 226, the plaintiffs sued for damage to goods shipped on *The Glendarroch*. The defendant shippers claimed that the case fell within an exemption clause excepting damage caused by perils of the sea. The plaintiffs argued that the loss did not come within the exemption clause as it was due to the fault of negligent navigation on the part of the defendant shippers. The Court of Appeal held that it was for the plaintiffs to prove the contract and non-delivery; for the defendants to bring the case within the exemption clause (perils of the sea); but for the plaintiffs to bring the case within the proviso to the exemption clause (defendants' negligence).

2.3.1.3   Statute

The incidence of the legal burden may be fixed by statute. For example, if, in proceedings referred to in the Consumer Credit Act 1974, s 139(1), the debtor or any surety alleges that the credit bargain is extortionate within the meaning of ss 137 and 138 of the Act, then, under s 171(1), it is for the creditor to prove the contrary.

2.3.2   Standard of proof

In *Miller v Minister of Pensions* [1947] 2 All ER 372, Denning J described the standard of proof in civil cases as follows:

> If the evidence is such that the tribunal can say; 'We think it more probable than not', the burden is discharged, but, if the probabilities are equal, it is not.

There are, however, some exceptional cases where the criminal standard of proof is required:

(a) Contempt of court (*Re Bramblevale Ltd* [1970] Ch 128, CA; *Dean v Dean* [1987] 1 FLR 517, CA).

(b) Where a person's livelihood is at stake (*R v Milk Marketing Board, ex p Austin* The Times, 21 March 1983).

(c) Allegations of misconduct amounting to a criminal offence in disciplinary hearings (*Re A Solicitor* [1993] QB 69, DC; *R (on the application of S) v Governing Body of YP School* [2003] EWCA Civ 1306).

(d) Where statute requires the criminal standard of proof (*Judd v Minister of Pensions and National Insurance* [1966] 2 QB 580).

In civil cases where allegations are made of misconduct so serious that it could have formed the basis of a criminal prosecution, although the standard remains the balance of probabilities, a higher degree of probability may be required. The more serious the allegation the less likely it is to be true and so the stronger should be the evidence before the court concludes that it is proved on the balance of probabilities (*Re H (Minors) (Sexual Abuse: Standard of Proof)* [1996] AC 563, HL; *Hornal v Neuberger Products Ltd* [1957] 1 QB 247; *R v Home Secretary, ex p Khawaja* [1984] AC 74, HL).

Presumptions

3.1 Introduction

There are two types of presumption:

- presumptions without proof of basic facts; and
- presumptions with proof of basic facts

3.2 Presumptions without proof of basic facts

This type of presumption is simply a way of stating where the burden of proof lies in certain situations. It is not a 'true' presumption in that it does not require that a basic, or preliminary, fact be proved before the presumption can be made. The most common examples of this type of presumption are:

3.2.1 Presumption of innocence

The presumption of innocence requires that in a criminal trial the court must conclude that the defendant is innocent unless the contrary is proved. It is simply a way of expressing the common law rule that the prosecution bears the legal burden of proving the accused's guilt beyond reasonable doubt.

3.2.2 Presumption of sanity

The presumption of sanity requires that in a criminal trial the court must conclude that the defendant is sane until the contrary is proved. It is simply a way of expressing the common law rule that where the defence of insanity has been raised, the accused bears the legal burden of proving it.

3.2.3 Presumption of mechanical regularity

Where a mechanical device is of a type that is ordinarily in working order, the court must conclude that it was working on the particular instance in question. A party wishing to prove that such a device was not working properly bears an evidential burden. This presumption has been used to prove that mechanical devices such as traffic lights (*Tingle Jacobs and Co v Kennedy* [1964] 1 WLR 638) and speedometers (*Nicholas v Penny* [1950] 2 KB 466) were operating properly. This presumption applies to both civil and criminal proceedings.

3.3 Presumptions with proof of basic facts

This type of presumption is a 'true' presumption in that it only permits a court to conclude the existence of a fact ('the presumed fact') on the proof of a preliminary fact ('the basic fact'). For example, where it is proved that two persons went through a marriage ceremony with the intention to marry ('the basic fact'), the court may presume that all the formalities required for a valid marriage were complied with ('the presumed fact'). This type of presumption operates as an evidential short-cut enabling a party to prove a fact in issue without having to call any further evidence on the point.

Presumptions with proof of basic facts may be separated into three categories:

(a) irrebuttable presumptions of law;

(b) rebuttable presumptions of law; and

(c) presumptions of fact.

3.4 Irrebuttable presumptions of law

Definition: Upon proof of the preliminary fact the court must conclude the existence of the presumed fact, and no evidence may be adduced to the contrary. Thus, the presumption is said to be irrebuttable. In practice, irrebuttable presumptions are simply rules of substantive law. The following examples may be given:

3.4.1 Civil Evidence Act 1968, s 13(1)

Section 13(1) of the Civil Evidence Act 1968 provides:

In an action for libel or slander in which the question whether a person did or did not commit a criminal offence is relevant to an issue arising in the action, proof that at the time when that issue falls to be determined, that person stands convicted of that offence shall be conclusive evidence that he committed that offence; and his conviction thereof shall be admissible in evidence accordingly.

3.4.2 Children and Young Persons Act 1933, s 50

Section 50 of the Children and Young Persons Act 1933 provides:

It shall be conclusively presumed that no child under the age of 10 years can be guilty of an offence.

3.4.3 Sexual Offences Act 2003, s 76

Section 76 of the Sexual Offences Act 2003 provides:

(1) *If in proceedings for an offence to which this section applies it is proved that the defendant did the relevant act and that any of the circumstances specified in subsection (2) existed, it is to be conclusively presumed—*

(a) *that the complainant did not consent to the relevant act, and*

(b) *that the defendant did not believe that the complainant consented to the relevant act.*

(2) *The circumstances are that—*

(a) *the defendant intentionally deceived the complainant as to the nature or purpose of the relevant act;*

(b) *the defendant intentionally induced the complainant to consent to the relevant act by impersonating a person known personally to the complainant.*

Section 76 of the Sexual Offences Act 2003 applies to offences under sections 1 to 4 of that Act. Commentators have questioned the compatibility of this provision with the Human Rights Act 1998. It is thought that it might contravene the ECHR, Article 6(2) as it deprives the defendant of the opportunity to put forward a defence, namely that the victim was aware of the deception but consented nonetheless. However, the point has yet to be raised on appeal.

3.5 Rebuttable presumptions of law

Definition: Upon proof of the preliminary fact the court must conclude the existence of the presumed fact, unless sufficient evidence to the contrary is adduced. For this reason, the presumption is said to be rebuttable.

3.5.1 Civil proceedings

In civil proceedings rebuttable presumptions of law may be further divided into:

(a) *Evidential presumptions*. An evidential presumption places only an evidential burden on the party against whom it operates. Thus, in order to rebut the existence of the presumed fact, the party disputing it need only adduce some evidence on the point.

(b) *Persuasive presumptions*. A persuasive presumption places a persuasive, or legal, burden on the party against whom it operates. Thus, in order to rebut the existence of the presumed fact, the party disputing it must disprove it.

3.5.2 Criminal proceedings

In criminal proceedings the position is slightly different. As noted in **Chapter 2**, the prosecution bears the burden of proving the accused's guilt. As a result, where the prosecution rely on a common law rebuttable presumption, only an evidential burden can be placed on the defence. Similarly, where the defendant relies upon a common law rebuttable presumption, a legal burden must be placed on the prosecution. Statutory presumptions, on the other hand, may operate so as to place a legal burden on the accused. The prosecution is further restricted in its use of presumptions by virtue of the fact that it cannot rely on a presumption to prove facts which are central to an offence (*Dillon v R* [1982] AC 484, PC).

3.5.3 Presumption of marriage

There are two presumptions of marriage:

3.5.3.1 Formal validity

Where it is proved that the parties to the marriage went through a marriage ceremony with the intention to marry, it is presumed that the marriage complied with the formalities required for a valid marriage (*Piers v Piers* (1849) 2 HL Cas 331; *Mahadervan v Mahadervan* [1964] P 233). There is little authority on the point but it is thought that this presumption applies to both civil and criminal proceedings. In civil proceedings it operates as a persuasive presumption.

3.5.3.2   Essential validity

Where it is proved that a formally valid marriage ceremony was conducted, it is presumed that the parties to the marriage had the requisite capacity and gave their consent. Again, it is thought that this presumption applies to both civil and criminal proceedings. Insofar as it applies to civil proceedings it is probably a persuasive presumption although the authorities are not entirely clear on the point (*Re Peete* [1952] 2 All ER 599 and *Taylor v Taylor* [1967] P 25).

3.5.4   Presumption of legitimacy

Where paternity is in dispute, and it is proved that a child was either conceived whilst the mother was married (*Maturin v Attorney-General* [1938] 2 All ER 214) or born to her whilst she was lawfullly married (*The Poulett Peerage Case* [1903] AC 395), it is presumed that the child is the legitimate offspring of the parties to the marriage. This presumption applies to civil proceedings only. It is expressly made a persuasive presumption by the Family Law Reform Act 1969, s 26.

3.5.5   Presumptions of death

3.5.5.1   Common law

In *Chard v Chard* [1956] P 259 it was held that the court must presume a person's death where it is proved that:

(a) there is no acceptable affirmative evidence that the person was alive during a seven-year period;

(b) there are several people who would be expected to have heard from the person during that seven-year period;

(c) those people have not heard from that person; and

(d) all due enquiries that are appropriate have been made in respect of the person.

There is conflicting authority as to the date on which the fact of the deceased's death may be presumed. Some authorities suggest that the presumption only allows the court to conclude that the deceased died at the end of the seven-year period (*Re Phené's Trusts* (1870) LR 5 Ch App 139; *Chipchase v Chipchase* [1939] P 391). Other authority suggests that death can only be presumed to have occurred can on the date of trial (*Lal Chand Marwari v Manhant Ramrup Gir* (1925) 42 TLR 159, PC).

This presumption applies in both civil and criminal proceedings. In civil proceedings it is probably only an evidential (*Prudential Assurance v Edmonds* (1877) 2 App Cas 487, HL). This is also implicit from the first of the basic facts identified in *Chard v Chard*.

3.5.5.2   Matrimonial Causes Act 1973, s 19(3)

Section 19(3) of the Matrimonial Causes Act 1973 provides:

> *. . . the fact that for a period of seven years or more the other party to the marriage has been continually absent from the petitioner and the petitioner has no reason to believe that the other party has been living within that time shall be evidence that the other party is dead until the contrary is proved.*

This is a persuasive presumption and applies in matrimonial proceedings only.

3.5.5.3 Law of Property Act 1925, s 184

Section 184 of the Law of Property Act 1925 provides:

In all cases where . . . two or more persons have died in circumstances rendering it uncertain which of them survived the other or others, such deaths shall (subject to any order of the court) . . . be presumed to have occurred in order of seniority, and accordingly the younger shall be deemed to have survived the elder.

This is a persuasive presumption that applies in any civil proceedings concerning claims to property. An example of its application may be found in *Hickman v Percy* [1945] AC 304 where the residents of a house were all killed from a bomb explosion.

3.5.6 Sexual Offences Act 2003, s 75

Section 75 of the Sexual Offences Act 2003 provides:

(1) If in proceedings for an offence to which this section applies it is proved—

    (a) that the defendant did the relevant act,

    (b) that any of the circumstances specified in subsection (2) existed, and

    (c) that the defendant knew that those circumstances existed, the complainant is to be taken not to have consented to the relevant act unless sufficient evidence is adduced to raise an issue as to whether he consented, and the defendant is to be taken not to have reasonably believed that the complainant consented unless sufficient evidence is adduced to raise an issue as to whether he reasonably believed it.

The circumstances set out in s 75(2) include:

- the use of violence against the complainant at, or immediately before, the commission of the relevant Act (s 75(2)(a));

- the complainant's inability to communicate consent to the defendant due to his or her physical disability (s 75(2)(e)); and

- the administration of a substance to the complainant which was capable of causing or enabling the complainant to be stupefied or overpowered at the time of the relevant act (s 75(2)(f)).

The wording of the provision ('*unless sufficient evidence is produced*') and the fact that the burden is borne by the defence clearly make this an evidential presumption. As a result, it is thought that this provision is compatible with the Human Rights Act 1998. The Sexual Offences Act 2003, s 75 only applies to offences under ss 1 to 4 of the Act.

3.5.7 Presumption of official regularity

Where it is proved that a person has acted in a judicial, official or public capacity, it will be presumed that the person had been properly appointed and that the act complied with all necessary formalities. This presumption applies in both civil and criminal proceedings. In civil proceedings it operates as a persuasive presumption. Two examples may be given. In *R v Cresswell* (1873) 1 QBD 446, it was proved that a building had been used for marriage ceremonies, and so it was presumed that the building had been duly consecrated. In *R v Roberts* (1874) 14 Cox CC 101, CCR, it was proved that a person had acted as a deputy county court judge, and so it was presumed that that person had been properly appointed.

3.6   Presumptions of fact

Definition: Upon proof of the preliminary fact the court may conclude the existence of the presumed fact. Presumptions of fact are no more than commonly occurring examples of inferences that may be drawn on the basis of certain circumstantial evidence.

There are two key differences between presumptions of law and presumptions of fact. First of all, a presumption of fact does not compel the court to conclude the existence of the presumed fact, rather it simply permits it to do so. Secondly, a presumption of fact has no effect on the burden of proof, instead it places a 'tactical' burden on the party against whom it operates. In other words, because the presumption permits the tribunal of fact to find in favour of one party on a certain issue, it places a tactical obligation the other party to call evidence on that point, because if it fails to do so there is a danger that it may lose on that issue.

3.6.1   Presumption of intention

Section 8 of the Criminal Justice Act 1967 provides:

> *A court or jury, in determining whether a person has committed an offence,—*
>
> (a) *shall not be bound in law to infer that he intended or foresaw a result of his actions by reason only of its being a natural and probable consequence of those actions; but*
>
> (b) *shall decide whether he did intend or foresee that result by reference to all the evidence, drawing such inferences from the evidence as appear proper in the circumstances.*

The effect of this provision is that the tribunal of fact is not obliged to conclude that a defendant intended or foresaw the natural and probable consequence of his or her actions, but is permitted to infer that the defendant did so in the light of all the evidence. This presumption obviously only applies in criminal proceedings.

3.6.2   Presumption of guilty knowledge

This presumption applies where a person is charged with theft, handling stolen goods or an offence which has theft as an ingredient, such as burglary. Where evidence is given that the accused was found in possession of the property soon after it had been stolen, and he either offered no explanation as to how it came to be in his possession, or offered an explanation that the tribunal of fact find to be untrue, then the tribunal of fact may infer that the accused was either the thief, the handler of the stolen goods or the burglar. This presumption is more commonly known by practitioners as the doctrine of recent possession.

3.6.3   Presumption of continuance of life

Where a person is proved to have been alive on a particular date they may be presumed to have been alive on a subsequent date. Whether the presumption will be made in a particular case depends on factors such as the age and health of the person and the circumstances in which he or she was last seen. Clearly, the longer it is since the person was seen, the less likely it is that the tribunal of fact will reach the conclusion that he or she is still alive. This presumption applies in both civil and criminal proceedings.

3.7 *Res ipsa loquitur*

In *Scott v London and St Katherine Docks Co* (1865) 3 Hurl & C 596, it was held that, per Erle CJ:

... where the thing is shown to be under the management of the defendant or his servants, and the accident is such as in the ordinary course of things does not happen if those who have management use proper care, it affords reasonable evidence, in the absence of explanation by the defendants, that the accident arose from want of care.

Thus, in a claim for negligence, where it is shown that:

(a) something (whether an object or a location) is under the control of the defendant;

(b) that thing caused an accident; and

(c) the accident would not have happened if the thing had been properly managed,

then it may be presumed that the accident arose due to the negligence of the defendant. There is contradictory authority as to whether the doctrine of *res ipsa loquitur* is properly classified as a presumption of fact (see, for example, *Ng Chun Pei v Lee Chuen Tat* [1988] RTR 298, PC), a persuasive presumption (see, for example, *Woods v Duncan* [1946] AC 401) or an evidential presumption (see, for example, *The Kite* [1933] P 154). It has been argued that this presumption defies classification; the strength of the inference of negligence that may be drawn in a particular case will differ depending on the facts, and so the presumption can operate so as to place either a tactical, evidential or legal burden on the other party.

3.8 Conflicting presumptions

Where two presumptions of equal strength apply to the facts of a case, the one leading to a conclusion which conflicts with that of the other, the authorities are unclear as to the approach that the court should adopt. *Monckton v Tarr* (1930) 2 BWCC 504 is authority for the view that conflicting presumptions of equal strength should cancel each other out. However, *Taylor v Taylor* [1967] P 25 suggests that the court may choose between the different presumed facts by a comparison of their likelihood, or even on the basis of policy considerations.

Witnesses

The most common way for evidence to be adduced is through the testimony of a witness. In this chapter we will consider the rules that determine which persons may give evidence, when a person may be compelled to give evidence and how a person's evidence will be given.

4.1 Oaths and affirmations

4.1.1 Sworn evidence

Generally, evidence in both civil and criminal proceedings will be given on oath. Evidence given on oath is known as sworn evidence. The present law is governed by the Oaths Act 1978.

Section 1(1) of the 1978 Act directs the form and manner in which oaths are to be administered and taken by Christians and Jews. In *R v Chapman* [1980] Crim LR 42 it was held that failure to comply with s 1(1), which was directive only, did not necessarily invalidate the whole taking of the oath. The oath was valid if taken in a way binding and intended to be binding upon the conscience of the witness.

Section 1(3) of the 1978 Act provides that for those of other religious beliefs the oath shall be administered 'in any lawful manner'. An oath is lawfully administered where:

- it appears to the court that the oath is binding on the conscience of the witness; and
- the witness considers the oath to be binding on his or her conscience.

In *R v Kemble* [1990] 3 All ER 116, CA, the evidence of a Muslim witness was held to have been lawfully administered even though it had been administered on the New Testament, whereas Islam requires that a binding oath must be made on a copy of the Koran that is written in Arabic.

To prevent persons with no religious belief from taking an oath and later alleging that, because of their beliefs, the oath was of no effect, s 4(2) of the 1978 Act provides that the fact that a person taking an oath has no religious belief does not prevent it from being binding on him. Section 5(1) permits any person who objects to being sworn to make a solemn affirmation instead of taking an oath. A solemn affirmation is of the same force and effect as an oath (s 5(4)).

4.1.2 Criminal proceedings

Competence to give sworn evidence is governed by the Youth Justice and Criminal Evidence Act 1999 ('the YJCEA 1999'). Section 55(2) of the Act provides:

The witness may not be sworn . . . unless—
(a) he has attained the age of 14, and
(b) he has sufficient appreciation of the solemnity of the occasion and of the particular responsibility to tell the truth which is involved in taking the oath.

Under the YJCEA 1999, s 55(3), a person who is able to give intelligible testimony, ie

- is able to understand questions put to him or her; and
- is able to give answers that can be understood (s 55(8)),

is presumed to have sufficient appreciation of the solemnity of the occasion and of the responsibility to tell the truth, as long as no evidence tending to show the contrary is adduced. If such evidence adduced, it is for the party seeking to have the witness sworn to prove, on a balance of probabilities, that the witness has attained the age of 14 and has a sufficient appreciation of the matters mentioned (s 55(4)).

Section 55 of the YJCEA 1999 provides that the determination of whether a witness may be sworn (which can be raised by either party or the court) must take place in the absence of the jury (s 55(5)), but in the presence of the parties. Expert evidence can be received (s 55(6)).

A witness who is not permitted to give sworn evidence by virtue of the YJCEA 1999, s 55(2) must give his or her evidence unsworn (s 56(2)) and a court may properly receive unsworn evidence in such circumstances (s 56(4)).

Children and persons of unsound mind are those who most commonly give evidence unsworn. The amount of weight to be attached to the evidence of such a witness is a matter for the jury. Clearly, if the evidence is so tainted with insanity as to be unworthy of credit, the jury will properly disregard it (*R v Hill* (1851) 2 Den 254). Equally, however, a person suffering from a mental illness may be a reliable witness. In *R v Barrat* [1996] Crim LR 495, CA, the witness was suffering from fixed belief in paranoia and held bizarre beliefs about certain aspects of her private life, but the court could see no reason to suppose that on matters not affected by her condition, her evidence was not as reliable as that of any other witness.

4.1.3 Civil proceedings

The general rule is that a witness who is not sworn cannot give evidence at all and a judgment based on such evidence will be set aside as a nullity (*R v Marsham, ex p Lawrence* [1912] 2 KB 362). However, a person may give unsworn evidence if:

- the case is brought on the small claims track and the court does not require evidence on oath (CPR, r 27.8(4));
- the witness is producing a document that can be identified by another witness on oath (*Perry v Gibson* (1834) 1 Ad & El 48);
- the evidence is of the terms of an agreement between parties and the witness is counsel for one of the parties (*Hickman v Berens* [1895] 2 Ch 638); or
- the witness is a child and is not competent to give sworn testimony (Children Act 1989, s 96).

Unlike criminal cases, there is no general power on the part of the civil courts to accept the unsworn testimony of a person suffering from a mental illness or other mental disability.

4.2 Competence and compellability

A witness is said to be 'competent' if he or she can as a matter of law be called by a party to give evidence. A witness is said to be 'compellable' if, being competent, he or she can as a matter of law be compelled by the court to give evidence. A compellable witness who, having been ordered to attend court, refuses to do so, or on attending court, refuses to give sworn evidence is liable to be imprisoned for contempt of court in proceedings before the High Court or the Crown Court, committed to prison in proceedings before a magistrates' court or fined up to £1,000 in proceedings before a county court.

4.2.1 General rule

The general rule at common law has two limbs:

- all persons are competent; and
- all competent persons are compellable.

In criminal proceedings the first limb of the general rule has been put on a statutory footing in the YJCEA 1999, s 53(1), which provides:

At every stage in criminal proceedings all persons are (whatever their age) competent to give evidence.

The general rule that all persons are competent and that all competent witnesses are compellable is subject to a number of statutory and common law exceptions in both civil and criminal proceedings.

4.2.2 Exceptions in criminal proceedings

4.2.2.1 Children and persons under a disability

As noted at **4.2.1** above, all persons, whatever their age, are competent to give evidence in criminal proceedings. Thus, a child witness is not prevented from giving evidence by virtue of his or her age. However, the YJCEA 1999, s 53(3) provides:

A person is not competent to give evidence in criminal proceedings if it appears to the court that he is not a person who is able to—
(a) understand questions put to him, and
(b) give answers to them which can be understood.

This exception applies to all witnesses but will most commonly affect children and persons who are under a disability.

As the requirements of the test for competence in the YJCEA 1999, s 53(3) are the same as the basic facts needed to trigger the presumption of a sufficient appreciation of the solemnity of the occasion and of the responsibility to tell the truth in s 55(3) (see **4.1.2** above), a competent witness, who is over 14 years of age, will be presumed to be capable of giving sworn evidence.

4.2.2.2 The accused

For the prosecution

Section 53(4) of the YJCEA 1999 provides:

A person charged in criminal proceedings is not competent to give evidence in the proceedings for the prosecution (whether he is the only person charged, or is one of two or more persons charged in the proceedings).

Section 53(5) states that 'a person charged in criminal proceedings' does not include a person who is not, or is no longer, liable to be convicted of any offence in the proceedings. An accused is thus competent to give evidence for the prosecution:

- on acquittal;
- where a *nolle prosequi* has been entered on the direction of the Attorney-General;
- on pleading guilty; or
- where separate trials are ordered.

Where the accused pleads guilty and intends to give evidence for the prosecution against his former co-accused, there is a danger that he may tailor his evidence in the hope of receiving a more lenient sentence. Thus, the court in this situation has a discretion whether or not to sentence him before he gives evidence (*R v Palmer* (1993) 99 Cr App R 83). A similar situation arises where the prosecution wish to call an accomplice against whom proceedings are pending. There is a rule of practice, but not law, that the prosecution should only be allowed to call such witnesses where it has given an undertaking to discontinue proceedings or not prosecute him (*R v Pipe* (1966) 51 Cr App R 17; *R v Turner* (1975) 61 Cr App R 67). As it is only a rule of practice, it is ultimately a matter of judicial discretion whether or not to allow the accomplice to be called.

For the accused

By virtue of YJCEA 1999, s 53(1), the accused is competent to give evidence on his or her own behalf. However, he or she is not compellable. Section 1(1) of the Criminal Evidence Act 1898, provides:

A person charged in criminal proceedings shall not be called as a witness in the proceedings except upon his own application.

Where the accused does elect to give evidence, two important consequences follow. First, any evidence that the accused may give is admissible against any co-accused (*R v Rudd* (1948) 32 Cr App R 138). Secondly, he or she is open to cross-examination by both the prosecution and any co-accused. Thus, while an accused is neither competent nor compellable for the prosecution when appearing in his or her own defence, he or she may be cross-examined by the prosecution about the guilt of the co-accused (*R v Paul* [1920] 2 KB 183).

If an accused decides not to testify it should be the invariable practice of counsel to record the decision, and to cause the accused to sign the record, giving a clear indication that he has by his own will decided not to testify bearing in mind the advice, if any, given to him by his counsel (*R v Bevan* (1994) 98 Cr App R 354, CA; *R v Chatroodi* [2001] All ER (D) 259 (Feb)). In practice, this is done by endorsing the decision on the brief itself.

Concerning the inferences that may be drawn from the failure of an accused to give evidence, see **Chapter 13**.

For the co-accused

The accused is competent as a witness for a co-accused (YJCEA 1999, s 53(1)) but is not compellable (Criminal Evidence Act 1898, s 1(1)). Once the accused is no longer a 'person charged' in the proceedings, he or she will become compellable. An accused ceases to be a person charged:

- on pleading guilty;
- on acquittal; or
- where separate trials are ordered.

4.2.2.3 Spouse or civil partner of the accused

Competence

A spouse or civil partner is competent for any party in criminal proceedings (YJCEA 1999, s 53(1)). However, as a person charged in the proceedings is not competent to give evidence for the prosecution, where the accused and the spouse or civil partner are both charged in the proceedings neither will be competent for the prosecution (s 53(4)).

Compellability

The compellability of the spouse or civil partner of the accused is governed by the Police and Criminal Evidence Act 1984, s 80:

(2) *In any proceedings the spouse or civil partner of a person charged in the proceedings shall, subject to subsection (4) below, be compellable to give evidence on behalf of that person.*

(2A) *In any proceedings the spouse or civil partner of a person charged in the proceedings shall, subject to subsection (4) below, be compellable—*

    (a) *to give evidence on behalf of any other person charged in the proceedings but only in respect of any specified offence with which that other person is charged; or*

    (b) *to give evidence for the prosecution but only in respect of any specified offence with which any person is charged in the proceedings.*

(3) *In relation to the spouse or civil partner of a person charged in any proceedings, an offence is a specified offence for the purposes of subsection (2A) above if—*

    (a) *it involves an assault on, or injury or a threat of injury to, the spouse or civil partner or a person who was at the material time under the age of 16;*

    (b) *it is a sexual offence alleged to have been committed in respect of a person who was at the material time under that age; or*

    (c) *it consists of attempting or conspiring to commit, or of aiding, abetting, counselling, procuring or inciting the commission of, an offence falling within paragraph (a) or (b) above.*

(4) *No person who is charged in any proceedings shall be compellable by virtue of subsection (2) or (2A) above to give evidence in the proceedings.*

(4A) *References in this section to a person charged in any proceedings do not include a person who is not, or is no longer, liable to be convicted of any offence in the proceedings (whether as a result of pleading guilty or for any other reason).*

(5) *In any proceedings a person who has been but is no longer married to the accused shall be compellable to give evidence as if that person and the accused had never been married.*

(5A) *In any proceedings a person who has been but is no longer the civil partner of the accused shall be compellable to give evidence as if that person and the accused had never been civil partners.*

(6) *Where in any proceedings the age of any person at any time is material for the purposes of subsection (3) above, his age at the material time shall for the purposes of that provision be deemed to be or to have been that which appears to the court to be or to have been his age at that time.*

(7) *In subsection (3)(b) above 'sexual offence' means an offence under the Sexual Offences Act 1956, the Indecency with Children Act 1960, the Protection of Children Act 1978 or Part 1 of the Sexual Offences Act 2003.*

For the prosecution

A spouse or civil partner, subject to one exception, is compellable to give evidence on behalf of the prosecution against the accused or any co-accused, in respect of any specified offences (Police and Criminal Evidence Act 1984, s 80(2A)(b)). Section 80(3)(a) to (c) provides that an offence is a specified offence if:

- it involves an assault on, or injury or threat of injury to, the spouse or civil partner (s 80(3)(a));
- it involves an assault on, or injury or threat of injury to, a person under the age of 16 (s 80(3)(a));
- it is a sexual offence committed in relation to a person under the age of 16 (s 80(3)(b)); or
- it is an offence that consists of attempting or conspiring to commit, or of aiding, abetting, counselling, procuring or inciting the commission of any of the above offences (s 80(3)(c)).

The drafting of section 80 gives rise to an apparent problem. This stems from the use of the word 'involves' in s 80(3)(a). The question arises whether the test is factual or legal, ie whether s 80(3) only refers to those offences which include assault, injury or threat of injury as an element of the offence, or whether it also includes those offences which involve an assault, injury or threat of injury, on the facts but not as a legal requirement.

The exception referred to above is that where the spouse or civil partner is a charged in the same proceedings, he or she is not compellable unless he or she is no longer likely to be convicted (s 80(4), (4A)).

For the accused

The spouse or civil partner of the accused is generally compellable for the accused (Police and Criminal Evidence Act 1984, s 80(2)). The only exception is that where the spouse or civil partner is a charged in the same proceedings, he or she is not compellable unless he or she is no longer likely to be convicted (s 80(4), (4A)).

For the co-accused

A spouse or civil partner is compellable to give evidence on behalf of any co-accused, but only in respect of specified offences (Police and Criminal Evidence Act 1984, s 80(2A)(a)). Where the spouse or civil partner is a charged in the same proceedings, he or she is not compellable unless he or she is no longer likely to be convicted (s 80(4), (4A)).

Former spouse or civil partner

Under the Police and Criminal Evidence Act 1984, s 80(5) and (5A), the provisions of s 80 do not apply where the spouse is no longer married to the accused or the civil partnership has ended. If a marriage is void ab initio there never was a spouse. Thus in *R v Khan* (1987) 84 Cr App R 44, CA, it was held that a woman with whom a man had gone through a bigamous ceremony of marriage was a competent witness against him for the prosecution. (This case was decided at a time when s 80(5) governed competence as well as compellability.) On the other hand parties who are married remain married where they are judicially separated, or a simply not cohabiting (whether by reason of an informal arrangement, a separation agreement or a non-cohabitation order).

Cohabitees

In *R v Pearce* [2002] 1 WLR 1553, it was held that the Police and Criminal Evidence Act 1984, s 80 does not cover the cohabitee of an accused who is not married to the accused. This case was decided prior to the amendment by the Civil Partnerships Act 2004 which introduced civil partners to s 80, but it is submitted that the same principle will continue to apply so that s 80 will only apply to spouses or civil partners.

4.2.2.4 Heads of state

The Sovereign and the sovereign or head of foreign states are competent (YJCEA 1999, s 53(1)) but not compellable. Furthermore, diplomats and consular officials, and their and staff, have immunity from compellability pursuant to a wide variety of statutory provisions.

4.2.2.5 Bankers

Bankers and bank officials are competent (YJCEA 1999, s 53(1)). Their compellability is governed by the Bankers' Books Evidence Act 1879. Section 6 of that Act provides that bankers and bank officials shall not be compellable, in legal proceedings to which the bank is not a party, to produce any banker's book the contents of which may be proved under the Act, or to appear as witnesses to prove the matters recorded therein, unless by order of a judge.

4.2.2.6 Judges

Judges and masters are competent (YJCEA 1999, s 53(1)) but cannot be compelled to give evidence relating to judicial function.

4.2.2.7 Procedure

Where there is an issue regarding the competence of a witness it should be determined at the beginning of the trial (*R v Yacoob* (1981) 72 Cr App R 313, CA). It is determined by the court in the absence of the jury (YJCEA 1999, ss 53(3) and 54(4)). It may be raised either by a party to the proceedings or by the court of its own motion (s 54(1)). The party calling the witness must satisfy the court, on the balance of probabilities, that the witness is competent to give evidence in criminal proceedings (s 54(2)). Any questioning of the witness is conducted by the court in the presence of the parties (s 54(6)).

The parties may call expert evidence (s 54(5)). Under different provisions of the YJCEA 1999 the court has the power to make special measures directions to facilitate the giving of evidence by a vulnerable or incapacitated witness (see **4.9** below). The court, in determining competence under s 53(3), is required to treat the witness as if they have the benefit of any special measures directions that the court would make if the witness were to give evidence at trial (s 54(3)).

4.2.3 Exceptions in civil proceedings

The general rule in civil proceedings is that all persons are competent and that all competent persons are compellable. The only exceptions to this rule are children, persons of unsound mind, the Sovereign, foreign heads of state, diplomats, bankers and judges.

4.2.3.1 Children

Section 96 of the Children Act 1989 provides:

(1) *Subsection (2) applies where a child who is called as a witness in any civil proceedings does not, in the opinion of the court, understand the nature of an oath.*

(2) *The child's evidence may be heard by the court if, in its opinion—*

(a) *he understands that it is his duty to speak the truth and;*

(b) *he has sufficient understanding to justify his evidence being heard.*

A 'child', for these purposes, is a person under the age of 18 (s 105). The court must first determine whether or not a child witness understands the oath (s 96(1)). In deciding this issue the courts are likely to be guided by the decision of the Court of Appeal in *R v Hayes*

[1977] 1 WLR 238. *Hayes* is a criminal case that was decided at a time when the position in criminal proceedings was similar to that provided by s 96. The test laid down in *Hayes* was:

Whether the child has a sufficient appreciation of the solemnity of the occasion and the added responsibility to tell the truth, which is involved in taking an oath, over and above the duty to tell the truth which is an ordinary duty of normal social conduct.

In civil proceedings, if a child fails this test, he or she may only give evidence if the conditions in s 96(2) are satisfied and, if given, any evidence must be unsworn.

On matters of procedure, the courts are also likely to draw on previous criminal authority. As the competence of the witness is a matter for the judge, he or she should put to the child preliminary questions so as to be able to form an opinion (*R v Surgenor* (1940) 27 Cr App R 175). Whether a child is sufficiently young to warrant examination to see whether he or she can give sworn evidence is a matter for the judge to decide on the particular facts of the case. However, in *R v Khan* (1981) 73 Cr App R 190, CA, it was held that although much depends on the type of child before the court, as a general working rule inquiry is necessary in the case of a child under the age of 14.

4.2.3.2 Persons of unsound mind

In civil cases the competence of a person of unsound mind is determined by his or her ability to understand the nature and sanction of the oath. If the witness of unsound mind does not understand the nature of the oath then he or she cannot testify (*R v Hill* (1851) 2 Den 254). In determining whether such a witness understands the nature of the oath, the courts have adopted the test in *R v Hayes* [1977] 1 WLR 234, namely whether a witness has a sufficient appreciation of the solemnity of the occasion and the added responsibility to tell the truth, which is involved in taking an oath, over and above the duty to tell the truth which is an ordinary duty of normal social conduct. If the witness understands the nature of the oath, and is therefore competent to testify, it is a matter for the tribunal of fact to decide how much weight should be attached to his or her evidence (*R v Hill* (1851) 2 Den 254).

4.2.3.3 Heads of state, bankers and judges

The rules concerning the competence and compellability of the Sovereign, foreign heads of state, diplomats, bankers and judges in criminal proceedings (see **4.2.2.4** to **4.2.2.6** above) apply equally to civil proceedings with one exception, namely that in civil proceedings competence is determined by the common law and not the YJCEA 1999.

4.3 Form of witness evidence

The general rule is that evidence must be given orally by a witness who is present in court. However, there are a number of exceptions to this rule.

4.3.1 Criminal proceedings

In criminal proceedings the exceptions are that:

- evidence may be read with the agreement of both parties (Criminal Justice Act 1967, s 9);
- evidence may be given through a live link (Criminal Justice Act 2003, s 51; YJCEA 1999, s 24; Criminal Justice Act 1988, s 32); and

- evidence may be given by a pre-recorded video (Criminal Justice Act 2003, s 137; YJCEA 1999, ss 27 and 28)

4.3.1.1   Evidence read by agreement

By virtue of the Criminal Justice Act 1967, s 9, a written statement shall be admissible to the same extent as oral evidence by the maker of the statement where:

(a) the statement purports to be signed by the maker (s 9(2)(a));

(b) the statement contains a declaration by that person to the effect that it is true to the best of his knowledge and belief and that he made the statement knowing that if it were tendered in evidence, he would be liable to prosecution if he wilfully stated in it anything which he knew to be false or did not believe to be true (s 9(2)(b));

(c) a copy of the statement has been served on each of the other parties (s 9(2)(c)); and

(d) within seven days of service none of the parties have served a notice objecting to the statement being tendered in evidence (s 9(2)(d)).

A party wishing to rely on this provision must therefore serve the statement at least seven days in advance of the hearing. This provision is usually relied upon where a witness does not give controversial evidence.

4.3.1.2   Evidence through a live link

Criminal Justice Act 2003, s 51

Under the Criminal Justice Act 2003, s 51, the court has a general power to direct that a witness, other than the defendant, give evidence through a live link. The live link will usually be a closed circuit television link, but could be any technology with the same effect such as video conferencing facilities or the internet. Evidence may only be given through a live link where it is in the interests of the efficient or effective administration of justice for that person to do so. In deciding whether to make a direction the court must consider all the circumstances in the case, including:

(a) the availability of the witness;

(b) the need for the witness to attend in person;

(c) the importance of the witness's evidence to the proceedings;

(d) the views of the witness; and

(e) whether a direction might tend to inhibit any party to the proceedings from effectively testing the witness's evidence.

Criminal Justice Act 1988, s 32

Under the Criminal Justice Act 1988, s 32, a witness who is outside the United Kingdom may give his or her evidence by live television link but only in the following proceedings:

- trials on indictment;

- appeals to the criminal division Court of Appeal;

- references by the Criminal Cases Review Commission;

- proceedings in youth courts; and

- appeals to the Crown Court arising out of such proceedings.

These provisions are presently only in force in relation to proceedings for offences involving the killing of any person and certain offences involving serious fraud.

Special measures directions
Under the YJCEA 1999, s 19, the court has the power to make a 'special measures direction' in respect of certain types of vulnerable witnesses. Where the court makes a special measures direction it may order that the witness may give evidence by live link (YJCEA 1999, s 24).

4.3.1.3 Pre-recorded video evidence

Special measures directions
When making a special measures direction under YJCEA 1999, s 19, the court may also direct that a pre-recorded video interview with a witness stand as his or her evidence-in-chief (YJCEA 1999, s 27) and that cross-examination or re-examination be pre-recorded (YJCEA 1999, s 28). Special measures directions will be considered in more detail at **4.9**.

Where the prosecution rely on a pre-recorded video of a child's evidence-in-chief, the judge may allow the jury to have transcripts of the recording if this would assist them in following the recording. The judge should make it clear that the transcript is only for that limited purpose and should give them directions both at the time, and during summing up, so as to safeguard against the risk of disproportionate weight being given to the transcript (*R v Welstead* [1996] 1 Cr App R 59, CA). The judge has a discretion to permit a jury to view a video of a child's evidence again in court (*R v Rawlings* [1995] 1 WLR 178). However, the judge must always warn the jury not to attach disproportionate weight to the evidence and remind them of the cross-examination and re-examination of the complainant.

Criminal Justice Act 2003, s 137
Under s 137 of the Criminal Justice Act 2003 the court has a general power to direct that all, or part, of the pre-recorded video evidence of a witness, other than the defendant, shall stand as a witness's evidence-in-chief where:

(a) a person is called as a witness in proceedings for an offence that is either triable on indictment only or is a prescribed either-way offence (s 137(a));

(b) that person witnessed the offence, part of the offence, or events closely connected with the offence (s 137(b));

(c) the witness has given a video recorded account of those events at a time when they were still fresh in his or her memory (s 137(c),(d) and (e));

(d) the witness's recollection of the events in question is likely to have been significantly better when he or she gave that account (s 137(3)(b)(i));

(e) the witness in oral evidence in the proceedings asserts the truth of the statements made by him or her in the recorded account (s 137(2)); and it is in the interests of justice for the recording to be admitted (s 137(3)(b)(ii)) having regard to:
  (i) the interval between the time of the events in question and the time when the recorded account was made (s 137(4)(a));
  (ii) any factors that might affect the reliability of what the witness said in that account (s 137(4)(b));
  (iii) the quality of the recording (s 137(4)(c)); and
  (iv) any views of the witness as to whether his evidence in chief should be given orally or by means of the recording (s 137(4)(d)).

It does not matter if the statements in the recorded account were made on oath (s 137(5)). Once a video recording has been admitted, the witness may not give evidence-in-chief otherwise than by means of the recording as to any matter which, in the opinion of the court, has been dealt with adequately in the recorded account (s 138). It is submitted that the same principles that have been applied in relation to a child witness's pre-recorded video evidence will be adopted in relation to evidence adduced under s 137.

4.3.2   Civil proceedings

Under CPR, r 32.2, the general rule is that any fact which needs to be proved by the evidence of a witness is to be proved:

(a) at trial, by his or her oral evidence given in public; and

(b) at any other hearing, by his or her evidence in writing.

However, this provision is subject to any provision to the contrary contained in the CPR or elsewhere, or to any order of the court (CPR, r 32.2(2)). For example, under CPR, r 32.3, the court may allow a witness to give evidence through a video link or by other means.

Under CPR, r 35(1), where a party has served a witness statement, and wishes to rely at trial on the evidence of the witness who made the statement, the witness must be called to give oral evidence unless the court orders otherwise or the statement is put in as hearsay evidence. By r 35(2), where a witness is called to give oral evidence under r 35(1), his or her witness statement shall stand as his or her evidence-in-chief unless the court orders otherwise. However, the court may permit a witness to amplify his or her witness statement and give evidence in relation to new matters that have arisen since the witness statement was served if it considers that there is a good reason for not confining the evidence of the witness to the contents of his or her statement (r 32.5(3), (4)).

For details of the formal requirements of witness statements and discussion of other procedural issues such as disclosure see the *Civil Litigation Manual* and *Blackstone's Civil Practice* 2005.

4.4   Power of a party to choose its witnesses

4.4.1   No property in a witness

In both criminal and civil proceedings a party may call any witness even if the witness has previously agreed to give evidence for the opposing party. In *Harmony Shipping Co SA v Saudi Europe Line Ltd* [1979] 1 WLR 1380, CA, a handwriting expert was approached by the plaintiffs to authenticate a particular document. The expert's view was that it was a forgery (which was unfavourable to their case). Later, the defendants asked him to advise on the same issue and, forgetting his previous involvement in the case, he expressed the same view as before. On discovering that the plaintiffs had already retained him, the expert refused to accept any further instructions from the defendants. The defendants then issued a subpoena against him. The Court of Appeal held that, as there is no property in a witness, the expert witness was compellable on behalf of the defendants. It should be noted that any communications between the expert and the plaintiffs might have been protected by legal professional privilege (see **Chapter 17**). However, in *Harmony Shipping* it was not the communications that were in issue but the evidence.

4.4.2   Criminal proceedings

4.4.2.1   The accused

The accused may call such witnesses to support his or her case as he or she thinks fit (subject to the rules of competence and compellability). Although, once a witness has given evidence for the prosecution, he or she cannot be called to give evidence for the defence (*R v Kelly* The Times, 27 July 1985, CA).

4.4.2.2   The prosecution

As for the prosecution, the relevant rules for trials on indictment were set out in *R v Russell-Jones* [1995] 3 All ER 239, CA:

(a) the prosecution must bring to court all the witnesses whose statements have been served as witnesses on whom the prosecution intends to rely, if the defence want them to attend. (In deciding which statements to serve, the prosecution has an unfettered discretion, but must normally disclose material statements not served.)

(b) the prosecution enjoys a discretion, which must be exercised in the interests of justice to promote a fair trial, whether to call, or tender for cross-examination, any witnesses it requires to attend;

(c) the prosecution ought normally to call, or offer to call, all the witnesses who give direct evidence of the primary facts of the case, even if there are inconsistencies between one witness and another, unless for good reason the prosecutor regards the witnesses' evidence as unworthy of belief;

(d) it is for the prosecution to decide which witnesses can give direct evidence of the primary facts;

(e) the prosecutor is also the primary judge of whether or not a witness is unworthy of belief; and

(f) the prosecutor is not obliged to proffer a witness merely in order to give the defence material to attack the credit of other prosecution witnesses.

In *R v Haringey Justices, ex p DPP* [1996] QB 351, DC, it was held that the principles set out in *Russell-Jones* also applied to criminal trials in magistrates' courts. However, the problem was determining at what point the procedure in a magistrates' court is equivalent to the service of statements in proceedings on indictment. The court concluded that, in the case of an offence triable either way, that point was reached when the prosecution served copies of witness statements by way of advanced information, but that in other cases the prosecutor should retain an unfettered discretion until the case starts.

There is conflicting authority as to whether a judge has the power to direct the prosecution to call a witness. In *R v Sterk* [1972] Crim LR 391, prosecution counsel referred to a witness in opening but later formed the view that he was unreliable and declined to call him. The Court of Appeal held that the judge should have ordered the prosecution to at least tender the witness for cross-examination. However, in *R v Oliva* [1965] 1 WLR 1028 it was held that the judge has a discretion to invite the prosecution to call a witness, but that if they refuse the ultimate sanction is for the judge to call the witness himself. This approach was followed in *R v Haringey Justices, ex p DPP* [1996] QB 351, DC.

4.4.3   Civil proceedings

Prior to the implementation of the Civil Procedure Rules, parties to civil proceedings had an unfettered choice as to which witnesses they would call (*Briscoe v Briscoe* [1966] P 501). However, CPR, r 32.1 provides that:

(1)   The court may control the evidence by giving direction as to—
    (a)   the issues on which it requires evidence;
    (b)   the nature of the evidence which it requires to decide those issues;
    (c)   the way in which the evidence is to be placed before the court.

(2)   The court may use its power under this rule to exclude evidence that would otherwise be admissible.

However, the judge has no power to order a party to call a particular witness (*Society of Lloyd's v Jaffray* The Times, 3 August 2000).

4.5 Order of witnesses

Parties are generally free to call witnesses in the order of their choice. The only major restriction concerns the order of defence witnesses in criminal trials. The Police and Criminal Evidence Act 1984, s 79 provides that:

If at the trial of any person for an offence—

(a) *the defence intends to call two or more witnesses to the facts of the case; and*

(b) *those witnesses include the accused,*

the accused shall be called before the other witness or witnesses unless the court in its discretion otherwise directs.

The court may exercise its discretion to permit the defence to call a witness to fact other than the defendant first where, for example:

(a) the witness's evidence relates to some formal or uncontroversial matter; or

(b) the witness's evidence concerns events which occurred before the time of the events about which the accused will give evidence and the defence case will be more readily understood if told in chronological order.

Section 79 of the Police and Criminal Evidence Act 1984 is of no application to persons who are not witnesses to fact eg expert witnesses.

4.6 Calling a witness after the close of the case

The general rule is that a party must adduce all of its evidence before the close of its case. Thus, a party will generally not be allowed at some later stage to remedy defects in its case, or contradict the evidence of the other party, by adducing additional evidence.

4.6.1 Criminal proceedings

In criminal proceedings there are two well-established exceptions to this general rule.

(a) Matters arising *ex improviso*. Where a matter arises which could not reasonably have been foreseen then the judge has a discretion to allow a party who has already closed its case to call evidence in rebuttal (*R v Scott* (1984) 79 Cr App R 49; *R v Hutchinson* (1986) 82 Cr App R 51, CA).

(b) Formal evidence omitted through inadvertence or oversight. The court will normally allow evidence in rebuttal to be called in order to make good a purely formal omission. For example, in *Price v Humphries* [1958] 2 QB 353, DC, the prosecutor failed to prove that the Director of Public Prosecutions had given leave to bring the proceedings.

However, the discretion of the trial judge to permit the prosecution to call evidence after the close of its case is not restricted to the above exceptions. It has been held that the judge has a wider discretion, the limits of which should not be precisely defined, but which should be exercised only rarely outside the two established exceptions (*R v Francis* [1991] 1 All ER 225, CA), especially when the evidence is tendered after the case for the accused has begun (*R v Munnery* [1992] Crim LR 215, CA). In *Francis*, evidence having been given that at a group identification the man standing at position number 20 was identified, the prosecution were allowed to recall the inspector in charge of the identification procedure to say that it was the appellant who was standing at position number 20. Counsel for the prosecution was under the impression that the name of the person standing in that position was not in issue. In *Jolly v DPP* [2000] Crim LR 471, DC, the Divisional Court held that it was now 'beyond argument' that there was a general discretion to permit the calling of evidence after the close of the prosecution case which must be exercised having regard to the interests of justice and to any possible prejudice to the defendant. The court stated that the discretion would be sparingly exercised but it doubted whether it assisted the court any longer to speak in terms of exceptional circumstances. Each case had to be considered on its own facts.

There is a sacrosanct rule that once the jury have retired to consider their verdict, no witnesses may be called or recalled (*R v Owen* [1952] 2 QB 362). However, the judge has a discretion to permit witnesses to be called up to that point and witnesses have even been called while the judge is summing up the case (*R v Sanderson* [1953] 1 WLR 392).

4.6.2   Civil proceedings

A similar approach to that taken in criminal proceedings has been followed in civil cases. In *Stocznia Gdanska SA v Latvian Shipping Co* (2000) LTL 12/2/2001, the claimants made an application to adduce further evidence after the close of the trial but before judgment had been handed down. It was held that the claimants ought to be allowed to adduce it as to ignore it would neither be just nor in accordance with the overriding objective (CPR, r 1.1).

4.7   Judge's powers to call and examine witnesses

4.7.1   Criminal proceedings

In criminal proceedings in the Crown Court the judge, without the consent of either party, may call and examine any witnesses not called by the parties (*R v Chapman* (1838) 8 Car & P 558; *R v Harris* [1927] 2 KB 587). Magistrates have a similar power (*R v Haringey Justices, ex p DPP* [1996] QB 351, DC).

4.7.2   Civil proceedings

Prior to the implementation of the Civil Procedure Rules, apart from cases for civil contempt, the judge could not call a witness without the consent of the parties (*Re Enoch and Zaretsky, Bock and Co.'s Arbitration* [1910] 1 KB 327, CA). Under CPR, r 32.1, the court now has the power to direct the nature of the evidence which it requires to decide an issue and the way in which such evidence is to be placed before the court. Thus, the judge has the power to direct that a witness give evidence without the consent of either party.

4.8 Securing the attendance of witnesses

4.8.1 Criminal proceedings

Where the prosecution or defence anticipate that a witness will not attend the Crown Court voluntarily, they may apply for a witness summons under the Criminal Procedure (Attendance of Witnesses) Act 1965, s 2. The party seeking the summons must show that the witness is likely to be able to give material evidence, or produce a material exhibit, but will not voluntarily attend as a witness or will not voluntarily produce the exhibit. Failure to comply with a witness summons may be summarily punished as contempt of court by up to three months' imprisonment (s 3).

In a magistrates' court the attendance of witnesses may be secured by a witness summons or a warrant under the Magistrates' Court Act 1980, s 97. A witness summons may similarly be issued where the witness is likely to be able to give material evidence, or produce a material exhibit, but will not voluntarily attend as a witness or will not voluntarily produce the exhibit. However, should the witness fail to attend court in answer to the summons, the court may issue a warrant for his or her arrest (s 97(3)). Refusal to be sworn or give evidence may be imprisoned for up to one month and/or fined up to £2,500 (s 97(4)).

4.8.2 Civil proceedings

The attendance of a witness in a civil case is secured by the issuing of a witness summons under CPR, r 34. A civil witness summons may similarly require a witness to attend court to give evidence or to produce a document. Failure to obey a witness summons issued by the High Court is contempt of court and the contemnor may be committed to prison for up to 2 years and/or fined (*Wyatt v Wingford* (1729) 2 Ld Raym 1528; Contempt of Court Act 1981, s 14(1)). Refusal to be sworn or give evidence also amounts to contempt of court (*R v Daye* [1908] 2 KB 333). A person failing to answer to a witness summons issued by a county court may be fined up to £1,000 (County Courts Act 1984, ss 55(1) and (2)). Refusal to be sworn or give evidence may also be punished by a fine (ss 55(1)).

4.9 Special measures directions

The YJCEA 1999 introduced in criminal proceedings a statutory regime of 'special measures directions'. A special measures direction is an order that may be made by the court, either of its own motion or on application by either party, which is intended to protect vulnerable and intimidated witnesses and facilitate the giving of their evidence.

4.9.1 Eligibility

A witness will be eligible in principle for a special measures direction if he or she comes within any of the following three categories:

(a) he or she is under the age of 17 at the time of the hearing (s 16(1)(a));

(b) the court considers that the quality of evidence given by the witness is likely to be diminished because the witness:

(i) suffers from a mental disorder within the meaning of the Mental Health Act 1983;

(ii)   has a significant impairment of intelligence and social functioning; or

(iii)   has a physical disability or is suffering from a physical disorder (s 16(1)(b)).

(c) The court considers that the quality of evidence given by the witness is likely to be diminished by reason of fear or distress on the part of the witness in connection with testifying in the proceedings (s 17(1)). In determining this issue, s 17(2) requires the court to take into account factors such as:

(i)   the nature and alleged circumstances of the offence;

(ii)   the age of the witness;

(iii)   the social and cultural background and ethnic origins of the witness;

(iv)   the religious beliefs and political opinions of the witness; and

(v)   the behaviour of the accused, his or her family or associates towards the witness.

The accused is not eligible for a special measures direction (YJCEA 1999, ss 16(1) and 17(1)). In *R (S) v Waltham Forest Youth Court* [2004] 2 Cr App R 21, it was held that non-availability of special measures directions to the accused did not breach ECHR, Article 6.

4.9.2   Availability

Witnesses who are eligible for a special measures direction by virtue of their age (s 16(1)(a)) or physical or mental incapacity (s 16(1)(b)) may have the special measures directions available under ss 23 to 30. Witnesses who are eligible by virtue of their fear or distress (s 17(1)) may have the special measures directions available under ss 23–28. See Table 4.1.

Table 4.1 Special measures directions

Section authorising direction	Special measures direction available	Available		Limits
		s 16	s 17	
23	Witness prevented from seeing accused by screen or other means	Yes	Yes	
24	Evidence given by live link	Yes	Yes	
25	Exclusion of specified person from court	Yes	Yes	Only if: • sexual offence; or • reasonable grounds for believing that person other than accused has sought or will seek to intimidate the witness about testifying.
26	Wigs and gowns not worn	Yes	Yes	
27	Pre-recorded video interview with witness to stand as evidence in chief	Yes	Yes	
28	Cross-examination or re-examination to be pre-recorded	Yes	Yes	Only if s 27 direction has been made.
29	Examination of witness through interpreter or court-approved intermediary	Yes	No	
30	Use of devices to enable communication between witness and others during examination	Yes	No	

Where the court determines that the witness is eligible, it must then go on to consider:

(a) whether any of the special measures available (or any combination of them) would be likely to improve the quality of evidence given by the witness; and, if so,

(b) which of those special measures (or any combination of them) would be likely to maximise so far as practicable the quality of the witness's evidence.

It should then give a direction providing for the appropriate measures to apply (s 19(2)(a) and (b)). The court must have regard to all the circumstances of the case and, in particular, the views of the witness and the extent to which any special measure might tend to inhibit the witness's evidence being effectively tested by a party to the proceedings (s 19(3)).

4.9.3 Child Witnesses

A 'child witness' is a witness who is eligible for a special measures direction because he or she is under 17 years of age (ss 16(1)(a) and 21(1)(a)). Section 21(3) of the YJCEA 1999 provides that, in relation to a child witness, the court must make a special measures direction that:

(a) provides for any video recorded interview to stand as evidence-in-chief under s 27 of the YJCEA 1999 (s 21(3)(a)); and

(b) provides for any evidence which is not given by means of a video recording (whether in-chief or otherwise) to be given by means of a live link under s 24 of the YJCEA 1999 (s 21(3)(b)).

However, the court need not make such a special measures direction where:

(a) the facilities are not available (s 21(4)(a));

(b) having regard to all the circumstances it is in the interests of justice not to admit a video recording of the witness's evidence-in-chief (s 21(4)(b)); or

(c) the court is satisfied that neither direction would be likely to maximise the quality of the witness's evidence so far as is practicable (for example, where some other special measures available would have that effect) (s 21(4)(c)).

4.9.4 Child witnesses in need of special protection

Under the YJCEA 1999, s 21(1)(b) a child witness is 'in need of special protection' where he or she is a witness to one or more of the offences specified in YJCEA 1999, s 35(3), namely:

(a) sexual offences under either Part 1 of the Sexual Offences Act 2003 or the Protection of Children Act 1978 (s 35(3)(a));

(b) kidnapping, false imprisonment or child abduction (s 35(3)(b));

(c) child cruelty (s 35(3)(c)); or

(d) any other offence involving an assault on, or injury, or threat of injury to any person (s 35(3)(d)).

4.9.4.1 Offences other than sexual offences

Where a child witness is deemed in need of special protection by virtue of being a witness to an offence other than a sexual offence (categories (b) to (c)), the court must make a special measures direction as outlined above in the case of an ordinary child witness (s 21(3)). However, the court need not make such a special measures direction where:

- the facilities are not available (s 21(4)(a)); or
- having regard to all the circumstances it is in the interests of justice not to admit a video recording of the witness's evidence-in-chief (s 21(4)(b)).

4.9.4.2 Sexual Offences

By virtue of ss 21(3) and (6) of the YJCEA 1999, where a child witness is deemed in need of special protection because of his or her being a witness to a sexual offence (category (a) above), the court must make a special measures direction that:

(a) provides for any video recorded interview to stand as evidence-in-chief under s 27 of the YJCEA 1999 (s 21(3)(a));

(b) provides for video recorded cross-examination (otherwise than by the accused in person) and re-examination to be admitted under s 28 of the YJCEA 1999 (s 21(6)(a) and (b)); and

(c) provides for any evidence which is not given by means of a video recording (whether in chief or otherwise) to be given by means of a live link under s 24 of the YJCEA 1999 (s 21(3)(b)).

However, the court need not make such a special measures direction where:

- the facilities are not available (s 21(4)(a) and (7)(a));
- having regard to all the circumstances it is in the interests of justice not to admit a video recording of the witness's evidence-in-chief (s 21(4)(b)); or
- the witness has informed the court that he or she does not want a special measure under s 28 (video recording of cross-examination and re-examination) to apply (s 21(7)(b)).

5

Corroboration and suspect witnesses

5.1 Introduction

The general rule is that a court's decision may properly be based on the evidence of a single witness. However, in criminal proceedings the law of evidence recognises two exceptions to this rule:

- offences requiring corroboration; and
- suspect witnesses.

5.2 Offences requiring corroboration

Corroboration is required before a person can be convicted of the following offences.

5.2.1 Perjury

Section 13 of the Perjury Act 1911 provides:

A person shall not be liable to be convicted of any offence against this Act, or of any offence declared by any other Act to be perjury or subornation of perjury, or to be punishable as perjury or subornation of perjury, solely upon the evidence of one witness as to the falsity of any statement alleged to be false.

The jury must be directed by the judge to look for evidence which is capable of corroborating the evidence given by the main witness as to the falsity of the statement made by the accused; if they can find none, the should acquit the accused (*R v Rider* (1986) 83 Cr App R 207). Corroboration need not be by the testimony of a witness and may take the form of documentary evidence.

5.2.2 Speeding

Section 89(1) of the Road Traffic Regulation Act 1984 creates the offence of speeding. Subsection (2) provides:

A person prosecuted for such an offence shall not be liable to be convicted solely on the evidence of one witness to the effect that, in the opinion of that witness, the person prosecuted was driving the vehicle at a speed exceeding a specified limit.

The need for corroboration arises from the possible inaccuracy of a witness's evidence as to the speed of the vehicle. However, in most cases evidence of the vehicle's speed comes from a reading taken by an automatic camera or radar gun. As this is factual evidence, rather than opinion evidence, s 89(2) of the 1984 Act will not apply.

5.2.3 Attempt

Where an accused is charged with attempting to commit either of the two preceding offences, the same requirement for corroboration applies to the trial for the attempt as it would in a trial for the completed offence (Criminal Attempts Act 1981, s 2(1) and (2)(g)).

5.3 Suspect witnesses

A witness is said to be suspect where there is a danger that he or she may give unreliable evidence.

5.3.1 Children, complainants in sexual cases and accomplices

Historically, the common law recognised three categories of suspect witness. The judge was required to warn the jury of the danger of convicting the accused on the basis of such a witness's uncorroborated evidence. The three categories were:

- complainants in sexual cases;
- children; and
- accomplices giving evidence for the prosecution.

The requirement on the judge to give such warnings to the jury was abrogated by the Criminal Justice Act 1988, s 34 (in the case of children) and the Criminal Justice Act 1994, s 32 (in the case of complainants in sexual offences and accomplices).

Following the abolition of the requirement to give corroboration warnings for complainants in sexual offences and accomplices, the Court of Appeal gave guidance on how the court should approach the evidence of unreliable witnesses in *R v Makanjuola* [1995] 2 Cr App R 469. Lord Taylor of Gosforth CJ summarised the new position in eight points:

(a) Section 32(1) [of the Criminal Justice and Public Order Act 1994] abrogated the requirement to give a corroboration direction in respect of an alleged accomplice or a complainant of a sexual offence, simply because a witness falls into one of those categories.

(b) It is a matter for the judge's discretion what, if any, warning he considers appropriate in respect of such a witness as indeed in respect of any other witness in whatever type of case. Whether he chooses to give a warning and in what terms will depend on the circumstances of the case, the issues raised and the content and quality of the witness's evidence.

(c) In some cases, it may be appropriate for the judge to warn the jury to exercise some caution before acting upon the unsupported evidence of a witness. This will not be so simply because the witness is a complainant of a sexual offence nor will it be necessarily be so because the witness is alleged to be an accomplice. There will need to be an evidential basis for suggesting that the evidence of the witness may be unreliable. An evidential basis does not include mere suggestion by cross-examining counsel.

(d) If any question arises as to whether the judge should give a special warning in respect of a witness, it is desirable that the question be resolved by discussion with counsel in the absence of the jury before final speeches.

(e) Where the judge does decide to give some warning in respect of a witness, it will be appropriate to do so as part of the judge's review of the evidence and his comments as to how the jury should evaluate it rather than as a set-piece legal direction.

(f) Where some warning is required, it will be for the judge to decide the strength and terms of the warning. It does not have to be invested with the whole florid regime of the old corroboration rules.

(g) Attempts to reimpose the straightjacket of the old corroboration rules are strongly to be deprecated.

(h) Finally, the Court of Appeal will be disinclined to interfere with a trial judge's exercise of his discretion save in a case where that exercise is unreasonable in the *Wednesbury* sense.

Lord Taylor gave further guidance as follows:

> The judge will often consider that no special warning is required at all. Where, however, the witness has been shown to be unreliable, he or she may consider it necessary to urge caution. In a more extreme case, if the witness is shown to have lied, to have made previous false complaints, or to bear the defendant some grudge, a stronger warning may be thought appropriate and the judge may suggest it would be wise to look for some supporting material before acting on the impugned witness's evidence. We stress that these observations are merely illustrative of some, not all, of the factors which the judges may take into account in measuring where a witness stands in the scale of reliability and what response they should make at that level in their directions to the jury.

> The crucial factor is that the judge always has a discretion whether to warn or not. He or she has to decide:

> - whether any warning is appropriate; and
> - what form the warning should take.

> The decision will depend on the issues raised in the trial, the circumstances of the case and the judge's view of the content and quality of the witness's evidence. In those cases where the judge suggests that the jury might look for supporting material, he or she ought to identify for the jury any evidence which is capable of being supporting evidence and also any evidence which a jury might think offers support but which in law cannot do so (*R v B (MT)* [2000] Crim LR 181).

5.3.2   Analogous cases

The common law also recognised several further categories of witness which, while not requiring a full corroboration warning from the judge, nevertheless required a warning as to a special need for caution. They became known collectively as the 'analogous cases' and included categories such as co-defendants and witnesses tainted by an improper motive. In *R v Muncaster* [1999] Crim LR 409, CA, it was held that the guidance in *R v Makanjuola* applied equally to these cases.

5.3.2.1   Co-defendants

Where a defendant gives evidence incriminating a co-defendant a warning should normally be given by the trial judge in which the jury should be directed to examine the evidence of such a witness with care because he or she may have his or her own interests to serve (*R v Knowlden* (1983) 77 Cr App R 94; *R v Jones* [2004] 1 Cr App R 60). In *R v Petkar*

[2004] 1 Cr App R 270, it was held that a failure to give a warning would not be fatal in a case where it was obvious that the accused had an axe to grind. Where an accused gives evidence in or her co-accused such a direction would be wrong (*R v Burley* [2001] EWCA Crim 731).

5.3.2.2   Witnesses with improper motive

A judge should warn a jury to treat with caution the evidence of a witness where there is material to suggest that a witness's evidence may be tainted by improper motive (*R v Beck* [1982] 1 WLR 461). Evidence given by a fellow prisoner of a cell confession allegedly made by the accused is inherently unreliable and, while it is undesirable to restrict the circumstances in which a judge might warn the jury to exercise caution in regard to a particular witness's evidence, and the terms in which any such warning might be given, the judge in such a case ought to draw the attention of the jury to any indications that the evidence might be tainted by improper motive and their possible significance. He should then advise the jury to be cautious before accepting his or her evidence (*Benedetto v R* [2003] 1 WLR 1545, PC).

5.4   Identification witnesses

The Court of Appeal has recognised that identification evidence is also potentially unreliable and has taken a similar approach to that taken in relation to suspect witnesses. Whenever the prosecution case rests wholly or substantially on the correctness of one or more identifications of the accused, which the defence allege to be mistaken, the judge should warn the jury of the special need for caution. Where the quality of the identifying evidence is poor, the judge should withdraw the case from the jury unless there is evidence to support the reliability of the identification. The judge should identify to the jury the evidence which he or she adjudges to be capable of being supporting evidence and any evidence which the jury might think was supporting but which does not have that quality (*R v Turnbull* [1977] QB 224). Identification evidence will be considered further at **Chapter 14**.

5.5   Confessions by mentally handicapped defendants

Section 77(1) of the Police and Criminal Evidence Act 1984 requires the trial judge to warn the jury of the special need for caution before convicting a defendant where the prosecution evidence depends wholly or substantially on a confession by a defendant suffering from a mental handicap and the confession was not made in the presence of an independent person. The same requirement applies to summary trials (s 77(2)) and trials on indictment without a jury (s 77(2A)). 'Independent person' does not include a police officer or a person employed for or engaged on police purposes (s 77(3)). 'Mentally handicapped' means a state of arrested or incomplete development of mind which includes significant impairment of intelligence and social functioning (s 77(3)).

The warning should be given by the trial judge when summing up the case. However, where the prosecution case depends wholly upon confession evidence, the accused suffers from a significant degree of mental handicap, and, in the opinion of the judge, the confession evidence is unconvincing to a point where the jury, properly directed by the judge, could not properly convict in reliance on that evidence, then the judge should withdraw the case from the jury (*R v Mackenzie* (1993) 96 Cr App R 98).

Witness evidence

6.1 Introduction

There are three stages to the examination of a witness:

- examination-in-chief;
- cross-examination; and
- re-examination.

We will consider each stage in turn.

6.2 Examination-in-chief

Examination-in-chief is the questioning of a witness by the party calling him or her.

6.2.1 Leading questions

6.2.1.1 General rule

Leading questions are those questions that either suggest the answer sought or assume the existence of a fact not yet established. For example, in a case where the prosecution case is that A stole money from B, a question that suggests the answer sought would be:

'Did you see A taking money from B's wallet?'

A question that assumes the existence of a fact not yet established would be:

'How much money did you see A take from B?'

The rationale of this rule is to prevent the witness from being led into giving answers that are favourable only to the party calling him or her and thereby giving a distorted account of the events. If evidence is elicited by leading questions, it remains admissible, but the weight to be attached to it may be reduced (*Moor v Moor* [1954] 1 WLR 927).

6.2.1.2 Exceptions to the rule

There are three main exceptions to the rule:

(a) Introductory matters. Leading questions may be asked in relation to matters that are introductory, such as the witness's name and occupation.

(b) Undisputed matters. Where a matter is not in dispute, leading questions may be asked.

(c) Hostile witnesses. Where the court has given leave for party to treat its own witness as hostile, leading questions may be put (see **6.2.5.2**).

6.2.2 Refreshing memory out of court

The rules regarding the circumstances in which a witness is permitted to refresh his or her memory out of court apply to both civil and criminal proceedings.

In *R v Richardson* [1971] 2 QB 484, the Court of Appeal approved the practice of permitting a witness to refresh his or her memory from a copy of his or her witness statement before giving evidence. The Court recognised that requiring witnesses to give evidence without the opportunity to do so would reduce their testimony in the witness box to more of a test of memory than of truthfulness. It would tend to create difficulties for the honest witness but would be likely to do little to hamper dishonest witnesses. The Court warned that it would be wrong for several witnesses to be handed their statements in circumstances which enabled one to compare with another what each had said. Likewise, such statements should not be read to witnesses in each other's presence (*R v Skinner* (1994) 99 Cr App R 212, CA).

Where prosecution witnesses in a criminal trial have refreshed their memory before giving evidence, it is desirable that the defence should be informed (*Worley v Bentley* [1976] 2 All ER 449). However, a failure to do so will not, by itself, be a ground for acquittal (*R v Westwall* [1976] 2 All ER 812). The defence are entitled to inspect and cross-examine the witness on a document used to refresh his or her memory. Where such cross-examination extends to matters contained in the document to which the witness has not referred, then the party calling the witness is entitled to put the whole of the document in evidence so that the court may see the document on which the witness has been cross-examined.

The judge has a discretion to permit a witness who has started to give evidence to refresh his or her memory from a witness statement where the witness indicates:

(a) that he or she cannot now recall the details of events because of the lapse of time since they took place;

(b) that he or she made a statement much nearer the time of the events and that the contents of the statement represent his or her recollection at the time he made it;

(c) that he or she had not read the statement before coming into court; and

(d) that he or she wishes to have an opportunity to read the statement before continuing to give evidence.

The witness may either withdraw from the witness box or remain there to read the statement. However, there must be no communication with the witness during that time. The statement must be removed when witness comes to give evidence and he or she should not be permitted to refer to it again (*R v Da Silva* [1990] 1 All ER 29). It would appear from *R v South Ribble Magistrates' Court, ex p Cochrane* [1996] 2 Cr App R 544, DC that the conditions set out in *Da Silva* are not strict requirements; whether to allow a witness to refresh their memory from a statement once they have started to give evidence is always a matter of discretion for the court. In *ex p Cochrane*, a witness who had read his statement before giving evidence, but had not taken it in properly, was allowed to refresh his memory. The court could see no logical distinction between a witness in that position and someone who has not read his or her statement at all. In criminal proceedings this discretion must now be read subject to the Criminal Justice Act 2003, s 139 (see **6.2.3.2**).

6.2.3   Refreshing memory in court

6.2.3.1   Civil proceedings

In the vast majority of cases a witness's witness statement will stand as his or her evidence-in-chief (CPR, r 32.5(2)). However, a witness may nevertheless benefit from being able to refresh his or her memory while giving evidence. The witness will be permitted to refresh his or her memory from any document where:

(a) the document was made or verified at the time of the events in question or so shortly thereafter that the facts were still fresh in the witness's memory;

(b) the document is produced in court for inspection by the court and any other party; and

(c) that, in cases where the witness has no recollection of the events in question but simply swears to the accuracy of the contents of the document, it is the original or, if the original is not available, an accurate copy.

Past recollection revived

This rule applies not only where a witness's memory is refreshed, but also where the witness has no actual recollection of the past event and simply swears to the accuracy of the record in the document. These two types of memory refreshing are often referred to as 'present recollection revived' and 'past recollection recorded' respectively. An example of the latter may be found in *Maugham v Hubbard* (1828) 8 B & C 14 where an issue arose as to whether a sum of money had been paid. A witness was permitted to prove receipt of the money by looking at a written acknowledgement initialled by himself and stating in evidence that, on the basis of seeing his initials, he was sure that he had received the money, although he had no actual recollection of doing so.

Stage of proceedings

A witness may even be allowed to refresh his or her memory at any stage of the proceedings, even in re-examination (*R v Sutton* [1991] Crim LR 836, CA).

Making and verifying

A memory-refreshing document must either be made by the witness or made by another and verified by the witness.

Verification may be visual or aural. In *Anderson v Whalley* (1852) 3 Car & Kir 54, it was held that entries in a ship's log made by the mate and inspected by the captain could be used by the latter to refresh his memory. In *R v Kelsey* (1982) 74 Cr App R 213, it was held that a witness could refresh his memory from a note dictated to a police officer and read back to the witness where the police officer was called to prove that the note was the one he had taken down and read back. Verification must take place when the facts are still fresh in the memory of the witness (*Eleftheriou v Eleftheriou* [1993] Crim LR 947).

Originals and copies

Where the witness has no recollection of the past event but simply swears to the accuracy of the contents of a document (see *Maugham v Hubbard* (1828) 8 B & C 14 above), then the original must be produced (*Doe d Church and Philips v Perkins* (1790) 3 TR 749). However, if the original is not available, an accurate copy can be used (*Topham v McGregor* (1844) Car & K 320).

The court may permit a witness to refresh his or her memory from a document based on an original note and containing substantially what was in it. In *R v Cheng* (1976) 63 Cr App R 20, a police officer made a statement based upon notes that he had made shortly after the defendant's arrest. By the time of the trial the original notes had been lost but the officer was permitted to refresh his memory from the statement because the statement substantially reproduced what was in the original notes, even if it was not an exact copy.

In *Attorney-General's Reference (No 3 of 1979)* (1979) 69 Cr App R 411, the court allowed a witness to refresh his memory from a document that he had compiled from jottings taken during the course of an interview, the events being fresh in his mind at the time he made the note, even though he was unable to decipher the jottings at trial and the note was not a complete record of the interview.

Inspection and cross-examination

A memory-refreshing document must be made available for inspection by any other parties to the proceedings who may then cross-examine the witness on its contents. Where course-examination goes beyond those parts used by the witness to refresh his or her memory, the party calling the witness is entitled to put the document in evidence (*Gregory v Tavernor* (1833) 6 Car & P 280; *Senat v Senat* [1965] P 172). Once put in evidence, a memory-refreshing document is evidence of consistency and/or the truth of the matters stated in it (Civil Evidence Act 1995, ss 1 and 6(4) and (5)).

6.2.3.2   Criminal proceedings

Criminal proceedings were formerly subject to the common law rules. However, the Criminal Justice Act 2003, s 139 provides:

> (1) *A person giving oral evidence in criminal proceedings about any matter may, at any stage in the course of doing so, refresh his memory of it from a document made or verified by him at an earlier time if—*
>
> (a) *he states in his oral evidence that the document records his recollection of the matter at that earlier time; and*
>
> (b) *his recollection of the matter is likely to have been significantly better at that time than it is at the time of his oral evidence.*

It follows that in criminal proceedings there is no requirement that the memory-refreshing document be made contemporaneously or even while the events were still fresh in the memory. Instead, all that is required is that:

- the witness states in evidence that the document records his recollection at an earlier time; and
- his or her recollection at that time is likely to have been significantly better than when giving evidence.

Once those matters are proved there is a presumption that the witness will be permitted to refresh his or her memory from the document.

Prior to the implementation of the Criminal Justice Act 2003 ('CJA 2003'), the common law rules applied to criminal proceedings. It is submitted that where appropriate the principles established at common law and set out above in relation to civil proceedings will continue to apply. For example, the CJA 2003, s 139 applies both where 'past recollection is recorded' and where 'present recollection is revived'. Similarly, under the CJA 2003 a document may still be verified by the witness visually or aurally (*Anderson v Whalley* (1852) 3 Car & Kir 54; *R v Kelsey* (1982) 74 Cr App R 213).

Evidential status of a memory-refreshing document: Examination-in-chief.
The CJA 2003, s 120 provides:

> (1) *This section applies where a person (the witness) is called to give evidence in criminal proceedings.*
>
> . . .

> *(4)   A previous statement by the witness is admissible as evidence of any matter stated of which oral evidence by him would be admissible if,—*
>
> *(a)   any of the following conditions is satisfied, and*
>
> *(b)   while giving evidence the witness indicates that to the best of his knowledge and belief he made the statement, and that to the best of his belief it states the truth.*
>
> *. . .*
>
> *(6)   The second condition is that the statement was made by the witness when the matters stated were fresh in his memory but he does not remember them, and cannot reasonably be expected to remember them, well enough to give oral evidence of them in the proceedings.*

In essence, where a witness cannot remember, and cannot reasonably be expected to remember, the events about which he or she has been called to testify, a statement made by the witness when those events were still fresh in his or her memory may be admitted as part of that witness's evidence-in-chief. The statement is admitted as evidence of the matters stated. However, if there is anything contained in the statement about which the witness would not have been permitted to give oral evidence (ie because it is inadmissible by virtue of some other rule of evidence) that part of the statement will remain inadmissible. The fact that the witness has to rely on a document to give evidence is a matter that may affect the weight that is attached to the evidence.

Evidential status of a memory-refreshing document: cross-examination. As in civil proceedings, a memory-refreshing document must be made available for inspection by the other party who may then use it in cross-examination. Where cross-examination on the document goes beyond those parts used to refresh memory, then the party calling the witness is entitled to put the document in evidence (see also *Gregory v Tavernor* (1833) 6 Car & P 280; *Senat v Senat* [1965] P 172). Additionally, in *R v Sekhon* (1987) 85 Cr App R 19, the Court of Appeal held that where the nature of the cross-examination involves a suggestion that the witness has subsequently made up his or her evidence, which will usually involve, either expressly or impliedly, an allegation that the memory-refreshing document is concocted, the document may be admissible to rebut this suggestion and to show that it is a genuine contemporaneous record which has not subsequently been altered.

The Criminal Justice Act 2003, s 120 provides:

> *(1)   This section applies where a person (the witness) is called to give evidence in criminal proceedings.*
>
> *. . .*
>
> *(3)   A statement made by the witness in a document—*
>
> *(a)   which is used by him to refresh his memory while giving evidence.*
>
> *(b)   on which he is cross-examined, and*
>
> *(c)   which as a consequence is received in evidence in the proceedings,*
>
> *is admissible of any matter stated of which oral evidence by him would be admissible.*

Thus, where a memory-refreshing document is admitted as evidence as a result of cross-examination it is evidence of authenticity, consistency, and the truth of its contents.

In *R v Sekhon* (1987) 85 Cr App R 19, the Court of Appeal identified two other circumstances in which a memory-refreshing document may go before a jury:

(a) where it is difficult for the jury to follow the cross-examination of the witness who has refreshed his or her memory, without having the record before them; and

(b) where it is convenient to use the record as an aide-mémoire as to the witness's evidence where that evidence is long and involved.

The Court of Appeal stated that whether it was appropriate to treat a memory-refreshing document put before the jury in these circumstances as an exhibit was of no practical importance. However, this case was decided at a time when a memory-refreshing document could only be admitted as evidence of consistency or authenticity. It is submitted that, in the light of the CJA 2003, s 120, such a document will not be formally exhibited as evidence because, if it is, it will then be evidence of the truth of its contents.

6.2.4   Previous consistent statements

The general rule, in both civil and criminal proceedings, is that a witness may not be asked in examination-in-chief about his or her previous oral or written statement, consistent with his or her testimony, in order to show the witness's consistency (*R v Gregson* [2003] 2 Cr App R 521). Nor may a party seek to adduce evidence of such a statement through another witness. The rationale for the rule is that such evidence is too easy for a witness to fabricate. It has also been suggested that such evidence is, in any event, superfluous as a witness's evidence should be taken as true until there is a reason for impeaching it.

Two examples may be given. In *Corke v Corke* [1958] P 93, the Court of Appeal held that a wife, whose husband had accused her of having committed adultery with a lodger, should not have been permitted to adduce evidence that she had telephoned her doctor immediately after the accusation had been made, requesting him to come at once and examine both her and the lodger, with a view to establishing their innocence of misconduct. In *R v Roberts* [1942] 1 All ER 187, the accused was charged with the murder of a girl by shooting her. At the trial he gave evidence that the gun went off accidentally while he was trying to make up a quarrel with the girl. Two days after the alleged offence, the accused had told his father that his defence would be one of accident. The Court of Appeal held that held that proof of this conversation was not permissible if tendered to bolster the credibility of the accused by showing his consistency.

There are a number of exceptions to the rule in both civil and criminal proceedings.

6.2.4.1   Exceptions in civil proceedings

Section 6 of the Civil Evidence Act 1995 provides:

> (2)   *A party who has called or intends to call a person as a witness in civil proceedings may not in those proceedings adduce evidence of a previous statement made by that person except—*
> (a)   *with leave of the court, or*
> (b)   *for the purpose of rebutting a suggestion that his evidence has been fabricated.*
> . . .
> (4)   *Nothing in this Act affects any of the rules of law as to the circumstances in which, where a person called as a witness in civil proceedings is cross-examined on a document used by him to refresh his memory, that document may be made evidence in the proceedings.*

Therefore, there are three exceptions to the general rule in civil proceedings:

- the statement is admissible with the leave of the court (s 6(2)(a));
- the statement is admissible to rebut an allegation of recent fabrication (s 6(2)(b)); and
- the statement is admissible as a memory-refreshing document (s 6(4)).

Leave of the court

Under the Civil Evidence Act 1995, s 6(2)(a) the court has a wide discretion to admit previous consistent statements where it would be just to do so. In *Morris v Stratford-on-Avon Rural District Council* [1973] 1 WLR 1059, a decision under the equivalent provision in the Civil Evidence Act 1968, the trial was held 5 years after the accident which gave rise to the action. A witness whose recollection of the facts was hazy was allowed to adduce in his evidence-in-chief a statement that he had made to an insurance company 9 months after the accident.

Evidence in rebuttal of an allegation of recent fabrication

The mere fact that the cross-examination of a witness suggests that the witness is not worthy of belief does not allow the proof of a previous statement by the witness to reinforce his or her credibility. This is so even if the cross-examination exposes a previous inconsistency or contradiction between his or her evidence and a statement made on a previous occasion (*R v Coll* (1889) 25 LR Ir 522; *R v Beattie* (1998) 89 Cr App R 302). However, where it is suggested that the witness has recently fabricated his or her evidence, evidence is admissible in rebuttal to show that on an earlier occasion the witness made a statement consistent with that testimony (*R v Oyesiku* (1971) 56 Cr App R 240, CA; *Fox v General Medical Council* [1960] 1 WLR 1017). For example, in *Flanaghan v Fahy* [1918] 2 IR 361, it was put to a witness, who had testified that a certain document was a forgery, that he had invented his evidence because of the hostility which existed between him and the defendant. The witness was then allowed to call evidence to show that he had told someone else that it was a forgery before the cause of the hostility between him and the defendant arose.

In *R v Oyesiku* (1971) 56 Cr App R 240, the Court of Appeal approved the judgment of Dixon CJ in the Australian case *Nominal Defendant v Clement* (1961) 104 CLR 476 in which he held that:

(a) where it is suggested that the witness's account is a recent invention or reconstruction, even though not with conscious dishonesty, a previous consistent statement is admissible;

(b) the previous statement must have been made either contemporaneously with the event or at a time sufficiently early to be inconsistent with the suggestion that the allegation that his or her evidence is a recent invention or reconstruction;

(c) the judge must exercise great care in determining whether a previous statement is admissible. In particular, he or she must be satisfied that:

(i) the account given by the witness has been attacked on the ground of recent invention or reconstruction or that foundation for such an attack has been laid;

(ii) the contents of the previous statement are in fact to the like effect as the account given by the witness in evidence; and

(iii) having regard to the time and circumstances in which it was made, it rationally tends to the answer the attack.

The facts in *R v Oyesiku* were as follows. After the defendant had been arrested, and while he was still in custody, his wife made a written statement to his solicitor. At trial, prosecution counsel suggested in cross-examination that she had made up her evidence to help her husband. The Court of Appeal held that in re-examination she had properly been permitted to adduce evidence of her previous consistent statement. However, the conviction was quashed as the trial judge had not allowed the document to go before the jury which would have assisted them in determining the extent to which the previous statement answered the attack.

A previous consistent statement can be proved either during the re-examination of the witness or by calling the other person to whom the statement was made (*R v Wilmot* (1989) 89 Cr App R 341).

Memory-refreshing document

See **6.2.3.1** above.

Evidential status of a previous consistent statement

A previous consistent statement admissible under the Civil Evidence Act 1995, s 6 is admissible as evidence of consistency and the truth of the matters stated (ss 1 and 6(5)).

6.2.4.2   Exceptions in criminal proceedings

Memory-refreshing documents

See **6.2.3.2** above.

Previous identifications

At common law, evidence of a previous identification of the accused by a witness out of court is permissible (*R v Christie* [1914] AC 545). However, the common law rules have been superseded by the Criminal Justice Act 2003, s 120 which provides:

(1)   *This section applies where a person (the witness) is called to give evidence in criminal proceedings.*

...

(4)   *A previous statement by the witness is admissible as evidence of any matter stated of which oral evidence by him would be admissible if,—*

   (a)   *any of the following conditions is satisfied, and*

   (b)   *while giving evidence the witness indicates that to the best of his knowledge and belief he made the statement, and that to the best of his belief it states the truth.*

...

(5)   *the first condition is that the statement identifies or describes a person, object or place.*

Recent complaint

For a long time it was a part of the common law that where a complainant, in the a case of a sexual offence, made a voluntary complaint shortly after the alleged incident, then evidence could be given of the complaint. Such evidence was not evidence of the matters stated, but evidence of consistency between the complainant's conduct and his or her testimony, and to disprove consent (*R v Lillyman* [1896] 2 QB 167, CCR). Again, the common law has now been superseded by the Criminal Justice Act 2003, s 120 which provides:

(1)   *This section applies where a person (the witness) is called to give evidence in criminal proceedings.*

...

(4)   *A previous statement by the witness is admissible as evidence of any matter stated of which oral evidence by him would be admissible if,—*

   (a)   *any of the following conditions is satisfied, and*

   (b)   *while giving evidence the witness indicates that to the best of his knowledge and belief he made the statement, and that to the best of his belief it states the truth.*

...

(7)   *The third condition is that—*

   (a)   *the witness claims to be a person against whom an offence has been committed,*

   (b)   *the offence is one to which the proceedings relate,*

   (c)   *the statement consists of a complaint made by the witness (whether to a person in authority or not) about conduct which would, if proved, constitute the offence or part of the offence,*

   (d)   *the complaint was made as soon as could reasonably be expected after the alleged conduct,*

   (e)   *the complaint was not made as a result of a threat or a promise, and*

   (f)   *before the statement is adduced the witness gives oral evidence in connection with its subject matter.*

(8)   *For the purpose of subsection (7) the fact that the complaint was elicited (for example, by a leading question) is irrelevant unless a threat or promise was involved.*

Section 120(7) broadens the previous common law exception so as to permit evidence of recent complaint in relation to any offence, not just a sexual offence. Previously, evidence of a complaint elicited as the result of a leading question was inadmissible (*R v Osborne* [1905] 1 KB 551). However, the CJA 2003 now expressly permits the admission of complaints made in answer to such questions as long as no threat or promise was involved (s 120(8)). Of course, such questioning may nevertheless affect the weight that the tribunal of fact attach to such evidence.

A recent complaint is evidence of the truth of the matters stated, consistency between a complainant's conduct and his or her evidence at trial and, where consent is in issue, lack of consent (s 120(4)).

Statements in rebuttal of recent fabrication

The Criminal Justice Act 2003, s 120(2) provides that:

> (1) *This section applies where a person (the witness) is called to give evidence in criminal proceedings.*
>
> (2) *If a previous statement by the witness is admitted as evidence to rebut a suggestion that his oral evidence has been fabricated, that statement is admissible as evidence of any matter stated of which oral evidence by the witness would be available.*

The CJA 2003, s 120(2) puts on to a statutory footing the previous common law rule which continues to apply in civil proceedings (see **6.2.4.1**). It is submitted that the law relating to the circumstances in which such statements may be admitted remains the same as at common law. The significant change is that whereas, at common law, a previous consistent statement in rebuttal of an allegation of recent fabrication was only evidence of consistency and to rebut the allegation of recent fabrication (*R v Benjamin* (1913) 8 Cr App R 146, CCA), under the CJA 2003 the statement may also be admitted for the truth of its contents.

Statements upon accusation

An accusation of involvement in a criminal offence will most often be made by police officers in an informal conversation with the suspect, on arrest or in interview. The law of evidence recognises three types of statement that could be made by a person when confronted by such an accusation:

- an admission;
- an exculpatory statement;
- a mixed statement.

(a) Admissions

A statement which contains an admission is admissible as a confession under the Police and Criminal Evidence Act 1984, s 76(1) as evidence of the facts stated. Confessions will be considered further in **Chapter 12**.

(b) Exculpatory statements

An exculpatory statement is a statement denying any involvement in the offence. It is admissible as evidence of the reaction of the accused when taxed with incriminating facts and, thus, evidence of the consistency of the accused's defence, but it is not evidence of the truth of the matters stated (*R v Storey* (1968) 52 Cr App R 334).

In *R v Storey*, the prosecution lead evidence that when a quantity of cannabis had been found in the accused's flat, she had explained that it belonged to a man who had brought it there against her will. The defence relied on this statement in a submission of no case to answer. The Court of Appeal upheld the judge's ruling that the statement was not evidence of the facts stated, it was evidence of the reaction of the accused which formed part of the general picture to be considered by the jury.

In *R v Pearce* (1979) 69 Cr App R 365, it was held that this exception to the rule against previous consistent statements is not limited to statements made on the first encounter with the police. However, the longer the time that has elapsed after the first encounter the less the weight which will be attached to the denial.

Where a previous exculpatory statement adds nothing to the evidence already before the court it may be excluded on the basis that it is not relevant and is, therefore, inadmissible. This was the reasoning of the Court of Appeal in *R v Tooke* (1989) 90 Cr App R 417, when upholding the trial judge's decision to exclude a spontaneous written statement made to the police within an hour of the incident because during the course of the trial, a statement made at the scene to the same effect had already been admitted. The Court recognised that in such a case it is not an easy task for the judge to decide, in his or her discretion, where the dividing line falls.

If the accused produces a carefully written statement to the police with a view to it being made part of the prosecution evidence, the trial judge may also rule it inadmissible (*R v Pearce* (1980) 71 Cr App R 325, CA).

(c) Mixed statements

A mixed statement is one that is partly incriminatory and partly exculpatory. For example, 'I hit W, but only because I was trying to defend myself'. The whole of a mixed statement is admissible, because it would obviously be unfair for the prosecution to exclude those parts that are favourable to the accused, while relying on those parts favourable to the prosecution (*R v Storey* (1968) 52 Cr App R 334). Moreover, the whole statement is to be taken into consideration in determining where the truth lies. While it could be argued that the exculpatory parts should be admitted as evidence of reaction only, and not as evidence of the truth of the matters stated, it is considered too difficult to explain this legal nicety to a jury. However, the judge may point out that the incriminating parts are likely to be true (otherwise why say them?), whereas excuses do not have the same weight (*R v Sharp* [1988] 1 All ER 65, HL; *R v Aziz* [1996] AC 41, HL).

In *R v Garrod* [1997] Crim LR 445, the Court of Appeal addressed the question of how to identify when a statement contained enough in the nature of admissions to justify calling it 'mixed'. The Court, acknowledging that many statements could be said to contain some admissions of relevant fact, as well a statement of innocence and a denial of guilt, held that a statement should be regarded as mixed if it contained an admission of fact which was significant to any issue in the case, ie capable of adding some degree of weight to the prosecution case on an issue which was relevant to guilt.

In *R v Aziz* [1996] AC 41, HL, it was held that mixed statements are only admissible as evidence of the truth of the matters stated if tendered by the prosecution. However, where the prosecution tender a mixed statement but do not rely on it as proof of any part of their case against the accused, the accused may rely upon it for the truth of its contents (*Western v DPP* [1997] 1 Cr App R 474, DC).

Res gestae *statements*

Under the doctrine of *res gestae*, evidence is admissible of any act or statement so closely associated in time, place and circumstances with some matter in issue that it can be said to be a part of the same transaction. A *res gestae* statement is admitted for the truth of its contents. In *R v Fowkes* The Times, 8 March 1856 (Assizes), the defendant was charged with murder. The son of the victim and another person present at the scene were permitted to give evidence that on seeing a face at the window through which a shot was fired, the son had said, 'There's Butcher' (a name by which the defendant was known). The doctrine of *res gestae* will be considered in greater detail at **11.3.3**.

6.2.5   Unfavourable and hostile witnesses

A party may not impeach the credibility of its own witness, whether by:

- asking leading questions; or
- asking about or calling evidence to prove prior inconsistent statements, prior discreditable conduct, bad character, previous convictions or bias.

6.2.5.1   Unfavourable witnesses

An unfavourable witness is one who either fails to prove that which he or she was expected to prove ('fails to come up to proof') or who gives evidence unfavourable to the party by whom he or she has been called. In accordance with the general rule, the party calling the witness may not impeach his or her credibility but may only call other witnesses to prove the matters that the unfavourable witness failed to prove (*Ewer v Ambrose* (1825) 3 B & C 746).

6.2.5.2   Hostile witness

A hostile witness is one who, in the opinion of the judge, 'is not desirous of telling the truth to the court at the instance of the party calling him' (Stephen, *Digest of the Law of Evidence*, 12th edn., Article 147).

In criminal proceedings, the prosecution may call a person even if he or she has shown that he or she is likely to be a hostile witness, for example, by retracting an earlier statement and/or making a second statement (*R v Mann* (1972) 56 Cr App R 750, CA).

An application for leave to treat the witness as hostile must be made to the judge and, in criminal proceedings, should generally be made in the presence of the jury (*R v Darby* [1989] Crim LR 817; *R v Khan* [2003] Crim LR 428). Normally, the application will be made during examination-in-chief. However, in rare cases in which a witness shows hostility in re-examination, an application can be made at this later stage (*R v Powell* [1985] Crim LR 592). The judge should have regard to the demeanour of the witness, the evidence the witness gives, the evidence the witness does not give and the witness's willingness to cooperate. If a witness gives evidence contrary to an earlier statement or fails to give the evidence expected, the party calling the witness and the judge should not immediately proceed to treat him or her as hostile, unless that is the only appropriate course because of the degree of hostility, but should consider first inviting the witness to refresh his or her memory from appropriate material (*R v Maw* [1994] Crim LR 841).

Where the judge grants leave to treat a witness as hostile, the party calling the witness may, at common law, ask leading questions (*R v Thompson* (1976) 64 Cr App R 96, CA).

Section 3 of the Criminal Procedure Act 1865, which applies in both civil and criminal proceedings, makes provision for the party calling a hostile witness to prove previous inconsistent statements made by that witness. Section 3 provides that:

A party producing a witness shall not be allowed to impeach his credit by general evidence of bad character, but he may, in case the witness shall in the opinion of the judge prove adverse, contradict him by other evidence, or, by leave of the judge, prove that he has made at other times a statement inconsistent with his present testimony; but before such last-mentioned proof can be given the circumstances of the supposed statement, sufficient to designate the particular occasion, must be mentioned to the witness, and he must be asked whether or not he has made such a statement.

The first part of s 3 of the 1865 Act merely restates the common law rule that a party cannot impeach its own witness. The remainder of the provision applies only to adverse witnesses. In *Greenough v Eccles* (1859) 5 CB NS 786, it was held that 'adverse' means hostile. Thus, the section allows a party calling a hostile witness:

- to contradict the witness, in the same manner as an unfavourable witness, by calling other evidence; or
- to prove a previous inconsistent statement against the witness.

If the witness, under cross-examination on the previous inconsistent statement, confirms its contents, then that will stand as his or her evidence and can be accepted by the tribunal of fact subject to assessment of the witnesses credibility (*R v Maw*). Where the witness does not admit the truth of the previous statement, the statement is admissible as evidence of the matters stated in both civil proceedings (Civil Evidence Act 1995, ss 1 and 6(3) and (5)) and criminal proceedings (CJA 2003, s 119(1)). Thus, where a witness does not admit making the previous inconsistent statement, and it is proved against him or her, it will be open to the tribunal of fact to accept the present testimony of the witness or the previous inconsistent statement and determine the weight to be attached.

6.3 Cross-examination

Cross-examination is the questioning of a witness by any party other than the party calling him or her. The purpose of cross-examination is:

- to elicit evidence favourable to the cross-examining party's case;
- to qualify, weaken or cast doubt upon the witness's evidence-in-chief.

6.3.1 Liability to cross-examination

All witnesses who have been called by a party and taken the oath are liable to cross-examination except:

- those who produce documents without being sworn (*Sumners v Mosely* (1834) 2 Cr & M 477);
- those called by mistake who cannot give material evidence (*Wood v Mackinson* (1840) 2 Mood & R 273); and
- those who have been called by the judge, unless the judge grants leave (*Coulson v Disborough* [1894] 2 QB 316).

If a witness dies before being cross-examined (*R v Doolin* (1832) 1 Jebb CC 125) or the judge determines that the witness is incapable of answering further questions, the evidence adduced up to that point may be used if the judge can adequately direct the jury as to the prejudice faced by the accused in not having the opportunity to cross-examine the witness (*R v Stretton* (1986) 86 Cr App R 7; *R v Wyatt* [1990] Crim LR 343; *R v Lawless* (1994) 98 Cr App R 342).

In criminal proceedings, a witness is examined in-chief before being cross-examined. However, sometimes a witness will simply be tendered by the prosecution for cross-examination. This typically happens where one police officer gives evidence of observations he made with a second officer, and the second officer's witness statement does no more than confirm the first officer's evidence in all material details. The prosecution would call the second officer, after the first has given evidence in full, ask the officer sufficient questions to identify him or her and permit the officer to use any memory-refreshing document, before leaving the witness to be cross-examined by the defence.

In civil proceedings, as the witness statement will usually stand as a witness's evidence-in-chief (CPR, r 32.5(2)), evidence-in-chief would ordinarily consist simply in the witness identifying the witness statement and confirming his or her belief in the truth of its contents. Cross-examination follows immediately after.

6.3.2 Restrictions on cross-examination

6.3.2.1 The accused in criminal proceedings

Generally, a witness called by one party to the proceedings and liable to cross-examination, may be cross-examined by the accused in person. However, there are a number of restrictions placed upon cross-examination by the accused.

At common law, the judge can restrict both the length of the cross-examination and the issues to which it relates (*R v Brown* [1998] 2 Cr App R 364).

The Youth Justice and Criminal Evidence Act 1999 ('YJCEA 1999') places significant restrictions on the accused's ability to cross-examine certain witnesses in person. Section 34 of the YJCEA 1999 provides:

> *(1)   No person charged with a sexual offence may in any criminal proceedings cross-examine in person a witness who is the complainant, either—*
> *(a)   in connection with that offence, or*
> *(b)   in connection with any other offence (of whatever nature) with which that person is charged in the proceedings.*

'Sexual offence' is defined in YJCEA 1999, s 62 as any offence under the Sexual Offences Act 2003, Part 1.

Section 35 of the YJCEA 1999 provides:

> *(1)   No person charged with an offence to which this section applies may in any criminal proceedings cross-examine in person a protected witness, either—*
> *(a)   in connection with that offence, or*
> *(b)   in connection with any other offence (of whatever nature) with which that person is charged in the proceedings.*

A 'protected witness' is a witness who:

(a) is either the complainant or a witness (s 35(2)(a)) to one or more of the offences specified in YJCEA 1999, s 35(3), namely:

(i)   sexual offences under either Part 1 of the Sexual Offences Act 2003 or the Protection of Children Act 1978 (s 35(3)(a));

(ii)   kidnapping, false imprisonment or child abduction (s 35(3)(b));

(iii)   child cruelty (s 35(3)(c)); or

(iv)   any other offence involving an assault on, or injury, or threat of injury to any person (s 35(3)(d));

and

(b) either

(i)   where the offence is a sexual offence, the witness is under the age of 17 or falls to be cross-examined having given evidence-in-chief when under that age (s 35(2)(b)), or

(ii)   in the case of any other specified offence, the witness is under the age of 14 or falls to be cross-examined having given evidence-in-chief when under that age (s 35(2)(b)).

Section 36 of the YJCEA 1999 permits the court to make a direction prohibiting the accused from cross-examining a witness in person where neither YJCEA 1999, ss 34 nor 35 operate if:

> (2)   . . . it appears to the court—
>   (a)   that the quality of evidence given by the witness on cross-examination—
>   (i)   is likely to be diminished if the cross-examination . . . is conducted by the accused in person, and
>   (ii)   would be likely to be improved if a direction were given under this section, and
>   (b)   that it would not be contrary to the interests of justice to give such a direction

In determining whether the YJCEA 1999, s 36(2)(a) applies, the court must take into account the various factors set out in s 35(3) including any views expressed by the witness, the nature of the questions likely to be asked and the behaviour of the accused both towards the witness and generally. 'Witness' for the purposes of this section does not include a co-accused (s 36(4)(a)).

In cases where cross-examination by the accused is prevented under any of the above provisions, YJCEA 1999, s 38 requires that the court must invite the accused to arrange for a legal representative to act for him or her for the purposes of cross-examining, and require the accused to notify the court whether such a person is to act. If the accused fails to arrange for a legal representative or, failing notification, it appears that there will be no such representative, the court must consider whether it is necessary in the interests of justice for the witness to be cross-examined by a legal representative appointed to represent the accused's interests. If so, the court must appoint a qualified legal representative to cross-examine the witness in the interests of the accused.

Under YJCEA 1999, s 39, a judge is required to give such warning as necessary (if any) to the jury, in a case where cross-examination in person has been prevented, to ensure that the accused is not prejudiced by any inferences that might be drawn from the fact that he or she has been prevented from cross-examining, and, where there is a court-appointed legal representative acting, that that person was not acting as the accused's own legal representative.

6.3.2.2   Cross-examination of complainants in sexual cases

The YJCEA 1999, also places strict limits on the extent to which a complainant to a sexual offence may be cross-examined about previous sexual experience. This will be considered in detail at **9.3**.

6.3.2.3   Judicial discretion

The judge has a common law discretion to prevent counsel from conducting unnecessary or improper cross-examination. Counsel should not waste time by protracted and irrelevant cross-examination but should cross-examine with restraint and the courtesy and consideration which witnesses are entitled to expect (*Mechanical and General Inventions Co. Ltd v Austin* [1935] AC 346, HL; *R v Kalia* (1974) 60 Cr App R 200).

In civil proceedings, the court has an additional power to limit cross-examination under CPR, r 32.1(3).

6.3.2.4   Code of Conduct for the Bar

There are also a number of rules to be observed which are set out in the Code of Conduct of the Bar of England and Wales, including in particular, the following paragraphs of Part VII (conduct of work):

> *701. A barrister:*
>   (a)   *must in all his professional activities be courteous and act promptly conscientiously diligently and with reasonable competence and take all reasonable and practicable steps to avoid unnecessary expense or waste of the Court's time. . . .*

> 708. A barrister when conducting proceedings in Court:
>
> . . .
>
> (e) must not adduce evidence obtained otherwise than from or through the client or devise facts which will assist in advancing the lay client's case;
>
> . . .
>
> (g) must not make statements or ask questions which are merely scandalous or intended or calculated only to vilify insult or annoy either a witness or some other person;
>
> (h) must if possible avoid the naming in open Court of third parties whose character would thereby be impugned;
>
> (i) must not by assertion in a speech impugn a witness whom he has had an opportunity to cross-examine unless in cross-examination he has given the witness an opportunity to answer the allegation;
>
> (j) must not suggest that a victim, witness or other person is guilty of crime, fraud or misconduct or make any defamatory aspersion on the conduct of any other person or attribute to another person the crime or conduct of which his lay client is accused unless such allegations go to a matter in issue (including the credibility of the witness) which is material to the lay client's case and appear to him to be supported by reasonable grounds.

While the Code of Conduct is not binding on the court, it does have persuasive force (*R v McFadden* (1975) 62 Cr App R 187, a case concerning the Bar Council Rules which the Code of Conduct replaced).

6.3.3   Consequences of failing to cross-examine

In *R v Wood Green Crown Court, ex p Taylor* [1995] Crim LR 879 it was held that a party who fails to cross-examine a witness on a fact is deemed to have accepted what the witness says on that fact and therefore cannot invite the tribunal of fact to disbelieve him or her on that matter. There is therefore a duty to put one's case and it is a fundamental requirement of cross-examination. However, if it is proposed to invite the jury to disbelieve a witness on a particular matter, it does not follow that it is always necessary to put to the witness explicitly that he or she is lying, provided that the overall tenor of the cross-examination is designed to show that his or her account is incapable of belief (*R v Lovelock* [1997] Crim LR 821, CA). It has been held that the rule in *ex p Taylor* does not apply to proceedings before lay justices (*O'Connell v Adams* [1973] RTR 150). If counsel omits to cross-examine on a particular point by reason of inadvertence, the judge has a discretion to allow the witness to be recalled (*R v Wilson* [1977] Crim LR 553, CA).

6.3.4   Cross-examination and inadmissible evidence

The rules governing the admissibility of evidence apply equally to cross-examination and examination-in-chief. Therefore, questions seeking to elicit evidence that would not be admissible in examination-in-chief cannot be put to a witness in cross-examination. For example, it has been held to be improper for a cross-examining party to attempt to elicit hearsay evidence (*R v Thomson* [1912] 3 KB 19).

Many of the cases in this area concern the use to which admissions and confessions may be put. In *R v Treacy* [1944] 2 All ER 229, it was held that the prosecution should not have been permitted to cross-examine the accused so as to reveal that he had made a confession that had been ruled inadmissible as part of the prosecution case. This rule also obtains in favour of any co-accused of the maker of a confession (*R v Rice* [1963] 1 QB 857). However, where an accused's inadmissible confession is relevant to the defence of the co-accused, and the accused gives evidence inconsistent with the statement, the co-accused can cross-examine him or her on it, provided that the judge makes clear to the jury that it is not evidence of the accused's guilt (*R v Rowson* [1986] QB 174, CA; *Lui Mei Lin v R* [1989] 1 All ER 359, PC).

6.3.5 Cross-examination on documents

Counsel may show a document to a witness during cross-examination, ask the witness to read it to himself or herself and then ask the witness if the contents are true. If the witness admits that they are and he or she would have been permitted to give oral evidence of the matters stated, then, they become the witness's evidence and can be revealed (*R v Gillespie* (1967) 51 Cr App R 172; *R v Cooper* (1985) 82 Cr App R 74).

6.3.6 Previous inconsistent statements

6.3.6.1 Criminal Procedure Act 1865, ss 4 and 5

Where a previous inconsistent statement is put to the witness and he or she admits to having made it, then it becomes part of the witness's evidence and no further proof of the statement is required (*R v P (GR)* [1998] Crim LR 663). Where the witness does not admit making the previous statement, its admissibility will be determined, in both criminal and civil proceedings, by the Criminal Procedure Act 1865, ss 4 and 5. Section 4 provides:

If a witness, upon cross-examination as to a former statement made by him relative to the subject matter of the indictment or proceeding, and inconsistent with his present testimony, does not distinctly admit that he has made such statement, proof may be given that he did in fact make it; but before such proof can be given the circumstances of the supposed statement, sufficient to designate the particular occasion, must be mentioned to the witness, and he must be asked whether or not he has made such statement.

In *R v Derby Magistrates' Court, ex B* [1996] AC 487, HL, Lord Taylor of Gosforth CJ confirmed that s 4 of the 1865 Act applies to both oral and written statements, s 5 of the Act is confined to written statements.

The phrase 'relative to the subject matter of the indictment or proceeding', which is used in ss 4 and 5 of the 1865 Act, means relevant to the facts in issue as opposed to some collateral matter such as, for example, matters going solely to the credit of the witness (*R v Funderburk* [1990] 1 WLR 587). Thus where the previous inconsistent statement is relevant only to the credibility of the witness, the 1865 Act does not apply. However, it is not always easy to determine whether an issue is relevant to a fact in issue or merely credibility. This is particularly true where the disputed issue is a sexual one between two persons in private as, in those circumstances, the difference between questions going to credit and questions going to the issue is reduced almost to vanishing point (see **6.3.7.1** below).

Section 5 of the Criminal Evidence Act 1865 provides:

A witness may be cross-examined as to previous statements made by him in writing, or reduced into writing, relative to the subject matter of the indictment or proceeding, without such writing being shown to him; but if it is intended to contradict such witness by the writing, his attention must, before such contradictory proof can be given, be called to those parts of the writing which are to be used for the purpose of so contradicting him: Provided always, that it shall be competent for the judge, at any time during the trial, to require the production of the writing for his inspection, and he may thereupon make such use of it for the purposes of the trial as he may think fit.

Under s 5 of the 1865 Act, counsel can cross-examine a witness on a document without showing it to the witness. However, even if counsel does not intend to show the writing to the witness with a view to contradicting the witness, the document must be in court because the judge may require the document to be produced (*R v Anderson* (1929) 21 Cr App R 178).

The usual practice is for counsel to hand the document to the witness and ask the witness to read the relevant part to himself or herself. This does not make the document an exhibit. Counsel will then ask the witness, whether he or she still stands by the evidence given to the court. If the witness accepts that the previous consistent statement is true, then that becomes part of his or her evidence. If the witness stands by his or her evidence, then counsel can choose whether or not to prove the previous statement. If counsel wishes to do so he or she may prove it by reading, or asking the witness to read, the relevant part to the court. It is then open to the court to examine the document to see the extent of the inconsistency.

Where a witness has been cross-examined on a previous inconsistent statement, then, because under s 5 of the 1865 Act the judge may make such use of it for the purposes of the trial as he may think fit, it is open to the judge to allow the whole of the statement to go before the jury, but the judge has a discretion to allow the jury to see only those parts on which cross-examination was based.

A previous inconsistent statement is admissible, in both criminal proceedings (Criminal Justice Act 2003, s 119(1)) and civil proceedings (Civil Evidence Act 1995, ss 1 and 6(3) and (5)), as evidence of credibility and the truth of its contents.

6.3.7 The rule of finality

6.3.7.1 General rule

A witness's answer to a question concerning a collateral issue is final in that the cross-examining party cannot attempt to call any further evidence to prove the contrary (*Harris v Tippett* (1811) 2 Camp 637). However, the tribunal of fact are under no obligation to accept the answer give by the witness as true. As noted at **6.3.6** above, a collateral issue is one that is not directly relevant to the facts in issue in the case. The classic, if somewhat circular, test for identifying a collateral issue was given in *Attorney-General v Hitchcock* (1847) 1 Exch 91 by Pollock CB:

> The test whether a matter is collateral or not is this: if the answer of a witness is a matter which you would be allowed on your own part to prove in evidence — if it have such a connection with the issues, that you would be allowed to give it in evidence — then it is a matter on which you may contradict him.

For example, in *R v Burke* (1858) 8 Cox CC 44, it was held that whether a witness giving evidence through an interpreter had spoken in English to two people in the court building was a collateral issue and, as the witness denied it, evidence to the contrary could not be called. In *R v Marsh* (1985) 83 Cr App R 165, by contrast, a witness's denial that he had threatened the accused was not treated as a collateral issue, part of the defence being that the accused believed that the witness had intended to attack him.

The principal rationale for the rule is that it prevents a proliferation of the issues at trial. However, it would also be unfair to ambush a witness with questioning on issues that he or she had not anticipated.

Determining whether a particular issue is a fact in issue or a collateral issue can be very difficult and may require the court to draw some very fine distinctions. In *R v Funderburk* [1990] 1 WLR 587, the Court of Appeal urged a flexible, rather than an overly pedantic, approach to such questions, even recognising that the test may be instinctive and depend upon the prosecutor's and the court's sense of fair play. Where the disputed issue is a sexual one between two persons in private, the difference between questions going to credit and questions going to the issue is reduced almost to vanishing point because sexual intercourse, whether or not consensual, usually takes place in private and leaves few visible traces of having occurred, so that the evidence is often limited to that of the parties and much is likely to turn on the balance of credibility between them.

Whether an issue is collateral or not is a decision to be made by the judge, and it is a decision with which the Court of Appeal will only interfere if it is wrong in principle or clearly wrong on the facts of the case (*R v Sommers* [1999] Crim LR 744).

6.3.7.2 Exceptions

The general rule is subject to four exceptions:

- evidence of disability affecting reliability;
- evidence of bias or partiality;
- previous convictions; and
- evidence of reputation for untruthfulness.

Where a question concerning any one of the above issues is put to the witness and answered in the negative, the cross-examining party will be permitted to call evidence in rebuttal.

Evidence of disability affecting reliability

Medical evidence is admissible to show that a witness suffers from a physical or mental disability that affects the reliability of his or her evidence (*Toohey v Metropolitan Police Commissioner* [1965] AC 595, HL). Such evidence is not restricted to a general opinion of the unreliability of the witness, but may include evidence of the foundations of, and reasons for, the diagnosis and the extent to which the credibility of the witness is affected.

For example, in *R v Eades* [1972] Crim LR 99, the prosecution were properly allowed to call a consultant psychiatrist to prove that the accused's account of how he had recovered his memory after an accident was not consistent with current medical knowledge.

Bias, previous convictions and evidence of reputation for untruthfulness

As the remaining three exceptions concern the character of the witness, they will be considered at **7.3.2.1**.

6.4   Re-examination

After cross-examination a witness may be re-examined by the party calling him or her. Re-examination is subject to the same rules as evidence-in-chief. Except with leave of the judge, re-examination must be restricted to the matters which arose in cross-examination (*Prince v Samo* (1838) 7 Ad & El 627).

In *R v Beattie* (1989) 89 Cr App R 302, CA, it was held that a party is not entitled, merely by reason of cross-examination on a previous inconsistent statement, to re-examine the witness on a previous statement consistent with the witness's testimony. However, in *R v Ali* [2004] 1 Cr App R 501, the Court of Appeal recognised that the court does have a residual discretion to allow re-examination on a previous consistent statement, to prevent the jury from being positively misled as to the existence of some fact or the terms of an earlier statement.

Character evidence: introduction and civil cases

This chapter introduces the use of the character evidence generally and deals with the particular rules that govern the use of character evidence in civil proceedings.

7.1 Introduction

7.1.1 Meaning of character evidence

In most cases the character of a party is an issue. A person tried with a major criminal offence, if found guilty, is clearly being shown to be of bad character. Furthermore being found liable in various civil trials can portray a party in a bad light (for example as 'negligent'). This is the consequence of the trial process. This chapter is concerned with the way in which the previous or current behaviour or characteristics of a person can be used to establish guilt or liability at trial.

7.1.2 Evidential value of character evidence

Evidence of the character of a person is relevant to one of two issues. First, is the person in question likely to have acted in a particular way that is relevant to a matter in issue at trial? Secondly, should the person be believed as a witness at trial?

Consider the following example: Alex is alleged to have taken a computer from the shop in which he works. Proof of this allegation is based upon Ben's allegation that this happened. Ben is a fellow employee of Alex. If you were asked to determine whether Alex had taken the computer consider how your conclusion would be affected by evidence that:

- Ben is a compulsive liar.
- Ben accused Alex after Ben himself had been alleged to have taken the computer.
- Ben has a previous conviction for theft from his employer.
- Alex has a previous conviction for theft from his employer.
- Alex had been dismissed from his previous job on the grounds of having taken money from the till of that shop (but has no conviction for having done so).
- Alex has never been in trouble with the police before and is a model employee.

In all of these situations, one is considering the character either of the person making the allegation (Ben) or the character of the person against whom the allegation is being made (Alex). Not everyone would reach the same conclusions on all of the above facts. For example, different people are willing to 'forgive and forget' previous instances of what might be called bad behaviour and the willingness to do so may depend on exactly what was done previously, how long ago it was done and what evidence there is of a change of personality since that date. These are, ultimately, matters for the fact-finder at trial. The function of the rules of evidence, as ever, is to determine in what circumstances the evidence can go to the fact-finder in the first place. In other words when should a fact-finder be presented with, and entitled to use, evidence of the character of a party or a witness to a case? Furthermore, how should the fact-finder use (or, in the case of a jury, be directed to use) evidence of character?

7.1.3   Distinctions

Before looking at the rules of evidence in depth it is worth making five important distinctions.

7.1.3.1   Civil vs criminal proceedings

As you will have noted already, the approach of the civil and criminal courts to evidence is different. The difference of approach is often due to a consciousness of a need to protect criminal defendants against prejudicial evidence and the imposition of stronger safeguards to ensure the fairness of the trial process for criminal defendants. However, it will be seen that the rules in this area often share a common origin and that there is an extent to which the principles in criminal cases may be used by a lawyer in making an application in a civil court and vice versa.

This chapter will set out the rules for civil proceedings while **Chapters 8** and **9** concern the rules in criminal proceedings.

7.1.3.2   Good character vs bad character

It is important not to forget that both good character and bad character can be relevant to a trial issue. If one accepts the argument (as the law does) that the fact that Alex had committed thefts in the past makes it more likely that he committed a theft on the occasion in question then it should follow (and the law accepts that it does follow) that the fact that Alex has never committed thefts in the past makes it less likely that he did so on this occasion. It is worth noting that the law is willing to accept as its starting point that a person who is not proven to have committed an offence in the past is a person who has not in fact committed an offence. However, as we shall see below, the absence of previous criminal convictions does not force a court to conclude that a person is of good character.

7.1.3.3   Character evidence relevant to a fact in issue vs character evidence relevant to credibility

In most cases, both civil and criminal, evidence of character is used to establish whether a person's evidence should be believed. To take the example above, evidence that Ben is a compulsive liar does not directly effect our decision whether or not Alex took the computer. The evidence that directly affects this decision is Ben's accusation that Alex did so. That Ben is a compulsive liar influences our willingness to accept that what Ben said was true. In other words, that character evidence is relevant to Ben's credibility or credit as a witness. The distinction between character evidence relevant to a fact in issue and evidence relevant to credibility should be remembered at all points when considering character evidence. They can be treated differently by the courts in many situations.

7.1.3.4 Character evidence relevant to a fact in issue vs character as a fact in issue

Even among those situations in which character evidence is adduced to prove a fact in issue at trial, there is an important distinction to be drawn. Sometimes the conclusion that someone has a particular character is central to the trial issue. It is one of the major facts in issue. For example, in defamation proceedings, it is necessary to determine the truth of the defamatory statement. Therefore the particular bad characteristic of the claimant that the defendant alleged has to be proven or disproven. In such circumstances, the character of the claimant is a fact in issue, in the strict sense of the word. Equally, if a criminal defendant were charged with driving a vehicle whilst disqualified, then it would be necessary to prove as an element of the offence that the defendant was disqualified. Again, the character of the defendant is one of the facts in issue at trial.

However, you will remember from **Chapters 1** and **2**, that sometimes the main facts in issue in a case are proven by combinations of evidence (circumstantial evidence). Therefore, to take the example of Alex above, if he were tried with theft, the main facts in issue would be the elements of the offence of theft. Alex's character is not one of the elements of that offence. The relevance of any evidence of character on Alex's part goes to the questions (a) whether he should be believed when he denies committing the offence (which is 'credibility' considered at **7.1.3.3** above) and (b) whether he may have had the disposition to commit the offence of theft. For question (b) the evidence is (if admissible) relevant as circumstantial evidence of Alex's guilt. In other words, the jury would have to look at it along with other evidence in the case to decide whether the prosecution had proven all of the elements of the offence of theft beyond reasonable doubt. It will be seen below that it is this use of character evidence in criminal cases that has proven the most controversial in the past and that is still now subject to the most safeguards and protections.

7.1.3.5 Witnesses vs parties

It will be seen in the remainder of the chapter that there are different rules in operation for parties to proceedings and witnesses in proceedings. The different is more apparent in criminal than in civil cases but in both it should be remembered that witnesses play a different part in proceedings to parties and that they are therefore subject to different rules.

In this chapter the rules concerning parties to and witnesses in civil proceedings are dealt with in turn. The rules concerning the defendant in criminal proceedings are dealt with in **Chapter 8** and the rules for other witnesses in criminal cases are covered in **Chapter 9**.

7.2 Parties in civil proceedings

7.2.1 Character as a fact in issue

The character of a party to a case is admissible if the character is a fact in issue in the case. Think again of the example of Alex set out above. Consider the situation if a newspaper printed an allegation that Alex was a thief. At the trial of a defamation claim, if the newspaper ran the defence of justification, the truth of the statement would be a fact in issue. Any evidence logically relevant to that issue (either that he has committed theft in the past or that he stole from his employer) is admissible.

Of course, whether a fact is a fact in issue in a civil case depends on whether it remains so after the statement of case have been served. In other words character is only admissible to prove a fact that has not already been admitted by a party.

7.2.2 Character relevant to a fact in issue

Furthermore, the good or bad character of a party to a case is admissible if it is relevant to prove one of those facts in issue. In *Mood Music Publishing Co Ltd v De Wolfe Ltd* [1976] Ch 119, CA, an action was brought for infringement of the plaintiff's copyright in relation to a piece of music. The defendant alleged that any similarities between the plaintiff's music and the defendant's music was coincidental. The plaintiff was held to have been entitled to adduce evidence of three other pieces of music that the defendant had copied. The Court of Appeal noted that such evidence would be admissible if 'logically probative' (per Lord Denning at p 126).

Using Alex again, consider the situation if Alex's employer brought a civil action for return of the computer taken. Alex's character is not a fact in issue. What the employer would have to prove is that the computer was his and not Alex's. However, the fact of the theft from the employer is logically relevant in establishing who truly owns the computer. As the proceedings are of a civil nature, any evidence of Alex's good or bad character that is logically relevant to the issue of ownership of the computer could be admissible.

In contrast to criminal cases (see **Chapters 8** and **9**), there are no rules specific to character evidence that give a trial judge in a civil case a discretion to exclude such evidence on the grounds of fairness or prejudice. In *Mood Music*, Lord Denning did state that evidence of previous instances of the conduct of which the plaintiff complained would only be admissible if not 'oppressive or unfair'. It seems from *Berger v Raymond Sun Ltd* [1984] 1 WLR 625 that this test is concerned more with the amount of notice given to the party against whom the evidence is to be admitted and any difficulties that party would have with disproving such evidence rather than any concerns about prejudicial thinking on the part of the fact finder. It is likely that the restrictions on the admissibility of such evidence are now covered by the general discretion to exclude evidence civil proceedings pursuant to CPR, r 32.1 and that the restrictions on admissibility identified in *Mood Music* and *Berger* are now reflected in that provision and the 'overriding objective' in CPR, rr 1.1 and 1.2.

7.2.3 Evidence of character relevant to credibility

A party in civil proceedings is treated in the same way as any other witness insofar as evidence relevant to his or her credibility is concerned. Therefore the rules identified at **7.3.2** below apply.

7.3   Other witnesses in civil proceedings

7.3.1 Evidence of character relevant to a fact in issue

It is possible that a witness in a civil case could be asked a question concerning his or her character not to discredit testimony given by him or her but to prove that a particular fact in issue in a civil case is not proven against one of the parties. For example, in an action brought by Alex's employer for the return of the missing computer, the proof that Ben has a previous conviction for theft against a previous employer could be relevant to prove that he, and not Alex, had taken the computer. As such, the rules in *Mood Music* would appear to apply. The test would be whether proof of Ben's previous conviction is logically probative of an issue in the case (ie who took the computer) and not to the issue of whether Ben is an honest person and therefore an honest witness.

7.3.2   Evidence of bad character relevant to credibility

As will be seen below, there are more restrictions upon the extent to which evidence of the character of a witness may be admitted. Clearly the good or bad character of a witness is not a fact in issue in the case. Rather it is of incidental importance, being useful to the tribunal of fact in deciding what weight to attach to that witness's evidence. In other words, it is a type of collateral evidence. As shall be seen its collateral nature means that the courts are concerned to limit the extent to which parties will take up court time and use public resources to investigate matters of incidental importance.

It is worth remembering that not all cross-examination as to the credit of a witness necessarily is cross-examination as to their character. For example to put to a witness that she is short-sighted does not impeach her character but would have a clear effect on her credibility as an eye witness. The general rule for cross-examination as to credit in both civil and criminal cases was set out by Lawton J in *R v Sweet-Escott* (1971) 55 Cr App R 316 where he said:

Since the purpose of cross-examination as to credit is to show that the witness ought not to be believed on oath, the matters about which he is questioned must relate to his likely standing after cross- examination with the tribunal which is trying him or listening to his evidence.

In other words, if the cross-examination will not affect the weight which the tribunal will attach to the witness's evidence, it is not permissible. This principle reflects the approach identified in *Hobbs v C T Tinling and Co Ltd* [1929] 2 KB 1, CA, where the court observed that cross-examination should not be allowed if the bad character in question occurred in the distant past or that it is out of proportion with the matters on which the witness will give evidence.

The court will therefore consider the potential probative value of the matters raised in cross-examination to determine whether such matters could assist the jury in deciding whether or not to believe the witness in question. This can cause difficulties if the evidence that the witness has acted dishonestly in the past is not clear. For example, *R v Edwards* [1991] 1 WLR 207 concerned allegations that a police officer had previously been disciplined for improper conduct. The court considered a number of options and concluded:

(a) An officer could be asked about previous convictions or disciplinary charges that had been found proved against him or her.

(b) An officer should not be asked about disciplinary charges that had not yet been proved against him or her.

(c) An officer should be asked about discreditable conduct of other officers in his or her squad.

(d) An officer could be asked about other cases in which he had been involved in certain limited circumstances:

(i)   The mere fact that the officer had given evidence in previous cases and that the accused in those cases had been acquitted did not suggest anything about the credibility of the officer and therefore were not appropriate matters for cross-examination.

(ii) However, if it was alleged that (a) in the previous case the officer in question had given evidence that that accused person had made a confession, and (b) that accused person had been acquitted, and (c) the circumstances of that case suggest that the acquittal involved the tribunal of fact disbelieving the evidence of the officer about the confession, and (d) the officer was alleging that the current defendant had confessed, then the officer could legitimately be asked about that previous acquittal.

R v Edwards provides a useful example of the approach that the court will adopt in determining what sort of matters should be considered. That it was stating general principles rather than laying down rigid rules is supported by the fact that in a different case, *R v Edwards* [1996] 2 Cr App R 345, the Court of Appeal concluded that there could be circumstances in which unproven allegations of perjury and other misconduct on the part of police officers *could* be legitimate matters for cross-examination. What appears to have made a difference in that case was that the numerous allegations had led prosecuting authorities to drop charges against other defendants in cases with which those police officers were involved. In other words the test is simply that laid down in *R v Sweet-Escott*: will the cross-examination affect the standing of the witness in the eyes of the tribunal? This is a matter of fact and argument in each case rather than rigid principle.

7.3.2.1 The rule of finality

A witness's answer to a question concerning a collateral issue is final in that the cross-examining party cannot attempt to call any further evidence to prove the contrary (see **6.3.7.1**). The rule is subject to four exceptions:

- evidence of disability affecting reliability;
- bias;
- previous convictions;
- evidence of reputation for untruthfulness.

Evidence of disability affecting reliability was considered at **6.3.7.2**. The remaining three exceptions all concern character evidence and will be dealt with here. It should be noted that these are common law exceptions and apply equally to criminal proceedings. However, the adduction of evidence of bad character of the accused or witnesses in criminal proceedings is subject to further restrictions which are set out in **Chapters 8** and **9**.

Bias or partiality

The prohibition on calling evidence to prove the lack of credibility of a witness does not apply where the witness has denied that he or she is biased against a party or has something to gain from giving the evidence in the way that he or she has. In such circumstances a party other than the one calling the witness can call evidence to prove that witness's bias or partiality (*R v Mendy* (1976) 64 Cr App R 4; *Dunn v Aslett* (1838) 2 Mood & R 122).

Quite what could amount to bias or partiality will vary from case to case. However the courts will look closely at the alleged bias or partiality before allowing evidence to be called under this exception. For example, it is not the fact of having been *offered* but the fact of having *accepted* a bribe that is evidence of partiality (*Attorney-General v Hitchcock* (1847) 1 Exch 91).

Previous convictions

Where it has been suggested in cross-examination to a witness that he or she has previous convictions and the witness denies the allegation, those convictions can be proved (Criminal Procedure Act 1865, s 6). The trial judge has a discretion to limit such cross-examination both at common law (following *R v Sweet-Escott*) and under CPR, r 32.1: *Watson v Chief Constable of Cleveland Police* [2001] EWCA Civ 1547.

If a conviction is "spent" under the Rehabilitation of Offenders Act 1974, s 4 the previous conviction cannot be adduced in evidence without leave of the trial judge (Rehabilitation of Offenders Act 1974, s 7). Leave should only be granted if justice cannot be done without admitting the evidence. Therefore such evidence will only admitted if one of the parties could not have a fair trial without proving the previous conviction (*Thomas v Commissioner of the Police for the Metropolis* [1997] 1 All ER 747, CA). For a detailed explanation of rehabilitation under the Rehabilitation of Offenders Act 1974, s 4, see *Blackstone's Criminal Practice*, 2005, E 27.3.

Reputation for untruthfulness

This is a common law exception to the rule of finality that is seldom used. In *R v Richardson* [1969] 1 QB 299, the following elements of the rule were identified:

(a) A witness may be called to give evidence of the general reputation for untruthfulness of another witness and whether *on the basis of that knowledge* he or she would believe the sworn testimony of the other witness.

(b) The witness may also give his or her personal opinion as to whether the person ought to believed on oath.

(c) Such a witness cannot identify in his or her evidence-in-chief particular details of the testimony he or she would not believe (but may do so in cross-examination).

In *R v Colwill* [2002] EWCA 1320 the evidence of witnesses that a complainant was untruthful was held not to fall within this exception where the opinion of those witnesses was based on specific instances of untruthful behaviour.

7.3.3   Evidence of good character relevant to credibility

A party calling a witness cannot call evidence to bolster the credibility of that witness. In *R v Turner* [1975] QB 834, Lawton LJ said (at p 842), 'in general evidence can be called to impugn the credibility of witnesses but not led in chief to bolster it up'.

Character evidence: the defendant in criminal proceedings

8.1 Introduction

Chapter 7 considered what is meant generally by character evidence and how the rules of evidence regulate its use in civil proceedings. In civil proceedings the rules governing character evidence are primarily common law rules. However, it will be seen that in criminal cases the common law rules have been extensively modified by statute law, most recently by the Criminal Justice Act 2003 (the CJA 2003).

This chapter concentrates on the rules concerning evidence of the character of a defendant in criminal proceedings. **Chapter 8** identifies the rules that currently govern evidence of the character of witnesses other than the defendant.

8.2 Good character

A defendant is entitled to have his or her good character taken into account both in determining whether the defendant is to be believed in his or her testimony and in determining whether the defendant is likely to have committed the offence (*R v Aziz* [1996] AC 41).

Imagine that John is on trial for burglary and produces evidence of his good character. He gives evidence that he was nowhere near the house that was burgled at the relevant time because he was walking to his girlfriend's house. The jury would be invited to use the evidence of good character in two ways: first to determine whether his account of where he was is more likely to be true as John appears to be an essentially honest person and secondly to determine whether, John is less likely to have committed a burglary offence because he is a person of an honest disposition. While both might appear to lead to the same conclusion, clearly, they are in fact two different conclusions and the jury could accept one and still reject the other.

8.2.1 When a good character direction should be made

The defendant is entitled to assert his or her good character without proving the absence of previous convictions (*R v Aziz* [1996] AC 41). However, the prosecution can rebut any assertion made by an accused that is not accurate (CJA 2003, ss 101(1)(f) and 105; see **8.3.9** below), whether the bad character amounts to a previous conviction or not (CJA 2003, s 98).

In the face of the defendant's assertion of good character it is for the trial judge to determine whether to provide a good character direction during the summing up. Where a good character direction is appropriate, the trial judge is under a duty to make such a direction to the jury (*R v Aziz*).

Where a defendant has no previous convictions but is clearly of bad character, the trial judge retains a discretion either to withhold the good character direction or to provide a modified direction (*R v Aziz; R v Zoppola-Barraza* [1994] Crim LR 833). A modified direction should be given unless to do so would be 'meaningless or absurd' (*R v Gray* [2004] EWCA Crim 1074) or would cause prejudice do the defendant (*R v Alkaitis* [2004] EWCA Crim 1072). The judge may either withhold or modify the direction (*R v Martin* [2000] 2 Cr App R 42; *R v Sanchez* [2003] EWCA Crim 735).

Behaviour short of previous convictions that may lead to the withholding of the good character direction includes being cautioned for criminal activity (*R v Martin*), drug use (*R v Alkaitis*), lying to the police during police interview (*R v Sharp* [1994] QB 261) or violent conduct immediately before the crime charged (*R v Gray*).

The court has a discretion to allow a defendant with minor previous convictions to receive a full or qualified good character direction (*R v Nye* (1982) 75 Cr App R 247). This discretion extends both to previous convictions that are spent in accordance with the Rehabilitation of Offenders Act 1974, s 4 (*R v Nye*) or where the previous conviction is for an offence that bears no relation to the offence for which the defendant is being tried (*R v Timson* [1993] Crim LR 59; *R v H* [1994] Crim LR 205).

Where a defendant has pleaded guilty to a lesser offence or to another offence with which he or she was charged at the same time, then the defendant is no longer of good character and may only obtain a good character direction if the judge decides in his or her discretion to provide one (*R v Challenger* [1994] Crim LR 202 but see for a contrary view, *R v Teasdale* [1993] 4 All ER 290, CA).

8.2.2 The good character direction

In *R v Vye* [1993] 1 WLR 471, it was recognised that the full direction consisted of two limbs. In that case, Lord Taylor of Gosforth provided the following guidance to trial judges:

(a) A direction as to the relevance of his good character to a defendant's credibility is to be given where he has testified or made pre-trial answers or statements. (The first limb.)

(b) A direction as to the relevance of his good character to the likelihood of his having committed the offence charged is to be given, whether or not he has testified, or made pre-trial answers or statements. (The second limb.)

It will therefore be seen that, once it is established that the defendant is entitled to a good character direction, the exact nature of the direction will depend on his or her conduct at trial.

A second limb direction is available to all defendants of good character. Therefore the issue at trial is whether a defendant will be entitled to both a first limb and a second limb direction (ie credibility and propensity directions) or only to a second limb direction (ie propensity direction only).

8.2.2.1 Both first and second limb direction

As the first limb direction assists the jury in determining the credibility of the defendant it will only be given where there is evidence that depends on the credibility of the defendant for its probative force. In other words, the defendant must have made some sort of statement that is admissible evidence before the jury (*R v Vye*).

The most obvious statement that a defendant will have made upon which he would wish a jury to rely would be his or her testimony. Therefore, any defendant of good character who testifies in his or her own defence is entitled to both a first limb direction (effectively that the jury can take the defendant's good character into account when deciding whether to believe what he said in evidence) and a second limb direction (ie that the jury can also take the defendant's good character into account when deciding whether he is likely to have committed the offence at all).

The first limb direction is also available where a defendant has made non-testimonial statements which are admissible as evidence (*R v Aziz*). There are two main situations in which this is likely to happen:

(a) As was noted at **6.2.4.2** a statement made on being accused of involvement in a criminal offence which is wholly exculpatory is not admissible as evidence of the truth of its contents. Furthermore, a defendant would clearly not wish to have the credibility of a wholly inculpatory statement (a confession) enhanced with a good character direction (even though such statements will be admissible: see **Chapter 12**). However, a 'mixed' statement (one that is partly exculpatory and partly inculpatory) is admissible to prove the truth of the matters stated both for and against the defendant. In *R v Aziz* the House of Lords ruled that the first limb direction should be made in relation to such statements.

(b) Statements made by the defendant may also be admitted as hearsay evidence (see **Chapters 10** and **11**). Where such statements are admitted on behalf of the defendant, it would follow that a first limb direction should be made in relation to them.

8.2.2.2   Second limb direction only

Where a defendant of good character does not give evidence and has not made any admissible pre-trial statements in his or her defence, a first limb direction is not required (*R v Vye*). Clearly, in such cases the defendant is still entitled to a second limb direction.

8.2.2.3   Modified direction

Where a defendant is not of entirely good character, a modified direction may be given (*R v Aziz*). Therefore, a judge should consider whether it is possible to give a qualified direction to the jury where a person is of essentially, but not entirely, good character. However, such a modified direction should not be given if it would have the effect of causing prejudice against the defendant (*R v Alkaitis* [2004] EWCA Crim 1702, where the defendant to a charge of importing heroin had no previous convictions but admitted having used heroin previously).

8.2.2.4   Co-defendants of bad character

Where there is more than one defendant on trial and only one of them is of good character, there is the risk that a good character direction for one defendant will highlight the absence of good character on the part of the other. As will be seen later in this chapter, there may be reasons why evidence of bad character on behalf of that other defendant may not be admitted at trial. Clearly, the risk is that the jury may infer from the absence of a good character direction that a defendant has bad character and may reach inappropriate conclusions as to what that bad character involves and the evidential effect of bad character generally.

In *R v Vye*, the Court of Appeal held that in such a situation the defendant of good character is entitled to a good character direction whatever the effect on the other defendant. Such a direction will not support a ground of appeal for the defendant of bad character. According to *R v Shepherd* [1995] Crim LR 153, the judge has a discretion as to whether or not to give a direction to the jury as to the character of any co-defendant who has not received a good character direction if no evidence of bad character of that defendant has been adduced at trial.

8.2.3 Proving good character

R v Rowton (1865) Le & Ca 520 held that the character of the accused must be proven by evidence of general reputation rather than by specific acts. Nor should a character witness give evidence of his or her own opinion of the defendant. Therefore, a character witness (or the defendant in his or her own evidence) should prove good character by testifying as to the reputation of the defendant not specific good acts. This rule is generally not enforced particularly stringently: it would not be unusual for a character witness to state that the defendant is of good character or that the witness has known the defendant for a certain period of time and that the defendant has not been in trouble during that period. However the rule was given a further lease of life in *R v Redgrave* (1982) 74 Cr App R 10, where the Court of Appeal held that the defendant, charged with a crime of a homosexual nature, was not entitled to prove specific acts that proved that he was of a heterosexual disposition. All that he was entitled to do was prove that he was by reputation not the sort of person who would have committed a homosexual crime. The rule in *Rowton* therefore still appears to prevent the calling of evidence of specific acts to disprove a propensity to commit a particular offence.

It is also common practice to cross-examine prosecution witnesses, particularly a police officer, as to the accused's lack of previous convictions. This appears not to offend the rule in *Rowton*, probably by stretching the definition of 'reputation' to include reputation within the Criminal Records Bureau.

8.3 Bad character

8.3.1 Introduction

Before the CJA 2003 came into force, the admissibility of the defendant's bad character was governed by a combination of statute and common law. The CJA 2003 provided a statutory framework for the admissibility and exclusion of such evidence and abolished all but one of the common law rules governing the admissibility of evidence of bad character (s 98(1)). However, while there are some significant changes to the law in this area, in many respects the CJA 2003 has restated, in identical or modified form, the pre-existing law. For this reason the principles stated in cases under the previous legal regime are likely to be used by the courts in applying the CJA 2003. Therefore, in this chapter there will be occasional reference to cases and statutes under the old law.

Unfortunately, there are many aspects of the CJA 2003 that are unclear in their effect. Therefore, much of what follows involves predictions as to the likely effect of its provisions. In *R v Hanson* The Times, 24 March 2005, the Court of Appeal gave preliminary guidance upon this part of the Act in which it was stated that the starting point of analysis is that the purpose of the legislation is to ensure 'the evidence-based conviction of the guilty without putting those who are not guilty at risk of conviction by prejudice'.

8.3.2   Admissibility of evidence of bad character

Section 101(1) provides the bases for admissibility of evidence of bad character:

(1)   *In criminal proceedings evidence of the defendant's bad character is admissible if, but only if—*

    (a)   *all parties to the proceedings agree to the evidence being admissible,*

    (b)   *the evidence is adduced by the defendant himself or is given in answer to a question by him in cross-examination and intended to elicit it,*

    (c)   *it is important explanatory evidence,*

    (d)   *it is relevant to an important matter in issue between the defendant and the prosecution,*

    (e)   *it has substantial probative value in relation to an important matter in issue between the defendant and a co-defendant,*

    (f)   *it is evidence to correct a false impression given by the defendant, or*

    (g)   *the defendant has made an attack on another person's character.*

Therefore there are seven bases ('gateways') upon which evidence of bad character can be admitted. No other grounds will render evidence of bad character admissible no matter what probative value the evidence might contain. Each basis for admissibility is dealt with in turn below.

8.3.3   Meaning of bad character

Section 98 provides:

References in this Chapter to evidence of a person's 'bad character' are to evidence of, or of a disposition towards, misconduct on his part, other than evidence which—

    (a) *has to do with the alleged facts of the offence with which the defendant is charged, or*

    (b) *is evidence of misconduct in connection with the investigation or prosecution of the offence.*

8.3.3.1   Bad character not regulated by the CJA 2003

Therefore, the rules regulating the admissibility of evidence of the commission of the offences being tried are not affected by any of the analysis of this chapter. Clearly, such evidence is admissible despite the fact that it shows the defendant in a bad light. The restrictions of the CJA 2003, ss 98 to 112 are limited to evidence of bad character on occasions other than the one being tried (or disposition in general). Note also that acts concerning the investigation of the offences being tried are also exempted from the restrictions under the CJA 2003.

In other words, where a defendant is charged with burglary, evidence that he committed the burglary alleged on the indictment and evidence that he attempted to intimidate the victim of the burglary would not be regulated by the CJA 2003 even though it happens to put the defendant in a bad light. Evidence that the alleged burglar had previous convictions for burglary on other occasions, that he had a general inclination to steal, that he was of a dishonest nature or reputation would all be regulated by the Act. They are extraneous to the offence being tried.

Therefore, bad character that has to do with the commission or the investigation of the offence with which the defendant is charged is not regulated by the CJA 2003. Such evidence may still be excluded within the discretion of the court under the Police and Criminal Evidence Act 1984, s 78 or the common law discretion to ensure a fair trial (see **8.3.11**).

8.3.3.2 Types of bad character

Section 98 identifies two types of bad character:

- evidence of misconduct on the defendant's part (ie specific bad acts); and
- evidence of a disposition towards misconduct (ie evidence that the defendant is the type of person inclined to particular bad acts) on the defendant's part.

Misconduct is further defined in the CJA 2003, s 112(1) as 'the commission of an offence or other reprehensible behaviour'. Therefore, bad character is not limited to previous convictions and can be extended to behaviour that, while criminal, did not lead to a previous conviction. Examples from cases decided before the CJA 2003 include:

(a) *Makin v Attorney-General of New South Wales* [1894] AC 57, PC, where the defendants were on trial for the murder of a baby they had adopted for a fee. The prosecution had been allowed to call evidence of the finding of corpses of other babies on the property of the defendants, who, the prosecution alleged, had also been adopted for a fee by the defendants and then murdered.

(b) *R v Smith* [1914–15] All ER Rep 262, CA, in which the defendant was tried for the murder of his wife. His defence was that she had died by accident in her bath following an epileptic fit. The prosecution were allowed to call evidence that showed that two previous wives of the defendant had also died and upon each occasion the defendant had said that the deaths were accidents that took place in the bath following some form of fit or seizure. The prosecution case was that on each occasion the wife had been murdered by the defendant who had a particular system for killing his wives to inherit their wealth.

However, the use of 'other reprehensible behaviour' in section 112(1) clearly establishes that the definition of bad character also includes conduct short of criminal behaviour. It is likely that the principles adopted in the following cases will continue to apply:

(a) *R v Ball* [1911] AC 47, HL, in which evidence of conduct that was not criminal at the time it was undertaken (incest) was admissible to prove, in combination with other evidence, that such conduct may have continued after the criminalisation of the conduct in question.

(b) *R v Barrington* [1981] 1 WLR 419, CA, in which the defendant was charged with indecent assaults upon girls employed to babysit his children. The prosecution were allowed to admit evidence of approaches and requests made to other girls who were not victims of assaults because they left when the requests were made. The requests were not necessarily criminal in nature but, by being similar to the ways in which the victims of the assaults were approached, they added credibility to the testimony of the assault victims.

However, the phrase 'reprehensible behaviour' was not used in this area of the law of evidence before the CJA 2003. It has been subject to critical academic evaluation (R Munday, 'What Constitutes "Other Reprehensible Behaviour" under the Bad Character Provisions of the Criminal Justice Act 2003?' [2005] Crim LR 24). The use of evidence of behaviour or disposition short of the commission of a criminal offence under the legal regime before the CJA 2003 was often confused and may have been reflective of the values and standards of the judiciary or of society more generally at the point each case was decided. The word 'reprehensible' does little to distinguish between socially unacceptable behaviour and behaviour that is properly used to prove criminality. Its meaning will soon have to be resolved by the courts. In doing so, it will be necessary to have regard to the evidential purpose and value of the evidence in question (ie its relevance and weight) and to the need to secure fair trials in accordance with Article 6 of the European Convention of Human Rights and the provisions of the Human Rights Act 1998.

In addition to the types of character defined in s 98, s 99(2) has preserved the common law rule that evidence of a person's general reputation in society may also be admissible evidence of that person's bad character, a rule stated in *R v Rowton* (1865) Le & Ca 520, CCR (see **8.2.3** above).

Therefore there are three types of bad character which are regulated by the CJA 2003:

- the previous commission of criminal or reprehensible acts;
- a disposition to criminal or reprehensible acts; and
- a general reputation of bad character.

8.3.3.3 Offences committed when the defendant was a child

Section 108 of the Act provides:

> (2) In proceedings for an offence committed or alleged to have been committed by the defendant when aged 21 or over, evidence of his conviction for an offence when under the age of 14 is not admissible unless—
> (a) both of the offences are triable only on indictment, and
> (b) the court is satisfied that the interests of justice require the evidence to be admissible.
> (3) Subsection (2) applies in addition to section 101.

8.3.4 Agreement of the parties (s 101(1)(a))

Evidence of bad character can be admitted if agreed to by 'all parties to the proceedings' (s 101(1)). Therefore the agreement of all co-defendants is required before evidence can be admitted on this ground.

8.3.5 Evidence adduced by the defendant himself (s 101(1)(b))

Practice prior to the implementation of the CJA 2003 allowed the defendant to adduce evidence of his or her own previous convictions. This would generally have allowed the defendant to present the previous convictions in a controlled way and to explain them in examination-in-chief. Volunteering the convictions was often considered by advocates to be less damaging then having them revealed under cross-examination.

Section 101(1)(b) of the CJA 2003 provides that evidence of bad character can be admitted either by the defendant as part of his or her case, or as a result of cross-examination. In this latter case, the evidence is only admissible if the question is intended to reveal the previous convictions, as opposed to the previous convictions being revealed unexpectedly. Note that it is the questioner's intent to ask about the bad character rather than the defendant's intention to provide the information about the bad character that determines its admissibility. The CJA 2003 is silent as to how the questioner's intent is to be proven should the matter be disputed.

8.3.6   Important explanatory evidence (s 101(1)(c))

There is no restriction as to which parties can admit evidence under s 101(1)(c). Therefore either the prosecution or a co-defendant could admit important explanatory evidence.

Section 102 provides the following definition of important explanatory evidence:

> For the purposes of section 101(1)(c) evidence is important explanatory evidence if—
>   (a) without it, the court or jury would find it impossible or difficult properly to understand other evidence in the case, and
>   (b) its value for understanding the case as a whole is substantial.

Section 101(1)(c), in allowing such evidence to be admitted, is simply placing on a statutory footing the pre-existing common law rule that allowed background evidence to be admitted. 'Background evidence' is evidence of previous bad character (usually specific behaviour) that explains the commission of the offence with which the defendant is charged. For example where the defendant is on trial for a violent attack on the victim, evidence that the defendant had made threats against the victim on previous occasions would be admissible to prove that the defendant had intended to carry out the attack (*R v Pettman* (2 May 1985)). However, the CJA 2003, s 98(a) provides that evidence of bad character that 'has to do with' the alleged facts of the offence is not 'bad character' under the Act. Therefore, where there is evidence of criminal or reprehensible behaviour immediately or closely preceding the actual commission of the offence it may be admissible either if it 'has to do with' the commission of the offence (s 98) or if the jury would find it impossible or difficult properly to understand the rest of the evidence in the case (ss 101(1)(c) and 102).

An example of background evidence at a greater remove from the offence which was held to be admissible under the common law and would be admissible under s 101(1)(c) is to be found in *R v M (T)* [2000] 1 WLR 421. In that case, the defendant was on trial for two counts of rape upon his sister. The prosecution had been allowed to adduce evidence of previous sexual acts carried out other members of his family. The Court of Appeal refused to quash the defendant's conviction. The evidence was admissible because without it the jury would have difficulty understanding how the defendant was able to commit the crimes for which he was being tried without fearing that his acts would be reported to other family members. The prosecution case was that non-consensual sexual intercourse between members of the extended family was a regular occurrence. The evidence showed the culture of abuse within the defendant's family and therefore made what would otherwise have seemed an incredible prosecution case capable of belief. The evidence in *R v M(T)*, would be admissible under s 101(1)(c) because without it the jury would find it 'impossible or difficult properly to understand other evidence in the case' (the circumstances in which it was possible for such a rape to take place without challenge by family members).

Note the following points about the definition in CJA 2003, s 102:

(a) Section 102(a) uses the word 'properly'. Therefore, the explanatory evidence is not only admissible to make sense of a case that would otherwise be meaningless but is also admissible where it will make the case presented by the party adducing it understandable. This would appear to be the situation in *R v M(T)*.

(b) Section 102(b) requires that the evidence should have 'substantial' value. This does not directly require a high degree of probative value. In other words there is no filter or precondition on the credibility of background evidence before it will be admissible. All that is required is that it has substantial value in explaining those parts of the case that would otherwise be difficult or impossible to understand.

(c) However the requirement of substantial value for understanding the case as a whole would appear to prevent the admissibility of evidence of bad character adduced to clarify minor or unimportant matters in the case.

8.3.7 Matter in issue between the prosecution and defence (s 101(1)(d))

The test under s 101(1)(d) is that the evidence of bad character must be 'relevant to an important matter in issue between the defendant and the prosecution'.

Only the prosecution can admit evidence under this paragraph (s 103(6)). The use of the word 'important' in s 101(1)(d) does not add much to the conditions for admissibility under this paragraph. It is the 'matter in issue' that must be 'important' not the evidence or its relevance. Therefore, the word does not require any probative value of the evidence. Section 112(1) defines 'important matters' as 'a matter of substantial importance in the context of the case as a whole'. Insofar as 'matters in issue' means the facts in issue in the case, clearly there can be little doubt that evidence relevant to such matters is 'important'; they are the matters upon which conviction or acquittal depend.

Furthermore, as will be seen, s 103(2) also provides that propensity to offend or to be untruthful are matters in issue. Having been expressly included in s 103, they must be deemed important within the terms of the CJA 2003 too. It is therefore likely that the word 'important' does little more than restrict evidence of bad character under this paragraph to the facts in issue, propensity to offend and propensity to truthfulness, and restricts evidence of the defendant's bad character that might be relevant to other issues of collateral or incidental importance to the issues at trial. For a different interpretation of 'important' in the context of background evidence, see *Blackstone's Criminal Practice*, 2005, F12.10.

8.3.7.1 Matters in issue other than propensity

Clearly the facts in issue at trial are matters in issue. Evidence of bad character was admissible at common law to prove any fact in issue, other than the propensity of the defendant to commit the offences with which she was charged, under the 'similar fact doctrine' (*Makin v Attorney-General of New South Wales* [1894] AC 57, PC). At common law the test was whether the evidence of the defendant's bad character was sufficiently probative of the relevant fact in issue to outweigh any risk of prejudice the evidence might present (*R v P* [1991] 3 All ER 337, HL).

In contrast, s 101(1)(d) makes the evidence admissible in principle simply if it is relevant to an important matter in issue, without regard to the degree of probative force. If it is relevant to such a matter the evidence may nevertheless be excluded under s 101(3) or under the other powers to exclude evidence such as the Police and Criminal Evidence Act 1984, s 78 (see **8.3.11** below). It is at this point that the probative force and likely prejudicial effect of the evidence in question will be considered.

Therefore evidence of bad character may be relevant:

- to prove the identity of the defendant;
- to prove that the defendant committed the *actus reus* of the offence;
- to prove that the defendant possessed a relevant *mens rea* for the offence;
- to disprove any defences that the defendant may raise.

Proof of the identity of the defendant by use of evidence of bad character at common law was subject to difficulties. In *R v P* it appeared to have been suggested by Lord Mackay that evidence of previous bad character on the part of the defendant could only be admitted to prove that the defendant had committed the offence for which he was being tried if it was 'strikingly similar'. However, that requirement of a high degree and specific type of probative force was rejected in *R v W (John)* [1998] 2 Cr App R 289. The Court of Appeal in that case stated that such evidence would be admissible to prove the defendant was the person who committed the offence once it had sufficient probative force to pass the *R v P* test (ie more probative force than prejudicial effect). The effect of the CJA 2003 is that such evidence will be admissible simply if it is relevant to prove the identify of the defendant. Issues surrounding the weight and the prejudicial effect will be resolved in deciding whether such evidence should be excluded under s 101(3). The same approach will be adopted for cases where the defence allege that the *actus reus* of the offence has not been proven, for example where the defendant raises the defence that the death of the victim was an accident to deny the allegation that he murdered her (as was the case in *R v Smith* noted at **8.3.3.2** above) or that the offence never took place (as was the defence case in *R v Barrington* also at **8.3.3.2** above).

Where evidence of bad character is admitted to prove the *mens rea* of the offence, the argument will often be that the defendant, having carried out similar acts in the past, is likely to have known the consequences of the act being carried out on the occasion for which he is being tried (for example, *R v Rance* (1975) 62 Cr App R 118 in which the defendant was on trial for bribery and evidence of the signing of previous documents of a similar nature was used to show that the defendant was likely to have known that, when he signed a similar document on this occasion, he was authorising a bribe). Equally, repetition of an act may show that a particular consequence was intended as was the case in *R v Mortimer* (1936) 25 Cr App R 150 where the prosecution were entitled to prove that the defendant had attempted to knock two ladies off bicycles on previous occasions to rebut the defendant's contention that he did not intend to murder the woman he finally killed by driving his car into her bicycle. Again, the test of admissibility is simply relevance. Probative value in proving the mens rea is considered at the exclusion stage.

At common law, the use of similar fact evidence to rebut defences was subject to a complicated history. In *Harris v DPP* [1952] AC 694 and *DPP v Boardman* [1975] AC 421, the House of Lords rejected the argument that evidence of bad character was admissible only if it rebutted certain specified categories of defence, an error that had crept into the case law since *Makin*. Rather, the House held in *Boardman*, that the admissibility of evidence of bad character could be relevant to any defence raised and whether it did so was a matter of logic and common sense. The CJA 2003 has now ensured that the test of admissibility of such evidence is simply its relevance to such matters. Again, how effective evidence is in rebutting the defence raised by the defendant will simply be an issue relevant to any decision whether or not to exclude such evidence rather than a test for its admissibility.

8.3.7.2   Propensity evidence

Section 103(1) extends the definition of 'matters in issue' to include the propensity of the defendant to commit the offence charged or to give untruthful testimony:

(1)   For the purposes of section 101(1)(d) the matters in issue between the defendant and the prosecution include—

    (a)   the question whether the defendant has a propensity to commit offences of the kind with which he is charged, except where his having such a propensity makes it no more likely that he is guilty of the offence;

    (b)   the question whether the defendant has a propensity to be untruthful, except where it is not suggested that the defendant's case is untruthful in any respect.

It is important to note how radical a change to the law this is. In *Makin v Attorney-General of New South Wales* [1894] AC 57, PC, Lord Herschell stated that evidence that happens to reveal evidence of the defendant's bad character was not admissible 'for the purpose of leading to the conclusion that the accused is a person likely from his criminal conduct or character to have committed the offence for which he is being tried.' However, it was recognised in *Makin* that evidence probative of issues in the case might happen to reveal the previous bad character of the defendant. For example, the finding of 13 corpses of babies in properties owned by the Makins showed that their defence to the charge of killing the baby for which they were tried was less worthy of belief. They alleged that they had had nothing to do with the baby in question. The evidence of other corpses showed that the defendants were in the practice of 'baby farming' (taking babies from poor mothers and promising to look after them for a fee but killing them and keeping the money paid over). The revelation of bad character evidence was therefore not admitted to prove that the Makins were the sort of people who killed babies but to disprove their defence.

Therefore the pre-CJA 2003 common law attempted to draw a distinction between bad character evidence that was probative of a fact in issue in the case and bad character evidence that 'merely' went to prove propensity to commit the type of offences under with which the defendant was charged ('prejudicial evidence'). Cases since *Makin* had to resolve the difficulty of identifying both what bad character evidence could prove, other than a propensity to commit offences, and when evidence that might prove something other than propensity should be admitted at trial despite the risk that it might lead tribunal of fact to decide that the defendant had committed the offence because of the evidence of his propensity to do so (what Lord Hailsham in *DPP v Boardman* [1975] AC 421 called the 'forbidden line of reasoning'). The position of the common law when the CJA 2003 came into force had been resolved in *R v P* [1991] 3 All ER 337, HL, where it was ruled that evidence showing the defendant to have a propensity to commit offences could be admitted where the probative value of that evidence in proving some fact other than a propensity to commit offences outweighed the prejudicial effect of the evidence in showing that the defendant had a propensity to commit such offences.

The CJA 2003 has therefore preserved the admissibility of evidence to prove facts other than a propensity to commit offences while also allowing for the admissibility of evidence of propensity. Therefore, evidence of bad character will be admissible in principle to prove both a fact in issue and the accused's propensity to commit offences of the same type with which he is charged. Evidence that is relevant to propensity will be admissible subject to the power to exclude for inadequate probative value.

Both s 103(1)(a) and (b) seek to qualify when propensity evidence will be admissible. Section 103(1)(b) is simpler: a propensity for untruthfulness is not a 'matter in issue', and therefore evidence of such propensity is not admissible, if it is not suggested that the defendant's case is untruthful in any respect. This would most obviously apply where the defendant accepts the prosecution case but argues that the effect of the facts presented is different from the effect alleged by the prosecution, for example whether the force used by the defendant in self-defence was reasonable or where the issue at trial is whether a mental illness that the defence and prosecution agree the defendant suffered from is capable of raising the defence of diminished responsibility. In such cases, there is no value in admitting evidence that the defendant has a propensity to be untruthful. Section 103(1)(b) does not, however, make clear whether it is just the prosecution who must suggest that the defendant's case is untruthful. If a co-defendant makes such a suggestion, but the prosecution does not, the co-defendant could potentially rely on s 101(1)(e) to admit evidence of any propensity to untruthfulness. However, could the prosecution admit such evidence? It may be that such evidence would technically be admissible but excluded under the duty in CJA 2003, s 101(3) and more generally (see **8.3.11**).

The qualification in s 103(1)(a) is less clear in its meaning. Evidence of a defendant's propensity to commit the offence in question will not be admitted 'where his having such a propensity makes it no more likely that he is guilty of the offence'. As was seen in **Chapter 1**, evidence that does not make a fact more likely to be true than not is irrelevant and therefore inadmissible. This phrase may therefore do little more than state the legally obvious: that irrelevant evidence is inadmissible. It is difficult to interpret the phrase in any other way. What it does not appear to do is to place any requirement as to the probative value of such evidence, above and beyond simple relevance, before it is admitted to prove the propensity in question.

In *R v Hanson* The Times, 24 March 2005, the Court of Appeal offered the following guidance:

> Where propensity to commit the offence is relied upon by reference to s 101(1)(d) and s 103(1)(a), there are essentially three questions to be considered: (i) whether the history of conviction(s) establishes a propensity to commit offences of the kind charged; (ii) whether that propensity makes it more likely that the defendant committed the offence charged; and (iii) whether it is unjust to rely on the conviction(s) of the same description or category and, in any event, whether the proceedings will be unfair if they are admitted.

The first question does not require any elaboration. The next question then addresses the potential irrelevance of the propensity evidence referred to in s 103(1)(a) and noted above. The third question refers to the powers to exclude propensity evidence in s 103(3) (**8.3.7.4** below) and to the duty to exclude under s 101(3) (**8.3.11** below).

8.3.7.3   Proving propensity evidence

Section 103 provides:

> (2)   *Where subsection (1)(a) applies, a defendant's propensity to commit offences of the kind with which he is charged may (without prejudice to any other way of doing so) be established by evidence that he has been convicted of—*
> > (a)   *an offence of the same description as the one with which he is charged, or*
> > (b)   *an offence of the same category as the one with which he is charged.*
> (4)   *For the purposes of subsection (2)—*
> > (a)   *two offences are of the same description as each other if the statement of the offence in a written charge or indictment would, in each case, be in the same terms;*
> > (b)   *two offences are of the same category as each other if they belong to the same category of offences prescribed for the purposes of this section by an order made by the Secretary of State.*
> (5)   *A category prescribed by an order under subsection (4)(b) must consist of offences of the same type.*

Therefore, it is possible to prove a propensity to commit offences of the kind with which the defendant is charged by:

(a) Proof that the defendant has been convicted of an offence of the same description as the one with which he is charged (s 103(2)(a)). An offence is of the same description if it would be written on a charge or indictment in the same terms (s 103(4)(a)).

(b) Proof that the defendant has been convicted of any offences that have been specified by statutory instrument as being in the same category as the one with which he is charged (s 103(2)(b), (4)(b)).

(c) Any other means (s 103(2) states 'without prejudice to any other way of doing so').

In *R v Hanson* the Court of Appeal stated that in deciding whether the convictions established a propensity to commit the type of offence with which the defendant was charged the following facts should be taken into account whether s 103(2)(a) or (b) or some other means was used to justify the admissibility of the previous convictions. There was no particular number of convictions that would prove propensity, the fewer the previous convictions the less likely they were to prove propensity. In principle, a single previous conviction could do so by showing a tendency to unusual behaviour or by otherwise possessing strong probative force. The Court apparently adopting the approach in *R v P*, also stated that there was no need for 'striking similarity' between the previous offences, although such similarity could be one of the ways in which the propensity of the defendant could be proven from his previous convictions.

The Court of Appeal also drew a distinction between a propensity to untruthfulness and a propensity to dishonesty. Therefore, the mere presence of previous convictions for offences involving dishonesty does not have any more value in proving that the accused is prone to untruthfulness than do any other convictions. What will matter is the extent to which the manner in which the offences were committed show a propensity for untruthfulness, or the previous convictions show that the defendant was disbelieved at trial.

Offences of the same description

Exactly what is meant by 'the same terms' under s 103(2)(a) is not clear. Where the defendant is charged with inflicting grievous bodily harm contrary to the Offences Against the Person Act 1861, s 20, a previous conviction for the same offence would clearly be admissible to prove his or her propensity to commit such offences under s 103(2)(a). However, it would appear, that one or more previous convictions for offences contrary to s 18 of the 1861 Act (causing grievous bodily harm with intent) might not be admissible as the description for such an offence on an indictment is not 'in the same terms'. It remains to be seen whether 'the same terms' is interpreted by the courts to mean identical or containing similar content without being identical. Given that it is open to the Home Secretary to specify categories of offences of a similar type under s 103(2)(b), a restrictive interpretation of s 103(2)(a) would appear to be more appropriate.

Offences of the same category

As for offences under s 103(2)(b), the Home Secretary issued the Criminal Justice Act 2003 (Categories of Offences) Order 2004 (SI 2004/3346) which created two categories of offences. Any offence specified in a category will potentially be admissible under s 102(2)(b) to prove propensity to commit any other offence in the same category. The offences in each of the two categories are:

The Theft Category
(SI 2004/3346, Sch, Pt 1)

Theft	Handling stolen goods
Robbery	Going equipped to steal
Burglary/aggravated burglary	Making off without payment
involving theft, attempted theft or	Aiding, abetting, counselling or
intention to steal	procuring any of the above offences
Taking a motor vehicle without	Attempting any of the above
authority	offences (but conspiracy or
Aggravated vehicle taking	incitement are not included)

The Sexual Offences (Persons under 16) Category
(SI 2004/3346, Sch, Pt 2)

Thirty six offences under the Sexual Offences Act 2003 and preceding Acts are specified in this category. Some are criminal because the victim is under a specified age (such as intercourse with a girl under the age of 16 contrary to the Sexual Offences Act 1956, s 6). However, this category also includes offences that can be committed against persons of any age (such as rape contrary to the Sexual Offences Act 1956, s 1 or the Sexual Offences

Act 2003, s 1). However, insofar as the offence can be committed with a person of any age, the offences only fit into this category for the purposes of admissibility under s 101(1)(d) if the victim of the offence was under the age of 16. Again, aiding, abetting, counselling or procuring such offences and attempting them also fit within the category but neither conspiracy nor incitement to commit any such offence do.

Other means

In *R v Hanson* The Times, 24 March 2005, the Court of Appeal confirmed that s 103(2) did not provide an exhaustive list of methods by which convictions could be proven. It would appear that the other means by which propensity may be proved could include evidence of commission of previous acts which were not prosecuted (as happened in *Makin* and in common law similar fact cases like *R v Smith*, *R v Ball* and *R v Barrington* referred to at **8.3.3.2**). Furthermore, it is possible that propensity might be proven by the possession of incriminating articles. At common law, the possession of incriminating articles was only admissible if it there was a probative link between the article and the commission of the offence with which the defendant was charged but not if the evidence merely showed a disposition to commit offences of the type charged (*R v B* [1997] 2 Cr App R 88). However in *Thompson v R* [1918] AC 221, the House of Lords had approved the admission of evidence that the defendant was arrested near public toilets in possession of powder puffs and had indecent photographs of young boys at his house. The prosecution had admitted these items to prove that the defendant was the person who had visited those public toilets to commit acts of indecency with young boys on the previous day. While in *Thompson*, the House of Lords stated that the items found were not being admitted simply to show that the defendant had a disposition to commit such offences and was therefore guilty, the items were justified in that case as evidence that hallmarked the defendant as a particular kind of person and who was therefore likely to be the same person who had visited the toilets on the previous occasion. Clearly the 'hallmark' stemmed from Thompson's disposition to commit offences.

This tension in the common law system has been removed by s 101(1)(d) and s 103(2). It would appear that evidence of propensity to commit offences can be proven by evidence of bad character which includes (according to s 98) evidence of a disposition to commit offences or carry out 'other reprehensible behaviour'. It is likely therefore that if a case like *Thompson* were to occur again, the evidence of the indecent photographs would probably be admissible (subject to the power to exclude) under s 101(1)(d) as relevant to an important matter (propensity to offend) and could be proved by means other than previous convictions. However, it is submitted that the possession of powder puffs would not be admissible. Whatever the attitudes to such items found in the possession of men in the early 20th century, it is unlikely that the powder puffs would be evidence of 'other reprehensible behaviour' today.

Section 103(2) may also, technically, include cases prosecuted where the accused was acquitted as occurred in the pre-CJA 2003 case of *R v Z* [2000] 2 AC 483, HL. However the previous case would have to have some relevance to the propensity to commit the offence with which the defendant is charged. In determining the breadth of the phrase 'other way of doing so' it is worth remembering that the court has the power to exclude evidence (see **8.3.11** below). It therefore seems likely that the court will simply determine whether the evidence proposed by the prosecution may prove a propensity to commit the offence charged (ie whether it is relevant to that issue) without considering the weight to be attached to the evidence when applying the test under s 103(2) but will consider any arguments as to the weight to be attached to such evidence when considering whether or not to exercise its power to exclude it.

8.3.7.4   Inadmissible evidence of propensity

In addition to the rules allowing for the exclusion of evidence under s 101(1)(d) generally, s 103(3) creates a specific power to exclude previous convictions of limited probative value:

> (3)   *Subsection (2) does not apply in the case of a particular defendant if the court is satisfied, by reason of the length of time since the conviction or for any other reason, that it would be unjust for it to apply in his case.*

The subsection only applies where the previous conviction is used to prove the propensity of the defendant to commit the offence or to be untruthful. It allows the court to rule that any previous convictions adduced for such purposes will not be admissible if they are either old or would cause injustice 'for any other reason'. There is likely to be an overlap with the general exclusionary duties and discretions that are considered at **8.3.11**. The subsection appears to allow the court to rule that previous convictions that are adduced by the prosecution to prove propensity may be ruled inadmissible if they are so lacking in probative value that their admission would cause injustice. The most likely interpretation that will be placed on this subsection by the courts is that the probative value of the convictions would be outweighed by the prejudicial effect of admitting them.

Although the subsection makes specific reference to previous convictions, as s 103(2) allowed proof of propensity by other means and as s 103(3) provides that the court can disapply s 103(2) 'for any other reason', clearly the duty not to admit other evidence of propensity is also provided for under that subsection.

8.3.7.5   Directions to the jury

In *R v Hanson* The Times, 24 March 2005, the Court of Appeal stated that where evidence of the defendant's propensity is admitted, the judge should warn the jury against placing undue reliance on that evidence and should direct them that they cannot simply use such evidence to bolster a weak case. The court went on to make suggestions as to the content of a direction:

- the jury should not conclude that the defendant is untruthful or guilty merely because he has the convictions;

- although convictions show propensity they do not prove the commission of the particular offence(s) with which he is charged (or is untruthful);

- whether the convictions prove propensity is a question for the jury to decide;

- the jury should consider anything the defendant has said about his previous convictions; and

- propensity should be considered alongside all the other evidence in the case.

It is probable that, although not expressly stated in *R v Hanson*, in accordance with directions given on inferences from the defendant's silence and in respect of alleged lies (see **Chapter 13**), the judge will be expected to remind the jury of any explanations that the defendant has given for his previous convictions.

8.3.8   Substantial probative value to an important matter in issue between co-defendants (s 101(1)(e))

Section 101(1)(e) allows one defendant to admit evidence of the bad character of a co-defendant in limited circumstances. Prior to the CJA 2003, there were two bases upon which a co-defendant could adduce evidence of the bad character of a co-defendant:

- (a)   Where the defendant adduced similar fact evidence that was relevant to his or own defence. For example, in *R v Miller* [1952] 2 All ER 667 it was held that evidence that the criminal activity in question ceased when the co-defendant was in prison should have been admitted. In *R v Randall* [2004] 1 WLR 56, the House of Lords held that a defendant should be entitled to adduce evidence showing the propensity of the co-defendant to commit the offence where the issue was which of the two defendants was more likely to have committed the offence.

(b) Where the defendant became entitled to adduce evidence of the bad character of the co-defendant under the Criminal Evidence Act 1898, s 1(3)(iii) because the co-defendant had 'given evidence against' the defendant. In *Murdoch v Taylor* [1965] AC 574, the House of Lords held that evidence was given against a defendant where the co-defendant supported the prosecution case or undermined the defence of another person charged in the same proceedings.

The effect of s 101(1)(e) is to provide for both of the situations under the pre-existing law. The requirements are that:

- there is an important matter in issue between the defendant and the co-defendant;
- the evidence has substantial probative value on that matter.

8.3.8.1 Important matter in issue between the defendant and co-defendant

The same meaning of 'important matter' that applies in s 101(1)(d) applies in s 101(1)(e): the matter must have 'substantial importance in the context of the case as a whole' (s 112(1)). This will include the sorts of circumstances that arose in the similar fact cases at common law (see eg *R v Miller*; *R v Randall*).

Section 104, which makes further provision for the application of s 101(1)(e), does not repeat the provisions of s 103 concerning the proof of propensity and the specific ways in which propensity may be proven, nor does s 104 adopt the provisions of s 103 in any way. As was noted above, at common law, a co-defendant was entitled to prove another co-defendant's propensity to commit offences where to do so was relevant to the defendant's defence. However the rules of common law have been expressly abolished (s 99). This leaves an unfortunate gap. While the CJA 2003 has specifically provided for the admissibility of evidence of propensity adduced by the prosecution, it has made no such provision for the co-accused except to place restrictions on the admissibility of evidence of a propensity to be untruthful (see below). There seems no reason in principle why only the prosecution could admit evidence of the propensity of a defendant to commit particular offences but it will probably be necessary for the appellate courts to make a ruling to clarify this matter and whether a co-defendant is entitled to prove previous convictions in accordance with s 103(4) and SI 2004/3346 should the prosecution not do so. The best view is that the sweeping abolition of the common law rules by s 99 and the silence of s 104 was not intended to deprive a co-defendant of a right to adduce evidence that would assist in raising a defence in the way envisaged in *R v Randall*.

Section 104 does make provision for proof of a propensity of untruthfulness:

(1) Evidence which is relevant to the question whether the defendant has a propensity to be untruthful is admissible on that basis under section 101(1)(e) only if the nature or conduct of his defence is such as to undermine the co-defendant's defence.

The effect of this subsection is to restate, in slightly different language, the right of the defendant to adduce evidence affecting the credibility of a co-defendant where a 'cut-throat' defence was being run. The complicated case law under the Criminal Evidence Act 1898, s 1(3)(iii) has been simplified in the CJA 2003 by simply providing that there must be an important matter in issue between the two defendants. This means that if the co-defendant has adduced evidence that suggests that the defendant may have committed the offence (or is more likely to have done so), there is an important issue between them.

However, one aspect of the law under the Criminal Evidence Act 1898 (CEA 1898) must be considered in more detail: is there a matter in issue between the two defendants simply because their accounts differ or is there a requirement that the evidence of one defendant renders the conviction of the other more likely? In *Murdoch v Taylor* [1965] AC 574, it was stated that evidence must assist the prosecution case or undermine the defence case. Under the CJA 2003, as the importance must, under s 112(1), be 'substantial' this would therefore support an argument that the approach identified in *Murdoch v Taylor* also applies under the CJA 2003. If this is the case, what if the conflict between the account of the co-defendant does not directly suggest that the defendant committed the offence but increases the risk that the defendant will be convicted by rendering his account less credible? This could happen, for example, because the co-defendant adduces evidence that conflicts with the defendant's account in a way that implies that the defendant is lying.

In *R v Varley* [1982] 2 All ER 519 the mere denial of participation in a joint venture was not enough to amount to evidence against a co-accused under the CEA 1898, s 1(3)(c). It was only where the denial of participation by the co-defendant 'must lead to the conclusion that if the [co-defendant] did not participate then it must have been the [defendant] who did' that the CEA 1898, s 1(3)(iii) would apply to allow the defendant to adduce evidence of bad character against the co-defendant. Under the CJA 2003 it would seem equally likely that there could be an 'important matter in issue' between co-defendants where one defendant simply denies involvement in an offence in a way that undermines the case of a co-defendant. Whether this is so will depend on the facts of the case. For example in *Varley*, V and D were charged with robbery. D alleged that he only took place in the offence because of V's threats against him. V denied any involvement at all. The Court of Appeal held that V's denial was evidence against D because the effect of V's denial was to deprive D of his defence of duress in addition to suggesting that D was less worthy of belief.

Equally, the court may find that there is a 'matter in issue' between two defendants where one defendant advances a defence which is inconsistent with the co-defendant's original defence, even if it provides the co-defendant with an alternative defence. In *R v Hatton* (1976) 64 Cr App R 88, another case concerning the CEA 1898 s 1(3)(iii), three defendants were charged with theft of scrap metal. A's defence was that he, B and C had agreed to take the metal but that they had not been dishonest because B had told A and C that he had permission to take it. However, B's defence was that he had witnessed A and C taking the metal and had helped them when he was convinced that they had paid for the metal. A was found to have given evidence against B even though it provided him with another defence. B could therefore cross-examine A as to his previous convictions. The Court of Appeal held that A's evidence assisted the prosecution case in a material way (that there was a plan to take the metal) and that even though it provided B with another defence, the inconsistency did more to undermine his defence than to enhance it. It is submitted that a similar approach should be adopted under s 101(1)(e): it is not the mere inconsistency of evidence that puts a matter in issue; the inconsistency should, on balance, render the conviction of the defendant more likely.

8.3.8.2   Substantial probative value

In contrast to the evidence adduced by the prosecution, before a defendant can adduce evidence of the bad character of a co-defendant, that evidence has to have substantial probative value. In the explanatory note accompanying the Criminal Justice Bill, it was explained that 'substantial' meant 'more than trivial' rather than any higher standard of probative value. The rationale for imposing a probative standard for evidence adduced by defendants but not for prosecution evidence is that prosecution evidence is subject to an exclusionary discretion under s 101(3) whereas defence evidence under s 101(1)(e) is not. Nor is evidence adduced by a defendant against a co-defendant subject to discretionary exclusion under the Police and Criminal Evidence Act 1984, s 78 or at common law (*Lobban v R* [1995] 1 WLR 877).

In assessing the probative value of evidence the court should assume that the evidence is true (s 109(1)) unless, on the evidence before the court, including evidence received during a voir dire, no jury or court could reasonably find the evidence to be true (s 109(2)).

8.3.8.3   Proof of the bad character of the defendant by a co-defendant

Section 104(2) provides that evidence of bad character can be proven by a co-defendant either by his or her own witnesses (s 104(2)(a)) or by cross-examination of prosecution or other defence witnesses (s 104(2)(b)). In contrast to the position under the CEA 1898, s 1(3)(iii), the CJA 2003, 104(2) only allows evidence to be admitted by defendants. The prosecution cannot use conflicts between co-defendants as a justification for adducing evidence of the bad character of either defendant.

8.3.9   Evidence to correct a false impression (s 101(1)(f))

Only the prosecution can adduce evidence under s 101(1)(f) to correct a false impression (s 105(7)).

8.3.9.1   Correcting a false impression

Section 105 provides:

> (1)   *For the purposes of section 101(1)(f)—*
>> (a)   *the defendant gives a false impression if he is responsible for the making of an express or implied assertion which is apt to give the court or jury a false or misleading impression about the defendant;*
>
>> . . .
>
> (4)   *Where it appears to the court that a defendant, by means of his conduct (other than the giving of evidence) in the proceedings, is seeking to give the court or jury an impression about himself that is false or misleading, the court may if it appears just to do so treat the defendant as being responsible for the making of an assertion which is apt to give that impression.*
> (5)   *In subsection (4) 'conduct' includes appearance or dress.*

Note that the test is broader than 'false fact' or 'false express assertion'. The 'impression' can be made by implication, by conduct and by appearance or by what a defendant wears.

Before the implementation of the CJA 2003, evidence of the defendant's bad character was admissible both at common law and under the CEA 1898, s 1(3)(ii) where the defendant had given evidence of his good character. It seems clear that the CJA 2003 has continued this rule. However, given that neither s 101(1)(f) nor s 105 use the phrase 'good character' the ambit of s 101(1)(f) is wider than the pre-existing law.

One effect of this is that the prosecution could use evidence of bad character to correct a false impression other than an impression that the defendant is of good character. For example, if a defendant were charged with burglary of a house in London, where the burglary took place at 1 pm on 4 March and the defendant alleged that he was in Manchester at that time visiting his mother all day, the prosecution could use s 101(1)(f) to prove that he had, in fact, been appearing at a Magistrates' Court in London at 11 am that day in connection with another offence. Unless such evidence of bad character is covered by CJA 2003, s 98 (because it 'has to do with the alleged facts of the offence with which the defendant is charged'), it would be admissible under s 101(1)(f) to create the false impression of the alibi.

Another effect of the difference in the language is that it is unclear to what extent case law preceding the CJA 2003 can be used to interpret s 101(1)(f). The approach adopted under the CEA 1898, s 1(3)(ii) was that, in addition to the assertion by a defendant that he had no previous convictions, a defendant had asserted his good character where he had advanced a positive case as to his disinclination to commit the offence or as to his credibility as a witness. The courts interpreted such assertions broadly so that an assertion by a defendant that he was in regular employment (*R v Baker* (1912) 7 Cr App R 252) or that he was of a religious character (*R v Ferguson* (1909) 2 Cr App R 250)) would allow cross-examination as to previous convictions. However, in *R v Robinson* [2001] Crim LR 478, the Court of Appeal held that a person who held onto a bible while testifying was not asserting his good character.

How would these issues be resolved under the CJA 2003? It is submitted that the courts should restrict the application of the law in this area to the test stated in s 101(1)(f), namely whether the defendant is giving a false impression. It must at least be arguable that a person asserting that he has regular employment is not giving a false impression unless, in doing so, he is either telling an untruth or is giving a misleading impression as to his general honesty or his inclination or motivation to commit the particular offence with which he is charged. In other words, whether a false impression has been created cannot be treated with the technicality that courts appear to have adopted in determining whether a person was asserting 'good character' under the CEA 1898. 'False impression' is a question of fact to be decided on a trial by trial basis on the basis of the testimony given.

The same approach should be adopted when considering the difficulties faced by a defendant in advancing her defence in a way that happens to show him or her in a favourable light. In *R v Samuel* (1956) 40 Cr App R 8, the defendant was charged with theft of a camera. He testified that he had found the camera and was going to give it back, as he had done on other occasions in the past. It was held that he had been properly cross-examined as to his previous convictions because he was asserting his good character with the object of showing that he was honest. Clearly, under the CEA 1898 the defendant had gone beyond denying the charge by simply saying that he intended to hand the camera back into attempting to bolster his credibility by asserting that he had been honest in the past. However, had he created a false impression? The matter is arguable not least because it could be said to be 'misleading' and could only appropriately be resolved by looking at exactly what was said during his testimony in the context of the trial as a whole. It is submitted that the mere fact that he made an assertion that could have counted as an attempt to establish 'good character' under the CEA 1898 would not necessarily justify the conclusion that he gave a 'false impression' under the CJA 2003; the false impression test is less technical and therefore depends more on the facts of each case.

In *R v Winfield* (1939) 27 Cr App R 139, it was held that once the defendant had put his character in issue by testifying as to his good character, then the whole of the defendant's character was put in issue (ie a defendant's character is indivisible). The defendant in *Winfield* was charged with indecent assault upon a woman. He sought to prove that he had an exemplary record with women. The Court of Criminal Appeal held that the prosecution had been properly allowed to adduce evidence as to his previous convictions for dishonesty offences. Given that the test of admissibility under s 101(1)(f) is a false or misleading impression, rather than simply a false fact or false assertion, it would appear that the principle that other aspects of a defendant's bad character may be admitted if doing so would correct a false impression will continue. However if a defendant like Winfield were to admit to having been in trouble in the past but asserting that it was for offending of a different nature, it might be difficult to argue that the defendant has given a false impression. It therefore seems that the old rule that a defendant's character is indivisible can be dispensed with insofar as those other aspects of the defendant's bad character have not contributed to a false impression. All will very much depend on what impression the judge considers the defendant to have given.

In theory, s 101(1)(f) could also be used to correct a false impression about a propensity to commit offences. This will often be exactly the impression that the defendant wishes to convey by asserting her good character, a fact recognised by Lord Goddard CJ in *R v Samuel* (1956) 40 Cr App R 8 at p 12. Furthermore, the law relating to good character recognises that the presence of good character is evidence of a lack of propensity to offend (see **8.2.2**). However propensity is also invariably a matter in issue between the parties and so evidence of propensity is specifically admissible under s 101(1)(d). The courts may adopt the approach of the Court of Appeal in *R v Fernandez* [2003] EWCA Crim 1151, decided before the implementation of the CJA 2003, in which the defendant was charged with indecency offences against a young golfer. The defendant's evidence was that he had previously assisted another young golfer and that there was no sexual relationship, in other words that he did not have a propensity to commit such offences. The Court of Appeal held that the prosecution had properly been allowed to admit in evidence photographs that suggested that there had been a sexual relationship on that earlier occasion. The evidence was directed to a 'positive part of the evidence of the appellant'.

In determining whether evidence has probative value, the court should treat the evidence as true (s 109(1)) unless no reasonable jury could conclude that the evidence is true (s 109(2)).

The law prior to the CJA 2003 made no specific provision for restricting evidence admitted in this way. The restrictions imposed on the use of evidence admitted at common law or under the CEA 1898, s 1(3)(ii) derived from the common law discretion to control such evidence, which balanced the probative value of the evidence and its prejudicial effect. As part of this analysis regard had to be given to what the evidence was seeking to prove. The rule before the CJA 2003 was that evidence of bad character admitted under the CEA 1898, s 1(3)(ii) or the common law went simply to the issue of the credibility of the defendant. However, proof of the defendant's propensity was permitted under the common law rules and the CEA 1898, s 1(3)(ii) to counter the defendant's contention that he or she lacked the disposition to commit the offence. Under s 101(1)(f), by virtue of s 105(1)(b), the purpose of the evidence is to correct the false impression. This means that what the evidence proves depends on the issue to which the false impression relates.

Insofar as s 101(1)(f) is used to correct a false impression as to the credibility or the testimonial honesty of the defendant, the courts will probably find some of the pre-existing case law of assistance. The general principles identified in connection with the discretion to exclude evidence under the CEA 1898 in *R v McLeod* [1994] 1 WLR 1500 would apply equally to the restriction on evidence under s 101(1)(f) insofar as the false impression relates only to credibility. The principles in *McLeod*, adapted to s 101(1)(f) are:

(a) The fact that evidence incidentally shows a propensity to commit the type of offence with which the defendant is charged does not preclude its use to disprove his or her credibility.

(b) Extensive detail of previous offences should generally be avoided where the issue is the defendant's credibility.

(c) Details of pleas entered and false defences used previously could be proven as they are relevant to credibility.

(d) Details that show the defendant in a particularly bad light are not automatically inadmissible but the judge should consider whether to exclude them on the grounds of their prejudicial effect.

(e) Objection to the admission of evidence of the defendant's bad character should be taken as soon as possible.

(f) The jury should be directed as to what use to make of the evidence admitted.

McLeod concerned evidence that would now be governed by s 101(1)(g) rather than s 101(1)(f) but the principles remain the same.

If s 101(1)(f) also applies to evidence of propensity then a lot more evidence might be admitted within the limits of s 105(6) because proof of propensity may often require detailed analysis of the facts of previous offences or of previous misconduct. However, the courts were prepared before the CJA 2003 to place restrictions the use of evidence in rebuttal on an issue of propensity. In *R v Davison-Jenkins* [1997] Crim LR 816, the defendant was charged with theft of cheap cosmetics from a shop. She alleged that, being wealthy, she did not need to steal the items. The Court of Appeal held that she was properly cross-examined as to her previous convictions as she had put her character in issue but that the cross-examination went too far: all that was required was proof of her previous convictions for dishonesty and not the detail of previous shoplifting offences that would undoubtedly have been prejudicial in effect.

8.3.9.2   When should the defendant be responsible for creating a false impression?

Section 105 provides:

> (2)   A defendant is treated as being responsible for the making of an assertion if—
>
>   (a)   the assertion is made by the defendant in the proceedings (whether or not in evidence given by him),
>
>   (b)   the assertion was made by the defendant—
>
>   (i)   on being questioned under caution, before charge, about the offence with which he is charged, or
>
>   (ii)   on being charged with the offence or officially informed that he might be prosecuted for it, and evidence of the assertion is given in the proceedings,
>
>   (c)   the assertion is made by a witness called by the defendant,
>
>   (d)   the assertion is made by any witness in cross-examination in response to a question asked by the defendant that is intended to elicit it, or is likely to do so, or
>
>   (e)   the assertion was made by any person out of court, and the defendant adduces evidence of it in the proceedings.
>
> (3)   A defendant who would otherwise be treated as responsible for the making of an assertion shall not be so treated if, or the extent that, he withdraws it or disassociates himself from it.

Therefore s 101(1)(f) can be used to correct any subsisting false impression whether made during trial or made before trial and admitted as evidence at trial. At trial the false impression can be given by either the defendant herself or by a witness called on her behalf.

Note that statements made to police officers or other investigators only create a false impression if made under caution or following charge. Therefore pre-caution statements do not create a false impression nor do statements made to investigative officers that are not admissible or admitted in evidence. Hearsay statements admitted at trial (other than the records of the questioning or charge of the defendant) do not create a false impression unless admitted by the defendant. Therefore a document admitted by a co-defendant that happened to suggest that the defendant was a person of good character would not create a false impression for the purposes of s 101(1)(f).

A false impression about the defendant relayed by a prosecution witness or one called by a co-defendant cannot be corrected under s 101(1)(f) if that evidence was either elicited by the prosecution or a co-defendant, or if it was the unexpected and unpredictable result of the questioning by the defendant. Section 105(3) allows a defendant to correct a false impression himself so as to prevent evidence of his bad character from being admitted. Therefore if the defendant were to assert that he had never been in trouble with the police before while being questioned under caution but was to admit at some later stage that he had been in trouble with the police then s 101(1)(f) would not apply although he would be at risk of cross examination about previous inconsistent statements (see **6.3.6**) or, possibly, for adverse inferences from any lies (see **13.3.1**).

However, it should be noted that the CJA 2003 represents a reordering of the categories of admissibility of evidence as well as a reform of the law relating to propensity. It is therefore submitted that evidence of propensity (being a matter in issue by virtue of s 103(2)) is better resolved under s 101(1)(d) than s 101(1)(f), particularly as the protections and restrictions afforded under s 101(1)(d) are both stronger and more specifically focussed on propensity evidence.

8.3.9.3   What may be proven under s 101(1)(f)

Evidence that may be admitted under s 101(1)(f) is more limited than under other provisions considered so far such s 101(1)(d) and (e). In other words, even if a false impression has been given, this does not open up all of the defendant's character.

Section 105 provides:

> *(1)   For the purposes of section 101(1)(f)—*
>
> *. . .*
>
> > *(b)   evidence to correct such an impression is evidence which has probative value in correcting it.*
> *(6)   Evidence is admissible under section 101(1)(f) only if it goes no further than is necessary to correct the false impression.*

The combined effect of these two provisions is that the court must oversee prosecution evidence called to rebut the false impression. Only evidence that can prove the falsity of the impression is admissible and then only insofar as it corrects the impression.

8.3.10   A defendant's attack on the character of another person (s 101(1)(g))

Section 101(1)(g) restates the rule in the CEA 1898, s 1(3)(ii) which provided that a defendant's bad character could be put to him in cross-examination if 'the nature or conduct of his defence is such as to involve imputations on the character of the prosecutor or the witnesses for the prosecution or the deceased victim of the alleged crime.' The CEA 1898 only applied if the defendant gave evidence (*R v Butterwasser* [1948] KB 4) whereas the CJA 2003 applies whether or not the defendant testifies. Furthermore, the CEA 1898, s 1(3)(ii) allowed both the prosecution and any co-defendant to cross-examine the defendant as to his or her previous convictions. However, the CJA 2003, s 101(1)(g) is restricted to the proof of bad character by the prosecution (s 106(3)).

Section 106 provides:

> *(1)   For the purposes of section 101(1)(g) a defendant makes an attack on another person's character if—*
> > *(a)   he adduces evidence attacking the other person's character,*
> > *(b)   he . . . asks questions in cross-examination that are intended to elicit such evidence or are likely to do so, or*
> > *(c)   evidence is given of an imputation about the other person made by the defendant—*
> > > *(i)   on being questioned under caution, before charge, about the offence with which he is charged, or*
> > > *(ii)   on being charged with the offence or officially informed that he might be prosecuted for it.*

(2)   *In subsection (1) 'evidence attacking the other person's character' means evidence to the effect that the other person—*

    (a)   *has committed an offence (whether a different offence from the one with which the defendant is charged or the same one), or*

    (b)   *has behaved, or is disposed to behave, in a reprehensible way;*

and 'imputation about another person' means an assertion to that effect.

8.3.10.1   Who is the victim of the attack?

While the CEA 1898 only applied where the imputations were cast upon prosecution witnesses or the deceased victim of an alleged offence, ss 101(1)(g) and 106 provide that the bad character of the defendant may be admitted if he attacks 'another person'. Therefore, if the defendant were to suggest that a person not called as a witness (or the victim) was responsible for the offence, then this gateway to the admissibility of his bad character has been opened. The relevance of the defendant's bad character in such a situation may be either to assist the jury in deciding whether to believe the defendant's attack on another person (ie a credibility issue) or in deciding whether the defendant was in fact more likely to have committed the offence than the person attacked in evidence (a propensity issue). However, it may be that in many situations where the attack is not upon a witness in the case or a victim of the offence, the court may be particularly inclined to exercise its powers to exclude the evidence of bad character (see **8.3.11**).

8.3.10.2   What amounts to an attack?

An attack or imputation (the CJA 2003 appears to give these two words the same meaning) is made where the defendant suggests that the other person committed the offence with which the defendant is charged, has behaved in a reprehensible way or is disposed to behave in such a way.

It did not matter for the purposes of determining whether an imputation had been cast under the CEA 1898, s 1(3)(ii) whether the attack on the other person was necessary to mount the defendant's defence (*Selvey v DPP* [1970] AC 304, HL). However this approach posed two difficulties under the CEA 1898 that will also have to be addressed under the CJA 2003.

First of all, when does the emphatic use of language in his own defence by the defendant become an attack on another person? In *Selvey*, the House of Lords recognised that a 'mere traverse' of the prosecution case would not amount to an imputation. Contrast the following cases:

    (a)   *R v Rouse* [1914] 1 KB 184, where the defendant's testimony that the prosecution evidence was a lie and the prosecution was a liar was held not to be an imputation.

    (b)   *R v Rappolt* (1911) 6 Cr App R 156, where an imputation was held to have been cast where the defendant alleged that the prosecution witness was such a horrible liar that even is brother would not speak to him.

    (c)   *R v Wignall* [1993] Crim LR 62, where the cross-examination on behalf of the defendant alleging that the prosecution witness's evidence was untrue and being made up as the witness testified was held not to be an imputation.

The approach of the courts in such cases was resolved on a case-by-case basis. However, the impression that was left by this approach was one of inconsistency.

Secondly, what was the position where the defence necessarily involved an implication that a prosecution witness was lying? For example, if a complainant alleged he had been sexually assaulted by the defendant, would the defendant be casting an imputation if his defence was that the complainant was fabricating the whole incident out of spite? In doing so, he is doing no more than raising his defence to the charge. Again, the courts appeared to have reached different conclusions. In some cases the courts refused to find an imputation where the effect of the defence was to call into question the truthfulness of the case presented by a prosecution witness, for example *R v Nelson* [1968] 68 Cr App R 12, where the defendant had alleged that a police officer had fabricated a detailed confession by the defendant. In other cases, such as *R v Tanner* (1977) 66 Cr App R 56, the courts readily found that an imputation had been cast where the defendant alleged the police had fabricated confession evidence. In *R v Britzmann* [1983] 1 WLR 350, police officers testified that the defendant had confessed to the offence with which he was charged and had shouted incriminating information to an accomplice in a different police cell. The defendant sought to avoid the application of the CEA 1898, s 1(3)(ii) by simply denying that he had made any confession or incriminating statements without making any express allegations against the police officers. Nonetheless, the trial judge allowed his previous convictions to be put to him. The Court of Appeal held that the defendant's case necessarily implied that the police witnesses had fabricated the evidence against him. In so doing, Lawton LJ observed, 'When allegations of the fabrication of evidence are made against prosecution witnesses . . . juries are entitled to know about the characters of those making them'. His Lordship went on to observe that the fact that the defendant had been effectively forced to cast such an imputation could be used in exercising the discretion to exclude the evidence. In effect, the judgment in *Britzmann* sought to impose a clear distinction between the imputations issue and the exercise of a discretion. Whether or not an imputation had been cast was determined by consideration of the potential effect of the defendant's evidence upon the reputation of the prosecution witness. Issues such as whether the defendant had been forced in some way into running such a defence and whether allowance should be made for the tensions of being on trial and in giving evidence and for the intelligence of the defendant were matters to be considered in exercising the discretion to exclude the evidence.

The CJA 2003 provides a similar regime and allows for a similar approach. In *R v Hanson* The Times, 24 March 2005, the Court of Appeal stated that pre-CJA 2003 authorities would continue to apply to the extent that they were compatible with s 106 of the Act. Therefore as s 101(1)(g) is subject to the duty to exclude evidence on the grounds of fairness under s 101(3) the court can adopt the approach enunciated in *Britzmann* in applying s 101(1)(g). It will be matter for the judge, in interpreting the evidence to determine whether there has been an attack on another person. If so, the judge will then have to consider whether to prevent the admission of evidence of the bad character of the defendant under s 101(3). The effect of this is that the principle stated in *Selvey* that a mere traverse of the prosecution evidence does not amount to an imputation will have to be treated cautiously under the CJA 2003. It may still apply in many situations but the test under s 106(2) is whether there has been a suggestion of criminal or reprehensible behaviour by another person. As is illustrated by *Britzmann*, a simple traverse could amount to an imputation under the old law and could amount to an attack under the new law. The definition of 'attack' in s 106(2) includes both the commission of offences and of other reprehensible behaviour. Therefore the allegation that police officers have fabricated evidence against the defendant would clearly be an attack as would a suggestion that a witness was making up testimony (as in *R v Wignall* above). The judge may have to exercise more care in determining whether emphatic denials of the accounts of other witnesses such as in *Rouse* and *Rappolt* are attacks. There will come a point at which the allegations of the defendant amount to an offence such as perjury. Furthermore, the use of the word 'reprehensible' does give the trial judge a yardstick (albeit an imprecise one) by which to judge allegations of dishonesty short of perjury.

On the other hand the principle in *Selvey* that the necessity of making the imputation does not prevent the admissibility of bad character evidence applies equally to attacks and s 101(1)(g). The necessity of making the attack is simply something to which the court should have regard in considering whether to exercise its discretion to exclude such evidence (see **8.3.11**).

8.3.10.3   What may be proven under s 101(1)(g)?

Under the CEA 1898, s 1(3)(ii) evidence of bad character was only relevant to the credibility of the defendant. It was not relevant to the issue of the propensity of the defendant (*R v McLeod* [1994] 1 WLR 1500). However, s 106 in no way specifies the uses to which evidence of the defendant's character can be put under s 101(1)(g). Section 103(2) to (4) specifically authorises the proof of the defendant's propensity to commit offences under s 101(1)(d). However evidence of the defendant's propensity may be relevant under s 101(1)(g) where the effect of the defendant's attack is to suggest that the other person is more likely to have committed the offence by reason of his or her previous convictions, behaviour or disposition. Nonetheless it is submitted that, given that evidence of propensity is admissible in principle under s 101(1)(d), is subject to more rigorous controls by virtue of s 103(2) to (5) and, as no provision is made as to how propensity evidence is to be proven under s 101(1)(g), s 101(1)(g) should not be used to justify the admission of propensity evidence. However until the matter is dealt with by the appellate courts, the position remains unclear.

8.3.10.4   When must the attacking statement have been made?

Like false impressions under s 101(1)(f), the defendant may trigger s 101(1)(g) by leading evidence on his own behalf (either by his own evidence or by calling witnesses to give such evidence for him). He may also do so where the attack is made by a witness being cross-examined by him or on his behalf but only if the questioning is intended to elicit such evidence or is likely to do so. In other words, the defendant does not become liable for unsolicited and unexpected utterances. Nor is he liable where the attacks are solicited by the questioning of others such as the prosecution of co-defendant.

Also, as with s 101(1)(f) the defendant may be liable for statements he or she makes before trial. Under s 101(1)(g) the defendant will be liable for attacks on prosecution witnesses made during investigative questioning under caution or upon charge where such statements are admitted as evidence. Also any attacks made in out of court statements and adduced by the defendant as hearsay evidence (see **Chapters 10** and **11**) will constitute an attack on another person (s 106(1)(a)). However, if another party adduces an out-of-court statement in which the defendant has attacked another person, s 101(1)(g) will not apply.

8.3.11   Exclusion of evidence

Section 101(3) makes specific provision for the exclusion of evidence admitted under s 101(1)(d) (important matter in issue between the prosecution and the defendant) and s 101(1)(g) (evidence admissible following an attack on another person's character). Section 101 provides:

(3)   *The court must not admit evidence under subsection (1)(d) or (g) if, on an application by the defendant to exclude it, it appears to the court that the admission of the evidence would have such an adverse effect on the fairness of the proceedings that the court ought not to admit it.*

(4)   *On an application to exclude evidence under subsection (3) the court must have regard, in particular to the length of time between the matters to which that evidence relates and the matters which form the subject of the offences charged.*

8.3.11.1   Nature of the exclusionary power

Section 101(3) is expressed in similar terms to the Police and Criminal Evidence Act 1984, s 78 which provides a discretion to exclude evidence where the admission of the evidence would have such an adverse effect on the fairness of the proceedings that the court ought not to admit it.

However, s 101(3) requires the court to exclude evidence where it is unfair (s 101(3) uses the word 'must' whereas s 78(1) of the 1984 Act uses the word 'may'). As such the court does not have a discretion under s 101(3) whether to exclude evidence if it reaches the conclusion that to admit the evidence would be unfair. However, unfairness in these circumstances is a balancing exercise as can be seen from the observation of Lord Lane CJ in *R v Quinn* [1990] Crim LR 581 concerning s 78, where he said:

> The function of the judge is therefore to protect the fairness of the proceedings, and normally proceedings are fair if a jury hears all relevant evidence which either side wishes to place before it . . .

Therefore the court will undoubtedly have a great deal of latitude in deciding whether it must exercise its power to exclude under s 101(3).

In *R v Hanson* The Times, 24 March 2005, in providing guidance for the use of s 101, reiterated the significance of probative value and prejudicial effect in determining fairness under s 101(3).

8.3.11.2   Applying the fairness test

It will be remembered that, in essence, s 101(1)(d) replicates the rules at common law that allowed the admission of evidence of 'similar facts' and s 101(1)(g) is a development of the rule under the CEA 1898, s 1(3)(ii) that evidence of the defendant's bad character could be admitted where the defendant had cast imputations on prosecution witnesses. Both of those grounds of admissibility were subject to judicial control using similar principles. The admissibility of similar fact evidence (now replaced by s 101(1)(d)) was governed by the rule in *R v P* [1991] 3 All ER 337, HL, that evidence of the bad character of the defendant would only be admissible if its probative value in proving some issue relevant at trial was greater than the prejudicial effect of admitting such evidence. Where evidence was admitted under the CEA 1898, s 1(3)(ii) there was a judicial discretion to exclude such evidence if its prejudicial effect outweighed its probative value (*Selvey v DPP* [1970] AC 304, HL). This discretion to exclude evidence is a common law power that has been exercised either in its own right or under the Police and Criminal Evidence Act 1984, s 78 (*Attorney General's Reference (No 1 of 2003)* EWCA Crim 1286). As the common law power to exclude evidence has been based on the principle of fairness under s 78 of the 1984 Act, there is little reason to believe that, in using the same test in s 101(3), Parliament intended to develop a different test for exclusion than that which was used in pre-CJA 2003 cases. Put more simply: fairness requires that evidence posing the risk of prejudice be excluded unless it has such probative value that it would be fairer to admit it than to exclude it. On the other hand, it is worth noting that weighing the probative value of evidence against its prejudicial effect is not the only way in which fairness could be assessed under either s 101(3) or s 78 of the 1984 Act. The exclusion of evidence under s 78 is much wider in scope than the common law prejudicial effect/probative value test (see **Chapter 12** for more details).

Therefore, the focus, but not exclusive concern, of s 101(3) will be the comparison of the prejudicial effect of evidence and its probative value. The court will probably be greatly assisted by analysis of the principles identified in pre-CJA 2003 case law, although suitably adapted to take into account the changes of approach to bad character evidence required by the new law. The main change that must be taken into account when considering the case law is that the s 101(1)(d) now renders evidence of the propensity of the defendant to commit the offence charged admissible. Therefore, insofar as the 'prejudice' to a defendant consisted of the jury succumbing to the 'forbidden chain of reasoning' (that propensity to offend equates to actual commission of the offence), old statements as to what prejudice means must be altered. However, there are still ways in which evidence of propensity may be prejudicial. It is useful at this point to identify the distinction identified by the Law Commission (Law Commission Consultation Paper No 141, *Previous Misconduct of a Defendant* (HMSO, 1996)) between:

(a) Reasoning prejudice: this represents the risk that the tribunal of fact will attach too much weight to evidence of a defendant's bad character or will reach inaccurate conclusions from such evidence.

(b) Moral prejudice: this represents the risk that the jury will dispense with the reasoning process completely and convict the defendant despite the evidence simply out of disgust or outrage at his bad character.

The change to the law concerning propensity evidence represents a limited change in the law regarding reasoning prejudice. The state of the law before the CJA 2003 was that mere evidence of propensity could not support the conclusion that the defendant had committed the offence (*Makin v Attorney-General of New South Wales*; *R v P*). However, the law relating to reasoning prejudice has not changed completely: there is still a risk that the jury will attach too much weight to evidence of propensity, ie that it will overshadow other evidence in the case or that the jury will find propensity proven on insufficient evidence. Further, there is nothing about the CJA 2003 that suggests that the law relating to moral prejudice has changed. The practical result of this is that in considering fairness under s 1(3) the court should have particular regard to (a) the risk that the jury will attach too much weight to the evidence of bad character or (b) that they will be so outraged at the defendant that they will cease to consider the case in a rational manner on the evidence before them in accordance with their oaths as jurors.

8.3.11.3   Factors to be considered in applying the fairness test under s 101(3)

Because there is no specific reference to probative value in the test of exclusion under s 101(3), s 109 does not apply. That section requires the court to treat evidence as true when determining its probative value. The implication of this is that in assessing the probative value of the evidence for the purposes of determining whether it should be excluded on the grounds of fairness the court is not obliged to treat the evidence as though it is true. Therefore the court should be able to consider the credibility of the evidence in addition to what it might prove if it is true.

The court is specifically enjoined to consider the length of time between the previous bad character and the alleged offence (s 101(4)). However, other factors may be relevant in assessing the probative value of the evidence. In determining what other factors may be of assistance, it is likely that the courts will find pre-CJA 2003 case law useful.

Where s 101(1)(d) is used to prove a matter in issue other than a propensity to offend, it is likely that the courts will apply the *R v P* test. After all, that test was devised to regulate the admissibility of evidence of bad character to prove facts in issue. Therefore, the courts will consider whether the evidence of bad character has sufficiently strong probative value in proving the relevant fact in issue to outweigh any risk of prejudice from the proof of the bad character. The only revision to the *R v P* test is likely to be that, as noted above, the mere fact that the evidence proves a propensity to offend does not amount to prejudice. In *R v Hanson* the probative value of the evidence in proving a propensity to offend appears to have been used at the admissibility stage of analysis. However, the Court of Appeal also stated that in considering the issue of fairness under s 101(3) the judge should consider the degree of similarity between the previous convictions and the offence charged even when they fit within the same description or prescribed category. Further the trial judge should have regard to the respective gravity of the previous and current offences, substantial gaps between the past and current alleged offending. The details of the commission of each previous offence would generally have to be considered. Furthermore, it was stated, it would be unlikely to be just to admit evidence of propensity where there was little other evidence against the defendant.

Therefore, quite where fairness lies will turn on the totality of the facts of the case. Other factors, such as changes in the defendant's lifestyle or circumstances or unusual reasons for previous offending behaviour, would clearly affect the probative force of the previous convictions on the issue of propensity. In *R v Hanson* it was stated that the court would be slow to interfere where the trial judge had directed himself correctly or where the defendant pleaded guilty following a ruling that bad character evidence would be admitted.

It should be borne in mind that s 103(2) allows the admission of evidence of previous convictions to prove a propensity to commit the particular offence with which the defendant is charged. It does not allow proof of previous convictions generally to prove a general propensity to offend. Therefore, the court should exercise its power to exclude some or all of a lengthy list of previous convictions that are not probative of the particular propensity to commit the particular offence.

Further, the principles in *R v McLeod*, noted at **8.3.9.2** above, will apply particularly in relation to applications to admit evidence of credibility under s 101(1)(g) or to prove a propensity for untruthfulness under s 101(1)(d). Therefore, where the evidence is being admitted for those purposes, rather than the propensity to commit offences, some level of detail will be appropriate but the court's concern will be to focus the evidence on those aspects of the bad character that are probative of the credibility of the defendant (such as false defences and the pleas on previous occasions).

Finally the courts will, as was noted at **8.3.10.2** above, find the guidance in *R v Britzmann* useful, once it has been decided that an attack has been made triggering s 101(1)(g), in deciding whether to exclude the evidence of bad character. In *Britzmann* Lawton LJ said (at p 373) of the discretion to exclude evidence:

First, it should be used if there is nothing more than a denial, however emphatic or offensively made, of an act or even a short series of acts amounting to one incident or in what was said to have been a short interview. Examples are provided by the kind of evidence given in pickpocket cases and where the defendant is alleged to have said, 'Who grassed on me this time?' The position would be different however if there were a denial of evidence of a long period of detailed observation extending over hours . . . or . . . denials of long conversations.

Second, [evidence of bad character] should only be allowed if the judge is sure that there is no possibility of mistake, misunderstanding or confusion and that the jury will inevitably have to decide whether the prosecution witnesses have fabricated evidence. Defendants sometimes make wild allegations when giving evidence. Allowance should be made for the strain of being in the witness box and the exaggerated language which sometimes results from such strain or lack of education or mental instability. Particular care should be used when a defendant is led into making allegations during cross-examination.

8.3.11.4   Exclusion under s 103(3)

Section 103(3) provides that evidence of propensity admissible under s 101(1)(d) by virtue of s 103(2) should not be admissible if it would be unjust to admit it having regard to the length of time since the conviction or for any other reason. Neither s 101(3) nor s 103(3) are explicitly made subject to one another and there will be considerable overlap between the two subsections. It is submitted that evidence of propensity could be excluded under either one subsection or the other.

8.3.11.5   Exclusion of evidence under the other gateways

Section 101(3) only applies to exclude evidence admitted under s 101(1)(d) or (g). What of the other gateways?

The gateways to admissibility in ss 101(1)(a) (agreement by all parties) and 101(1)(b) (evidence adduced the defendant himself) make no provision for the exclusion of evidence.

Sections 101(1)(c) and 102 concerning important explanatory evidence also provide no exclusionary power. With background evidence, the courts recognised the existence of the common law discretion to exclude prejudicial evidence (*R v W* [2003] EWCA Crim 3024). Given that explanatory evidence is admissible to overcome the impossibility, or difficulty, of understanding the case without it, it is generally unlikely that the evidence would not be more probative than prejudicial. However as is noted in *Blackstone's Criminal Practice*, 2005 at F 12.31, where the evidence is admitted because it would be 'difficult' (as opposed to impossible) to understand the evidence without it, there is room for the operation of a power to exclude evidence, as was recognised in the pre-CJA 2003 case law.

Sections 101(1)(e) and 104 concern evidence admitted on behalf of the co-defendants. The absence of a power to exclude evidence of bad character for such evidence simply reflects the established position of the law before the CJA 2003, namely that the law should not provide for the exclusion of evidence by one co-defendant to protect another co-defendant (*R v Lobban* [1995] 2 All ER 602).

So far as ss 101(1)(f) and 105 (correction of a false impression) are concerned, s 105(5) imposes a restriction on the uses to which such evidence may be put which reflects (as was noted above) the judicial discretion to exclude prejudicial evidence. Insofar as evidence goes further than is necessary to correct a false impression, it would have been excluded as more prejudicial than probative for that purpose. However, it is possible that the protection offered by s 105(5) will be less extensive than the broad power to exclude evidence under s 101(3). Furthermore, whereas it is likely that the power under s 101(3) allows the court to exclude evidence because its has weak probative value due to issues surrounding its credibility, this does not appear to apply to the restriction under s 105(5). For example where the defendant suggests that he has never been in trouble before, it might be possible for the prosecution to call evidence that he left his previous employment under suspicion of theft from his employer. In determining the admissibility under s 101(1)(f) the court would be required (s 109(1)) to consider the evidence to be true when evaluating its probative force. On the assumption that it is true, it would be possible to argue that the evidence goes no further than necessary to rebut the suggestion of good character made by the defendant. The real problem with the evidence is that that it may lack probative force simply because it may not be true. In such circumstances, the restrictions in s 105(5) do not offer the protection that the power to exclude under s 101(3) or the exclusionary discretions under the Police and Criminal Evidence Act 1984 and the common law appear to offer.

Therefore, there is the possibility that the right of defendants to a fair trial will be adversely affected if they have no means to exclude evidence on the grounds of fairness or prejudice under s 101(1)(c) and (f) in particular. There is also a possibility that evidence admitted under s 101(1)(a) and (b) could have been obtained unfairly (for example by the prosecution deceiving the defendant). Section 99 provides that 'the common law rules governing the admissibility of evidence of bad character' are abolished. Does this include the common law power to exclude evidence that is more prejudicial than probative? Tapper ('Criminal Justice Act 2003: Part 3: Evidence of Bad Character' [2004] Crim LR 533) argues that it does not because the exclusionary discretion is not a rule governing admissibility. Furthermore, the CJA 2003 has not in any way affected the discretion to exclude prosecution evidence under the Police and Criminal Evidence Act, s 78.

It seems likely that both discretions to exclude evidence continue to apply and will apply to all prosecution evidence under the Act (ie s 101(1)(a) to (d), (f) and (g)). While there would be little reason to rely on these discretions under s 101(1)(d) and (g), particularly due to the mandatory nature of the exclusion of evidence under those paragraphs under s 101(3), it is likely that the exclusionary discretions will prove useful for some or all of paragraphs (a) to (c) and paragraph (f).

8.3.12   Contaminated evidence

Section 107 provides:

(1)   If on a defendant's trial before a judge and jury for an offence—
  (a)   evidence of his bad character has been admitted under any of paragraphs (c) to (g) of section 101(1), and
  (b)   the court is satisfied at any time after the close of the case for the prosecution that—
    (i)   the evidence is contaminated, and
    (ii)   the contamination is such that, considering the importance of the evidence to the case against the defendant, his conviction of the offence would be unsafe, the court must either direct the jury to acquit the defendant of the offence or, if it considers that there ought to be a retrial, discharge the jury.
(2)   Where—
  (a)   a jury is directed under subsection (1) to acquit a defendant of an offence, and
  (b)   the circumstances are such that, apart from this subsection, the defendant could if acquitted of that offence be found guilty of another offence, the defendant may not be found guilty of that other offence if the court is satisfied as mentioned in subsection (1)(b) in respect of it.
(3)   . . .
(4)   This section does not prejudice any other power a court may have to direct a jury to acquit a person of the offence or to discharge a jury.
(5)   For the purposes of this section a person's evidence is contaminated where—
  (a)   as a result of an agreement or understanding between the person and one or more others, or
  (b)   as a result of the person being aware of anything alleged by one or more others whose evidence may be, or has been, given in the proceedings, the evidence is false or misleading in any respect, or is different from what it would otherwise have been.

The effect of s 107 is that 'contaminated' evidence may lead to the termination of the case where the contamination renders the potential conviction unsafe (s 107(1)). Equally, a defendant may not be found guilty of an alternative offence in such a situation (s 107(2)). Termination may lead either to the jury being directed to acquit the defendant or for the jury to be discharged to allow a retrial of the offences.

Section 107(4) preserves other powers to terminate a case such as the power to stay proceedings for an abuse of process or to discharge a jury.

Character evidence is contaminated if it is false or misleading either because of agreements between witnesses or one witness and other people (s 107(5)(a)) or because the witness is aware of the evidence of other witnesses (s 107(5)(b)). Section 107 reflects the state of the common law before the CJA 2003 as established in *R v H* [1995] AC 596, where the House of Lords held that the issue of collusion should, generally, be resolved by the jury but if, after the evidence has been admitted, the judge concludes that no reasonable jury could regard the evidence as free from contamination then they should be directed to disregard it.

Section 107 therefore provides an additional protection for defendants. It only applies after the evidence of bad character has been admitted. Where there is evidence of collusion the court must consider whether the collusion renders the conviction unsafe. If it does, the jury must be discharged or directed to acquit. Whether the conviction will be unsafe may depend on whether the jury can continue to perform their function despite the contamination of the evidence. Therefore, if the jury could disregard the evidence as stated in *R v H* and could continue to decide the case without being prejudiced by it then a conviction would not be unsafe.

8.3.13   Duty to give reasons

Section 110 provides:

> (1)   *Where the court makes a relevant ruling—*
>> (a)   *it must state in open court (but in the absence of the jury, if there is one) its reasons for the ruling;*
>> (b)   *if it is a magistrates' court, it must cause the ruling and the reasons for it to be entered in the register of the court's proceedings.*
> (2)   *In this section 'relevant ruling' means—*
>> (a)   *a ruling on whether an item of evidence is evidence of a person's bad character;*
>> (b)   *a ruling on whether an item of such evidence is admissible under section 100 or 101 (including a ruling on an application under section 101(3));*
>> (c)   *a ruling under section 107.*

8.3.14   Rules of procedure

Section 111 allows the creation of rules of court concerning the admission of the evidence of character. The Criminal Procedure Rules, r 34 sets out the procedure by which the court and other parties must be notified of an application to adduce evidence of the defendant's bad character. The procedure may be summarised as follows:

(a) The prosecutor must give notice using the requisite form within 14 days of the defendant being sent to the Crown Court. In the magistrates' court it must be given at the same time as primary disclosure (r 35.4).

(b) A co-defendant must give notice, again using the requisite form, within 14 days of the prosecutor purporting to serve primary disclosure (r 35.5).

(c) The defendant must make any application to exclude the bad character evidence with 7 days after receiving notice under rules 35.4 or 35.5 (r 35.6).

8.4   Previous misconduct under the Theft Act 1968

Section 27(3) of the Theft Act 1968 provides:

> (3)   *Where a person is being proceeded against for handling stolen goods (but not for any offence other than handling stolen goods), then at any stage in the proceedings, if evidence has been given of his having or arranging to have in his possession the goods the subject of the charge, or of his undertaking or assisting in, or arranging to undertake, or assist in, their retention, removal, disposal or realisation, the following evidence shall be admissible for the purposes of proving that he knew or believed the goods to be stolen goods—*
>> (a)   *evidence that he has had in his possession, or has undertaken or assisted in the retention, removal or disposal or realisation of, stolen goods from any theft taking place not earlier than 12 months before the offence charged; and*

(b)   *(provided that seven days' notice in writing has been given to him of the intention to prove the conviction) evidence that he has within the five years preceding the date of the offence charged been convicted of theft or of handling stolen goods.*

Section 27(3) allows the proof of the defendant's previous convictions to establish the defendant's knowledge that goods were stolen. It neither proves the dishonesty of the defendant (*R v Duffas* (1994) 158 JP 224) nor that the goods were in the possession of the defendant nor that they were stolen. The fact that the defendant disputes possession of the goods (or some of them) does not prevent the evidence being admitted under s 27(3) (*R v List* [1966] 1 WLR 9). However, where there are numerous charges, in some of which possession is in dispute and in some of which possession is admitted but knowledge disputed, the judge should consider whether to allow the admission of the evidence of the previous convictions at all and, if they are allowed, should direct the jury that the previous convictions are only relevant to knowledge and not to any other issue in the case (*R v Wilkins* [1975] 2 All ER 734).

Where the evidence of the previous convictions is admitted, evidence of the details of previous convictions is not admissible (*R v Bradley* (1979) 70 Cr App R 200). However, in *R v Hacker* [1994] 1 WLR 1659, the House of Lords held that the proof of the previous convictions could include proof of such detail of the convictions as was included on the certificate of conviction under the Police and Criminal Evidence Act 1984, s 73. The certificate of conviction would include detail of the subject matter of the conviction (in this context of handling offences, the property that was handled).

The CJA 2003 has not affected the admissibility of evidence of bad character under the Theft Act 1968, s 27. However, it may be that proof of the convictions under s 27(3) could be achieved under s 101(1)(d) as an important matter in issue between the prosecution and defence without the restrictions imposed under s 27(3). The effect of s 27(3) can be excluded either at common law or under the Police and Criminal Evidence Act 1984, s 78 (*R v Hacker*).

Character evidence: witnesses other than the defendant in criminal cases

9.1 Evidence of good character

The position with regard to evidence of the good character of a witness is the same in civil and in criminal proceedings. Therefore the rule in *R v Turner* [1975] QB 834 identified at **7.3.3** applies equally in criminal proceedings: a party calling a witness cannot call evidence to bolster his or her credibility.

9.2 Evidence of bad character

The admissibility of evidence of bad character is now governed by s 100 of the Criminal Justice Act 2003 (CJA 2003). Section 100(1) provides:

(1) In criminal proceedings evidence of the bad character of a person other than the defendant is admissible if and only if—

    (a) it is important explanatory evidence,

    (b) it has substantial probative value in relation to a matter which—

        (i) is a matter in issue in the proceedings, and

        (ii) is of substantial importance in the context of the case as a whole, or

    (c) all parties to the proceedings agree to the evidence being admissible.

Therefore, evidence of bad character is generally inadmissible against a witness other than a defendant in criminal proceedings. Only evidence that fits within the three situations provided for by s 100(1) will be admissible. Evidence under s 100(1)(a) or (b) also requires the leave of the trial judge before it will be admitted (s 100(4)).

It should be remembered that s 100 protects the character both of prosecution witnesses and witnesses for the defence other than the defendant. Furthermore, the restriction applies both to the party calling the witness and any party seeking to cross-examine the witness (although it seems unlikely that if a party calling a witness wished to establish that witness's bad character there would not be agreement under s 100(1)(c)).

Section 99(1) abolishes the common law rules governing the admissibility of evidence of bad character with one exception, which is that evidence of the general reputation of a person proving their bad character is still admissible (s 99(2)). See **8.2.3** for further explanation of this rule.

9.2.1   Meaning of bad character

Section 112(1) provides that bad character for non-defendants has the same meaning as that provided for defendants in s 98 (see **8.3.3**). In the context of witnesses in criminal cases this means that it is possible to prove previous convictions, previous misconduct or a disposition to do either of those things. Clearly, the requirement of relevance would still need to apply so the bad character would have to satisfy one of the three grounds of admissibility identified in s 100(1).

Section 100 is silent on the rule of finality. Section 99 did not explicitly abolish the rule of finality but the common law rules governing the admissibility of evidence. However, it is arguable that the effect in s 100 of allowing proof of forms of misconduct that do not fit within any of the four classes of exception to the rule against finality (previous convictions, bias, a reputation for untruthfulness or insanity: see **6.3.7.2** and **7.3.2**) has had the effect of replacing the restrictions of proof of such facts under the rule of finality.

9.2.2   Important explanatory evidence

Section 100 provides:

(2)   . . . *evidence is important explanatory evidence if—*
   (a)   *without it, the court or jury would find it impossible or difficult properly to understand other evidence in the case, and*
   (b)   *its value for understanding the case as a whole is substantial.*

The text of s 100(2) is identical to s 102, which defines important explanatory evidence admitted against a defendant (see **8.3.6**) and the same principles apply. However, it should be remembered that s 100(2) concerns the proof of bad character of witnesses, so the issue will be whether the bad character of a prosecution witness, for example, has substantial value in making understandable other evidence in the case. An obvious example would be where the prosecution call an accomplice of the defendant to prove the defendant's commission of an offence. It will clearly be necessary to prove the involvement of the accomplice in the commission of the offence to explain his first hand knowledge of the matters that took place. Equally, if a defendant wished to prove that an offence was committed by the co-defendant alone and in order to do so wished to prove an admission to that effect by the co-defendant to a cellmate in a prison, if the cellmate is called to testify to the admission, it would be necessary to prove that he was in prison. As was noted at **8.3.6** the effect of admitting such evidence is really to bolster the credibility of the witness by plugging significant gaps in the background or context of the evidence.

9.2.3   Substantial probative value on a substantial matter in issue

Section 100(1)(b) allows proof of the bad character of witnesses where doing so has substantial probative value in relation to a matter of substantial importance in proceedings.

9.2.3.1   Substantial importance

Section 100(1)(b)(ii) has the effect of preventing gratuitous attacks on witnesses.

Clearly, facts in issue are always matters in issue of substantial importance. Any allegation that the witness committed the offence rather than the defendant, acted in such a way as to afford the defendant a defence such as self defence, or duress or was in some other way complicit in either the commission of the offence or the false accusation of the defendant, will be admissible subject to the requirement of substantial probative value (see **9.2.3.2**).

It seems equally clear that the credibility of witnesses is a matter in issue but to what extent is it a matter of 'substantial importance to the case as a whole'? This will depend on the part played in proceedings by the particular witness. In this sense, s 100(1)(b)(ii) reflects the principle identified in *R v Sweet-Escott* (1971) 55 Cr App R 316 (see **7.3.2**) that cross-examination as to credit should only be permitted where the questions affect the witness's likely standing after cross-examination. However, as s 100(1)(b) concerns the admissibility of evidence of character, the section has extended the *Sweet-Escott* rule beyond cross-examination. The principle in *Hobbs v Tinling* [1929] 2 KB 1 that cross-examination would not be allowed if the conduct occurred in the distant past or is out of proportion to the matters on which the witness will give evidence is also reflected by s 100(1)(b)(ii). Equally, the principles of *R v Edwards* [1991] 1 WLR 207 and *R v Edwards* [1996] 2 Cr App R 345 would apply in the application of s 100(1)(b)(ii).

9.2.3.2   Substantial probative value

Evidence of bad character that has a substantial importance to the proceedings as a whole will only be admissible if that evidence also has 'substantial probative value' (s 100(1)(b)(i)). Section 100 provides:

> (3)   *In assessing the probative value of evidence for the purposes of subsection (1)(b) the court must have regard to the following factors (and to any others it considers relevant)—*
>
>   (a)   *the nature and number of the events, or other things, to which the evidence relates;*
>
>   (b)   *when those events or things are alleged to have happened or existed;*
>
>   (c)   *where—*
>
>   (i)   *the evidence is evidence of a person's misconduct, and*
>
>   (ii)   *it is suggested that the evidence has probative value by reason of similarity between that misconduct and other alleged misconduct, the nature and extent of the similarities and the dissimilarities between each of the alleged instances of misconduct;*
>
>   (d)   *where—*
>
>   (i)   *the evidence is evidence of a person's misconduct,*
>
>   (ii)   *it is suggested that that person is also responsible for the misconduct charged, and*
>
>   (iii)   *the identity of the person responsible for the misconduct charged is disputed, the extent to which the evidence shows or tends to show that the same person was responsible each time.*

Section 100(3) therefore makes some general provision for the probative value of the evidence such as the extent to which the evidence of bad character is probative of the character of the witness by reason of frequency of the misconduct (s 100(3)(a)), the pattern of misconduct (s 100(3)(a)) and the extent to which they are too old to be probative of the witness's current character (s 100(3)(b)). These general provisions will apply whatever the matter in issue is (ie, relevance to a fact in issue or the credibility of the witness).

Section 100(3)(c) makes provision for the proof of the propensity of the witness towards particular misconduct (whether it is the commission of the offence charged, or a tendency to lie or a tendency to act aggressively and to cause fights) by requiring the court to consider the pattern of the offending behaviour. In this sense, the section is adopting the approach of the common law to similar fact evidence. The party wishing to prove bad character of the witness would seek to do so by showing a pattern of similar offending that suggests that such misconduct occurred on this occasion. For example, if the defendant (a person of Irish extraction) were relying on the defence of self-defence and sought to prove that the prosecution witness has caused fights with people who were or seemed to be Irish the court could consider that fact and any other similarities or differences on those previous occasions in addition to considering how often those attacks occurred (s 100(3)(a)) and how long it was since they last occurred (s 100(3)(b)). Section 100(3)(d) deals with situations in which the defendant alleges that the witness committed the offence (s 100(3)(d)(ii)) and seeks to prove this by establishing that the offence was committed in the same way in which the offence was committed by the witness on previous occasions. Proof of the identify of the offender by similar fact evidence was a difficult issue at common law and s 100(3)(d) has appears to have adopted the approach in *R v Downey* [1995] 1 Cr App R 547, CA, which is that the evidence could be combined in its effect to determine whether the person alleged had committed all of the offences.

In determining the probative value of evidence, the court should treat the evidence as thought it is true (s 109(1)) unless the evidence before it (possibly adduced at a voir dire) establishes that no reasonable tribunal could consider it true (s 109(2)).

9.2.4 Agreement of the parties

Section 100(1)(c) permits the admission of evidence of the bad character of a witness where all parties agree. Therefore, all co-defendants would have to agree to the admission of the evidence in addition to the prosecution.

9.2.5 Requirement of leave

Section 100(4) provides that save when the parties agree to admit the evidence of bad character under s 101(1)(c), such evidence must not be admitted without leave of the court.

9.3 Complainants in sexual cases

9.3.1 Restriction

The Youth Justice and Criminal Evidence Act 1999, s 41 places separate restrictions on the extent to which a complainant in a sexual offence may be cross-examined about his or her sexual history. Section 41 provides:

(1) *If at a trial a person is charged with a sexual offence, then, except with the leave of the court—*
    (a) *no evidence may be adduced, and*
    (b) *no question may be asked in cross-examination, by or on behalf of any accused at the trial, about any sexual behaviour of the complainant.*
(2) *The court may give leave in relation to any evidence or question only on an application made by or on behalf of an accused, and may not give such leave unless it is satisfied—*
    (a) *that subsection (3) or (5) applies, and*
    (b) *that a refusal of leave might have the result of rendering unsafe a conclusion of the jury or (as the case may be) the court on any relevant issue in the case.*
(3) *This subsection applies if the evidence or question relates to a relevant issue in the case and either—*
    (a) *that issue is not an issue of consent; or*
    (b) *it is an issue of consent and the sexual behaviour of the complainant to which the evidence or question relates is alleged to have taken place at or about the same time as the event which is the subject matter of the charge against the accused; or*

    (c)   *it is an issue of consent and the sexual behaviour of the complainant to which the evidence or question relates is alleged to have been, in any respect, so similar—*

        (i)   *to any sexual behaviour of the complainant which (according to evidence adduced or to be adduced by or on behalf of the accused) took place as part of the event which is the subject matter of the charge against the accused, or*

        (ii)   *to any other sexual behaviour of the complainant which (according to such evidence) took place at or about the same time as that event, that the similarity cannot reasonably be explained as a coincidence.*

  (4)   *For the purposes of subsection (3) no evidence or question shall be regarded as relating to a relevant issue in the case if it appears to the court to be reasonable to assume that the purpose (or main purpose) for which it would be adduced or asked is to establish or elicit material for impugning the credibility of the complainant as a witness.*

  (5)   *This subsection applies if the evidence or question—*

    (a)   *relates to any evidence adduced by the prosecution about any sexual behaviour of the complainant; and*

    (b)   *in the opinion of the court, would go no further than is necessary to enable the evidence adduced by the prosecution to be rebutted or explained by or on behalf of the accused.*

  (6)   *For the purposes of subsections (3) and (5) the evidence or question must relate to a specific instance (or specific instances) of alleged sexual behaviour on the part of the complainant (and accordingly nothing in those subsections is capable of applying in relation to the evidence or question to the extent that it does not so relate).*

  (7)   *Where this section applies in relation to a trial by virtue of the fact that one or more of a number of persons charged in the proceedings is or are charged with a sexual offence—*

    (a)   *it shall cease to apply in relation to the trial if the prosecutor decides not to proceed with the case against that person or those persons in respect of that charge; but*

    (b)   *it shall not cease to do so in the event of that person or those persons pleading guilty to, or being convicted of, that charge.*

  (8)   *Nothing in this section authorises any evidence to be adduced or any question to be asked which cannot be adduced or asked apart from this section.*

The CJA 2003, s 112 provides:

  (3)   *Nothing in this Chapter affects the exclusion of evidence—*

  . . .

    (b)   *under section 41 of the Youth Justice and Criminal Evidence Act 1999 . . .*

The effect of the CJA 2003, s 112(3) is that cross-examination of the complainant by the defendant about the complainant's sexual history is not subject to the CJA 2003, s 100 but only to the Youth Justice and Criminal Evidence Act 1999.

9.3.2 Extent of the restriction

The restriction imposed by s 41 only relates to questions or evidence about previous sexual behaviour; it does not restrict cross-examination about the sexual behaviour that is part of the incident or incidents for which the accused is being tried (s 42(1)(c)). In *R v Mukadi* [2003] EWCA Crim 3765, the Court of Appeal stated that it was not possible to define sexual behaviour. Rather what was meant by the term was a matter of 'impression and common sense'. The behaviour in that case was the act of getting into the car driven by an unknown man who had pulled up alongside the complainant and the exchange of telephone numbers in the car. In allowing the appeal of the defendant, the Court of Appeal concluded that in the circumstances such behaviour was either sexual behaviour relevant to the complainant's consent at a later point (see below) or it was not sexual behaviour and therefore could have been the subject of cross-examination as s 41 did not apply.

If the defence is that the complainant is making false allegations against the accused and the accused seeks to support this by eliciting evidence of false allegations made in the past, s 41 does not apply as the making of false allegations is not 'sexual behaviour' (*R v MH* [2002] Crim LR 73, CA). In *R v C and B* [2003] EWCA Crim 29 the Court of Appeal held that if the defence wished to question about previous false allegations, it would be necessary to determine whether there was a proper evidential basis for asserting that the allegation in question was (a) made and (b) false. If there were no such evidential basis the effect of questioning would be to prove the falsity of the previous allegation and would therefore be questioning about previous sexual behaviour. It is only if the falsity is shown by other seperate evidence that the previous allegation would not be sexual behaviour. Therefore, if the proof of falsity of the previous allegation wholly depends on cross-examination about sexual behaviour on that previous occasion, the false allegation is sexual behaviour within the meaning of s 41 (*R v H* [2003] EWCA Crim 2367) but if it can be established by evidence of a non-sexual nature, the false allegation is not sexual behaviour.

The previous sexual behaviour does not have to be between the accused and the complainant. However, where the behaviour was with a third person there would have to be very special facts before cross-examination would be permitted.

9.3.3   Restriction on cross-examination

Under s 41 such cross-examination will only be permitted if the court grants leave (s 41(1)). Leave can only be granted if:

- one of the four qualifying circumstances apply (s 41(2)(a)); *and*
- refusal to grant leave might render a conviction unsafe (s 41(2)(b)).

9.3.3.1   Qualifing circumstances

The four qualifying circumstances, one of which is required before cross-examination can be permitted, are:

(a) The cross-examination or evidence relates to an issue other than consent (s 41(3)(a)).

   (i)   Belief in consent is an issue 'other than consent' and therefore if the issue is belief in consent cross-examination may be permitted (subject to the other elements of the test) under this section (s 41(1)(b)).

   (ii)   It would also include, for example, the defence that no sexual act took place. Where there is medical evidence of a sexual act having taken place, the accused could seek to be allowed to prove that the complainant had had sexual intercourse with another person at that time.

(b) The cross-examination or evidence relates to the issue of consent and the previous sexual behaviour took place 'on or about the same time' as the offence (s 41(3)(b)).

   (i)   In *R v A* [2001] 3 All ER 1, HL, it was observed that this meant a matter of hours rather than days.

   (ii)   It would appear that this category of permissible questioning is aimed at defences using evidence of the complainant's promiscuity to prove that at the time of the alleged offence he or she was likely to have consented to the sexual act in question.

(c) The cross-examination or evidence relates to the issue of consent and the previous sexual behaviour in question is very similar either to the alleged offence or other sexual behaviour at about the same time as the alleged offence (s 41(3)(c)).

(i)   The exact phrase used by the Act is 'so similar . . . that the similarity cannot reasonably be explained as a coincidence'.

(ii) This is potentially quite complicated but appears to be aimed at evidence of previous consensual sexual behaviour of a distinctive nature that bears such a strong similarity to what appears to have taken place during the offence that this similarity may raise a reasonable doubt as to the complainant's lack of consent.

(iii) For example, evidence that the complainant regularly had sexual intercourse in a particularly distinctive way with the accused on previous occasions might be admissible under this circumstance if there was evidence that the sexual act forming the charge had very similar characteristics.

(iv) It is submitted that if the sexual behaviour on the previous and current occasions were, due to their nature, incapable of being consensual acts then such previous behaviour would not be admissible under s 41.

(v)   Note that s 41(3)(c) relates not only to a similarity between a previous incident and the alleged offence where the nature of the two incidents could prove the existence of consent. Under s 41(3)(c)(ii), evidence of previous sexual behaviour which is similar to behaviour 'at or about the same time' as the alleged offence could also be admitted. In *R v Tahed* [2004] All ER (D) 346 (Feb), where the alleged rape took place within a particular climbing frame at a public park, the conviction was set aside because the trial judge had not allowed cross-examination concerning a similar (consensual) sexual encounter within the same climbing frame three weeks earlier. The trial judge had wrongly considered that the similarity had to be between the acts comprising part of the sexual act and had neglected to consider acts that took place 'at or about the same time'.

(vi) In *R v Richardson* [2003] EWCA Crim 2754, the Court of Appeal concluded that evidence of a previous relationship and of a relationship after an alleged rape would not be permitted under s 41(3)(c) as the sexual behaviour in question (the relationship in general) would not bear sufficient similarity to the alleged offence.

(d) The cross-examination or evidence is tendered to rebut evidence tendered by the prosecution about the previous sexual behaviour of the complainant and only goes as far as is necessary to rebut that evidence (s 41(5)).

(i)   Note that this exception is not restricted to situations in which the defence is consent.

(ii) For example, if the prosecution tendered evidence that the complainant had no sexual experience before the act in question, the defence would be able to adduce evidence or ask questions that would establish that she had sexual experience in the past.

Note that no cross-examination will be permitted if its only purpose is to undermine the credibility of the complainant (s 41(4)).

In *R v M* [2004] All ER (D) 103, the Court of Appeal stated that where cross-examination would have the effect of undermining the credibility *and* of supporting the defendant's denial of the complainant's allegations then such evidence would not be excluded under s 41(4).

Even if the alleged sexual behaviour falls within the four categories of evidence set out in s 41(3)(5) identified above, such behaviour cannot be admitted unless it relates to specific incidents (s 41(6)). Therefore in *R v White* [2004] All ER (D) 103 (Mar), evidence of previous convictions of the complainant for prostitution were held to have rightly been excluded as such convictions would be too general.

9.3.3.2   Risk of unsafe conviction

The effect of s 41 is that the defence will have to convince the court to allow leave to question about *any* previous sexual behaviour of the complainant. The court cannot grant leave unless convinced both that there is some particular relevance to the evidence (ie, one of the qualifying circumstances set out above) and that the evidence is probative enough that a failure to allow it to be admitted would put the accused at risk of an unsafe conviction.

In *R v A*, the House of Lords considered the effect of this restriction in light of the right to a fair trial under Article 6 of the European Convention on Human Rights. They recognised that the right to a fair trial included the ability to put forward a full defence and that the restrictions imposed by s 41 of the 1999 Act created a risk that this would not be possible. They therefore invoked s 3 of the Human Rights Act 1998 to interpret s 41 to require that judges should consider the extent to which an accused would be deprived of a material defence and therefore a fair trial as a result of a refusal to grant leave. It would therefore appear that the restriction under s 41 is to be exercised narrowly by the courts.

In *R v Richardson* (above), the Court of Appeal concluded that the strict interpretation of s 41(3)(c) that excluded cross-examination about ongoing sexual relationships between the complainant and the defendant was unfair within the meaning of *R v A* and therefore quashed a conviction where the trial judge, applying s 41(3)(c), had not permitted such cross-examination.

In *R v Mukadi* (above), the issue was whether the complainant had consented to sexual intercourse. The complainant's evidence was that she had gone to the defendant's flat with him not intending any sexual acts to take place but that she had allowed him to carry out various sexual acts short of intercourse in the hope that he would then not have full intercourse with her but that he had subsequently carried out sexual intercourse without her consent. The case for the defendant was that the complainant had willingly consented to all the sexual acts that took place. The Court of Appeal held the behaviour of getting into a car with an unknown person and exchanging telephone numbers a matter of hours before the events alleged would be sufficiently relevant and probative to prove that she may have intended, in going to the defendant's flat, to carry out sexual acts. It was noted that if her evidence had been that she had gone to the defendant's flat willing to engage in sexual activity short of full sexual intercourse, the previous event would not have been particularly probative and therefore probably not admissible. However, as she had stated in evidence that she had not intended to engage in any sexual acts, the previous event was probative not only in proving that she may have been willing to consent but also that her denial of consent was probably untrue. As such the previous event should have been admitted. *R v Mukadi* therefore illustrates that any analysis of the probative value and therefore of the fairness of refusing to allow questioning will depend on detailed analysis of the issues raised by the evidence of the parties and cannot be determined by simple categorisation of the evidence.

The previous sexual behaviour does not have to have been between the accused and the complainant. However where the behaviour was with a third person more cogent evidence of potential consent would be required before cross examination will be permitted: *R v White* [2004] All ER (D) 103 (Mar).

Hearsay: introduction and hearsay in civil proceedings

10.1 Introduction to hearsay evidence

Chapters 10 and **11** consider the rules relating to hearsay evidence. **Chapter 10** concentrates upon the admissibility of hearsay in civil proceedings. **Chapter 11** considers the admissibility of hearsay evidence in criminal proceedings. However, before considering the admissibility of such evidence, this chapter will identify what is meant by hearsay evidence and the rationale for restricting its admissibility. Understanding what is meant by hearsay and why it has been felt that the rules of evidence should restrict the admissibility of such evidence is vital to understanding the rules themselves.

10.1.1 Out of court statements

The rules relating to hearsay evidence restrict the extent to which statements made out of court will be admitted as evidence. Hearsay statements are not the only 'out of court' statements so it is worth exploring out of court statements generally before looking at hearsay statements in particular.

Take a minute to visualise a trial. It is likely that you will be thinking about a witness in the witness box giving evidence about some matter, perhaps an assault. It is likely that the witness you are thinking about will be an 'eye witness' in that he or she will be saying what he or she saw. The reason such a witness is called to give evidence is that he or she will be the best person available to give such evidence. What makes him or her the best person is the first-hand experience of the events in question. It makes more sense to call the witness to say what happened than to bring to court someone else the witness spoke to about the incident. Equally, it makes more sense to call the witness than to rely upon a document the witness wrote about the event.

There are a number of aspects to this:

1. The court receives the information with appropriate formality. Testimony is generally given on oath (see **4.1.1**). Even if the witness does not hold religious beliefs, the formality of the court environment and threat of a conviction for perjury form strong encouragements to the witness to give truthful testimony. A person making a similar statement out of court may not feel an equal pressure to be honest.

2. There is less possibility of error. All witnesses can be mistaken in a number of ways. However, when witness B is used to prove what witness A saw by repeating what he has been told by A, we add to A's potential mistakes the chance that B has inaccurately repeated what witness A told him. B could have misheard, misinterpreted, forgotten or distorted what A had said or the account could simply be incomplete. Each extra

person in that the chain of communication between the actual witness to the event and the person testifying increases this risk of error.

3. If the testimony is given by the first-hand witness of the event, it will be possible to conduct the most critical examination of the account. A statement made out of court clearly cannot be cross-examined. Further, any possible explanation advanced by the party against whom the evidence is admitted cannot be put to the actual witness if his or her account is conveyed by another.

4. Where evidence is given by way of a statement made out of court, the tribunal of fact is deprived of an opportunity to assess the demeanour of the person making the statement.

5. Added to this is the risk that inexperienced tribunals of fact, such as juries, may not be sufficiently aware of the weakness of out of court statements identified above.

The courts have therefore been resistant to receiving out of court statements as evidence. There is a strong preference for receiving the evidence in court and from the person who had firsthand experience of the matters in question.

There are, however, various reasons for seeking to admit statements made out of court. A party may seek to prove that a statement was made out of court for the following purposes:

(a) To prove the thing said in the out of court statement by relying on the truth or accuracy of what was said. The logic in such cases is, 'If A said X then X is true'. If this is the purpose of the statement, it is a *hearsay* statement.

(b) To prove that the statement was made. These statements are called *original* statements. There are a number of reasons why this might be useful in the case:

(i)   to bolster the credibility of a witness by being consistent with his or her testimony. This is a *previous consistent statement*, which was considered at **6.2.3**;

(ii) to undermine the credibility of a witness by being inconsistent with his or her current testimony. This is a *previous inconsistent statement*, which was considered at **6.3.6**;

(iii) to prove that the maker held a particular belief or knew a particular fact. The logic is that if a person speaks about a particular thing, he or she knows of that thing. Therefore a statement, 'Hello, Caroline, have you recovered from your illness?', could prove that the maker knew Caroline had been ill as much as it could prove that she had in fact been ill. Insofar as it is used to prove Caroline's illness, the tribunal of fact would have to rely on the truth of the statement (or what it implies). Insofar as the statement is used to prove that the maker of the statement knew that Caroline was ill, the evidential purpose is to prove a fact (the maker's knowledge) by proving (a) the fact of certain things having been said and (b) that the things said were true (this being achieved by independent evidence): in other words, the statement does not prove the thing alleged (or implied) to be true;

(iv) to prove that someone other than the maker held a particular belief or knew a particular fact. For example, if the issue in the case was whether the accused acted under duress, evidence that a threat was made to that person would be relevant to prove that the accused *believed* that he or she had been threatened. It can do this whether or not the threat was genuine or true;

(v)   to prove that words were used because they have a particular legal significance. If I promise to sell you a painting for £100 and then refuse to do so, you could sue me for breach of contract. To prove the contract and its terms you would have to prove that I had made you an offer, which you accepted. To prove the offer, you would have to prove the statement I made out of court: 'I will sell you this painting for £100'. To amount to an offer the promise to sell you a painting for £100 does not have to be true. In fact, if you think about it, most promises in breach of contract cases will have been untrue up to a point: that is why the breach of contract action is being brought. To use a criminal example, it is an offence under s 4 of the Public Order Act 1986 to use 'threatening, abusive or insulting words or behaviour'. If the prosecution allege that the offence was committed by use of threatening words they will have to prove that the words were used. If, for example, the words were 'You bastard, you're dead,' that statement will have to be proved at court. Clearly what is said does not have to be true. The relevance to the case is that the statement was made at all;

(vi) to prove that the maker of the statement lied. Occasionally this sort of statement may overlap with the one above because proof that the maker of the statement lied may be a necessary feature of the case (for example in fraud, misrepresentation or deception cases). On other occasions the lie will be evidence that the maker was conscious of his or her own guilt and was trying to cover that guilt up (see **Chapter 13** for more detail on the probative value of lies). Obviously, the statement does not have to be true to be a lie!

10.1.2 What is hearsay evidence?

This chapter will first consider what evidence is hearsay and then consider the exceptions to the hearsay rule. The rule was originally a rule of common law. Many exceptions to the rule evolved because the rule, strictly applied, would lead to the exclusion of much evidence that (a) was highly probative and (b) could not be obtained by other sources. The common law rules have been replaced to a considerable extent in both civil and criminal cases by statute.

10.1.2.1 Definition

Hearsay evidence is essentially the use of a statement made out of court to prove something by getting the tribunal of fact to rely upon the truth of what the statement asserts. There is no single definition of hearsay. There are, however, definitions of hearsay in both civil and criminal proceedings and the courts and commentators have also provided definitions.

For civil proceedings, hearsay is defined by the Civil Evidence Act 1995, s 1(2) which provides:

(a)   'hearsay' means a statement made otherwise than by a person while giving oral evidence in the proceedings which is tendered as evidence of the matters stated

Section 13 provides:

'statement' means any representation of fact or opinion, however made.

In criminal proceedings, the Criminal Justice Act 2003 (CJA 2003), s 114(1) regulates the admissibility of 'a statement not made in oral evidence in the proceedings . . . as evidence of any matter stated'. CJA 2003, s 115 provides:

(1)   . . . references to a statement or to a matter stated are to be read as follows.

(2)   A statement is any representation of fact or opinion made by a person by whatever means; and it includes a representation made in a sketch, photofit or other pictorial form

> (3)   *A matter stated is one to which this Chapter applies if (and only if) the purpose, or one of the purposes,*
> *of the person making the statement appears to the court to have been—*
> *(a)   to cause another person to believe the matter, or*
> *(b)   to cause another person to act or a machine to operate on the basis that the matter is stated.*

Cross & Tapper on Evidence, 10th edn, OUP, 2004, at p 530, defines the rule against hearsay as:

An assertion other than one made by a person while testifying in the proceedings is inadmissible as evidence of any fact or opinion asserted.

An earlier version of this definition was approved in *R v Sharp* [1988] 1 WLR 7 by Lord Havers (at p 11) although that earlier definition did not contain a reference to opinion evidence.

With one important exception the definitions of hearsay are the same and include:

- a statement;

- the statement was made out of court (ie other than as 'oral evidence' or 'testimony'); and

- the statement is adduced to prove the truth of the matters asserted in it.

As was noted above, where out of court statements are not tendered to prove the truth of the matters asserted but to prove some other fact, the evidence will not be 'hearsay' evidence but 'original' evidence.

10.1.2.2   Implied hearsay

The important difference between the criminal definition of hearsay and that at common law and in civil cases is that the CJA 2003, s 115(3) states that implications from the statements are not hearsay statements if it was not the purpose of the maker to invite that implication.

At common law, implied statements were covered by the rule against hearsay as much as express statements. Therefore in *R v Kearley* [1992] 2 AC 228, HL, statements by unknown people requesting drugs and asking for the defendant, to the extent that they could be admitted as impliedly asserting that *Kearley* was a drug dealer, were hearsay. In the course of their speeches, their lordships approved another example of implied hearsay given in *Wright v Doe d Tatham* (1837) 7 Ad & El 313 of a ship's captain who inspects a ship and, having done so, sets sail in the ship with his family. In *Wright*, Parke B suggested that the ship captain's act was an implied statement as to the seaworthiness of the ship.

At common law, implied hearsay evidence was not without its difficulties. In *Ratten v R* [1972] AC 378, PC, a woman made a telephone call to the police in which she asked for the police in an hysterical manner. Her husband was tried for her murder and the court concluded that the statement was not a hearsay statement. In *Kearley*, the House of Lords concluded that the statement had in fact been an implied hearsay assertion although this was not part of the reasoning of the Privy Council. Furthermore, in contrast to *Wright*, in *Manchester Brewery v Coombs* (1901) 82 LT 347, Farwell J was of the view that the actions of people refusing to drink beer was admissible at common law in support of an allegation that the beer was unfit for consumption.

In civil law, the common law position is unaffected. Therefore implied statements can be hearsay statements.

Section 115(3) of the CJA 2003 has altered the definition of hearsay in criminal cases. By virtue of that section, a statement is not a hearsay statement unless one of the purposes of the statement was to cause the other person to believe the fact in question or to act on the basis that it is true. Therefore the statements in *Kearley*, *Ratten* and *Wright* would no longer be hearsay statements. The statute has confirmed the position in *Manchester Brewery*.

However, the CJA 2003, s115(3) has not taken all implied statements out of the ambit of the hearsay rule. Only statements in which there was no intention to convey the relevant fact are removed. Therefore, if a person were deliberately to imply a fact by making a particular statement that statement is still a hearsay. For example, if Anil wishing to give the impression that Ben was in hiding as a result of a crime were to say, 'Well, I would not expect see Ben on the High Street any time soon', the statement would still be a hearsay statement if it were established that Anil's purpose was to cause the person to whom the statement was made to believe that Ben was in hiding. The 2003 Act therefore reflects the ruling in *Teper v The Queen* [1952] AC 480, PC that a person made a hearsay statement identifying the defendant when she said to a person driving away from the scene of the crime, 'Your place burning and you going away from the fire'.

10.1.2.3   Representations by machines, etc

The rule against hearsay was developed by the common law in the 18th century. It was not therefore particularly well equipped to deal with the technological innovations of the 20th century.

The rule against hearsay was not designed with modern technology in mind. Technological devices produce information that may appear to be statements but which the courts have held occasionally not to be hearsay but real evidence. Whether or not this is so will depend on the extent to which the process of the device is mechanical or is dependent on human input. Where a person types information onto a computer and saves it into a file, it will clearly be as much a statement as if it had been said or written. However, where the courts conclude that the machine or device in question is producing the record automatically, it has been held to be real not hearsay evidence. Again, using the definition in *R v Sharp*, we might say that a calculation or automated message is not an 'assertion' nor is the mechanical process asserting any fact.

Consider the following examples:

(a) In *R v Wood* (1982) 76 Cr App R 23, CA, the prosecution had to prove the chemical composition of metal alleged to have been stolen. The Court of Appeal held that the printouts from the computer were not hearsay but real evidence as the computer was performing a calculation that could have been done manually. Note, however, it was still necessary to prove by non-hearsay evidence the formula that had been programmed into the computer and the data that had been fed into it. Once this had been done the computer itself was not making any statement for hearsay purposes.

(b) In *Castle v Cross* [1984] 1 WLR 1372, DC, an intoxometer reading was held not to be hearsay evidence. The reading was a mechanical calculation rather than a statement produced by human agency or interpretation. In contrast to the situation in *Wood* the machine did not rely upon data fed into it by human agency which would need to be proven by testimony at court.

(c) In *R v Governor of Brixton Prison, ex p Levin* [1997] 3 WLR 117, HL, the mechanical record was of fund transfers made over the internet. The bank's computer system automatically recorded transactions made. The issue in the case was whether the defendant had used a computer to make such fund transfers. The House of Lords held that the computerised records of the transactions were no more hearsay to prove the fact of such transactions than a photocopy of a fraudulent cheque.

(d) In *Taylor v Chief Constable of Cheshire* [1986] 1 WLR 1479, the Divisional Court held that police officers could give evidence as to what they had seen on a CCTV video of an offence even thought the video had been lost. Rather than the video being an out of court statement it was said by Ralph Gibson LJ to be no different in principle from having witnessed the event when it took place.

The identical definitions of 'statement' in the Civil Evidence Act 1995, s13 and the CJA 2003, s115 require 'representation . . . by a person', which reflects this common law position.

No specific further provision is made for mechanical devices in the Civil Evidence Act 1995. However, the CJA 2003, s 129 provides:

(1)   *Where a representation of any fact —*
    (a)   *is made otherwise than by a person, but*
    (b)   *depends for its accuracy on information supplied (directly or indirectly) by a person, the representation is not admissible in criminal proceedings as evidence of the fact unless it is proved that the information was accurate.*
(2)   *Subsection (1) does not affect the operation of the presumption that a mechanical device has been properly set or calibrated.*

Section 129 regulates statements made by a machine that has received information from a person such as the computer in *Wood* as opposed to intoxometer reading in *Castle v Cross*. Section 129(1) reflects the requirement in *Wood* that the information put into a machine has to be proven by non-hearsay evidence. However, it goes further than the requirement in *Wood* of proof of the information by non-hearsay evidence as the accuracy of the information is a pre-condition of admissibility. It would therefore appear to require that the tribunal of law determines the accuracy of the data supplied to such a machine before it can be adduced as evidence in front of the tribunal of fact.

10.1.2.4   Negative hearsay

As we saw from the definitions of hearsay in at **10.1.2.1**, a hearsay statement is one that is evidence of any fact asserted. But what if the things that a person states outside of the courtroom are notable not because of what the witness said but because of what the witness did not say. To what extent is this 'evidence of any fact asserted'?

Consider the following example. A theft takes place when some youths are on a hiking trip. The issue is whether the accused, Ed, was in a dormitory when an offence took place. Evidence is given that the person in charge of the trip, Peter, appointed 'Dormitory Monitors' for each dormitory and would call at each dorm asking the monitor who was there. At about the time the theft took place, the prosecution seek to prove that Ed was out of his dormitory.

To what extent should they be able to do so if the evidence they rely on is:

1.   That Peter called out to the monitor, 'Is there anyone missing from your dormitory' to which Michael replied 'Yes, Ed'.

2.   That Peter called out to the monitor, Michael, 'who is in there with you?' and that Michael replied, 'Me, Adrian, Jack, Steve and Asil'.

The courts have treated these two types of statements completely differently. In both cases the purpose of the statement is to prove that Ed was absent. The first statement does this by proving that what was said (or implied), namely that Ed is absent, was true. In the latter case, nothing has been asserted.

However the courts have taken the view that in the latter case it is not the truth of what was said that proves Ed was absent but the fact of not having said something and therefore the evidence that is used to prove Ed was absent is the silence from which absence is inferred.

This concept of proof by the absence of a statement (sometimes confusingly called 'negative hearsay') was recognised (obiter) in *R v Patel* (1981) 73 Cr App R 117, a case concerning illegal immigration, only to arise if:

- It was proved by an officer responsible for compiling records that a particular method was used for making and storing entries as to the existence of a fact in that record.
- It was proved by the same officer that due to the process, the absence of a particular entry on the record meant the non-existence of the fact.

For examples of the application of the rule see:

(a) *R v Shone* (1983) 76 Cr App R 72, CA. There the accused was charged with theft, to prove which the prosecution had to establish that the goods alleged to be stolen had not been legitimately sold on. The prosecution were allowed to call two employees who testified to the system adopted and the absence of a record of onward sale.

(b) *R v Muir* (1984) 79 Cr App R 153, CA. The accused was alleged to have stolen a video recorder but stated in his defence that the recorder had been repossessed by the hire company. The prosecution were allowed to call the district manager of the hire company who gave evidence that if there had been a repossession he would have been informed. This was held to have been original (negative hearsay) evidence. The Court of Appeal held that the district manager could have given evidence that he had checked with his Head Office to determine whether they had any such record. This judgment has been criticized for its inconsistency with the principle in *R v Patel* and *R v Shone* (see, for example, *Blackstone's Criminal Practice 2005* at F 15.13 and I.H. Dennis, *The Law of Evidence*, 2nd edn, 2002 Sweet & Maxwell at p 573).

10.1.2.5 Significance of hearsay evidence

It will be seen in this chapter and the next that hearsay evidence is subject to restrictions as to its admissibility and, even where admissible, rules of procedure regulating its use. Therefore, it is important to identify whether evidence is hearsay even where it will be admissible hearsay evidence. If it is not hearsay evidence but original evidence the restrictions and controls identified in this and the next chapter will not apply.

There is an essential two-stage process for considering hearsay issues:

- Is the evidence hearsay evidence at all?
- If it is hearsay, is it admissible under an exception to the rule against hearsay?

If the evidence is admissible hearsay for one purpose, it may still be inadmissible hearsay evidence for other purposes. In such situations the judge will have to direct the jury that they should not rely on the statement as evidence of truth in relation to any other issues. In *R v Nelson* [2004] EWCA Crim 333, the hearsay statement in question was a record of a call made to the police by the defendant's father. The defendant was alleged to have stabbed another man and raised the defence of automatism. The father's call to the police, which was made soon after the incident, showed that the father was aware that a stabbing had taken place and that the defendant might be blamed. It was accepted by the Court of Appeal that such a statement could have been admitted as original evidence (see below) to show that the father may have been aware of the stabbing, which may have proved that the father had been told about it by the defendant, who therefore would not have been suffering from automatism. However the conviction was quashed because the jury were not directed that they should only use the evidence to decide whether the defendant was not suffering from automatism. They were not directed that they should not use the statement to conclude that the defendant had in fact committed the offence (which would be a hearsay statement because the statement would then be used to prove a fact by virtue of its truth).

The rule against hearsay where it applies does not just prevent a witness from relating what he or she had heard; it also prevents a witness from adopting as his or her own knowledge something he or she has been told. Consider the example of the case of *R v Rothwell* (1994) 99 Cr App R 388, CA. The accused was charged with possession of heroin with intent to supply it. A police officer gave evidence that:

(a) He had seen the accused passing packages to other people and had seen him receive money in return.

(b) He knew that persons to whom the accused passed the money were drug dealers.

(c) He knew this because of his experience in the investigation of drugs offences and prosecutions in the Newcastle area where the events took place.

(d) (In cross-examination) he did not have first-hand experience of seeing the persons in question use drugs.

The Court of Appeal held that the police officer was not able to give such evidence as at this time it was inadmissible at common law. While it was not hearsay evidence in the obvious sense (his testimony was not 'PC Burnes told me that the persons were drug dealers') it was *based* on hearsay evidence (whatever he had in fact been told or heard in court at previous trials that led him to believe that the persons were drug dealers). It was just as inadmissible as if he had repeated every statement that he was relying on when he said that the people were drug dealers.

Nor will the courts allow the hearsay rule to be side-stepped by proving that there was a conversation and then proving what a person immediately did as a result where that would, in effect, suggest to the tribunal of fact what the conversation was about. Using the case of *Rothwell* again, it would not be possible to prove that the police officer giving evidence said that:

(a) He had a conversation with PC Ings.

(b) As a result of that conversation he arrested Rothwell for possession of heroin with intent to supply it.

Quite simply only the stupidest jury would fail to interpret the conversation as being about supplying heroin in some way, which would almost certainly be hearsay if it had been repeated.

10.1.3   Identifying hearsay evidence

Determining whether a statement is hearsay or original evidence is a skill that requires an understanding of proof and a logical approach to the evidence and, in particular, to relevance.

As the definitions above suggest, identifying hearsay evidence requires the addressing of three questions:

- Is the evidence a statement or assertion at all?
- Was the statement made other than as testimony in the current case?
- Is the statement being used 'as evidence of any fact asserted': ie to prove a fact simply by the statement being accepted as true.

If 'yes' to all three questions, the statement is hearsay evidence. If the answer is not 'yes' to all three questions quite what the evidence is will depend on which of the above questions is answered in the negative.

10.1.3.1   Is the evidence a statement or assertion at all?

This is not generally a difficult stage of the analysis. However it is worth noting the scope of the statement for these purposes. A 'statement' includes:

(a) Both oral and written statements. Matters written in a document are statements for this purpose. This would also include electronic communications.

(b) Statements made by gestures or conduct. In *Chandrasekera v The King* [1937] AC 220, PC, for example, a victim of an attack had had her throat cut and could not speak. To illustrate that the accused, a local cow-herd, committed the offence, she made gestures and signs (including putting her hands to her head to impersonate a bull) and nodded when asked questions. These gestures were determined to be statements for the purposes of the hearsay rule.

(c) Things stated whether or not there was an intention to communicate that information to another person (therefore a diary entry could be a statement for these purposes).

Note: the word 'statement' is commonly used in procedural rules to refer to a document written in preparation of proceedings. So far as the rule of hearsay is concerned, as can be seen from the analysis above, the word is being used in a much wider sense.

If the out of court fact is not a statement it will either be part of a witness's account of what he or she saw happen (for example, the accused hitting the victim is probably not a statement) or real evidence (such as a document proved in court not for the content but to prove that a particular type of paper was used).

10.1.3.2   Was the statement 'other than as testimony in the current case'?

Put quite simply this part of the test required a distinction between a statement that is made for the first time as testimony and a statement in testimony that is a repetition of something said at another time. A common (if slightly misleading) short-hand term for such a statement is 'out of court'.

Note the following points:

(a) Statements made outside of any court (in the pub, at home, on the street, in a police station, into a tape recorder) are clearly covered by this definition.

(b) Statements made in the witness box in *other* cases are also covered by this definition (*Berkeley Peerage Case* (1811) 4 Camp 401).

(c) Statements made in the courtroom but not in the witness box are also covered by this definition.

(d) Having been sworn does not prevent any of that witness's previous statements and utterances from potentially being hearsay evidence.

(e) However, a witness in a case will have made a statement to those preparing the case that outlines his or her testimony (a 'witness statement' or 'proof of evidence'). Insofar as the witness goes into the witness box and restates what is in that statement as his or her own testimony, the testimony is not the repetition of an out of court statement. All that document was doing was recording what the witness was intending to say as his or her evidence. However, if for some reason that statement must be produced before the court, it will be an 'out of court' statement for these purposes. When such statements will be admissible will depend on why they are admitted as evidence (see **10.1.4.3** below). See, for example, **6.2.3** (memory refreshing documents), **6.2.4** (previous consistent statements) and **6.3.6** (previous inconsistent statements).

(f) On the other hand, remember that there are certain rules of procedure that allow such earlier statements to stand as the evidence-in-chief of a party (CPR, r 32.5 and s 9 of the Criminal Justice Act 1967, for example: see **4.7.1**). The effect of these provisions is that these statements become the testimony of the witness in proceedings and cannot therefore be hearsay. This is because formalities and procedures have been complied with: without the required formalities such statements are just like any other 'out of court' statement.

It is important to look carefully at any statement or testimony to distinguish how much of it is (or will be) the testimony of the witness and how much will be the *repetition* of things said outside court. It is only the latter that will be potentially hearsay (ie to which you need to apply the third stage of the test, see **10.1.4.5**).

Merely because a statement is identified as an 'out of court' statement does not mean that it is automatically inadmissible or even that it is hearsay. It simply means that we need to apply the third stage of the test.

10.1.3.3   'Evidence of any fact asserted'

The really tricky but vital part of hearsay analysis is usually the third stage. It is this stage that distinguishes hearsay out of court statements from 'original' out of court statements.

The term 'hearsay' is only applied to 'out of court' statements or assertions with a particular purpose: those that are used to prove a fact by getting the tribunal to accept that the contents of the statement are true or accurate. If the statement has some other purpose, it will not be 'hearsay' but 'original' evidence. These are the various types of statements identified in **10.1**. By 'purpose' at this point we mean 'evidential purpose' (ie what it is adduced to prove) not the purpose of the maker of the statement in making it.

This third stage can be broken down into two further stages:

- What is the relevant purpose of the statement? (Note that it may have more than one.)

- Will the tribunal of fact have to rely on the truth of the statement for that purpose to be achieved?

The key to this part of the test is, therefore, 'purpose': what you are trying to achieve with the evidence? This is a question of logic and proof rather than law.

Consider this example: A's out of court statement is, 'B was on the High Street at 10 pm on Monday'. It has been put in evidence before a jury.

1. Assuming there is no other evidence in the case, if the jury decides that the statement is true or accurate, what does it prove?

2. What could the statement prove without being true or accurate?

If the statement is true, it proves what it says, namely that B was on the High Street at 10 pm on Monday. On these matters, the statement is evidence of those facts and they were asserted in the statement. Therefore for these purposes the statement is hearsay evidence.

In addition, by being true, the statement could also prove, for example, that A was on the High Street on Monday. This is done by:

(a) Proving the statement above was made.

(b) Proving that the statement was true (by use of evidence other than this statement).

(c) Arguing that the fact that the statement was made and that it was accurate shows that A was in a position to know that fact and that he was therefore probably on the High Street.

In the second situation the statement is not 'evidence of any fact asserted' because it is not seeking to prove what it states. While it requires the statement to be true to prove something useful in the case, the statement achieves its evidential purpose by being proved to be true by independent evidence.

The statement is 'evidence of *knowledge of the facts asserted*'. It is the fact of the particular statement having been made plus proof by other means that the statement was accurate that allows the tribunal of fact to *infer* that the maker of the statement knew (or believed) a particular fact. If the maker's knowledge or belief is relevant, the statement could be relevant *original* evidence.

What could such a statement prove without being true?

The statement can be relevant to prove the following facts without being true (and would therefore be original evidence of these facts):

(a) Facts it can prove by being false could include:
   (i)   B lied about A's presence at 10 pm on Monday;
   (ii) B is prone to misidentify A;
   (iii) B cannot tell the time;
   (iv) etc.

(b) Facts it can prove whether or not the statement is true:

   (i)   A knows B (proved by the fact of having been talking about them);
   (ii) A knows there is a High Street (he mentioned it);
   (iii) A believed B was on the High Street at 10 pm on Monday (A could *believe* this whether or not it was true).

At risk of over-simplification, where the purpose of the evidence is to prove a conclusion by simply proving that the statement was made, the statement is original evidence. Where the purpose of the evidence is to prove a fact by the statement being *true*, the statement is hearsay. The over-simplification is that sometimes (knowledge cases) the conclusion is proved by (1) the fact of the statement having been made and (2) it happening to be true (this being proven by other means). It is still, however, the fact of the statement having been made that determines its non-hearsay nature. The statement is not proving what it states.

While the word 'purpose' is of huge importance, do not overlook the word 'relevant'. Only relevant evidence is admissible. There is no point in determining that the statement could achieve some non-hearsay purpose if that purpose is not relevant in the proceedings. Have another look at **1.3.1.3** in this Manual and in particular the analysis of the cases of *R v Blastland* and *R v Kearley*. In both of those cases statements were determined to be inadmissible hearsay if used to prove that what the maker said was true. In each case they could also have proved what the maker of the statement knew or believed and would be admissible if relevant. In both cases the House of Lords concluded that the state of mind of the maker was not relevant (or not sufficiently relevant) in the case in question. While it might be possible to disagree with the conclusions of the House of Lords in each case on the issue of relevance, the principle that relevance remains an absolute requirement for admissibility in unquestionably correct.

Leaving to one side issues of relevance for the time being, let us go back to the concept of purpose. By identifying the purpose of the evidence we can then work out whether it is 'evidence of the facts stated' or is 'tendered for the truth of its contents' (another way of explaining how hearsay statements can be distinguished from original evidence).

The fact that statements are identified as hearsay does not necessarily mean that they are not admissible. Admissibility is regulated by the CJA 2003 in criminal proceedings and the Civil Evidence Act 1995 in civil proceedings. Other statements, although they would be inadmissible hearsay, could (and should) be proved from other sources. Remember that one of the purposes of the rule against hearsay evidence is to ensure that the evidence is given by the most authoritative source. Defining evidence as hearsay does not mean that the conclusion it proves can never be proven by any evidence. It simply means that it cannot be proven by the inadmissible hearsay statement.

10.1.4   Recap

Identifying whether evidence is hearsay is a matter of applying the technique of proof to the facts of a particular case. Case law can illustrate principle but cannot set universal rules that will determine whether a particular statement is hearsay or not.

The process for identifying hearsay evidence is:

(a) Determine whether it is a statement at all.

(b) Determine whether it has been made 'out of court' remembering quite how specific that is.

(c) Determine whether it is evidence of the facts stated by:

    (i)   determining the relevant purpose or purposes of the evidence;

    (ii) determining whether the statement has to be true to achieve those purposes.

(d) If hearsay, determine whether it is admissible or inadmissible hearsay.

10.1.5   Examples of original evidence

The following cases illustrate the approach that the courts have taken in determining whether a statement was hearsay evidence or original evidence. As usual, the cases are illustrations of the application of the principle. In all of the cases, the statements were held not be hearsay but original evidence. While the cases have been put into categories below, that is for illustrative purposes rather than an attempt to define distinct categories. Each turns on its own facts and the purpose of the evidence identified in each case, applying the central principle that the statement must not be used to prove what it alleges. The categories reflect the ways in which statements will prove facts without being 'evidence of a fact asserted' as we identified in **10.1.1** and **10.1.3.2**.

10.1.5.1   Cases in which the truth of the statement is irrelevant

In the following cases the relevant purpose of the evidence is achieved irrespective of the truth or falsity of the statement. Quite simply it is the fact that the statement was made that achieves a relevant purpose in the case. That this is so is generally a matter of the substantive law in question.

Subramaniam v Public Prosecutor [1956] 1 WLR 965, PC: The accused was charged with a terrorism offence and pleaded the defence of duress. He alleged that he had been threatened by terrorists with death if he did not carry ammunition for them. The Privy Council concluded that such statements were not hearsay. The defence of duress applies if a person is threatened *not* if the person actually faces the harm that has been threatened. In other words it is the *fact* of the threat that is relevant rather than its genuineness or truth. Therefore the relevant purpose was to prove that the threat had been made not that it had been a genuine or 'true' threat that the terrorists would in fact carry out.

R v Chapman [1969] 2 QB 436, CA: The accused was charged with driving with excess alcohol. He would have had a defence to the charge if a doctor had objected to the provision of a breath specimen on health grounds. The prosecution were entitled to prove that the doctor did not so object. It was the fact of the lack of objection rather than the genuineness of that lack of objection that was relevant as a matter of substantive law. The purpose of the statement was to show that there was in fact no objection rather than that the doctor was genuinely not objecting. Again this was a matter of substantive law.

Woodhouse v Hall (1980) 72 Cr App R 39, DC: The accused was charged with 'acting in the management of a brothel'. The property, which appeared to be a massage parlour, would be a brothel if the prostitution was conducted there. The Divisional Court held that this, as a matter of substantive law, would derive not from the actuality of the patrons having sex with the occupants but from the occupants soliciting sex from the patrons. In other words the property was a brothel if sexual acts were offered rather than either intended or performed. Therefore undercover police officers were allowed to give evidence of statements made on the property offering the sexual acts. The purpose was to show that sexual acts were offered not that they were intended or performed.

Ratten v R [1972] AC 378, PC: The accused was charged with the murder of his wife by shooting her. His defence was that his gun went off accidentally. The prosecution were allowed to call evidence from a telephone operator that at the time of the killing a phone call was received from the accused's address in which a woman said in an hysterical and sobbing voice, 'Get me the police, please'. The accused had denied that any such call was made. The Privy Council held that the purpose of the statement was to prove the fact of a phone call and the fact of the hysterical nature of the call not that the lady wanted the police as such.

R v O'Connell [2003] EWCA Crim 502: After having been arrested on suspicion of drugs offences, the police intercepted two calls on the defendant's mobile telephone in which the callers impliedly requested drugs. On both occasions, the defendant, who was present at the time, called out that it was not him but the police on the 'phone and that the callers should end the call. The Court of Appeal stated that what was said by the callers was hearsay evidence (see *R v Kearley* [1992] 2 AC 228 at **1.3.1.3**) but that what the defendant had said in reaction to those calls was admissible original evidence. The defendant's statement showed his reaction to requests on his telephone for drugs and therefore his awareness of his own guilt.

10.1.5.2   Cases in which the purpose was to prove the falsehood of the statement

Mawaz Khan v R [1967] 1 AC 454, PC: Two co-defendants were charged with murder. Each had made statements to the police that when the murder took place they were at a particular club. The prosecution were allowed to prove (a) that such statements were made and (b), by other witnesses, that the co-defendants were not at the club. The co-defendants appealed the admissibility of the statements as hearsay evidence. The Privy Council concluded that the statements were not hearsay evidence. The purpose of the statements was not to prove that the co-defendants *were* at the club but to prove the *fact* of having alleged that they were. This fact, combined with the fact that they were elsewhere would be relevant to prove that the co-defendants had lied about where they were (and therefore, potentially, that they were conscious of their guilty involvement in the crime). See also *R v B* [2003] EWCA Crim 2169. For further detail on the evidential value of lies, see **Chapter 13.**

10.1.5.3   Cases in which the purpose is the proof of knowledge of a fact that is either uncontested or proved by other means

To say that a statement is hearsay if it has to be true to achieve its relevant purpose simplifies matters a little too much. A statement does have to be true to achieve its purpose where what the relevant fact is that the person making the statement *knew* a particular fact. This is only achieved by proving it was correctly, accurately or truthfully stated. However the statement is not being used to prove that truth. Instead the fact is proved by other means and the statement is simply used to prove that the maker was aware of that fact. Have a look at the two cases that follow:

(a) *Thomas v Connell* (1838) 4 M & W 267: The issue was whether or not the defendant knew that he was insolvent. Proof of a statement in which he said that he was insolvent could prove *knowledge* of that fact. The fact that he was insolvent (another fact in issue in the case) was proved by other evidence.

(b) *R v Blastland* [1986] AC 41: In *Blastland* (referred to above and at **1.4.3.3**) it was accepted that the statements by M that showed he knew that there had been a murder would not be hearsay. While the statement had to be true to be achieve its purpose, the statement was *not proving the fact it alleged by being true*. Instead the fact that was alleged (there was a dead boy) was proved by other evidence. The purpose of the statement was to prove that M *knew* that fact. The statement was therefore not hearsay *insofar as it was used to prove that M knew of the death rather than to prove the death occurred*. However, the House of Lords concluded that M's knowledge was not (sufficiently) relevant to the trial issue (ie whether the accused killed him).

10.2   Admissibility of hearsay in civil cases

Most hearsay evidence is admissible in civil cases and the rules are therefore quite simple. The rules are stated in the Civil Evidence Act 1995. The 1995 Act has created a general rule of inclusion in civil cases, which is set out in s 1:

1.—(1)   *In civil proceedings evidence shall not be excluded on the ground that it is hearsay.*

(2)   *In this Act —*

(a)   *'hearsay' means a statement made otherwise than by a person while giving oral evidence in the proceedings which is tendered as evidence of the matters stated; and*

(b)   *references to hearsay include hearsay of whatever degree.*

(3)   *Nothing in this Act affects the admissibility of evidence admissible apart from this section.*

(4)   *The provisions of sections 2 to 6 (safeguards and supplementary provisions relating to hearsay evidence) do not apply in relation to hearsay evidence admissible apart from this section, notwithstanding that it may also be admissible by virtue of this section.*

In other words all hearsay evidence will be admissible in civil proceedings unless it is already admissible under another statute or is one of the common law exceptions preserved under s 7 of the Act. The 1995 Act applies to both documentary and oral statements and to 'multiple hearsay' (ie where the potentially hearsay statement itself contains or is based on hearsay).

It may not always be clear whether proceedings are civil or criminal. In *Clingham v Kensington and Chelsea London Borough Council* [2002] 3 WLR 1313, HL, proceedings in relation to an anti-social behaviour order under s 1 of the Crime and Disorder Act 1998 were determined to be civil because the order that would be imposed did not itself include a sanction (a sanction would have followed from non-compliance with the order).

These provisions do not allow the proof of out of court statements made by a person who would not be competent as a witness (s 5 of the 1995 Act: see **Chapter 4**).

The rule of admissibility under s 1 of the 1995 Act and the consequential provisions (set out below) do not apply if the statement is admissible under another statutory exception. Such exceptions include (but are not restricted to):

(a) Evidence in connection with the 'upbringing, maintenance or welfare of a child' will be admissible notwithstanding that it is hearsay evidence (Children (Admissibility of Hearsay Evidence) Order 1993).

(b) A copy of any entry in a banker's book is admissible to prove any transactions recorded in it (Bankers' Books Evidence Act 1879, s 3). For more detail, see *Blackstone's Civil Practice*, 2005.

10.2.1   The requirement of notice

Where a party proposes to rely upon hearsay evidence, he or she must comply with the notice requirements set out in s 2 of the 1995 Act. The notice requirements are set out in detail in the *Civil Litigation Manual* or *Blackstone's Civil Practice*, 2005, chapter 51. However in short the main points are:

(a) Failure to give notice:
  (i)   does not render evidence inadmissible (s 2(4));
  (ii) can lead the court to make procedural orders (for example the court could adjourn the hearing and/or order the party who has not complied with the notice requirements to pay costs) (s 2(4)(a));
  (iii) may lead the courts to attach less weight to the statement (s 2(4)).

(b) If the hearsay statement will be proved by the oral evidence of a witness (ie the witness will repeat what he or she has heard), service of the witness's statement is sufficient notice (CPR, r 33.2(1)).

(c) If the hearsay statement will be proved in a witness statement that stands as the evidence-in-chief, that witness statement constitutes compliance with the notice requirements (CPR, r 33.2(1)). Where the witness statement is going to be used instead of calling the witness, this fact must be identified to the other parties (CPR, r 33.2(2)).

(d) If the hearsay statement is not proved in the way set out above (for example the hearsay statement will be proved in a document) then a notice should be served on the other parties (CPR, r 33.2(3)). The reason for not calling the witness must be identified in the notice.

10.2.2   The requirement of leave

Generally leave is not required before such evidence will be admitted. The judge does not have to rule that the hearsay evidence is admissible.

There is one exception to the rule that evidence is admissible without leave. This exception is set out in s 6(2) of the 1995 Act:

6.— (2) *A party who has called or intends to call a person as a witness in civil proceedings may not in those proceedings adduce evidence of a previous statement made by that person, except—*
  (a) with the leave of the court, or
  (b) for the purpose of rebutting a suggestion that his evidence has been fabricated.

This shall not be construed as preventing a witness statement (that is, a written statement of oral evidence which a party to the proceedings intends to lead) from being adopted by a witness in giving evidence or treated as his evidence.

The effect of this is that leave will be required where a party seeks to both:

- call a person as a witness, *and*
- prove that the person has made a previous statement.

It is important to remember the rules relating to previous statements made by a witness. Re-read **6.2** of this Manual. Having done so you will remember that previous consistent statements are not generally admissible at common law. The effect of s 6 is that they now are generally admissible if the court grants leave. However, some of the types of previous statements have been mentioned specifically in s 6:

(a) *Previous inconsistent statements.* Generally a party calling a witness would not seek to prove the witness had made a previous *inconsistent* statement, however this might happen if the witness proves hostile (**6.2.5.2**). Section 6(3) provides that ss 3 to 5 of the Criminal Procedure Act 1865 still apply in such situations. The basic rule therefore has not changed the circumstances under which such statements can be proved.

(b) *Memory refreshing documents.* The common law rules concerning the admissibility of such documents as evidence (see **6.2.3.1**) has not been changed by this section (s 6(4)).

(c) *Statements admitted to rebut a suggestion of previous fabrication.* Such statements (formerly an exception to the common law rule against previous consistent statements: see **6.2.4.1**) are admissible *without leave.*

Any previous statements made by a witness to the proceedings, if admitted, will be evidence of the truth of what is alleged (s 6(5)). At common law such statements were only proof of the consistency of what the witness said (ie to bolster his or her credibility).

10.2.3 Proof of a hearsay statement

Although the 1995 Act renders hearsay statements admissible, they still must be proved. Where the statement is oral hearsay (ie the repetition of what someone *said* elsewhere), the statement is proved by the evidence of the person that heard it.

Where the hearsay statement is contained in a document, the document will be produced at court. The provenance of the document must be established (this is usually described as 'proving' the document). Section 8 provides that a document can be proved by producing it or a copy of it. This does not, however, mean that the document can simply be presented at court (*Ventouris v Mountain (No 2)* [1992] 1 WLR 817). A witness must establish that the document in question has something to do with the case. However this 'proof' of a document can be achieved by hearsay evidence. In *Ventouris v Mountain (No 2)*, the document in question was a tape recording of conversations between various people on matters relevant to an insurance fraud, which was being litigated. One of the participants to the conversation was G, who was not available to give evidence. A solicitor was allowed to 'prove' the tape recordings as relevant evidence of the conversations by repeating what G had told him about them.

Sections 9 and 10 of the 1995 Act make particular provisions for the admissibility of particular documents without having formally to 'prove' those documents.

(a) Section 9 concerns documents forming part of the records of a business or public authority. Instead of having to call a witness such a document will be proved if a certificate signed by 'an officer of the business or authority' is produced. 'Records' is defined, by s 9(4) as 'records in whatever form' and 'business' as 'any activity regularly carried on over a period of time, whether for profit or not, by any body . . . or by an individual'. 'Public authority' includes any government department or public undertaking.

(b) Section 10 provides for the admissibility of actuarial tables in personal injuries cases.

10.2.4 Challenging the hearsay statement

Clearly a party against whom a hearsay statement is made has little power to prevent the statement from being admitted. There is only a requirement for leave if the statement was made by a witness. Even a failure to comply with the notice requirements will not prevent the statement from being admitted.

However, under the 1995 Act there are a number of ways in which another party can challenge the weight to be attached to the statement:

(a) Where the hearsay statement has been made by a person not called as a witness any party may call the maker of the statement to cross-examine him or her if the court grants leave (s 3).

(b) Section 4 lays down guidance upon what weight should be attached to the hearsay evidence. Section 4(2) states that the court may take into consideration the following:

   (i)   Whether it would have been reasonable and practical to secure the attendance of the witness rather than using the hearsay statement (s 4(2)(a)).

   (ii) Whether the statement was made contemporaneously with the events to which they relate (s 4(2)(b)).

   (iii) Whether the hearsay itself is based on the repetition of information from another source ('multiple hearsay') (s 4(2)(c)).

   (iv) Any motive the maker has for concealing or misrepresenting matters (s 4(2)(d)).

   (v)   How complete the hearsay statement is as an account of the matters (s 4(2)(e)).

   (vi) Whether the statement was made by numerous people in collaboration (s 4(2)(e)).

   (vii) Why the statement was made (s 4(2)(e)).

   (viii) Whether the statement appears to have been produced in a way that would prevent other parties from fully testing or challenging it (s 4(2)(f)). In other words, failure to comply with notice requirements fully will probably lead the court to attach less weight to it.

(c) Where the witness does not attend for cross-examination, provision is made for attacking the credibility of the witness as if he or she had been called as follows:

   (i)   Evidence undermining the credibility of the witness may be called (s 5(2)(a)). This, however, would appear to be subject to the rule of finality (see **6.3.7**). Section 5(2)(a) states that the evidence is admissible for the purpose of attacking the credibility of the maker.

   (ii) Evidence of previous statements inconsistent with the hearsay statements may be proved (see **6.3.6**).

10.2.5   Preservation of the common law rules

Section 7 of the 1995 Act preserves some of the common law exceptions. These exceptions concern various statements in documents of a public nature and include:

(a) Statements contained in public documents (see **10.2.5.1** below).

(b) Statements made by deceased persons to prove matters of pedigree (see **10.2.5.2**).

(c) Statements made by deceased persons to prove the existence of a public or general right (see **10.2.5.3**).

(d) Evidence of a person's general reputation (see **10.2.6**).

Where these exceptions apply there is no need to comply with the notice requirements (**10.2.1**), the leave requirements (**10.2.2**) or the provisions in s 4 concerning the weight to be attached to such documents (**10.2.4**).

10.2.5.1   Statements contained in public documents

At common law hearsay statements in the following types of documents were admissible:

- published works dealing with matters of a public nature (such as dictionaries and maps);

- public documents (such as public registers, and returns made under public authority); and

- records (such as the records of courts, treaties, etc).

For detailed explanation of this exception, see *Blackstone's Civil Practice*, 2005. However, in outline, the exceptions apply where the document in question is available to the public as of right. 'Public' was stated in *Sturla v Feccia* (1880) 5 App Cas 623 not to mean the whole world but all persons interested in the subject matter in question.

10.2.5.2   Statements made by deceased persons to prove matters of pedigree

A statement made by a deceased person concerning a matter of pedigree (such as marriage, legitimacy, dates of birth, etc) will be admissible (*Butler v Mountsgarret* (1859) 7 HL Cas 633) to prove the truth of the facts stated if:

- the maker of the statement and the person about whom it was made are blood relations or the one is married to a blood relation of the other; and

- the pedigree matter is a fact in issue as opposed to a collateral matter.

10.2.5.3   Statements made by deceased persons to prove the existence of a public or general right

Where the existence of a public right is relevant to an issue, any statement by a deceased person affirming the existence of that public right that was made before the dispute arose shall be admissible to prove the existence of that right (see, for example, *Mercer v Denne* [1905] 2 Ch 638). The statement must relate to rights possessed by the general public or by particular classes of persons not to those possessed by an individual.

10.2.6   Evidence of a person's general reputation

The rule in *R v Rowton* (1865) Le & Ca 520, 169 ER 1497 provides that the character of a person should be proven by evidence of the general reputation of the person in the community rather than by evidence of specific acts. Proof by this means (honoured by the courts more in the breach than the observance) relies upon statements made by numerous other unidentified people and is therefore proof by hearsay evidence.

The rule in *Rowton* does not establish when evidence of character is admissible, simply how it is proven. For the rules concerning the admissibility of evidence of the character of parties and witnesses in civil cases see **Chapter 7**.

Hearsay evidence in criminal proceedings

11.1 Criminal Justice Act 2003

The admissibility of hearsay evidence is governed by the Criminal Justice Act 2003 (CJA 2003). Section 114(1) provides:

(1) In criminal proceedings a statement not made in oral evidence in the proceedings is admissible as evidence of any matter stated if, but only if—

    (a) any provision of this Chapter or any other statutory provision makes it admissible,

    (b) any rule of law preserved by section 118 makes it admissible,

    (c) all parties to the proceedings agree to it being admissible, or

    (d) the court is satisfied that it is in the interests of justice for it to be admissible.

'Statement' and 'matters stated' are defined in the CJA 2003, s 115 which was considered at **10.1.2.1**.

Section 114 therefore provides that there are four grounds of admissibility for hearsay evidence. If an out of court statement is a hearsay statement it is not admissible unless it fits within one of those four broad grounds. If, however, the evidence is not hearsay evidence but original evidence, then it does not have to fit within paragraph (a) to (d) to be admissible. Subject to all of the other rules of evidence, original evidence is admissible if relevant.

The four broad grounds for admissibility in s 114(1) are:

- that the statement is admissible under one of the sections of the 2003 Act (or any other statutory provision);

- that the statement is admissible under a preserved common law exception to the rule against hearsay;

- that all of the parties in the proceedings have agreed to the admissibility of the evidence; and

- that, in the absence of such agreement, the court has decided that it is in the interests of justice for the evidence to be admitted.

The CJA 2003 applies to 'criminal proceedings', which are defined in s 140 as 'criminal proceedings in relation to which the strict rules of evidence apply'. In *R v Bradley* [2005] EWCA Crim 20, the Court of Appeal concluded that this meant criminal trials and Newton hearings.

Specific provision is made for rehearings in s 131, which amends the Criminal Appeal Act 1968, sch 2. Paragraph 1 of sch 2 now provides that evidence at a rehearing should be oral if it was given orally at the first trial unless all the parties agree or the witness is unavailable either in the circumstances permitted in the CJA 2003, s 116 (see **11.2.1**) or otherwise unavailable but the court makes a ruling that such evidence is admissible in the interests of justice under the CJA 2003, s 114 (see **11.4**).

11.2   Admissibility under a section of the Criminal Justice Act 2003

The Act provides for the admissibility of evidence in two main situations:

- the maker or the statement is unavailable as a witness (s 116); and
- the statement was made in a business or professional document (s 117).

It is worth remembering that the CJA 2003, s 114(1)(d) allows the court to admit evidence in the interests of justice if it is not otherwise admissible. Therefore, any technicalities preventing the admissibility of evidence may (but not must) allow the court to admit the evidence under that inclusionary discretion.

11.2.1   Statements where the maker is unavailable as a witness

Section 116 of the Criminal Justice Act 2003 provides:

(1) In criminal proceedings a statement not made in oral evidence in the proceedings is admissible as evidence of any matter stated if—

  (a) oral evidence given in the proceedings by the person who made the statement would be admissible as evidence of that matter,

  (b) the person who made the statement (the relevant person) is identified to the court's satisfaction, and

  (c) any of the five conditions mentioned in subsection (2) is satisfied.

(2) The conditions are—

  (a) that the relevant person is dead;

  (b) that the relevant person is unfit to be a witness because of his bodily or mental condition;

  (c) that the relevant person is outside the United Kingdom and it is not reasonably practicable to secure his attendance;

  (d) that the relevant person cannot be found although such steps as it is reasonably practicable to take to find him have been taken;

  (e) that through fear the relevant person does not give (or does not continue to give) oral evidence in the proceedings, either at all or in connection with the subject matter of the statement, and the court gives leave for the statement to be given in evidence.

(3) For the purposes of subsection (2)(e) 'fear' is to be widely construed and (for example) includes fear of the death or injury of another person or of financial loss.

(4) Leave may be given under subsection (2)(e) only if the court considers that the statement ought to be admitted in the interests of justice, having regard—

  (a) to the statement's contents,

  (b) to any risk that its admission or exclusion will result in unfairness to any party to the proceedings (and in particular to how difficult it will be to challenge the statement if the relevant person does not give oral evidence),

  (c) in appropriate cases, to the fact that a direction under section 19 of the Youth Justice and Criminal Evidence Act 1999 (c. 23) (special measures for the giving of evidence by fearful witnesses etc) could be made in relation to the relevant person, and

  (d) to any other relevant circumstances.

(5) A condition set out in any paragraph of subsection (2) which is in fact satisfied is to be treated as not satisfied if it is shown that the circumstances described in that paragraph are caused—

  (a) by the person in support of whose case it is sought to give the statement in evidence, or

  (b) by a person acting on his behalf,

  in order to prevent the relevant person giving oral evidence in the proceedings (whether at all or in connection with the subject matter of the statement).

The precursor of the CJA 2003, s 116 was the Criminal Justice Act 1988, s 23 which has been repealed by the 2003 Act. Section 116 allows evidence to be admitted if:

- the statement being repeated would, if it had been stated in court as testimony would be admissible (in other words this section cannot be used to bypass the rest or the rules of evidence);

- the maker of the statement can be identified; and

- there is a specific good reason for the maker of the statement not to attend at court to give evidence.

In contrast to the Criminal Justice Act 1988, s 23 the statement admitted does not have to have been made in a document.

11.2.1.1   Oral evidence would have been admissible

The requirement that what has been stated must be admissible evidence is similar but not identical to the position under the 1988 Act. The effect is that the CJA 2003, s116 allows the use of statements to prove any statement that would be admissible if given as testimony. This could include multiple hearsay (ie the statement is the repetition of another out of court statement). However such multiple hearsay is subject to additional restrictions (see **11.5**).

The main effect of the CJA 2003, s 116 is that the repetition of a hearsay statement cannot be used to sidestep any of the other rules of evidence regulating the admissibility or exclusion of evidence. Therefore the mere fact that a person alleges that the defendant is of bad character in an out of court statement does not mean that that statement is admissible irrespective of the provisions of the Criminal Justice Act 2003, ss 98–112. Equally, irrelevant statements in hearsay statements are no more admissible than irrelevant testimony.

11.2.1.2   Maker of the statement can be identified

The requirement in the CJA 2003, s 116(1)(b) that the maker can be identified was not included in the Criminal Justice Act 1988, s 23. There is therefore no case law applying the requirement. It is the court that must be satisfied as to the identity of the maker, which may therefore require proof of the identity as a pre-condition of admissibility (and may therefore require a voir dire). When the court is entitled to be satisfied is unresolved. Consider the following example: Henry is charged with robbery. It is alleged that the crime occurred on a street near a place where a homeless person was sleeping and the homeless person provided the description of the attacker to a passer by, Irene, but had left by the time the police arrived and could not be found. Could the description by the home-less person be admitted under s 116? Is 'a homeless person' sufficient identity? Would it make a difference if the person was known to people in the area as 'Old Jack'? Would his full name and details be required? It is possible, but far from probable, that the evidence would be admitted in the interests of justice under the CJA 2003, s 114(1)(d) (see **11.4**).

11.2.1.3   Reasons for admitting the statement

Section 116 of the CJA 2003 is not intended to undermine the principle that persons with knowledge of the facts stated should attend court to give evidence of those matters if they can do so. The section only applies if one of the five good reasons for not doing so apply.

The party seeking to rely upon the document must prove one of the above reasons to the satisfaction of the judge. If it is the prosecution that is seeking to use the document, they must prove the reason beyond reasonable doubt (*R v Acton Justices, ex p McMullen* (1990) 92

Cr App R 98). The defence, when seeking to rely on one of the above reasons, need only prove it on the balance of probabilities (*R v Mattey* [1995] 2 Cr App R 409).

It is the state of the maker of the statement at the time of trial in all of the above situations which is important rather than the state when the statement was made.

None of the conditions for admissibility will apply if it is proven to the court that the condition in question was caused by the person seeking to admit the statement (s 116(5)(a)) or by a person acting on that person's behalf (s 116(5)(b)). It must be proven that the purpose in doing so was to prevent testimony in the proceedings. It would appear logical that the same rules as to the burden of proof would apply as in relation to proof of the s 116 conditions but here it is the party challenging rather than seeking the admissibility that must prove the relevant facts. Therefore, where the prosecution seek to challenge the use of a statement by a defendant on the grounds that the defendant, for example, put the maker in fear, that fact should be proven beyond reasonable doubt as should the purpose of the defendant in doing so.

11.2.1.4   Death of the maker

This is clear enough in its meaning.

11.2.1.5   Unfitness of the maker due to bodily or mental condition

The maker of the statement must be 'unfit to be a witness'. In *R v Setz-Dempsey* [1994] Crim LR 123, the Court of Appeal held that the Criminal Justice Act 1988, s 23 would apply equally where the witness was unable to attend court and where, due to the physical or mental condition the witness could not give meaningful testimony. However the test under the CJA 2003, s 116 means that where special measures can be used to assist the witness in giving testimony either in court or from some other place the witness would not be 'unfit' (see **Chapter 4** for special measures directions).

In *R v Lang* [2004] EWCA Crim 1701, the Court of Appeal held that the question under the equivalent provision of the Criminal Justice Act 1988 was whether the witness was fit to give evidence and that this was a matter for the trial judge. A judge could, therefore, reach a decision that was different to the medical evidence presented in support of an application. As the relevant language in the CJA 2003, s 116 is 'unfit to be a witness', the same principle would apply.

Insofar as the condition of the witness might affect his or her competence as a witness, this is now governed by the CJA 2003, s 123 (see **11.7.2**).

11.2.1.6   Maker is outside the United Kingdom

There are two aspects to this:

(a) *Outside the UK.* A diplomat resident in this country but who cannot be compelled to attend court is not 'outside the UK' (*R v Jiminez-Paez* [1993] Crim LR 596, CA).

(b) *Securing attendance.* Consider the following points:

    (i)   That it is not reasonably practicable to do so must be proved. In *R v Bray* (1988) 88 Cr App R 354 the maker of the statement had been suddenly sent to Korea. The prosecution were permitted to admit his statement as evidence of relevant facts. The accused successfully appealed on the grounds that the prosecution had not adduced evidence that it was not reasonably practicable to secure the attendance of the witness.

    (ii) Where a witness is not available at the date of trial, the judge should consider adjourning the case until he or she is available. However the judge should consider the practicability of securing attendance on the date of trial (or application to admit the statement) and should not have to look into the future to determine when a witness might be available (*R v French* (1993) 97 Cr App R 421, CA).

(iii) Note that the test is 'reasonably practical'. This means that it is not necessary to prove that it is not at all possible to get the witnesses to attend. In *R v Maloney* [1994] Crim LR 525, CA, the witnesses were Greek sea cadets and there was evidence that they were at sea, on leave or at college and that formal applications would have to be made to the Greek navy to secure their attendance. The Court of Appeal was satisfied that enough had been done in determining that they were not available for s 23 of the 1988 Act to apply. Clearly lengthy procedures could have been adopted but these went beyond what was 'reasonably practicable'. The same approach will apply to the CJA 2003.

(iv) Also as the phrase is 'reasonable practical to secure', a witness who could easily attend court *if he or she wished to do so* does not necessarily fall within s 116(1)(c). If there are no powers to secure the attendance of an unwilling witness because of the law of the country in which he or she is located, such a witness will fall within this category. In *R v French*, for example, the witness was Mexican and had already attended to give evidence at a trial that had been adjourned. There was no way of forcing the witness to attend again so the statement could properly have fallen within the identical test under s 23 of the 1988 Act.

(v) What is 'reasonably practicable' is a matter of fact to be determined in each case. However, in *R v Castillo* [1996] 1 Cr App R 438, the Court of Appeal stressed the following three factors:

* the importance of the evidence the witness could give;
* the expense and inconvenience in securing attendance; and
* the validity of the reasons put forward for not attending.

11.2.1.7   Maker cannot be found

The language of the CJA 2003, s 116(2)(d) has changed from that used in the Criminal Justice Act, s 23. There the test was whether 'all reasonable steps' had been taken. Now the test is 'such steps as it is reasonably practical to take'. As this is the test for the CJA 2003, s 116(2)(c), it is likely that the courts will adopt the same principles in applying this section. The principle that, in determining reasonableness, the serious of the charge should not be taken into consideration (*R v Coughlan* [1999] 5 Archbold News 2, CA) will probably continue to remain valid.

11.2.1.8   Maker in fear

Under the Criminal Justice Act 1988 witnesses in fear of giving evidence were governed by s 23(3). Section 116 of the CJA 2003 has extended this category. Any statement made by a person on a previous occasion who is now in fear of giving evidence will be admissible under s 116(2)(e). Section 116(2)(e) applies where the witness refuses to give any evidence, stops giving evidence or gives evidence avoiding reference to particular matters that will be proven by admitting the statement in place of the witness's testimony.

Unlike the other grounds for the application of the CJA 2003, s 116(2) evidence can only be admitted under this paragraph if the judge grants leave. Section 116(4) allows the court, in determining leave, to consider any 'relevant circumstances' but specifically requires consideration of the contents of the statement, whether any special measures directions could assuage the fear and the risk of unfairness to any party in the proceedings in either admitting or excluding the evidence. The last of those factors (fairness) will be considered in relation to the exclusionary discretions under s 126 (see **11.6.1**). It is also likely that the factors to be considered in relation to the inclusionary discretion under s 114(1)(d) will also be of some relevance.

Section 116(3) of the CJA 2003 requires fear to be widely construed and specifically mentions fear of death or injury to persons other than the maker of the statement and the fear of financial loss. Quite how much wider the definition of fear should extend will have to be resolved by the courts.

It is submitted that the following points made under the Criminal Justice Act 1988, s 23 will also apply under the CJA 2003 s 116:

(a) The judge must conclude that the fear will prevent the maker from giving evidence: *R v Singh* [2003] EWCA Crim 2320.

(b) There is no need to prove that the fear is reasonable or that it was caused by the incident that is being tried (*R v Acton Justices, ex p McMullen* (1990) 92 Cr App R 98). Further, it was resolved in *R v Martin* [1996] Crim LR 589, CA, that it is not necessary to prove that the fear was caused by a particular thing said or done by a particular person. In that case the fear had been triggered by a silent stranger outside the witness's house.

(c) In *R v H* [2001] Crim LR 815, the Court of Appeal stated that the court should consider whether the witness is in fear when the witness is due to give evidence rather than days or weeks beforehand. However it was recognised that there might be some practical necessity to resolve the matter at the beginning of the trial.

(d) The fear should preferably be established by oral evidence from the witness in fear (*R v H*). However, the evidence of the fear can be given by persons other than the person in fear (*R v Acton Justices, ex p McMullen*). In *R v Rutherford* [1998] Crim LR 490, the court stated that the fear could be proven by witness statement but in *R v Lobban* [2004] EWCA 1099, the Court of Appeal stated that a witness should be produced to give sworn oral evidence and should be subject to cross-examination unless the court concludes that this approach is not appropriate. Where cross-examination is not permitted by advocates in the case, the judge may conduct the questioning having consulted with the legal representatives as to the subject matter to be raised. In *Lobban* it was also stated that the questioning of a person in fear should take place in court and that the defendant should not be excluded. Other appropriate steps (such as special measures) should be taken to ensure that the person in fear is able to give evidence of that fear.

11.2.2   Statements in business documents

Section 117 of the CJA 2003 Act replaced the Criminal Justice Act 1988, s 24. Section 117 provides:

> (1) In criminal proceedings a statement contained in a document is admissible as evidence of any matter stated if—
>   (a) oral evidence given in the proceedings would be admissible as evidence of that matter,
>   (b) the requirements of subsection (2) are satisfied, and
>   (c) the requirements of subsection (5) are satisfied, in a case where subsection (4) requires them to be.
> (2) The requirements of this subsection are satisfied if—

(a) *the document or the part containing the statement was created or received by a person in the course of a trade, business, profession or other occupation, or as the holder of a paid or unpaid office,*

(b) *the person who supplied the information contained in the statement (the relevant person) had or may reasonably be supposed to have had personal knowledge of the matters dealt with, and*

(c) *each person (if any) through whom the information was supplied from the relevant person to the person mentioned in paragraph (a) received the information in the course of a trade, business, profession or other occupation, or as the holder of a paid or unpaid office.*

(3) *The persons mentioned in paragraphs (a) and (b) of subsection (2) may be the same person.*

(4) *The additional requirements of subsection (5) must be satisfied if the statement—*

(a) *was prepared for the purposes of pending or contemplated criminal proceedings, or for a criminal investigation, but*

(b) *was not obtained pursuant to a request under section 7 of the Crime (International Co-operation) Act 2003 (c. 32) or an order under paragraph 6 of Schedule 13 to the Criminal Justice Act 1988 (c. 33) (which relate to overseas evidence).*

(5) *The requirements of this subsection are satisfied if—*

(a) *any of the five conditions mentioned in section 116(2) is satisfied (absence of relevant person etc), or*

(b) *the relevant person cannot reasonably be expected to have any recollection of the matters dealt with in the statement (having regard to the length of time since he supplied the information and all other circumstances).*

(6) *A statement is not admissible under this section if the court makes a direction to that effect under subsection (7).*

(7) *The court may make a direction under this subsection if satisfied that the statement's reliability as evidence for the purpose for which it is tendered is doubtful in view of—*

(a) *its contents,*

(b) *the source of the information contained in it,*

(c) *the way in which or the circumstances in which the information was supplied or received, or*

(d) *the way in which or the circumstances in which the document concerned was created or received.*

As with the CJA 2003, s 116, s 117(1)(a) does not allow the admission of evidence that is inadmissible by other rules of evidence to be presented in a document.

11.2.2.1 Documents to which the CJA 2003, s 117 applies

Section 117 regulates the admissibility of two types of documents:

- ordinary business documents, and

- documents prepared for pending or contemplated criminal proceedings or during criminal investigations.

The section does not apply to all documents. To be admissible under the CJA 2003, s 117:

(a) The document must have been created or received by in the course of a trade, business or profession, etc (s 117(2)(a)). Note therefore that a letter written by someone in a non-professional capacity but received by someone in a professional/business capacity is covered by the section.

(b) The supplier of the information in the document is shown to have personal knowledge of the facts related (s 117(2)(b)). Section 117(2)(b) also allows the court to infer such personal knowledge from the nature of the document (see *R v Foxley* [1995] 2 Cr App R 523 and *Vehicle and Operator Agency v Jenkins Transport Ltd* [2003] EWHC 2879 (Admin)).

(c) Where the document represents information that has been passed from person to person, each person receiving the information did so in a trade, business, professional, etc capacity (s 117(2)(c)).

Consider the following example:

Alf is charged with theft of computer parts from Stock Room D of the building where he works as a packer. The prosecution allege that the goods went missing on the evening of 3 March. The computer parts were found in Alf's house and the serial numbers for each part was identified. Consider the following items of evidence:

1. A timesheet recording that Alf was due to pack in Stock Room D on 3 March from 3 pm to 11 pm. The person who filled out the timesheet, Anil, can attend court but cannot remember any details. The system for filling out the sheet is that each stock room has a foreman who informs Anil who was in that room on each day, when they started and when they left.

2. A checklist which records the serial numbers of all parts consigned to each warehouse. On the list the serial numbers for the computer parts found at Alf's house appear in the column headed 'Stock Room D'. A witness can prove that the usual process for recording the information is either for the person compiling the list to look at the parts himself or for him to have a colleague call the numbers out to him.

Both documents relate to hearsay evidence. Furthermore, neither of the documents would be admissible under s 116:

1. The first document is hearsay because its purpose is to prove that Alf had the opportunity to steal the computer parts when they must have gone missing. As Anil is available, the statement cannot be admitted under the CJA 2003, s 116.

2. The second document is hearsay, being an out of court statement admitted to prove that the stolen parts were in Stock Room D. However, it is not possible to prove the identity of the maker so as to comply with the CJA 2003, s 116(1)(b).

We shall see, however, that both documents fall within the CJA 2003, s 117 as they were both created in the course of a business.

There is little question that the filling out of the documents is a business activity. Furthermore, the information supplied in each case can be proven or inferred to be within the personal knowledge of the supplier of the information. The foreman may be inferred to have had personal knowledge of Alf's presence and either Anil himself or one of his colleagues will have had personal knowledge of the serial numbers.

11.2.2.2   Multiple hearsay

Section 117(2)(c) of the CJA 2003 makes particular provision for situations where the information has been received down a chain of communication. However such 'multiple hearsay' is only admissible if every person who received the *information* contained in the document *received* it in the course of a trade, business, etc. Note that the person who first *supplied* the information does not have to be acting in the course of a trade business or profession, etc. Consider the following examples:

(a) A guest tells a receptionist at a hotel that she saw a man outside room 203. The receptionist writes a note on piece of paper, which is then recorded in a daily log by an unknown employee. The hotel manager reads the daily log and makes an entry in a record book. Only the record book is now available. Can it be used to prove the man was outside room 203?

(b) Same as above but the guest says to the receptionist 'My husband says he saw a man outside room 203'.

In the first situation the record book could be admissible documentary evidence even though its author had no first-hand knowledge of the matters to which it relates. Each person received the information in the course of their business and it is reasonable to suppose that the guest had first-hand knowledge of the matters in question. However, in the second situation, the guest who passes on the information received it from her husband and therefore it has not been received in a trade or business capacity by 'every person through whom it was supplied'.

In the second scenario, it is unlikely that the statement would be admissible as multiple hearsay (see **11.5**)

In Alf's case the documents would fall within s 117(2)(c) because the information in both documents (Alf's presence for the first document and the serial numbers for the second document) was received by a person (Anil) in the course of business.

11.2.2.3 Documents prepared for criminal investigations or proceedings

Obviously a police officer or customs officer will be acting in the course of a profession and therefore any document created by them is potentially covered by s 117. Furthermore a police officer recording information given by a member of the public would be receiving such information in the course of his or her profession. To prevent s 117 from undermining the principle that witnesses attend to give evidence, the information contained a police notebook as a result of something a witness says (for example) is subject to same requirements as would be a document created by that witness. Before either can be used instead of the witness, there must be a good reason why the witness himself or herself cannot attend. However s 117 provides an additional justification for admitting the evidence. Therefore a s 117 statement created during a criminal investigation or for pending proceedings will be admissible if the maker of the statement is:

- dead;
- physically unfit to be a witness;
- mentally unfit to be a witness;
- abroad and cannot reasonably be made to attend court;
- not reasonably traceable;
- unwilling to give evidence through fear; or
- likely (for justifiable reasons) not to be able remember the details contained in the statement.

It is the person who supplied the information who must be unable to attend court as a witness or to remember the information and not the person who recorded and received the information.

11.2.2.4 Power to restrict admissibility under the CJA 2003, s 117

Section 117(6) of the CJA 2003 states that the court can direct that any document otherwise admissible under this section (whether created for criminal proceedings or not) will not be admissible. The court may do so if satisfied that the statement is unreliable having regard to the contents of the documents, the source of the information, how the information was supplied or received or the document was created or received (s 117(7)). This power to regulate the admissibility of the evidence focuses on questions of the reliability of the document rather than the effect of admitting the document on the parties in the case. Therefore, an anonymous note scribbled on a piece of paper and left at a police station that alleges that a particular person has committed a crime would not have to be admitted simply because it otherwise complies with the CJA 2003, s 117.

The courts will not, in determining admissibility at this point, consider issues other than reliability, for example whether a defendant is deprived of an opportunity to cross-examine the maker of the document or otherwise challenge its contents. Such matters will be relevant to the general exclusionary discretions (see **11.6.1** below).

11.2.3   Previous inconsistent statements

Whether a previous inconsistent statement is admissible is considered in **Chapter 6** of this Manual at **6.3.6**. Where such a statement is admissible, s 119(1) of the CJA 2003 provides that the statement is admissible as evidence of the truth of the contents. Before the 2003 Act the document was only admissible to diminish the credibility of the person who made the statement.

Insofar as a statement under s 119 is proven by a document and that document therefore becomes an exhibit in the case, s 122 provides that the document should not be taken to the jury room when the jury retires unless either the court considers it appropriate or all the parties in the case agree.

11.2.4   Other previous statements by witnesses

Section 120 of the CJA 2003 also changes the common law in relation to previous statements that are consistent with the testimony that they give at trial. Previous consistent statements were considered in **6.2.4.2**.

Section 120 of the CJA 2003 applies in relation to previous statements made by someone who does attend court to give evidence as a witness (s 120(1)). None of the statements considered under s 120 will be admissible if the witness does not attend to give evidence (although they could, of course be admissible if they comply with the requirements of ss 116 to 118).

Section 120 deals with three types of previous statements:

- previous statements admitted to rebut an allegation of fabrication;
- memory refreshing documents that, by reason of the cross-examination of the witness have become evidence in the proceedings;
- statements of identification or description etc.

The restriction on the use of the document by the jury when they retire to consider their verdict identified in relation to s 119 applies equally to any document proving a statement under any of the grounds in s 120.

11.2.4.1   Statements in rebuttal of fabrication and memory refreshing documents

Section 120 of the CJA 2003 provides:

(2)   *If a previous statement by the witness is admitted as evidence to rebut a suggestion that his oral evidence has been fabricated, that statement is admissible as evidence of any matter stated of which oral evidence by the witness would be admissible.*

(3)   *A statement made by the witness in a document—*

    (a)   *which is used by him to refresh his memory while giving evidence,*

    (b)   *on which he is cross-examined, and*

    (c)   *which as a consequence is received in evidence in the proceedings, is admissible as evidence of any matter stated of which oral evidence by him would be admissible.*

These two subsections have not changed the law relating to the admissibility of such evidence (see **6.2.4.2**). However the effect of these subsections is that the statements can be used as additional evidence of the facts alleged rather than simply to bolster the credibility of the testimony of the maker.

11.2.4.2   Statements of identification or description etc

Section 120(4) to (8) of the CJA 2003 provides for the admissibility of three types of statements where the witness gives evidence and adopts the statement as his own and truthful in the course of testimony (s 120(4)(b)).

Section 120 provides:

> (4) A previous statement by the witness is admissible as evidence of any matter stated of which oral evidence by him would be admissible, if—
>
>   (a) any of the following three conditions is satisfied, and
>
>   (b) while giving evidence the witness indicates that to the best of his belief he made the statement, and that to the best of his belief it states the truth.
>
> (5) The first condition is that the statement identifies or describes a person, object or place.
>
> (6) The second condition is that the statement was made by the witness when the matters stated were fresh in his memory but he does not remember them, and cannot reasonably be expected to remember them, well enough to give oral evidence of them in the proceedings.
>
> (7) The third condition is that—
>
>   (a) the witness claims to be a person against whom an offence has been committed,
>
>   (b) the offence is one to which the proceedings relate,
>
>   (c) the statement consists of a complaint made by the witness (whether to a person in authority or not) about conduct which would, if proved, constitute the offence or part of the offence,
>
>   (d) the complaint was made as soon as could reasonably be expected after the alleged conduct,
>
>   (e) the complaint was not made as a result of a threat or a promise, and
>
>   (f) before the statement is adduced the witness gives oral evidence in connection with its subject matter.
>
> (8) For the purposes of subsection (7) the fact that the complaint was elicited (for example, by a leading question) is irrelevant unless a threat or a promise was involved.

The statement will be admitted if it fulfils any one of the conditions set out below. They are:

First condition (s 120(5))

The statement is one of identification or description.

This is not restricted to a person but also includes identification or descriptions of objects or places. Therefore a witness attacked on a street could adopt a statement of the precise location and its layout, the appearance of the defendant and of the peculiar knife used in the attack.

Second condition (s 120(6))

There are three requirements:

- the statement was made when the matters were fresh in the witness's memory; and
- the witness cannot remember the matters; and
- the witness cannot reasonably be expected to remember the matters.

This condition applies to any witness. The witness would have to testify as to the failure of her recollection of the events. What a witness may reasonably be expected to give evidence of and how well matters must be remembered 'to be able to give oral evidence of them in proceedings' will be matters for the tribunal of law to decide in determining admissibility under this subsection. Clearly, the more intricate or remote the events about which the evidence is to be given, the more reasonable it is for the witness not to remember them. However, where the court is concerned with traumatic events there may be difficult arguments as to whether such events should be more or less memorable. It is likely, given the language used, that the courts will have to have regard to what it is reasonable for the particular witness to remember rather than to adopt any objective standard.

Third condition (s 120(7), (8))

The third condition expands the common law rule that recent complaints by victims of sexual offences are admissible to bolster the credibility of the testimony of the complainant. The requirements for the application of s 120(7) are:

- the witness is the alleged victim to an offence being tried (s 120(7)(a), (b)); and
- the statement is a complaint to any person that the offence has been committed (s 120(7)(c)); and
- the complaint was made as soon as could reasonably be expected after the alleged offence (s 120(7)(d)); and
- there was no pressure or threat leading to the complaint (s 120(7)(e)) although it can have been the result of leading questions (s 120(8)); and
- the witness has given some testimony on the offence (s 120(7)(f)) although one would assume by virtue of the second condition (s 120(6)) not detailed testimony.

Therefore, the CJA 2003, s 120(7) can only be used to prove statements by the victim of the crime who gives evidence of that crime. The crime no longer has to be a sexual offence and the statement is admissible to prove the truth of what was alleged in the statement. The following principles from the common law on previous complaints are likely to continue to apply:

(a) The subsection applies to statements made in private, such as entries in a diary not intended to be seen by any other person (*R v B* [1997] Crim LR 220).

(b) What is 'as soon as could reasonably be expected' is a question for the judge (*R v Cummings* [1948] 1 All ER 551, CA). However, s 120(7)(d) has removed the common law test of 'first reasonable opportunity', which the courts had, in any event, interpreted to allow some delay (*R v Valentine* [1996] 2 Cr App R 213, CA). On the other hand pre-CJA 2003 case law on this area was exclusively concerned with sexual offences. What is reasonable to expect of a victim of a crime without the perceived social stigma of a sexual offence will be different.

11.3 Admissibility under preserved common law exceptions

Section 118(1) of the CJA 2003 preserves the following common law exceptions to the rule against hearsay:

- public information;
- evidence of reputation;
- *res gestae*;
- confessions;
- admissions by agents;
- common enterprise;
- expert evidence;

Otherwise all of the common law rules concerning the admissibility of hearsay evidence in criminal proceedings are abolished by the CJA 2003, s 118(2).

11.3.1   Public information

Section 118(1) provides the following description of the common law rules preserved:

Public Information etc.

1   *Any rule of law under which in criminal proceedings—*
   (a)   *published works dealing with matters of a public nature (such as histories, scientific works, dictionaries and maps) are admissible as evidence of facts of a public nature stated in them,*
   (b)   *public documents (such as public registers, and returns made under public authority with respect to matters of public interest) are admissible as evidence of facts stated in them,*
   (c)   *records (such as the records of certain courts, treaties, Crown grants, pardons and commissions) are admissible as evidence of facts stated in them, or*
   (d)   *evidence relating to a person's age or date or place of birth may be given by a person without personal knowledge of the matter.*

Whether a document is 'public' is a question of degree and does not require proof that the document had to be of relevance to the whole world. Rather, it was necessary that it concerned all the people interested in the matter in question (*Sturla v Freccia* (1880) 5 App Cas 623). For details of the types of documents that fit within this exception see *Blackstone's Criminal Practice*, 2005 at F 16.25 to F 16.27.

11.3.2   Reputation

Section 118(1), paragraphs 2 and 3 preserve the following rules:

Reputation as to character

2   *Any rule of law under which in criminal proceedings evidence of a person's reputation is admissible for the purpose of proving his good or bad character.*

Note

The rule is preserved only so far as it allows the court to treat such evidence as proving the matter concerned.

Reputation or family tradition

3   *Any rule of law under which in criminal proceedings evidence of reputation or family tradition is admissible for the purpose of proving or disproving—*
   (a)   *pedigree or the existence of a marriage,*
   (b)   *the existence of any public or general right, or*
   (c)   *the identity of any person or thing.*

Note

The rule is preserved only so far as it allows the court to treat such evidence as proving or disproving the matter concerned.

Proof of the character of a person by reputation is only permitted where the proof of the character in question is admissible evidence: see generally **Chapters 7, 8** and **9**.

11.3.3   *Res gestae*

Section 118(1) states the rule which it preserves under the heading '*res gestae*' as follows:

4   *Any rule of law under which in criminal proceedings a statement is admissible as evidence of any matter stated if—*
   (a)   *the statement was made by a person so emotionally overpowered by an event that the possibility of concoction or distortion can be disregarded,*

   (b)   the statement accompanied an act which can be properly evaluated as evidence only if considered in conjunction with the statement, or

   (c)   the statement relates to a physical sensation or a mental state (such as intention or emotion).

The above is not intended to define the *res gestae* rule, merely to identify it. The definition of *res gestae* is a matter for the common law.

Statements forming part of the *res gestae* fall into a number of different categories. The phrase '*res gestae*' is used by the law to identify the event in question. The various *res gestae* exceptions loosely conform to a principle that the statement must be made at or about the same time as the matter to which it relates. In other words, there is some requirement of contemporaneity. Quite what the statement relates to for each exception varies as shall be seen below. The logic of these exceptions is that statements made at the time of the event or matter are less likely to be made up or distorted than statements made at a later point.

11.3.3.1   Statements contemporaneous to an emotionally overpowering event

This category of *res gestae* statement is one that is made by someone as an event is taking place and where the event is dominating or overwhelming the mind of the person making the statement.

The test for admissibility for this type of *res gestae* statement is set out in *R v Andrews* [1987] AC 281 where a man was attacked and mortally wounded by two others. The prosecution called police officers to give evidence that the victim told them that Andrews was one of the attackers. Clearly this was a hearsay statement adduced to prove that fact. The House of Lords held that nonetheless the statement was admissible under the *res gestae* exception. In doing so Lord Ackner defined the test of admissibility (at p 300) as follows:

(a) The primary question which the judge must ask himself or herself is — can the possibility of concoction or distortion be disregarded?

(b) To answer that question the judge must first consider the circumstances in which the particular statement was made, in order to satisfy himself or herself that the event was so unusual or startling or dramatic as to dominate the thoughts of the maker so that his utterance was an instinctive reaction to that event, thus giving no real opportunity for reasoned reflection. In such a situation the judge would be entitled to conclude that the involvement or the pressure of the event would exclude the possibility of concoction or distortion, providing that the statement was made in conditions of approximate but not exact contemporaneity.

Therefore:

(a) The primary test is whether concoction or distortion can be disregarded.

(b) This test is passed if the judge concludes (ie it is proved to him or her that):

   (i)   There was an 'unusual or *startling* or dramatic' *event*.

   (ii)   That event therefore *dominated the thoughts* of the maker of the statement.

   (iii)   As a result of that domination of the thoughts, the statement was an 'instinctive reaction' to the event. In other words, the statement was *spontaneous*.

   (iv)   The statement was *approximately contemporaneous*.

Lord Ackner made the following additional points:

(a) On the issue of spontaneity Lord Ackner said:

   (i)   The statement must be 'so closely associated with the event . . . that it can fairly be said that the mind of the declarant was still dominated by the event'.

(ii) The judge must be satisfied that the 'event, which provided the trigger mechanism was still operative'.

(iii) That the statement is a response to a question is only a factor to consider in deciding whether the statement was sufficiently spontaneous.

(b) The judge should consider any factors other than the passage of time that might, in the circumstances of each case, support any argument that the statement was concocted or distorted. In *R v Andrews*, for example, it was alleged that the victim had a malicious motive to fabricate evidence against Andrews. In such cases the judge must be satisfied that there was no possibility of any concoction or distortion having regard to the allegations of malice.

(c) Generally any risk that the person hearing and repeating the statement has made an error goes to the weight not the admissibility of the statement. However, where a special feature is alleged to have caused the mistake such as drunkenness (as was the case in *R v Andrews*) or short sightedness, the judge must 'consider whether he can exclude the possibility of error'. If not, it would seem the judge may have to exclude the statement.

Note the importance of proof of these matters. Whether or not a particular statement fits within this exception will have to be established by evidence. In *Teper v R* [1952] AC 480, PC, the statement was made to a police officer by an unknown person. It was held that as it was not known who had made the statement, it was *unlikely* to be possible to rely on this exception. This is because it is unlikely that it will be possible to prove that the maker's mind was dominated by the event if it is not known who the maker is. However, there may be circumstances in which there is evidence to suggest that the statement was made by an unknown person whose mind was dominated. This will be a matter of proof in each case.

The statement must be approximately contemporaneous. This will be a question of fact in each case. In *Tobi v Nichols* [1988] RTR 343, a statement made 20 minutes after a collision was determined not to be sufficiently contemporaneous. However it was also considered that the event was not sufficiently mind-dominating. It is submitted that there is a correlation between the nature of the event and how long after it a statement may be roughly contemporaneous. The more traumatic the event, the better the argument that it is still dominating the mind of the maker at a later point. In *R v Carnall* [1995] Crim LR 944, for example, a statement made an hour after a murderous assault was held to have been rightly admitted. As the statement must be a reaction to or part of the event, statements made before the event in question cannot be part of this category of *res gestae* exception (*R v Newport* [1998] Crim LR 581).

There are no particular requirements that the person who made the statement is dead or unavailable at the time of trial (*R v Nye* (1977) 66 Cr App R 252). Even statements made by the accused can be part of the *res gestae* and therefore admitted by either party. In *R v Glover* [1991] Crim LR 48, the accused said 'I am David Glover . . . we will not think twice about shooting you and your kids'. As the trial issue was identity, the prosecution were allowed to call this statement as part of the *res gestae*. However, in *R v Andrews*, Lord Ackner observed that it would be wrong to use this *res gestae* exception to avoid calling the witness in question so as to deprive other parties of an opportunity to cross-examine the maker of the statement. However, in *Attorney-General's Reference (No 1 of 2003)* [2003] 2 Cr App Rep 453, the Court of Appeal ruled that there was no requirement that a witness was unavailable before a statement made by that witness would be admissible under the doctrine of *res gestae*. However where the prosecution sought to rely on a *res gestae* statement made by a person who could be called as a witness but who the prosecution did not propose to call, the trial judge had a discretion under s 78 of the Police and Criminal Evidence Act 1984 to exclude the *res gestae* statements. In deciding whether to do so the court would have regard to the circumstances in which the statement was made and how easy it would have been to call the witness.

11.3.3.2   Contemporaneous statements accompanying an act

Such statements must be:

(a) Approximately contemporaneous to the act. In *Howe v Malkin* (1878) 40 LT 196, it was said that such a statement was admissible because it was mixed up with the event in question.

(b) Made by the person performing the act (*Peacock v Harris* (1836) 5 Ad & El 449).

(c) The act should itself be relevant to the issues in the case (in *R v McCay* [1990] 1 WLR 645, the statement 'It's number 8', was made at the same time as a person was identified in an identification parade).

11.3.3.3   Contemporaneous statements relating to the maker's physical or mental state

A statement made by a person in which he or she refers to his or her current physical state will be admissible to prove that physical state.

The statement can prove the physical state but not its cause (*R v Gloster* (1888) 16 Cox CC 471). Therefore in *R v Thomson* [1912] 3 KB 19 statements by a woman that she had recently operated upon herself were not admissible to prove the cause of a miscarriage.

The statements do not have to be made at the exact time that the feelings are being experienced: whether a statement is contemporary to the feeling is a question of degree. In *Aveson v Lord Kinnaird* (1805) 6 East 188, statements made by a woman as to symptoms she said she had been suffering for some time were admitted to prove that she not only was suffering those symptoms when she made the statement but also that she had suffered them some days earlier.

So far as the maker's state of mind is concerned, statements revealing that a person was of a particular frame of mind could be original evidence (eg *Thomas v Connell* (1838) 4 M & W 267, as confirmed by the approach of the courts in *R v Blastland* [1986] AC 41, and *R v Kearley*). This is probably the best approach to cases from which a state of mind is inferred (ie, because A said a particular thing we can infer a particular state of mind or particular emotional state). Clearly, however, where a person expressly states that he or she is of a particular state of mind (such as 'I hate that man,' or 'I believe he is the one who stole my watch') there can be little doubt that the statement is hearsay evidence.

However such a statement will be admissible as an exception to the rule against hearsay evidence if it is sufficiently contemporaneous. Statements of one's state of mind at an earlier time are not admissible (*R v Moghal* (1977) 65 Cr App R 56).

A particular difficulty arises from this rule where a statement of a contemporaneous fact is used to prove what happened at a later date. The usual case is one in which the statement reveals the intention of the maker and the issue is whether the maker later acted on that intention. Consider the following cases:

(a) *R v Buckley* (1838) 13 Cox CC 293: a statement made by a police officer that he intended to keep a watch on the accused was admitted to prove that he had later been keeping a watch on the accused when he was murdered.

(b) *R v Moghal* (above): a statement made by S that she intended to kill R was held to be admissible to prove that she and not the accused had killed R even though the statement had been made six months before.

(c) *R v Callender* [1998] Crim LR 337: statements made by a person two weeks before he was arrested on explosives charges that he intended to carry false explosive devices for publicity purposes was held not to be admissible.

The case law in this area appears confused. It is submitted that the best view to take of cases about current intentions is that such statements of intention are admissible under this exception but only if relevant. If the statements are not sufficiently relevant, they should not be admitted. This was the view taken in *R v Blastland* in which the statement in *R v Moghal* was criticised as insufficiently relevant. For a further criticism of *R v Callender*, see *Black- stone's Criminal Practice*, 2005, at F16.37.

11.3.4 Confessions and admissions

Section 118(1), paragraph 5 provides for the continued operation of the admissibility of confessions and mixed statements as an exception to the rule against hearsay. Confession evidence is dealt with in detail in **Chapter 12**. Mixed statements are considered at **6.2.4.2**.

Section 118(1), paragraph 6 provides for the continued operation at common law of the rule whereby admissions made by an agent (*R v Turner* (1975) 61 Cr App R 67) or a person appointed by the defendant to answer questions on the defendant's behalf (*Williams v Innes* (1808) Camp 364) will be admissible in evidence against the defendant. The agency must be proven by evidence independently of the agent's assertions (*R v Evans* [1981] Crim LR 699).

11.3.5 Common enterprise

Paragraph 7 of s 118(1) preserves:

> 7 *Any rule of law under which in criminal proceedings a statement made by a party to a common enterprise is admissible against another party to the enterprise as evidence of any matter stated.*

Where, in the course of committing a crime, A makes a statement which proves that B was also committing the same crime, the common law allows such matters to be admitted as proof of the fact that B committed the crime. This rule should be contrasted with the rule that generally a confession is only admissible against the person who makes it and not another person.

Before a statement will be admissible under this exception, however, it must be established that:

- there was a common criminal purpose or enterprise; and
- The statement was made to pursue or further that purpose.

11.3.5.1 Common purpose

A common purpose is wider than a conspiracy. In *R v Jones* [1997] 2 Cr App R 119, CA, for example, the doctrine was applied to the offence of evading the prohibition on the importation of drugs (drug smuggling) even though there was no charge of conspiracy on the indictment. However there does have to be some common element of commission of the offence. In *R v Gray* [1995] 2 Cr App R 100, there had been an allegation of a 'network' between various co-accused as to insider dealing but each accused was charged with separate offences. The Court of Appeal concluded that, in the absence of some allegation that the offences had been committed jointly, the rule did not apply. Usually such an allegation would arise from the way in which the accused persons were charged. Therefore even if there does not have to be conspiracy charged, the rule will generally only apply where the parties are jointly charged, whether as principals or as secondary parties. The court did leave open the possibility that future cases may involve a common purpose even if the various parties were charged with separate offences but did not define how that might be the case.

The existence of the common purpose must be proved by evidence independent to the statement to be admitted under the exception (*R v Blake* (1844) 6 QB 126). In other words, what is said in the statement cannot prove that there was a common purpose and the jury should be directed that they cannot rely on the statement itself to prove the existence of such a common purpose (*r v Williams* [2002] EWCA Crim 2208). However the court can conditionally admit the evidence of the statement subject to proof at some later stage of the common purpose (*R v Governor of Pentonville Prison, ex p Osman* [1990] 1 WLR 277). If the existence of a common purpose cannot subsequently be proven by independent evidence, the statement will have to be excluded from the case against any co-accused (*R v Donat* (1985) 82 Cr App R 173) and, in jury trials, a direction will have to be given directing the jury to ignore the evidence or they may have to be discharged.

11.3.5.2   Furtherance of the common purpose

A statement made after the criminal purpose has been achieved or one that simply explains what another member has done without advancing it in any way, will not be 'in furtherance' of the common purpose and therefore not admissible (*R v Walters* (1979) 69 Cr App R 115; *R v Steward* [1963] Crim LR 697).

What is capable of being a statement in furtherance of a common purpose will depend on the facts of the case. In *R v Devonport* [1996] 1 Cr App R 221, the statement concerned the intended division of proceeds from a drug deal. This was treated as in furtherance of the common purpose. However, in *R v Blake* (1844) 6 QB 126, a cheque proving that B had received his share of the proceeds from a conspiracy was held not to be in furtherance of the common purpose. In the former case the statement assisted or encouraged the commission of the offence whereas in the latter case it was simply a consequence of it.

Where the evidence that is alleged to prove the common purpose is a document, it will be necessary to prove (a) it was either made in a particular (and relevant) way or to have been found in an incriminating way, and (b) that it suggests the involvement of the defendants in the common purpose (*R v Jenkins* [2003] Crim LR 107). Merely producing the document without proving it in this way will not render it admissible as evidence of the common purpose.

The courts have interpreted what furthers the purpose quite loosely. In *R v Ilyas* [1996] Crim LR 810, the diary of A was admitted to prove that B, C an D had received stolen cars, Latham J appearing to extend the definition to documents 'created in the course of, or furtherance, of the conspiracy'.

11.3.6   Expert evidence

Section 118(1), paragraph 8 preserves:

> 8   *Any rule of law under which in criminal proceedings an expert witness may draw on the body of expertise relevant to his field.*

Expert evidence is considered in detail in **Chapter 15**. There it will be seen that experts are, understandably, entitled to rely upon hearsay in the sense that they can rely on the observations and writings of other experts in their field of expertise.

However, the rule that the data upon which the expert's opinion is based has to be proven by admissible evidence has been relaxed by the CJA 2003, s 127, which provides that an expert can base his or her opinion on information contained in a statement prepared for criminal purposes if the fact that the expert will do so is notified to the other parties. The other parties have the opportunity to object to such a use of the statement. Where such a statement is used, s 127(3) provides that the statement becomes evidence of its contents.

11.4   Admissibility in the interests of justice

Section 114(1)(d) of the Criminal Justice Act 2003 provides that the court may admit hearsay evidence in the absence of the agreement under s 114(1)(c) or any specific statutory or common law rule in s 114(1)(a) and (b) where to do so would be in the interests of justice.
   Section 114(2) provides:

(2)   *In deciding whether a statement not made in oral evidence should be admitted under subsection (1)(d), the court must have regard to the following factors (and to any others it considers relevant)—*

   (a)   *how much probative value the statement has (assuming it to be true) in relation to a matter in issue in the proceedings, or how valuable it is for the understanding of other evidence in the case;*

   (b)   *what other evidence has been, or can be, given on the matter or evidence mentioned in paragraph (a);*

   (c)   *how important the matter or evidence mentioned in paragraph (a) is in the context of the case as a whole;*

   (d)   *the circumstances in which the statement was made;*

   (e)   *how reliable the maker of the statement appears to be;*

   (f)   *how reliable the evidence of the making of the statement appears to be;*

   (g)   *whether oral evidence of the matter stated can be given and, if not, why it cannot;*

   (h)   *the amount of difficulty involved in challenging the statement;*

   (i)   *the extent to which that difficulty would be likely to prejudice the party facing it.*

Some of the factors under the CJA 2003, s 114 concern the probative value of the hearsay evidence. Under s 114(2)(a) the court must assume that the statement is true when assessing its probative value. This means that the question for the court is how much impact it would have on the case if accepted by the jury not whether they are likely to accept it as true. However, under paragraphs (e) and (f) the court can also consider any evidence of the reliability of both the maker of the statement and the circumstances of the making of the statement.

   Other factors concern the importance of the evidence to the trial process. Paragraph (a) requires the court to consider the impact of the evidence on the trial and paragraph (b) requires consideration of alternative means of proving the facts the statement would prove. Paragraph (c) requires consideration of the matter that is proven to the trial issues. Therefore, hearsay evidence going to a collateral issue such as the credibility of a witness that is not admissible under any other rule in the CJA 2003 is less likely to be admissible than hearsay evidence relevant that directly proves one of the facts in issue.

   Given that hearsay evidence is intended not to substitute oral evidence, the court is required to consider the availability of other oral evidence (s 114(2)(g)) and the difficulties of challenging the evidence given the lack of the opportunity to cross examine the maker (s 114(2)(h)).

   A final type of consideration concerns the extent to which the evidence could cause prejudice to the party facing it (paragraph (i)).

The court will probably use many of the principles developed in exercising the exclusionary powers under the Criminal Justice Act 1988, ss 25 and 26, which required consideration of similar factors. The following issues in particular should be noted:

(a) Where such a statement is admitted instead of calling the maker to give evidence, it will often not be possible to controvert it by cross-examination. Therefore the only way to challenge the statement will often be by the accused giving evidence. However the accused may wish not to do so. The fact that the accused would be put under pressure to give evidence as a result of the statement to be admitted will not dictate where the 'interests of justice' lie (*R v Cole* [1990] 2 All ER 108; *R v Gokal* [1997] 2 Cr App R 266).

(b) Whether the 'interests of justice' test can cause difficulties where there is more than one accused. In such circumstances admitting the evidence may cause difficulties for one accused while not admitting the evidence may cause difficulties for another. For example, in *R v Duffy* [1999] 1 Cr App R 307, CA, two accused, D and H, were charged with murder and robbery. The statement by the son of the victim suggested D had attempted to dissuade H from killing the victim. The prosecution sought to prove the statement, which H opposed under s 26 of the Criminal Justice Act 1988 on the ground that H would not be able to cross-examine the maker of the statement. The trial judge declined to grant leave to admit the statement. D, who had therefore been deprived of support for her defence, appealed. The Court of Appeal allowed her appeal. In doing so they contrasted the interests of justice of each accused. On the one hand, while H could not cross-examine the maker of the statement, he could still have controverted the statement by giving evidence himself. In contrast D had suffered by the decision not to admit the evidence as she was deprived of support for her evidence. Therefore the interests of justice should have favoured D over H and the statement should therefore have been admitted. In *R v Lake Estates Water sports Ltd* [2002] EWCA Crim 2067, the Court of Appeal considered that the trial judge should have had regard to the late stage in the proceedings at which the prosecution had sought to admit a statement. The court concluded that the statement should not have been admitted as the defendant had been deprived of a chance to call an expert witness to rebut the evidence contained in the statement.

(c) The quality of the evidence will be an important factor in determining whether or not to grant leave. Where the evidence is of marginal value, the court may decide not to admit it (see for example *R v Patel* (1993) 97 Cr App R 294, CA), whereas if the evidence is of high clarity and precision it is more likely to be admitted (*R v Fairfax* [1995] Crim LR 949).

(d) The significance of the evidence will also be an important factor. In *Neill v North Antrim Magistrates' Court* [1992] 1 WLR 1221, for example, the court concluded that if the statement contains evidence of identification, the court will generally be reluctant to admit it. Such evidence would be particularly difficult to challenge effectively given that the witness cannot be cross-examined. Where the evidence of the witness is central to the case, the approach of the courts has varied. In cases such as *R v French* (1993) 97 Cr App R 421, the courts have been reluctant to admit evidence where there is no other evidence on the issue. However, in cases such as *R v Dragic* [1996] 2 Cr App R 232, the courts have shown willingness to admit statements even when they are the only source of evidence on a crucial issue. The extent to which the statement provides the only evidence on a crucial issue would appear to be a strong factor. Furthermore, the court will have regard to the extent to which the loss of the opportunity to cross-examine the maker of the statement conflicts with the right to a fair trial under article 6 of the European Convention on Human Rights and in particular article 6(3)(d) which provides for the accused's right to cross-examine witnesses: see *R v Thomas* [1998] Crim LR 887, CA in which regard to article 6(3)(d) did not lead to the exclusion of evidence and *R v Radak* [1999] 1 Cr App R 187, CA, in which the court excluded a s 23 statement that it regarded as an essential link in the prosecution case. In *R v KM* The Times, 2 May 2003, the Court of Appeal overturned a conviction which was wholly based on a statement by a complainant witness who had been mentally unfit to attend. To base all of the prosecution case on evidence that the accused could not cross-examine was considered to be a breach of Article 6 of the European Convention.

Consider again the situation of the homeless person at **11.2.1.2.** It was noted there that the statement the person would not be admissible under the CJA 2003, s 116 as the maker was not identifiable. Nor would the statement of identification be admissible under the CJA 2003, s 120 as the maker did not give evidence. Nor would the statement fit within any of the preserved common law exceptions. Could the statement be admitted under s 114(1)(d)? There would be no certainty that it would: the evidence concerns an important issue in the case (s 114(2)(a)), namely identity, and nothing is known of the maker of the statement that would allow his credibility as a witness to be properly challenged (s 114(2)(e) and (h)). On the other hand, if, for example, the victim was unable to make an identification of her attacker, there may be no other evidence on this important matter (s 114(2)(a), (b), (c) and (g)).

11.5 Multiple hearsay

Consider the following example. Eric sees Frank one evening in a particular place where a robbery has occurred and says to Devon, 'Frank was near No 10 Gerrard Street last night'. Devon repeats this to Charlie. None of the people mentioned receives the information in any professional or business capacity. Clearly Eric could testify that he saw Frank: that is his personal experience. Devon could (in principle) also give evidence, under s 116(2), of what he heard Eric say if there is a reason why Eric is not available. But could Charlie also repeat the statement made by Devon?

The problem that is posed is that of multiple hearsay. Section 117 of the CJA 2003 makes specific provision for multiple hearsay contained in documents and received by people acting in the course of a trade, business, etc. For situations other than that, s 121 provides:

> (1) A hearsay statement is not admissible to prove the fact that an earlier hearsay statement was made unless—
>
> (a) either of the statements is admissible under section 117, 119 or 120,
> (b) all parties to the proceedings so agree, or
> (c) the court is satisfied that the value of the evidence in question, taking into account how reliable the statements appear to be, is so high that the interests of justice require the later statement to be admissible for that purpose.
>
> (2) In this section 'hearsay statement' means a statement, not made in oral evidence, that is relied on as evidence of a matter stated in it.

Section 121(1) requires consideration of the admissibility of the two hearsay statements: the first-hand hearsay statement (in our case what Devon said) and the second-hand hearsay statement (what Eric said). If either of those two statements is admissible under the CJA 2003, ss 117, 119 or 120 then both are admissible. In our case neither is. Therefore, the statement would only be admissible if all the parties agree to its admissibility (s 121(1)(b)) or it is in the interests of justice to admit it (s 121(1)(c)).

Note that the interests of justice test for these purposes is different to that in s 114. This test specifically links the interests of justice to the probative value of the evidence and does not require consideration of other factors. Furthermore, the CJA 2003 does not make clear whether the two tests are mutually exclusive. It would seem logical that, in defining this specific inclusionary power for multiple hearsay, Parliament intended the test in s 114 not to apply but the matter may be open to argument in the appellate courts.

Consider Frank's case with the following alternatives:

- Devon is a police officer, who wrote a note of what was said that somehow comes into the possession of Charlie other than in the course of a business;
- Eric gives evidence at trial and testifies that he and Frank were at a football match in another town at the time;
- Eric gives evidence but has difficulty remembering exactly where he saw Frank at the time but does remember having seen him that evening.

In each of these situations the statement would become admissible. In the first situation Devon's notebook would be admissible evidence under s 117. In the second situation, Eric has made a previous inconsistent statement that could be admissible under s 119 and in the third case the statement by Eric could be admissible under s 120(4). Therefore, for all three statements Charlie could give evidence as to the whole chain of statements. Charlie can prove Devon's statement under s 116. Devon's statement could be admitted as evidence of any fact of which admissible evidence could be given. By virtue of s 121 that includes what Eric said.

11.6   Exclusion of the evidence

11.6.1   General discretions to exclude evidence

Section 126(1) of the CJA 2003 creates a general discretion to exclude hearsay evidence and s 126(2) preserves the operation of the exclusionary discretions that apply to criminal law generally in relation to such evidence.

Section 126(1) states:

(1)   In criminal proceedings the court may refuse to admit a statement as evidence of a matter stated if—

(a)   the statement was made otherwise than in oral evidence in the proceedings, and

(b)   the court is satisfied that the case for excluding the statement, taking account of the danger that to admit it would result in undue waste of time, substantially outweighs the case for admitting it, taking account of the value of the evidence.

The exclusion applies to any hearsay evidence that would otherwise be admitted in criminal proceedings. Therefore, it could restrict the admissibility of hearsay evidence admitted under a common law exception preserved under s 118 as much as under any hearsay admitted under the CJA 2003. The section also applies to restrict hearsay evidence irrespective of which party is seeking to adduce it.

The meaning of the subsection is less than clear. There are two possibilities:

(a) There is a broad discretion to exclude evidence if the case for admitting the evidence is 'substantially outweighed' by the case for excluding it. The 'waste of time' and 'value of the evidence' are merely factors to be taken into account among other factors in exercising this discretion.

(b) There is a narrow discretion to exclude evidence where the risk of time being wasted creates a case for excluding the evidence that substantially outweighs the case for admitting it, having regard to the value of the evidence.

The authors of *Blackstone's Guide to the Criminal Justice Act 2003*, Oxford University Press, 2004 favour the broader ground not least because of the need to provide the safeguards of the article 6 right to fair trial. In addition to this, if the narrow interpretation is correct there is no specific provision within the CJA 2003 for the exclusion of evidence on the grounds that the evidence jeopardises the right to a fair trial or that it is contrary the interests of justice. Evidence admitted under the Criminal Justice Act 1988, ss 23 and 24 could be excluded under ss 25 and 26 of that Act, having regard to the interests of justice. These provisions were interpreted to preserve the right to fair trial. There might be a strong argument that the discretion under the CJA 2003, s 126 was intended by Parliament to continue that protection.

On the other hand, the CJA 2003, s 126(2) expressly retains the exclusionary discretions that apply the criminal law in general. Section 126(2) provides:

> (2) Nothing in this Chapter prejudices—
>> (a) any power of a court to exclude evidence under section 78 of the Police and Criminal Evidence Act 1984 (c. 60) (exclusion of unfair evidence), or
>> (b) any other power of a court to exclude evidence at its discretion (whether by preventing questions from being put or otherwise).

It is possible that the control over hearsay evidence that was effected by ss 25 and 26 of the Criminal Justice Act 1988 will now be achieved by use of the Police and Criminal Evidence Act, s 78 and the common law power to exclude evidence where its probative value is outweighed by its prejudicial effect.

Whether it is the CJA 2003, s 126 or the Police and Criminal Evidence Act, s 78 that allows for the exclusion of evidence in the interests of ensuring a fair trial, it is likely that the principles developed in applying the Criminal Justice Act 1988, ss 25 and 26 will continue to be adopted. These principles are set out at **11.4** above.

11.6.2 Stopping a case

In addition to the power to exclude evidence, the CJA 2003, s 125 provides the court with the power to stop a case where the evidence admitted poses the danger of an unsafe conviction.

Section 125 provides:

> (1) If on a defendant's trial before a judge and jury for an offence the court is satisfied at any time after the close of the case for the prosecution that—
>> (a) the case against the defendant is based wholly or partly on a statement not made in oral evidence in the proceedings, and
>> (b) the evidence provided by the statement is so unconvincing that, considering its importance to the case against the defendant, his conviction of the offence would be unsafe,
>
> the court must either direct the jury to acquit the defendant of the offence or, if it considers that there ought to be a retrial, discharge the jury.
>
> (2) Where—
>> (a) a jury is directed under subsection (1) to acquit a defendant of an offence, and

(b) *the circumstances are such that, apart from this subsection, the defendant could if acquitted of that offence be found guilty of another offence, the defendant may not be found guilty of that other offence if the court is satisfied as mentioned in subsection (1) in respect of it.*

(3) *. . .*

(4) *This section does not prejudice any other power a court may have to direct a jury to acquit a person of an offence or to discharge a jury.*

This section applies only to prosecution evidence (s 125(1)) and only where the case is based 'wholly or partly' on hearsay evidence (s 125(1)(b)). Where that is the case the court must consider both the probative value of the evidence and the importance that it has in determining trial issues. If the court considers it to have minimal probative value to the degree that, due to its importance to the trial issues, it poses the risk of an unsafe conviction, then the court must not simply exclude the evidence but must either direct the jury to acquit the defendant or must discharge the jury and order a retrial. This power is more extensive than the power to acquit following a submission of no case to answer as it can be exercised at any time after the close of the prosecution case.

Where the defendant is acquitted, by virtue of this section, of an offence to which a lesser verdict could be returned, that lesser verdict must not be returned if it also depends on the unconvincing hearsay evidence which has been withdrawn (s 125(2)). Therefore, if the hearsay evidence that is unconvincing relates to the identity of a defendant alleged to have intentionally caused grievous bodily harm on the victim contrary to the Offences Against the Person Act 1861, s 18 the withdrawal of the evidence would not permit a conviction for an offence contrary to the Offences Against the Person Act 1861, s 20. However, if the evidence related to the intention to cause such an injury to the victim, the acquittal for the s 18 offence would not necessarily preclude the jury from continuing to consider the s 20 offence.

11.7 Procedural Issues

11.7.1 Documents

A document must be 'proven' before it will be admissible. This means that the significance of the document to the trial issues must be established. Generally a document is proved by a witness who testifies as to its significance (ie that the witness wrote it or where the witness found it). However, the CJA 2003, s 133 makes further provision for proof of hearsay in documents:

Where a statement in a document is admissible as evidence in criminal proceedings, the statement may be proved by producing either—

(a) *the document, or*

(b) *(whether or not the document exists) a copy of the document or of the material part of it, authenticated in whatever way the court may approve.*

Therefore even if the original exists the court may accept in evidence a copy or a part of a copy of it.

11.7.2 Capacity

Hearsay evidence should not be used to sidestep the rules on competence of witnesses (see **Chapter 4**). Therefore, the CJA 2003, s 123 creates rules that regulate how the court should proceed when the issue of the competence is raised:

(1) *Nothing in section 116, 119 or 120 makes a statement admissible as evidence if it was made by a person who did not have the required capability at the time when he made the statement.*

(2) Nothing in section 117 makes a statement admissible as evidence if any person who, in order for the requirements of section 117(2) to be satisfied, must at any time have supplied or received the information concerned or created or received the document or part concerned—

    (a) did not have the required capability at that time, or

    (b) cannot be identified but cannot reasonably be assumed to have had the required capability at that time.

(3) For the purposes of this section a person has the required capability if he is capable of—

    (a) understanding questions put to him about the matters stated, and

    (b) giving answers to such questions which can be understood.

(4) Where by reason of this section there is an issue as to whether a person had the required capability when he made a statement —

    (a) proceedings held for the determination of the issue must take place in the absence of the jury (if there is one);

    (b) in determining the issue the court may receive expert evidence and evidence from any person to whom the statement in question was made;

    (c) the burden of proof on the issue lies on the party seeking to adduce the statement, and the standard of proof is the balance of probabilities.

This section does not apply in relation to statements admitted as exceptions to the rule against hearsay preserved under the CJA 2003, s 118.

Those classes of evidence that are primarily directed at first hand hearsay (ss 116, 119 and 120) simply provide that the maker of the statement must be 'capable' of giving evidence when the statement is made for the statement to be admissible. Capability is defined in s 123(3) in similar terms to the competence test under the Youth Justice and Criminal Evidence Act 1999, s 53(3), namely the witness must be able to understand questions put to him and able to give understandable answers to them.

Section 123(2) of the CJA 2003 applies the same test of competence to all persons involved in the transfer of information under the CJA 2003, s 117, that is to say, the supplier of the information and any person who received the information, or created any document with the information or received any document with the information. The relevant time for each person is the point at which they supplied, created or received the information or document. As tracing all persons in a chain of communication would be potentially impossible, s 123 requires to court to be consider whether any identifiable person was capable (s 123(2)(a)) and whether any unidentifiable person 'cannot reasonably be assumed to have the required capability at that time'. It seems likely on the language of paragraph (b) that the courts will be willing to presume that a person was capable unless there is evidence that prevents that being reasonably assumed.

Section 123(4) of the CJA 2003 makes provision for the proof of the capability of the person in question. The issue should be tried in the absence of the jury (s 123(4)(a)) and the burden of proof is upon the party seeking to prove competence on the balance of probabilities irrespective of whether it is the prosecution or defence seeking to adduce the hearsay statement. Clearly the court cannot (in contrast to practice under the Youth Justice and Criminal Evidence Act 1999, s 53) make its own inquiries as to the competence, at the time of the making of a statement, of the maker where the statement was made in the past. It will be reliant on such direct and circumstantial evidence of the maker's mental state at that time as it can obtain. It is submitted that insofar as s 123(4)(b) could be interpreted to restrict the proof of the maker's mental state to the person receiving the information and expert witnesses, the better view is that the evidence could be proven by any witness who can testify as to facts relevant to the issue and to experts who can offer admissible expert evidence on those issues.

11.7.3   Attacking the credibility of the maker of the statement

As was noted at the start of **Chapter 10**, one of the main problems with hearsay evidence is that it is not possible to test the reliability of the statement, or the credibility of the person who made the statement, by cross-examination. Section 124 of the CJA 2003 makes provision for challenges to the credibility of hearsay statements:

(1)   *This section applies if in criminal proceedings—*

(a)   *a statement not made in oral evidence in the proceedings is admitted as evidence of a matter stated, and*

(b)   *the maker of the statement does not give oral evidence in connection with the subject matter of the statement.*

(2)   *In such a case—*

(a)   *any evidence which (if he had given such evidence) would have been admissible as relevant to his credibility as a witness is so admissible in the proceedings;*

(b)   *evidence may with the court's leave be given of any matter which (if he had given such evidence) could have been put to him in cross-examination as relevant to his credibility as a witness but of which evidence could not have been adduced by the cross-examining party;*

(c)   *evidence tending to prove that he made (at whatever time) any other statement inconsistent with the statement admitted as evidence is admissible for the purpose of showing that he contradicted himself.*

(3)   *If as a result of evidence admitted under this section an allegation is made against the maker of a statement, the court may permit a party to lead additional evidence of such description as the court may specify for the purposes of denying or answering the allegation.*

(4)   *In the case of a statement in a document which is admitted as evidence under section 117 each person who, in order for the statement to be admissible, must have supplied or received the information concerned or created or received the document or part concerned is to be treated as the maker of the statement for the purposes of subsections (1) to (3) above.*

And the CJA 2003, s 119(2)(c) provides:

(2)   *If in criminal proceedings evidence of an inconsistent statement by any person is given under section 124(2)(c), the statement is admissible as evidence of any matter stated in it of which oral evidence by that person would be admissible.*

Section 124 of the CJA 2003 applies to any hearsay evidence admitted in criminal proceedings. It therefore also applies where the evidence was admitted under one of the exceptions to the rule against hearsay preserved in s 118 as much as it applies to other statements admissible under other sections of the CJA 2003. However, s 124 does not apply where the maker of the statement gives evidence. It, therefore, does not apply where the hearsay statement is admitted under ss 119 or 120. Nor will it apply to hearsay statements admitted under s 118 where the maker is called as a witness (for example where the defendant made a res gestae statement and gives evidence at trial as happened, for example in *R v Glover* referred to at **11.3.3.3**). Insofar as the statement is admitted under s 117, inconsistencies by any of the persons involved in the transfer of the information are potentially admissible under this section (s 124(4)).

Section 124(2) makes provision for the challenge of the witness in three ways that reflect what could have been done had the witness given evidence but in a way that makes allowance for the absence of the witness:

(a) Section 124(2)(a) allows evidence which would have been admissible as relevant to his credibility as a witness to be adduced (for example proof of his bad character under the Criminal Justice Act 2003, s 100 or proof of other facts permitted by the rule against finality).

(b) Section 124(2)(b) allows evidence to be given of a matter which could have been put in cross-examination as relevant to his credibility even though, had the maker actually been a witness at trial such evidence could not have been adduced. Remember that the rules concerning cross-examination allowed questions to be asked affecting the credit of a party but the rule of finality provided that only some of those matters could be proved in evidence if the witness denied the facts alleged during cross-examination. Because the maker of the statement is not present to give evidence, the questions cannot be put to him. Therefore, s 124(2)(b) allows the evidence to be put before the tribunal of fact. However, to maintain the distinction between those things admissible as exceptions to the rule against finality and those matters which are not, evidence of matters which do not fit within any of those exceptions are only admissible with the leave of the court. For the rule of finality see **6.3.7** and **Chapter 4**.

(c) Section 124(2)(c) allows proof of previous inconsistent statements. As the maker of the statement is not present to give evidence, the procedure for establishing inconsistency under the Criminal Procedure Act 1865, ss 3, 4 and 5 cannot be adopted. Therefore, a statement inconsistent with the hearsay statement admitted is admissible as of right.

Section 124(3) of the CJA 2003 allows any party to counter the attacks on the credibility of the maker of the statement under s 124(2) by proof of further evidence. The most likely ways in which this could occur would be by proof of previous consistent statements admissible as evidence of rebuttal of an allegation of fabrication under s 120(2) or evidence to disprove the evidence of the defendant's bias, criminality, reputation for untruthfulness or mental instability that would have been admitted as an exception to the rule of finality under s 124(2)(b). Where a party has admitted evidence under s 124(2)(c) to impeach the credibility of the maker of a statement as a substitute for cross-examination, s 124(3) would appear to allow another party (most probably the person who adduced the hearsay statement in the first place) to adduce evidence to counter any such challenge. Insofar as this would appear to undermine the rule of finality and that rule's aim to prevent extensive expenditure of time and resources on collateral issues, it should be remembered that the court has the discretion under the CJA 2003, s 126 to exclude evidence having regard to the danger that admitting it would be an 'undue waste of time'.

11.7.4 Rules of court

Section 132 of the CJA 2003 provides for the making of rules of court to regulate the process of proof of hearsay evidence, in particular about procedure to be followed and conditions for admissibility of such evidence (s 132(2)) and the provision of notices (s 132(3)). Section 132(4) provides that a failure of a party to challenge the admissibility of evidence under the notice procedure can amount to agreement as to the admissibility of that evidence.

The effect of failure to comply with the notice provisions is dealt with by the CJA 2003, s 132(5):

(5) *If a party proposing to tender evidence fails to comply with a prescribed requirement applicable to it—*
  (a) *the evidence is not admissible except with the court's leave;*
  (b) *where leave is given the court or jury may draw such inferences from the failure as appear proper;*
  (c) *the failure may be taken into account by the court in considering the exercise of its powers with respect to costs.*
(6) *In considering whether or how to exercise any of its powers under subsection (5) the court shall have regard to whether there is any justification for the failure to comply with the requirement.*
(7) *A person shall not be convicted of an offence solely on an inference drawn under subsection (5)(b).*

Rule 34 of the Criminal Procedure Rules regulates the notice provisions under the CJA 2003. The rule applies to evidence admitted on all of the grounds under s 114 of the Act and therefore includes evidence admitted as an exception to the rule against hearsay preserved under s 118 by virtue of s 114(1)(b). The notice procedure is as follows:

(a) The prosecution must give notice (under r 34.3) in the Crown Court within 14 days of committal to the Crown Court or an equivalent and in a magistrates' court as part of the disclosure process.

(b) The defendant must give notice of hearsay evidence within 14 days of the prosecution complying or purporting to comply with its obligation (r 34.4).

(c) Opposition to hearsay evidence must be given within 14 days of receipt of notice (r 34.5)

The court has the power to vary notice (r 34.7) and any party may waive their entitlement to notice (r 34.8). The court, in exercising the power to vary notice will have to have regard to the overriding objective of dealing with cases justly (rr 1.1 and 1.3).

11.8   Other statutory exceptions to the rule against hearsay in criminal cases

With the exception of confessions (which are covered in **Chapter 12**) the statutory exceptions to the rule against hearsay in criminal cases all relate to documentary evidence. Other statutes have created exceptions to the rule against hearsay, including:

(a) The Bankers' Books Evidence Act 1879, ss 3 and 4, which provide for the use of bankers books to evidence banking transactions.

(b) The Magistrates' Courts Act 1980, ss 5A–5F, which creates comprehensive rules for the admissibility of documentary evidence at committal proceedings in the magistrates' court.

(c) The Criminal Justice Act 1967, s 9, which provides that the written statement of a witness shall be admissible 'as evidence to the like extent as oral evidence' of the maker. This will only happen, however, if no other party has objected to the use of the statement instead of calling the witness. See 4.3.1.1.

(d) The Theft Act, s 27(4), which provides for the proof of facts by statutory declarations relating to goods in transmission.

The above list is far from comprehensive. See *Archbold* 2005 for a more extensive list and *Blackstone's Criminal Practice*, 2005, for a more extensive consideration of documentary evidence in criminal cases.

Confessions and illegally or improperly obtained evidence

12.1 Confessions

The admissibility of a confession is governed by the Police and Criminal Evidence Act 1984 (PACE).

12.1.1 The definition of confession

Section 82(1) PACE provides that:

'confession' includes any statement wholly or partly adverse to the person who made it, whether made to a person in authority or not and whether made in words or otherwise.

This is a very wide definition. However, the leading case, *R v Sat-Bhambra* (1988) 88 Cr App R 44, notes that there is a restriction on confessions in that the statement must have been adverse *when made*. Therefore, statements that were favourable when made, eg false alibis, but later proved to be adverse are not confessions: *R v Park* (1995) 99 Cr App R 270.

The whole statement is admissible, therefore a statement that is partly exculpatory and partly adverse (ie mixed) cannot be divided and is taken as one confession *R v Garrod* [1997] Crim LR 445. See **5.2.4.5** for more detail on mixed statements.

12.1.1.1 Section 76(1) PACE

Section 76(1) PACE provides that:

In any proceedings a confession made by an accused person may be given in evidence against him in so far as it is relevant to any matter in issue in the proceedings and is not excluded by the court in pursuance of this section.

The confession must generally be based on facts that are known to the person who makes it. In *R v Hulbert* (1979) 69 Cr App R 243, the defendant was charged with handling stolen goods and confessed that the person from whom she bought the goods told her that they were stolen. This confession could not prove that the goods were stolen, but only went to Hulbert's knowledge of the goods.

If a confession made by an accused person is evidence against him or her, it follows that the tribunal of fact must be satisfied that the accused was person who made the admission before they can use the statement as confession evidence against him or her. Thus, where the evidence of the identity of the maker of a confession comes from the confession itself, logic would seem to dictate that the confession should not be admitted. However, in *R v Ward* [2001] Crim LR 316, the accused denied being the person to whom a certain police officer had spoken on a particular occasion. It was held that the accused's statement to the police officer, giving his name and address, was admissible as a confession proving that the accused was the person to whom the officer had spoken. The Court of Appeal recognised that there was some circularity in its reasoning.

12.1.1.2   The confession is only admissible against the defendant who made it

A confession made by one defendant is generally not evidence against a co-defendant. However, when the statement is made in the presence of the co-accused and he or she acknowledges the incriminating parts so as to make them, in effect, his or her own, the statement will be admissible against both parties. Note also that evidence that a co-accused gives on oath is evidence for all purposes, including being evidence against the accused: *R v Rudd* (1948) 32 Cr App R 138.

Where X makes adverse statements about Y, X is entitled for the whole confession statement to be admitted even when parts incriminate Y: *R v Pearce* (1979) 69 Cr App R 365. Y is only protected by a direction by the judge to state that the confession is not evidence against Y.

The question of whether a statement should be edited was raised in *R v Silcot* [1987] Crim LR 765 and it was suggested that the trial judge had a discretion whether to do so. However, in *Lobban v R* [1995] 2 All ER 602, the Privy Council held that the discretion to exclude by balancing the probative value and prejudicial effect applies only to prosecution evidence and there is therefore no discretion in regard to defence evidence. This case was decided before the Human Rights Act and it would be interesting to see whether Article 6, right to fair trial, would have led to a different result.

12.1.2   Statutory restrictions on admissibility of confessions (s 76(1) PACE)

Section 76(1) is subject to subsection 76(2) which provides grounds on which such evidence will be excluded. Further, ss 78 and 82(3) provide discretionary grounds by which a confession may be excluded. The prosecution do not have to prove the admissibility of a confession unless:

- the defence raised an argument under s 76(2); or

- the court requires proof of admissibility.

The standard of proof is beyond reasonable doubt.

Further, the Codes of Practice provided for under PACE give weight to this issue. Section 67(11), PACE, provides that the court *shall* take account of the codes in determining any question (where relevant) arising in any proceedings.

12.1.2.1   The first barrier to admissibility, s 76(2) and (3), PACE

(2)   *If, in any proceedings where the prosecution proposes to give evidence of a confession made by an accused person, it is represented to the court that the confession was or may have been obtained—*

(a)   *by oppression of the person who made it; or*

(b)   *in consequence of anything said or done which was likely, in the circumstances existing at the time, to render unreliable any confession which might be made by him in consequence thereof, the court shall not allow the confession to be given in evidence against him except insofar as the prosecution proves to the court beyond reasonable doubt that the confession (notwithstanding that it may be true) was not obtained as aforesaid.*

(3)   *In any proceedings where the prosecution proposes to give in evidence a confession made by an accused person, the court may of its own motion require the prosecution as a condition of allowing it to do so, to prove that the confession was not obtained as mentioned in subsection (2).*

12.1.2.2   Making an objection under s 76

The leading case, pre-PACE, in relation to the admissibility of confessions was *Adjodha v The State* [1982] AC 204, PC. In this case Lord Bridge indicated that the confession should not be opened to the jury and the issue of admissibility would be resolved by a *voir dire*. A confession could be excluded where its 'voluntariness' was in doubt.

After PACE was enacted the procedure in *Adjodha* was followed. However, the case of *R v Sat-Bhambra* made no reference to *Adjodha* and did not see the defendant's position as one of choice. If there was to be an objection under s 76, the time to take the objection was before the confession was given in evidence. The court went on to state that where a confession was admitted, following an objection or not, if during the course of the trial it emerged that the issue of admissibility was in doubt the judge was precluded from re-opening the s 76 issue. However, the judge could direct the jury in several ways:

- to disregard the statement;
- direct their attention to the matters which might affect the weight attached to the confession; or
- if the matter could not be solved by a suitable direction, he or she could discharge the jury.

The judge's power to do the above derives from the preservation of the common law, under s 82(3), PACE, to take such steps that are necessary to prevent injustice.

12.1.2.3   Oppression and reliability in s 76(2)

Oppression is defined in s 76(8) of PACE as 'torture, inhuman or degrading treatment, and the use or threat of violence (whether or not amounting to torture)'.

In *R v Fulling* [1987] QB 426, Lord Lane held that 'oppression' was to be given its ordinary dictionary meaning:

The Oxford English Dictionary as its third definition of the word runs as follows: 'exercise of authority or power in a burdensome, harsh, or wrongful manner; unjust or cruel treatment of subjects, inferiors, etc., or the imposition of unreasonable or unjust burdens'

There is no reference to Article 3 of the European Convention on Human Rights nor are the words 'the use or threat of violence' further defined in PACE. 'Torture' is a criminal offence under s 134, Criminal Justice Act 1988 and 'violence' or 'force' is broadly defined in s 8, Public Order Act 1986 (where it includes violent conduct to property and person).

In *R v Paris* (1992) 97 Cr App R 99, CA, the fact that the defendant had a solicitor present did not deprive the interview of its oppressive character. The police had continued to shout at the suspect even though he had denied the charge over 300 times.

In *R v Parker* [1995] Crim LR 223, CA, and *Re Proulx* [2001] 1 All ER 57, it was held that any breach of the PACE Codes of Practice would not automatically exclude the confession. It was important to look at the context in which the term oppression was used to judge whether or not the confession had been obtained by oppression.

The assessment as to the nature of 'oppression' varies according to the character and attributes of the accused. In *R v Miller* [1986] 1 WLR 1191, it was said per Watkins LJ that it might be oppressive to put questions to an accused who is known to be mentally ill so as to 'skilfully and deliberately' induce a delusionary state in him. In *R v Seelig* [1992] 1 WLR 128, Henry J took account of the fact that the accused was an 'experienced merchant banker' and was 'intelligent and sophisticated' when he assessed whether he had been questioned in an oppressive way.

When considering the issue of the reliability of a confession, reference to pre-PACE law may be made to see whether the test has been passed. *R v Phillips* (1988) 86 Cr App R 18, CA relates to inducements: promises of bail and taking further offences into consideration, leading to unreliable confession. *R v Prager* (1972) 56 Cr App R 151 states 'questioning which by its nature or duration...excites hope (such as hope of release) or fears, or so affects the mind of the subject that his will crumbles and he speaks when otherwise he would have stayed silent'.

Therefore, s 76 (2)(b), unlike s 76 (2)(a), may be inadmissible *without any impropriety*.

The case of *R v Barry* (1992) 95 Cr App R 384 sets out some useful guidelines when considering the reliability of a confession taken during police interview:

1. Identify the thing 'said or done' (the judge must take into account every thing 'said or done' by the police).

2. Ask whether or not the thing 'said or done' was likely in the circumstances to render unreliable any confession made in consequence.

3. Ask whether the prosecution have proved beyond reasonable doubt that the confession was not obtained in consequence of the thing 'said or done'.

1 and 2 are objective and the third step is a question of fact. See Code C, PACE 1984.

The words 'said or done' do not include anything said or done by the person making the confession: *R v Goldenberg* (1989) 88 Cr App R 285, CA. In this case a heroin addict was interviewed at a time when he may have been withdrawing from the effects of heroin. The police agreed that they would not have interviewed if they had known he was withdrawing. However, the fact that the section states 'in consequence of' meant that a causal link had to be shown between what was said and done and therefore it followed that the words 'said or done' were limited to something external to the person making the confession.

Breaches of PACE Code C can amount to 'things done'. Examples include a failure to caution a suspect: *R v Doolan* [1988] Crim LR 747, CA, or improper denial of access to a solicitor: *R v McGovern* (1991) 92 Cr App R 228, CA. The test is whether the breach is significant: see *R v Delaney* (1989) 88 Cr App R 338, CA, where a confession made at the end of an interview which had not been recorded in accordance with Code C was ruled inadmissible. In *R v M* [2000] 8 Archbold News 2, M's solicitor, by intervening in the interview in an attempt to secure a confession, rendered the resultant confession unreliable.

12.1.2.4   Mentally handicapped persons

Section 77, PACE states *'the court shall warn the jury that there is a special need for caution before convicting the accused in reliance on the confession '* If the judge fails to give this warning it is likely that the conviction will be quashed: *R v Lamont* [1989] Crim LR 813, CA. See **5.5**.

The provisions for mentally handicapped and mentally disordered persons can be found in PACE Code C and are summarised in Annex E.

12.1.2.5   Confessions tendered by a co-accused

In *R v Myers* [1998] AC 124, HL, it was held that where the accused has made a confession, and that that confession is relevant to the defence of a co-accused, then the co-accused will be allowed to adduce evidence of that confession unless the way in which it was obtained would have rendered it inadmissible at the hands of the prosecution by virtue of PACE 1984, s 76(2). However, where a confession is inadmissible for the prosecution under PACE 1984, s 78, it could still be admissible for the co-accused. This rule has been put on a statutory footing in PACE 1984, s 76A which was inserted by the Criminal Justice Act 2003. Section 76A provides:

(1) *In any proceedings a confession made by an accused person may be given in evidence for another person charged in the same proceedings (a co-accused) in so far as it is relevant to any matter in issue in the proceedings and is not excluded by the court in pursuance of this section.*

(2)   If, in any proceedings where a co-accused proposes to give in evidence a confession made by an accused person, it is represented to the court that the confession was or may have been obtained—

(a)   by oppression of the person who made it; or

(b)   in consequence of anything said or done which was likely, in the circumstances existing at the time, to render unreliable any confession which might be made by him in consequence thereof, the court shall not allow the confession to be given in evidence for the co-accused except in so far as it is proved to the court on the balance of probabilities that the confession (notwithstanding that it may be true) was not so obtained.

12.1.3   The discretion(s) to exclude

Section 78, PACE provides that:

(1)   In any proceedings the court may refuse to allow evidence on which the prosecution proposes to rely to be given if it appears to the court that, having regard to all the circumstances, including the circumstances in which the evidence was obtained, the admission of the evidence would have such an adverse effect on the fairness of the proceedings that the court ought not to admit it.

(2)   Nothing in this section shall prejudice any rule of law requiring a court to exclude evidence.

Section 82(3) PACE preserves the common law discretion to exclude evidence pre-PACE and provides that:

Nothing in part of this Act shall prejudice any power of a court to exclude evidence (whether by preventing questions being put or otherwise) at its discretion.

12.1.3.1   Section 78 and the *voir dire*

A *voir dire* is necessary in the Crown Court to determine whether a confession should be excluded under s 78. However, s 78 has no application when magistrates are acting as examining justices, ie in committal proceedings (Criminal Procedure and Investigations Act 1996, Sch 1, para 26).

12.1.3.2   Deprivation of rights under the 1984 Act and Code C

The discretion to exclude a confession is likely to be exercised when deliberate impropriety or bad faith has obtained the confession and this has resulted in unfairness. Therefore, the fact that there has been a breach of the Code or a defendant's rights have been infringed by the actions of the police does not automatically lead to exclusion under s 78. Since the Human Rights Act 1998, the courts should be more 'rights oriented' in their application of s 78. One obvious example of this is where a confession has been obtained after an unjustified refusal of access to a solicitor.

12.1.3.3   Rights of access

A person who is arrested and held in custody at a police station has a right, at his request, to consult with a solicitor at any time, privately (s 58 Police and Criminal Evidence Act 1984). Article 6(3) ECHR requires that consultation must take place out of the hearing of a third party (in particular a police officer): *Brennan v UK* (2002) 34 EHRR 507. In the magistrates' court it is not a statutory right but it is a common law right to have access to a solicitor as soon as is reasonably practicable.

The right is a right to advice and not to be present during interview; however, Code C, para 6.8 states if the detainee has requested a solicitor and the solicitor is present before the interview starts, the detainee *must* be allowed to have the solicitor present during the interview.

The police may refuse access on the ground that allowing a particular individual access to the detainee may prejudice the investigation: *R (Thompson) v Chief Constable of the*

Northumberland Constabulary [2001] 1 WLR 1342. In *Samuel* [1988] QB 615, the Court of Appeal stated that if the police seek to deny access to a solicitor they must show more than a substantial risk of their fears being realised. If delay is authorised the reasons must be given and noted in the custody record.

12.1.4   Effects of excluding a confession

Section 76(4), (5) and (6) provides that:

(4)   *The fact that a confession is wholly or partly excluded in pursuance of this section shall not affect the admissibility in evidence—*
   (a)   *of any facts discovered as a result of the confession; or*
   (b)   *where the confession is relevant as showing that the accused speaks, writes or expresses himself in a particular way, of so much of the confession as is necessary to show that he does so.*

(5)   *Evidence that a fact to which this subsection applies was discovered as a result of a statement made by an accused person shall not be admissible unless evidence of how it was discovered is given by him or on his behalf.*

(6)   *Subsection (5) applies—*
   (a)   *to any fact discovered as a result of a confession which is wholly excluded in pursuance of the section; and*
   (b)   *to any fact discovered as a result of a confession which is partly so excluded, if the fact is discovered as a result of the excluded part of the confession.*

These provisions have no effect in committal proceedings, as examining magistrates cannot rule on the admissibility of a confession.

The effect of s 76(4)–(6) is that even where the confession is excluded, facts discovered as a result of the confession are admissible. However, the prosecution cannot prove that those facts were discovered due to the making of the excluded confession. If the confession is excluded under s 78 then s 76(4)–(6) cannot be invoked. However, the common law principles of relevance will apply should the prosecution wish to admit facts arising from the confession. Furthermore any evidence obtained as a result of a confession excluded under s 78 may also be subject to a s 78 argument.

12.2   Illegally or improperly obtained evidence other than confessions

It is well established that a judge has, under his or her overriding duty to ensure a fair trial, a discretion to exclude evidence that may be admissible prosecution evidence where the prejudicial effect of the evidence outweighs its probative value. This is therefore a principle that is applied on a case by case basis and, as was stated in *Sang*, should not be treated as a closed list of situations.

Where the police or State has obtained evidence unlawfully or improperly, a s 78 application may be made to exclude the evidence. In *R v Sang* [1980] AC 402 the House of Lords held that at *common law* the court did not have a discretion to exclude this type of evidence unless its probative value was outweighed by its prejudicial effect or the evidence could be equated with a confession. An example of the latter is where a defendant was induced into providing a specimen, which was then used to show that he was unfit to drive: *R v Payne* [1963] 1 WLR 637.

Under both case law and recent legislation, the defendant is not *entitled* to have unlawfully obtained evidence excluded simply because it has been so obtained, *R v P* [2002] 1 AC 146 and the Regulation of Investigatory Powers Act 2000.

Therefore, any s 78 application to exclude unlawful or improperly obtained evidence must turn on its facts.

In *R v Khan (Sultan)* [1997] AC 558, the House of Lords upheld the Court of Appeal decision that evidence obtained by a bugging device, attached by the police to a private house without the knowledge of the owner, was admissible. Lord Nolan (at p 582) stated that the significance of any breach of any relevant law or convention will normally be determined by its effect on the fairness on the proceedings rather than its irregularity or unlawfulness. This case went to the European Court: *Khan v UK* [2000] Crim LR 684. The case was that there had been a breach of Article 8, respect for private life and therefore breach of Article 6(1), fair trial. The Court decided that there was no breach of Article 6, despite finding the UK had violated Article 8. Since this decision the Regulation of Investigatory Powers Act 2000 now governs the actions of the police for covert surveillance.

In *R v Smurthwaite; R v Gill* (1994) 98 Cr App R 437, CA, the court held that entrapment itself did not result in the exclusion of evidence but laid down a number of criteria that should be followed by the police. The first criterion being whether the officer enticed the defendant to commit an offence he would not otherwise have committed. *R v Loosely; Att Gen's Reference (No 3 of 2000)* [2002] 1 Cr App R 29 reviewed the issue of entrapment and Lord Hoffman stated that the more appropriate remedy in cases of entrapment would be staying the prosecution as an abuse of process rather than excluding the evidence. For further comment on abuse of process see *R v Latif; R v Shahzad* [1996] 2 Cr App R 92, HL.

13

Lies and silence

13.1 Introduction

In the last chapter we considered how the courts will use confessions obtained (usually but not exclusively) by police officers investigating a criminal offence. Clearly not all persons questioned will confess. Others may seek to lie to deflect the police from investigating them further. So to what extent can the court use the fact either that someone remained silent or lied?

Consider the following scenario:

Ollie is alleged to have stolen a car. When arrested by the police he is in possession of a car radio (that, it later turns out, is the same as the car radio that has been taken from the stolen car). Ollie refuses to say anything about the radio when asked to do so by the police. Ollie is taken to the police station. He is interviewed and says that he does not know anything about the car in question and that when it went missing he was at work. The police tell him (correctly) that they found his wallet in the back of the car. He asks to see his solicitor and, having taken the solicitor's advice, he refuses to answer any other questions.

What if anything does Ollie's conduct prove? How might the following situations change the way in which a tribunal of fact might treat Ollie?

(a) At trial, Ollie alleged that he lied about his whereabouts because he was visiting his girlfriend, of whom his parents do not approve and he didn't want them to know. He found the radio on the road.

(b) In addition to (a) above, his solicitor advised him not to answer any questions because the police officer interviewing him had a reputation for planting evidence.

(c) Instead of (a) and (b) above, Ollie alleges at trial that he didn't answer questions because his solicitor advised him that he had a right to remain silent and that it was for the police to get all the evidence to prove the case against him without his help.

(d) Instead of (a) to (c) above, Ollie gives no evidence at trial in his own defence but his barrister has cross-examined the police witnesses to suggest that the wallet was planted in the car by racist police officers (Ollie is black and has been in trouble with the police before).

The detail of the answers to these questions will be considered below. However, for the time being, it is worth considering the issues that the questions have raised:

(a) What is the evidential value of a lie? Does it show that the liar is guilty of the offence about which he has lied? Should it be admitted in evidence in a criminal trial?

(b) What is the evidential value of refusing to answer questions or allegations at the time of arrest and questioning?

(c) What is the effect of raising a defence for the first time at trial? Does it show that the accused was trying to hide his defence from the prosecution until he put it before the jury? If so, does that mean that he is more likely to be guilty?

(d) What if the refusal to explain or answer questions is due to legal advice?

(e) What does the fact that an accused person does not testify in his own defence prove? Does this show that he or she is conscious of his or her own guilt?

(f) Does it make a difference if a person does not testify but gets his or her lawyer to advance the defence through cross-examination?

Before looking at these areas in more depth, it should be noted that what this chapter looks at is the evidential value of lies or silence on the part of a party. It is not about the evidential value of the thing that the party lied or was silent about. Consider the example above. Ollie was found with a car radio like the one from the car and his wallet was found in the car. These are items of circumstantial evidence unaffected by the law covered in this chapter. They are admissible insofar as they are relevant. What this chapter considers, amongst other things, is the evidential value of *failures to explain those other items of admissible evidence*. Do not mistake the two (it is very easy to do so).

As is common with the rules of evidence, we shall see that there is a very different approach between the civil and the criminal courts. We shall consider the civil rules first.

13.2   Civil cases

The common law governs the position in civil cases in respect of both lies and silence. The courts have treated the silence or lie like any other item of evidence: it is admissible if it is relevant to a fact in issue and the weight to be attached to it is a matter for the tribunal of fact and will depend on the facts and issues in each case. Examples include:

- *Bessela v Stern* (1877) 2 CPD 265 in which the plaintiff confronted the defendant over a promise to marry her. The defendant's silence was treated as admissible evidence to prove that there had been such a promise because he would have denied that fact if it had not been true.

- *Wiedmann v Walpole* [1891] 2 QB 534 in which the defendant did not reply to an accusatory letter written by the plaintiff. The court held that the letter was not admissible as evidence that the accusations were true. The failure to reply to the letter simply did not go far enough in proving that the accusation was true. There were a number of reasons why a person might not reply to such a letter.

- *Francisco v Diedrick* The Times, 3 April 1998 where a plaintiff had made out a prima facie case, the defendant's failure to testify was circumstantial evidence that supported the plaintiff's case.

13.3   Lies in criminal cases

The evidential value of lies, as opposed to silence in the face of accusation or questioning, is governed by the common law. Evidence of lies is generally admissible. The statements alleged to be lies will be admissible as original, as opposed to hearsay evidence (see **10.1.3.3**). The rules set out below apply to lies told both outside of court and in the witness box.

13.3.1   Directing the jury on lies

Where a lie is admitted, the judge will ensure that the jury is given careful guidance as to how they should deal with it as evidence. The leading case is *R v Lucas* [1981] QB 720, where Lord Lane CJ said (at p 724) that the jury must be directed that to be capable of being evidence against the accused the lie must be:

- Deliberate.
- Concerned with a material issue in the case.
- Motivated by a realisation of guilt and fear of the truth.
- Shown to be untrue.

All four matters must be identified to the jury in summing up and they must be told that before they use the alleged lie as evidence of the accused's guilt that they must be satisfied beyond reasonable doubt that the statement is a lie (*R v Burge* [1996] 1 Cr App R 163).

On the issue of the motive for the lie, Lord Lane said:

The jury should in appropriate cases be reminded that people sometimes lie, for example, in an attempt to bolster up a just cause, or out of shame or out of a wish to conceal disgraceful behaviour from their family.

Clearly, a statement made by the defendant that is alleged to be untrue will potentially be a lie within the meaning of *Lucas*. However, what if the statement is made by another person in the presence of the defendant? In *R v Collins* [2004] EWCA Crim 33, C and B were arrested together on suspicion of having recently kidnapped H. When B was asked where he had been he told the police officers (in C's presence) that both he and C had been at a particular public house. However, in interview and at trial C maintained that he had been with H but that he had not kidnapped him. At trial the judge gave a *Lucas* direction against C. The Court of Appeal quashed C's conviction. The court concluded that where a question was asked and an untrue answer was given in the presence of a defendant, the jury could conclude that his reaction to that question and answer could amount to his adoption of that answer, if the jury were satisfied that (a) the question called for some response from the defendant and (b) by his reaction, the defendant had adopted the answer made. In the circumstances of that case the jury had not been properly directed to adopt that approach and in any event there was not sufficient evidence adduced at trial for the jury to reach such a conclusion from the question and answer posed. Clearly, whether this is the case or not will depend on the particular facts of each case.

13.3.2   When a *Lucas* direction is required

The direction set out above is not always necessary. A *Lucas* direction is only required where lies are of direct relevance to the offence charged, eg false alibi (*R v Smith* [1995] Crim LR 305). In *R v Burge* [1996] 1 Cr App R 163 the Court of Appeal identified four situations in which such a direction would be necessary:

(a) Where the accused raised an alibi;

(b) Where the judge has directed the jury to look for supporting evidence for particular witnesses and has made reference to potential lies as corroboration (on the need for the judge to issue such a direction, see **Chapter 5**);

(c) Where the prosecution have sought to rely on an alleged lie as evidence of the accused's guilt;

(d) Where the prosecution have not explicitly sought to rely on the alleged lie but there is a real danger that the jury will do so.

Situation (d) mentioned in *R v Burge* clearly places an obligation on the trial judge to consider the likely effect of any untrue statements made during or before trial. In *R v Nash* [2004] All ER (D) 207 (Jan), no *Lucas* direction was given. The defendant was charged with criminal damage, it being alleged that he had fired pellets from an air gun at car windows. The only evidence against the defendant was that (a) he was seen near the scene of the crime acting suspiciously, (b) he denied owning an air rifle and (c) an air rifle was found at his flat. The Court of Appeal concluded that, in such circumstances, a direction should have been given as there was a real danger that the jury might use the defendant's lie as evidence of guilt even though the prosecution did not so rely upon it.

The list identified in *R v Burge* is not exhaustive. In *R v Jefford* [2003] EWCA Crim 1987, the Court of Appeal noted that the categories identified in *Burge* did not reduce the general principle that a direction is required where there is a danger that the jury may regard the fact that the defendant has told lies as probative of his guilt. In any such situation a *Lucas* direction may be required. In *Jefford*, the need for the direction arose due to the significance that the judge attached to potential lies and inconsistencies even though the prosecution had placed no particular reliance upon those lies.

Although it should generally be clear whether such situations arise in each case, this may not always be so. The court in *R v Burge* stated that the judge and counsel should consider the need for a *Lucas* direction before the judge starts summing up. Further the Court of Appeal would generally be unwilling to overturn a conviction due to the lack of a *Lucas* direction if defence counsel did not identify the need for one at trial. This is because the lawyers and the trial judge are in a better position than the Court of Appeal to evaluate the issues and to determine whether a *Lucas* direction should have been given in any particular case. If the lawyers did not identify the need for a direction at trial, the Court of Appeal is unlikely to conclude that the absence of a direction renders a conviction unsafe (*R v McGuinness* [1999] Crim LR 318).

On some occasions where the jury rejects the accused's account (ie concludes he or she is lying) they will have no choice but to convict. In such circumstances, there is no need for the judge to direct the jury in respect of the lie (*R v Patrick* [1999] 6 Archbold News 4). Clearly as the effect of rejecting the defence case is the conviction of the accused, there is little purpose to be served by also considering whether the lie is evidence that the accused was guilty of the offence.

13.4 Silence in criminal cases

Parliament has created a number of rules that allow the failure of the accused to answer allegations to be admitted as evidence of the accused's guilt.

It is not difficult to understand why a lie might prove that a person is guilty of an offence. A lie suggests that the person lying is trying to cover up for their guilty behaviour. But what about a refusal to answer questions or to explain matters? Clearly, it is possible to infer from such silence that the suspect does not have an explanation that will stand up to scrutiny. However, there are numerous reasons why a person might refuse to answer questions or explain incriminating evidence and being guilty is only one of them. Therefore, as we shall see, the courts have sought to ensure that juries are carefully directed only to use silence as evidence if any innocent explanations have been rejected.

Furthermore, using the silence of the accused as evidence of guilt offends some fundamental principles of the criminal justice process. Clearly such evidence runs contrary to the right to silence and the privilege against self-incrimination. These principles are enshrined in Article 6 of the European Convention on Human Rights. For this reason the statutory provisions set out below have been the subject of regular scrutiny to determine whether they comply with the right to a fair trial.

Instead of a single rule relating to inferences from silence, Parliament has provided different rules for inferences to be drawn in respect of silence at different stages in the criminal process. These stages are dealt with below.

13.4.1 Silence upon being questioned

Inferences may be drawn in certain circumstances if the accused has not explained his defence at an early opportunity. Before considering when this might happen, it is worth making sure that you understand the powers of the police to question suspects. Have a look at the *Criminal Litigation and Sentencing Manual*, **Chapter 2**.

13.4.1.1   The Criminal Justice and Public Order Act 1994, s 34

Section 34 of the Criminal Justice and Public Order Act 1994 states:

(1) *Where, in any proceedings against a person for an offence, evidence is given that the accused—*
   (a) *at any time before he was charged with the offence, on being questioned under caution by a constable trying to discover whether or by whom the offence had been committed, failed to mention any fact relied on in his defence in those proceedings; or*
   (b) *on being charged with the offence or officially informed that he might be prosecuted for it, failed to mention any such fact,*

   . . .

(2) *Where this subsection applies—*

   . . .

   (c) *the court, in determining whether there is a case to answer; and*
   (d) *the court or jury, in determining whether the accused is guilty of the offence charged, may draw such inferences from the failure as appear proper.*

Section 34 places a suspect under an obligation to explain his or her potential defence under specified circumstances. These circumstances will be discussed in more detail below. The duty is not absolute. There is no automatic sanction for failing to explain a defence: the failure to mention a fact simply allows the tribunal of fact the option of treating that failure as something that can strengthen the prosecution case.

13.4.1.2   No inference will be drawn if the fact relied on is true

In *R v Wisdom* (CA, 10 December 1989) it was stated that no inference should be drawn under s 34 if the fact in question has been shown to be true. This was approved in *R v Webber* [2004] 1 All ER 770.

13.4.1.3   The timing of the duty to explain

The court can draw inferences from the accused's failure to explain defences in two situations:

- Upon being questioned. But only if:
  - the accused has been cautioned;
  - the accused has not yet been charged with the offence.
- Upon being charged with the offence.

Therefore not all questions asked by a police officer are covered by s 34. There are situations in which questioning is possible both before caution and after charge (for detail, see Code C of the PACE Codes of Practice). However in such situations s 34 will not apply. To the extent that the prosecution seek to rely on a failure to provide answers to questions in those non-s 34 situations the common law rules apply (see below).

The text of the caution is:

You do not have to say anything. But it may harm your defence if you do not mention when questioned something which you later rely on in court. Anything you do say may be given in evidence. (PACE Code C, para 10.4)

It is likely that the second situation (failure to mention facts in response to charge) would arise in the sort of situations where the police did not feel that there was a need to question the accused because they have sufficient evidence to charge the defendant. It would be rare for an inference to be drawn in this situation as under para 16.1 of Code C even if the police have sufficient evidence to charge they should only do so if 'the person has said all he wishes to say'. However, s 34(1)(b) will also apply if no inferences can be drawn from the interview because it has been excluded under s 78 (see **Chapter 12**). In those circumstances, inferences can be drawn from the failure to mention a defence on charge even though the accused was questioned fully prior to charge (*R v Dervish* [2002] 2 Cr App R 105).

Note that s 34 applies to situations in which the prosecution will be commenced other than by charging the accused (see the *Criminal Litigation and Sentencing Manual*, **Chapter 1**). In such circumstances the obligation to explain facts arises upon the accused being told he or she will be prosecuted.

13.4.1.4   The fact that is not mentioned must later be relied upon as part of a defence

This is a very important feature of s 34. Inferences cannot be drawn simply because the accused did not answer questions during interview (or upon caution). They may only be drawn if the accused:

- relies on a fact in his defence, and
- did not mention that fact when questioned under caution or charged.

In other words, it is the last-minute use of a defence (or facts supporting a defence) that leads to the inference rather than the simple exercise of the right to silence. But in what circumstances has a person relied upon a fact in his defence? Where the accused gives evidence this is relatively simple, but what if either the accused does not give evidence or the question as to s 34 inferences arises before the accused has had an opportunity to do so (for example during a submission of no case to answer)?

Think again about the case concerning Ollie at **13.1**. Have a look at situations (a) and (d) identified there. In which of the two situations does Ollie rely on a fact in his defence?

In situation (a) it is clear that Ollie has relied upon an alibi defence (he was visiting his girlfriend) and also that he found the radio on the road. In addition to any adverse inferences that might result from having lied, he could be subject to adverse inferences under s 34.

Situation (d) has presented more difficulty for the courts. To what extent does a defendant rely on a fact if he or she does not give evidence or call any witnesses? Does cross-examination of the police witnesses that the wallet was planted amount to reliance upon a fact? In *R v Webber* [2004] 1 All ER 770, the House of Lords considered the meaning of 'fact' within s 34 at some length. Lord Bingham said (at [33]) that the word 'fact' in s 34, 'should be given a broad and not a narrow or pedantic meaning. The word covers any alleged fact which is in issue and is put forward as part of the defence case: if the defendant advances at trial any pure fact or exculpatory explanation or account which, if it were true, he could reasonably have been expected to advance earlier, s 34 is potentially applicable.' For this reason, the House concluded that a party relies on a fact within the meaning of s 34 not only when the defendant gives evidence of that fact but also when the defendant's advocate 'puts a specific and positive case to prosecution witnesses, as opposed to asking questions intended to probe or test the prosecution case' and that was the case whether or not the witness in question accepted the allegation put to them by defence counsel.

It is therefore necessary to distinguish between cross-examination that tests the prosecution evidence (such as suggesting that an identification witness was mistaken) and cross-examination that suggests a positive defence (putting to the same witness that the accused was at another place at the time of the offence). The former will not amount to reliance on a fact under s 34 but the latter probably will.

The use of the phrase 'facts relied on in defence' may appear to give the prosecution and the court an opportunity to invoke s 34 whenever there is a small detail raised by the defendant at trial that he or she did not mention during a previous interview. However, in *R v Brizzalari* The Times, 3 March, 2004, the Court of Appeal recognised that it was a matter for the trial judge to determine whether facts mentioned by the defendant were sufficiently important to fall within s 34.

13.4.1.5   **The failure to mention the fact must be unreasonable**

Section 34 states that a fact which is not mentioned must be 'a fact which in the circumstances existing at the time the accused could reasonably have been expected to mention'.

In many cases the defendant will have a reason for having failed to answer questions, which should be presented to the jury and which the jurors must consider. In *R v Cowan* [1996] 1 Cr App R 1, a case concerning s 35 of the 1994 Act, which also allows adverse inferences to be drawn unless there are good reasons for the defendant's silence, it was noted that there would have to be evidence before the jury of the reasons for silence. It was not possible for counsel simply to give those reasons in the absence of an evidential foundation.

In *R v Nickolson* [1999] Crim LR 61, the Court of Appeal held that a suspect could not be expected to give an innocent explanation of potentially incriminating evidence that was not presented to him at interview.

In *R v Turner* [2004] 1 All ER 1025, the Court of Appeal stated that, where possible, the prosecution should challenge the defendant about any unmentioned fact in cross-examination and give the defendant an opportunity to provide an explanation.

It would appear that s 34 will not apply if the accused mentioned the fact in a prepared statement even if he or she then refuses to answer questions (*R v Ali* [2001] All ER (D) 16).

Have another look at the scenarios concerning Ollie at **13.1**. Now consider situations (a), (b) and (c). In which of those situations should the jury be allowed to draw an adverse inference from Ollie's failure to explain his defence at the police station?

In relation to situation (a), the reason Ollie did not give the real explanation was fear of his parents. It will be a matter for the jury as to whether they believe this explanation. If not, they may decide that he did not give his defence because he was guilty. Note the similarity of approach adopted in relation to the lie he told: the jury will have to decide whether his reason for lying or not mentioning a fact was a consciousness of guilt. It should also be noted that no explanation appears to have been given for the failure to explain the radio. As he has not put forward any reason for failing to mention how he came by the incriminating radio, the jury would simply have to decide whether his failure to mention the finding of the radio was evidence that he might be guilty of the offence. In other words, where the defendant attempts to give an explanation for his failure to mention facts at trial, the jury will have to undertake a more complicated analysis before drawing adverse inferences against him or her.

In situations (b) and (c) Ollie's failure to put forward defences at the police station *are* explained at trial. However, the jury is not bound to accept the reasons he gives. Even legal advice does not determine whether or not inferences should be drawn. In *R v Condron* [1997] 1 Cr App R 185, two suspects being investigated for drug offences had been interviewed under caution but both remained silent. At trial the two accused put forward innocent explanations of all the prosecution evidence, which explanations could have been given at the police station. They also testified that their solicitor had advised them not to answer questions because he felt that they were suffering from heroin withdrawal. The police (acting on the advice of the police doctor) had decided the suspects were fit to be interviewed. The jury was directed that they could draw an inference from the failure of the accused to explain their defences at the police station. The Court of Appeal affirmed their convictions. Legal advice could not determine whether or not s 34 applied. Instead the jury should have regard to the reasons given by the accused (including legal advice) and consider whether it is the legal advice or the consciousness of guilt that is the reason for the failure to mention the fact. The matter was taken to the European Court of Human Rights (*Condron & Condron v UK* [2000] Crim LR 677) where it was decided that it was necessary that the jury be directed that they should only draw an adverse inference if they concluded (beyond reasonable doubt) that the *only* reason for failing to mention the fact was that the suspect had no answer to the questions (or none that would stand up to cross-examination). See *R v Daly* [2002] 2 Cr App R 201 and *R v Petkar* [2004] 1 Cr App R 270.

In *R v Argent* [1997] Crim LR 346, the Court of Appeal stated that the jury should take into consideration the circumstances in which advice was given and the personality of the accused in deciding the real reason for remaining silent. It was also said that the reasons for the legal advice should not determine whether or not adverse inferences should be drawn. The jury should not be concerned with the correctness of the advice but its impact upon the accused's conduct at the police station. Therefore it is not the fact (or the accuracy) of the legal advice that determines whether or not it amounts to a good reason for remaining silent. Rather the jury will have to consider whether the advice was the cause of the silence or whether it was some other matter and should only infer guilt where they conclude that other reason was the guilty mind of the accused. There is no real difference between situations (b) and (c) except insofar as the jury is likely to accept one or the other as more or less likely to have influenced Ollie's decision. The fact that the advice in situation (c) is clearly wrong (in that it overlooks s 34) is simply a matter for the jury to take into account.

As legal advice can (but not must) be a good reason for failing to mention a fact it will occasionally be necessary to prove what legal advice was given. The accused could testify as to what his legal advisor told him (this would not be hearsay evidence because it is admitted to prove the fact not the truth of the advice: see **Chapter 10**). However, it may be necessary to call the legal advisor to testify as to what advice he gave to assist in deciding whether the decision to remain silent was really based on the legal advice given (*R v Roble* [1997] Crim LR 449). In *R v Bowden* [1999] 4 All ER 43, it was said that where the accused or his solicitor had given evidence as to not just the fact of advice having been given to keep silent but also the reasons for that advice, the accused 'voluntarily withdrew the veil of privilege and having done so could not resist questioning directed to the nature of that advice and the factual premises on which it was based' (per Lord Bingham CJ at p 47). While it is not generally permissible for one party to enquire into the legal advice that another has received (see legal professional privilege in **Chapter 17**), it is possible for this rule to be waived and following *R v Bowden* the giving of evidence as to the legal advice received constitutes such waiver. The witness (whether the solicitor or his or her client) could be cross-examined about that advice.

13.4.1.6   The nature of the questioning

Section 34 only applies if the questioning relates to whether or by whom the offence has been committed. A failure to explain other matters cannot be used to support an inference under s 34 (although it may do so at common law: see **13.4.1.10**).

13.4.1.7   Who must conduct the questioning

While s 34(1) refers to a constable, the section also applies to 'persons (other than constables) charged with the duty of investigating offences or charging offenders' (s 34(4)) (*R v Ali* [2001] EWCA Crim 83). Where questioning is conducted by someone who does not have a duty of investigating offences the rules at common law apply.

13.4.1.8   Access to legal advice

When questioning takes place in an 'authorised place of detention' (which includes but is not limited to a police station: see s 38(2A)) then no inferences can be drawn if the suspect was not allowed an opportunity to consult a solicitor (s 34(2A)) (see *Murray v United Kingdom* (1996) 22 EHRR 29). If the accused declines the right to consult a solicitor, it would appear that inferences could be drawn (as the opportunity has been allowed) although the matter has not been determined by case law. However if the police exercise the power to delay access to legal advice under s 58 of the Police and Criminal Evidence Act 1984 (see **Chapter 12**) then inferences could not be drawn from the failure to mention a fact.

13.4.1.9   The effect of the failure to mention the fact

Where the jury decide that there has been a failure to mention a fact in the circumstances set out above they may draw 'such inferences as appear proper' (s 34(2)). However in *R v Petkar* [2004] 1 Cr App R 270, the Court of Appeal accepted that the trial judge should give guidance as to what inferences might be drawn in each case.

13.4.1.10   Direction to the jury

There will always be a need to direct a jury when the judge concludes that the defendant has relied upon a fact and that the jury could conclude the failure to mention it was unreasonable. However in *R v Mountford* [1999] Crim LR 575, the Court of Appeal held that if the defence is raised for the first time at trial and the reasons for not mentioning it earlier were so related that the rejection of the defence would necessarily involve a rejection of the reasons, then a direction to the jury was unnecessary. Mountford's defence was that a prosecution witness (W) had committed the offence and that he had not mentioned this before trial out of fear of that witness. If the jury rejected the defence ('W did it') they must necessarily reject the reasons for not mentioning that defence ('W would kill me for saying so') and so a direction would serve no purpose. However in *R v Daly* [2002] 2 Cr App R 201, the Court of Appeal doubted that s 34 required any such restriction and thought that the direction should be given in all cases. Further in *R v Webber* [2004] 1 All ER 770, the House of Lords questioned the judgment in *R v Mountford*, noting that the jury could find assistance in deciding whether to believe W or Mountford from considering why Mountford had not offered the explanation he did at an earlier point.

Where the prosecution have not sought to rely on section 34 the judge should not invite the jury to draw an adverse inference from the alleged failure of the accused to mention a defence without first discussing the matter with counsel (*R v Khan* [1999] 2 Archbold News 2).

The full specimen direction can be obtained from the Judicial Studies Board website (www.jsboard.co.uk). In essence the jury should be directed that:

(a) A suspect is not bound to answer police questions.

(b) An inference from silence cannot prove guilt on its own.

(c) The prosecution must have established a case to answer before any inference may be drawn.

(d) It is for them to decide whether the defendant could reasonably be expected to have mentioned the defence. If they think the defence should have been mentioned then the jury may, but not must, draw inferences against the accused.

(e) They can draw an inference *only* if satisfied that the defendant was silent because he had no answer or none that would stand up to investigation. See *R v Daly* [2002] 2 Cr App R 14.

The judge should identify the facts it is alleged the accused has relied upon that give rise to this inference (*R v Chenia* [2003] 2 Cr App R 83). Simple reference to a general failure to answer questions at interview creates the risk that the jury will convict on the silence at interview alone rather than on the failure to mention a fact later relied on in defence: *R v Turner* [2004] 1 All ER 1025.

The judge in summing up should not only identify any reasons given by the defendant for failing to mention a fact but should do so as part of the direction on s 34 rather than when summing up on the defence case: *R v Petkar* [2004] 1 Cr App R 270.

13.4.1.11   The position at common law

Section 34 will not apply if:

- The person questioning is not a police officer or authorised investigator.
- The questioning or accusation does not take place under caution.
- The questioning takes place after the accused has been charged.
- The accused does not rely on a fact in his defence.
- The questioning did not concern whether or by whom an offence had been committed.
- The failure to mention the fact now relied upon was not unreasonable.

As noted above, if s 34 does not apply the common law rules on inferences from silence may apply (*R v McGarry* [1999] 1 WLR 1500). However, the common law rules will be of limited application because:

(a) A person could only be subject to adverse inferences arising from his or her failure to answer questions or accusations if:
   (i) the accused had not been cautioned, and
   (ii) the questioner/accuser and the accused were on equal terms: *Parkes v R* [1976] 1 WLR 1251.

(b) Where the person questioning or making accusations is a police officer or equivalent they will not be on equal terms (*Hall v R* [1971] 1 WLR 298) although an obiter dictum in *R v Chandler* [1976] 1 WLR 585 suggested that a person might be on equal terms with a police officer if he or she was accompanied by a solicitor. Furthermore in *R v Horne*

[1990] Crim LR 188, CA an unprompted accusation was made by a victim of an attack in the presence of the defendant and police officers. The Court of Appeal ruled that the defendant's failure to respond to that accusation had been rightly admitted.

The main situation in which the common law rule will apply is where the person making the accusations or asking the questions is another member of the public (as was the case in *Parkes v R*).

13.4.1.12 'Counterweight' directions

If the accused does not advance a new defence or new facts in support of a defence at trial, s 34 will not apply. Because the accused was questioned under caution the common law rules concerning inferences do not apply either.

However, s 34(3) allows the prosecution to prove the silence under questioning (a 'no-comment' interview) before or after the accused relies on a fact. This is a pragmatic rule allowing to prove the accused's interview as an ordinary part of the prosecution case rather than requiring the prosecution to reopen their case when the accused later raises a new fact or defence and therefore triggers s 34. It is very rare in practice for an interview (other than those excluded under ss 76 or 78 of the Police and Criminal Evidence Act 1984) not to be proved during the prosecution case.

Where the prosecution have proved the interview but the accused does not then advance any new defence or facts, the tribunal of fact will have heard or read the interview and may draw an adverse inference of their own accord. In such situations not only should the judge not issue a s 34 direction, he or she should also issue a further direction (a 'counterweight direction') that they should not hold the accused's silence against him (*R v McGarry*). However, the judge should have regard to whether on the particular facts there is any real risk that the jury would draw an adverse inference in the absence of any comment by the judge on the matter (*R v La Rose* [2003] EWCA Crim 1471). Where, for example, a direction will be made under s 35 (see **13.4.5** below) the jury would have been sufficiently warned about the right to remain silent so any further direction would simply be confusing.

13.4.2 Silence upon confrontation about particular types of incriminating evidence

There are two inferences of a similar nature. Both arise when a person is confronted about particular types of incriminating evidence. Unlike inferences under s 34, they do not arise because the accused later relies upon a defence which he or she has not mentioned at an earlier point but simply because he or she does not offer an explanation when invited to do so. In other words, it is the simple exercise of the right to silence in incriminating circumstances that gives rise to the inferences.

13.4.2.1 Failure to account for objects, substances or marks

Section 36 of the Criminal Justice and Public Order Act 1994 provides:

(1) Where—
   (a) a person is arrested by a constable, and there is—
      (i) on his person; or
      (ii) in or on his clothing or footwear; or
      (iii) otherwise in his possession; or
      (iv) in any place in which he is at the time of his arrest,
   any object, substance or mark, or there is any mark on any such object; and
   (b) that or another constable ... reasonably believes that the presence of the object, substance or mark may be attributable to the participation of the person arrested in the commission of an offence specified by the constable; and

(c) *the constable informs the person arrested that he so believes, and requests him to account for the presence of the object, substance or mark; and*

(d) *the person fails or refuses to do so,*

then if, in any proceedings against the person for the offence…evidence of those matters is given, subsection (2) below applies.

(2) *Where this subsection applies—*

  (a) *…*

  (b) *…*

  (c) *the court, in determining whether there is a case to answer; and*

  (d) *the court or jury, in determining whether the accused is guilty of the offence charged,*

  may draw such inferences from the failure or refusal as appear proper.

(3) *Subsections (1) and (2) above apply to the condition of clothing or footwear as they apply to a substance or mark thereon.*

In addition to the above points, it should be noted:

(a) Section 36 allows the court to draw adverse inferences from the failure to explain the object, substance or mark only if the accused has been arrested and the effect of the failure to explain the incriminating object, etc, has been explained to the accused. Note, however, that the object, substance or mark itself is evidence in its own right and there are no particular rules or conditions for its admissibility (other than the usual rules of evidence).

(b) The inference can only be drawn if the suspect has been told of the reasons for suspicion and of the effect of failing to comply with this section (s 36(4)). The officer does not have to identify the precise offence. In *R v Compton* [2002] EWCA Crim 2835, CA, it was considered sufficient that the police officer had said that he was investigating 'drug trafficking'.

(c) Code C sets out the text of the special warnings that should be given to the accused under s 36 at para 10.5A.

(d) Section 36 applies to questions raised by customs and excise officers as well as police officers (s 36(5)). However, in contrast to s 34, other officers with a duty of investigating offences are not specifically mentioned. It would therefore appear that only confrontations or questions about objects, substances or marks by police or customs officers will lead to adverse inferences.

(e) Where the accused was in a place of authorised detention, inferences are only possible if the accused was offered access to a solicitor. This is likely to be a common feature of s 36 inferences as the section only arises upon arrest at which stage the police should generally take a suspect to a police station before questioning him.

13.4.2.2   Failure to account for presence at the scene of a crime

Section 37 of the 1994 Act provides:

(1) *Where—*

  (a) *a person arrested by a constable was found by him at a place at or about the time the offence for which he was arrested is alleged to have been committed; and*

  (b) *that or another constable investigating the offence reasonably believes that the presence of the person at the place at that time may be attributable to his participation in the commission of the offence; and*

  (c) *the constable informs the person that he so believes, and requests him to account for that presence; and*

  (d) *the person fails or refuses to do so,*

  then if, in any proceedings against the person for the offence, evidence of those matters is given, subsection (2) below applies.

(2)   Where this subsection applies—
  (a) . . .
  (b) . . .
  (c)   the court, in determining whether there is a case to answer; and
  (d)   the court or jury, in determining whether the accused is guilty of the offence charged,
may draw such inferences from the failure or refusal as appear proper.

The points noted in relation to s 36 above apply equally to s 37. However the text for the special warning is at Code C, para 10.5B.

13.4.3   Refusal to give body samples

Body samples are used to prove issues by scientific evidence, usually be DNA profiles. During the investigation of a crime samples or substances such as blood or semen might be taken, for example from the scene of the crime or from a victim. To prove that the accused committed the offence, the DNA profile of the sample and a profile from a sample taken from the accused must be matched.

The taking of bodily samples is governed by ss 62 and 63 of the Police and Criminal Evidence Act 1984. This is covered in more detail in **Chapter 14**. However at this point it is worth noting that bodily samples are defined in two classes:

(a) Non-intimate samples: such samples can be taken without the consent of the owner in certain circumstances (s 63). If the conditions for taking such a sample without consent do not apply and the owner declines to consent without good reason, the court may draw inferences of guilt from that refusal at common law (*R v Smith* (1985) 81 Cr App R 286).

(b) Intimate samples: such samples cannot be taken without the consent of the owner in any circumstances. However if the owner refuses to consent to the taking of such samples without good cause the court may draw such inferences from that refusal as appear proper. These inferences can be used in determining the issue of guilt and in determining whether there is a case to answer.

13.4.4   Failure to disclose the defence case

The inferences that we have already considered all relate to pre-trial investigation. Those that follow all relate to the trial process itself.

The Criminal Procedure and Investigations Act 1996, s 5 places the accused under an obligation to disclose his or her defence by way of a defence statement. See the ***Criminal Litigation and Sentencing Manual***, *Blackstone's Criminal Practice*, 2005 or *Archbold*, 2005 for the detailed rules of procedure. In outline a defence statement should set out in general terms the nature of the accused's defence and matters with which he or she takes issue with the prosecution case and the basis of any such dispute (s 5(6)). The logic of this procedure is that the accused is then committed to the defence to be run at trial. Where the accused intends to rely on an alibi defence (ie that he was at some other specific place at the time of the offence) there are additional obligations. Section 11 of the 1996 Act makes provision for any failure on the part of the accused to comply with his obligations under s 5. The court may draw inferences when deciding the guilt of the accused *but not when deciding whether there is a case to answer* if the accused:

- does not give a defence statement;
- gives the defence statement late;

- runs a defence at trial which is inconsistent with that in his or her defence statement;
- seeks to establish an alibi without having complied with the additional notice requirements for alibi defences.

In summary proceedings, the giving of a defence statement is voluntary (s 6) but must comply with the requirements in s 5 as to the form and content of the statement. However under s 11 inferences can be drawn if the accused:

- gives the defence statement late;
- runs a defence at trial which is inconsistent with that in his or her defence statement;
- seeks to establish an alibi without having complied with the additional notice requirements for alibi defences.

The accused cannot be convicted solely on the basis of an inference under s 11 (s 11(10)). The court should take care to ensure that the jury is properly directed as to the nature of any discrepancy and the reasons that the accused may give for it (*R v Wheeler* (2000) 164 JP 565). There may be particular difficulties where the accused states that the defence statement was not drafted under his or her instructions (in other words that a solicitor drafted it) and that therefore that its contents do not reflect his or her intended defence. It is not possible to force the accused to sign the statement (*R (Sullivan) v Crown Court at Maidstone* [2002] 1 WLR 2747, CA). However, under the Criminal Procedure and Investigations Act 1996, s 6E(1) where an accused's solicitor purports to give a defence statement on behalf of the accused there is a rebuttable presumption that it was given with the accused's authority.

There is no specimen direction concerning inferences under s 11 but it would appear likely that such a direction should contain the features of an adverse inference direction: that the inconsistency is proven, deliberate, material and motivated by a consciousness of guilt.

13.4.5   Failure to testify

The traditional right of an accused not to testify has been modified by s 35 of the Criminal Justice and Public Order Act 1994, which provides:

> (1)   *At the trial of any person for an offence, subsection . . . (3) below applies unless—*
> (a)   *the accused's guilt is not in issue; or*
> (b)   *it appears to the court that the physical or mental condition of the accused makes it undesirable for him to give evidence;*
>
> . . .
>
> (3)   *Where this subsection applies, the court or jury, in determining whether the accused is guilty of the offence charged, may draw such inferences as appear proper from the failure of the accused to give evidence or his refusal, without good cause, to answer any question.*

Such inferences can only be drawn if the accused has either been warned by the court of the effect of the failure to give evidence (s 35(2)) or has stated that he will give evidence and then fails to do so (s 35(1)). The text of any warnings to the accused is set out in the *Practice Direction (Criminal: Consolidated)* [2002] 3 All ER 904, para 44. The section applies to a person who refuses to answer questions in evidence unless the refusal is justified (under s 35(5)):

(a) on the grounds of legal privilege (see **Chapter 17**),

(b) because another statute excludes the evidence that would be contained in the answer; or

(c) because the court rules that the question need not be answered.

Note that inferences can only be drawn when determining whether the accused is guilty. Inferences cannot be used to determine whether there is a case to answer not least of all because the accused has not had the opportunity to give evidence by that point in proceedings (*Murray v DPP* [1994] 1 WLR 1, HL).

Section 35 allows the judge to direct the jury (or requires the magistrates) to take into account the failure of the accused to testify if the conditions in s 35(1) are satisfied and the warnings have been issued under s 35(2). Further the prosecution are entitled to comment on the failure of the accused to testify.

13.4.5.1   The accused's guilt is not in issue

There are situations in which the accused could give evidence in his or her 'defence' even though his or her guilt is not in issue. The most obvious example is a 'Newton' hearing at which the issue is not whether the accused committed a particular crime but how serious his or her commission of the offence was so that an appropriate sentence can be passed: see the ***Criminal Litigation and Sentencing Manual***, *Blackstone's Criminal Practice*, 2005, or *Archbold*, 2005.

13.4.5.2   'Physical or mental condition'

There must be evidence that the physical or mental condition of the accused is such that an inference should not be drawn (*R v A* [1997] Crim LR 883).

In *R v Friend* [1997] 1 WLR 1433, F was tried for murder. He did not give evidence and sought to avoid a s 35 inference on the grounds that he had a mental age of nine (he was 15 years old). The judge did invite the jury to draw an inference under s 35 on the grounds that, in light of the fact that he had been able to give a clear account of what he said had happened before trial, his mental age did not make it undesirable that he give evidence. The conviction was upheld by the Court of Appeal. Insofar as F would have had any special needs in giving evidence the court could have met these needs so the prejudice of having to give evidence could be accommodated.

13.4.5.3   The direction to the jury

In *R v Cowan* [1996] 1 Cr App R 1, CA, Lord Taylor stated that a direction to the jury should contain the following elements:

(a) The accused has a right not to give evidence but he has been warned that a failure to do so may lead to the jury drawing inferences.

(b) A failure to give evidence cannot on its own prove guilt but it can assist in deciding whether the accused is guilty.

(c) If a reason for not testifying has been advanced the jury should consider it and:
   (i)   If they accept the reason advanced, they cannot draw any inference against the accused.
   (ii) If they reject they reason advanced, they may draw an inference but are not obliged to do so.

(d) If the jury conclude that the only sensible explanation for his decision not to give evidence is that he has no answer to the case against him, or none that could have stood up to cross-examination, then it would be open to them to hold against him his failure to give evidence. It is for the jury to decide whether it is fair to do so.

In *R v Birchall* [1999] Crim LR 311, CA, a conviction was overturned where the trial judge had not required the jury to decide whether the prosecution had established a prima facie case before they could draw an inference, such consideration being an absolute requirement before an inference could be drawn under s 35.

Note that the jury can be invited to infer the fact of guilt from the failure to testify if a prima facie case has been made out. Lord Mustill described the matter in this way in

Murray v DPP (a case concerning Northern Ireland legislation with provisions that were materially the same):

> If . . . the defendant does not go on oath . . . the fact finder may suspect that the defendant does not tell his story because he has no story to tell or none which will stand up to scrutiny; and this suspicion may be sufficient to convert a possible prosecution case into one which is actually proved.

Lord Mustill also said that whether such inferences should be drawn depended upon whether the accused should be able to give his or her own account of the particular matter in question. Developing this point, the Court of Appeal concluded in *R v McManus* [2001] EWCA Crim 2455 that a direction under s 35 was inappropriate where there was no factual dispute in the case. The only issue in that case was whether a particular property could in law constitute a 'disorderly house', the facts that supported such a conclusion being agreed between the defence and prosecution. The accused's testimony could not have assisted on this matter so a s 35 inference was inappropriate.

13.4.5.4   The practical effect of s 35

While s 35 has not removed the right of the accused to remain silent, it has put a considerable practical burden on some defendants to give evidence.

In *R v Cowan*, Lord Taylor CJ observed that it would not be appropriate to permit an accused with numerous previous convictions to avoid a s 35 inference when he did not give evidence to avoid being cross-examined on them under s 1(3) of the Criminal Evidence Act 1898 (see **Chapter 8**). To do so would put an accused with no previous convictions in a worse position than an accused with a number of previous convictions. This was affirmed in *R v Becouarn* [2004] All ER (D) 369 (Feb), but the Court of Appeal certified a question of law of general public importance as to whether or not a s 35 direction was appropriate in such a situation. However, it is submitted that this issue has been superseded by the implementation of the CJA 2003 which permits the prosecution to adduce the defendant's bad character as part of its case as well as in cross-examination.

13.4.6   Failure to call evidence

At common law it is permissible for the judge to comment on the failure of the accused to call a particular witness. The principle is that the judge should exercise care before doing so and the comments made to the jury should not generally invite the court to equate the failure to call the witness with the accused's account being untrue (*R v Weller* [1994] Crim LR 856). It is especially important that no comment should be made about the failure to call a witness if there may be a valid reason for not calling the witness (*R v Couzens* [1992] Crim LR 822, CA).

The Police and Criminal Evidence Act 1984, s 80A, provides that the failure to call a spouse should not be commented upon by the *prosecution* (the spouse of an accused person not being compellable on his or her behalf under s 80 of that Act: see **Chapter 4**). However, there is no prohibition on the *judge* commenting on the failure to call a spouse. However in *R v Naudeer* [1984] 3 All ER 1036, the Court of Appeal took the view that great care should be exercised by the judge before any such comment was made.

13.4.7   Conclusion on inferences from silence in criminal cases

There are two broad categories of inferences:

    (a) Silence before a criminal prosecution is commenced:
        (i)   Silence under questioning (Criminal Justice and Public Order Act 1994, s 34).

    (ii) Failure to explain objects substances or marks on the suspect's person (Criminal Justice and Public Order Act 1994, s 36).

    (iii) Failure to explain presence at the scene of the crime (Criminal Justice and Public Order Act 1994, s 37).

    (iv) Failure to provide bodily samples (Police and Criminal Evidence Act 1984, s 62).

(b) Silence after a criminal prosecution has been commenced:

    (i) Failure to produce a defence statement (Criminal Procedure and Investigations Act 1996, s 11).

    (ii) Failure of the accused to testify in his own defence (Criminal Justice and Public Order Act 1994, s 35).

    (iii) Failure to call witnesses (common law).

There are many differences between the various sections but the essential difference between the two categories is that silence before commencement of a prosecution case can be used to raise a case for the accused to answer while silence after commencement cannot.

All of the inferences in criminal cases, however, have certain common features whether as a result of statute or common law. While expressed differently in different situations, the common features are that:

(a) Before an inference can be drawn it must be established that the motive for the failure must be a realisation of guilt rather than some other reason (and the jury should be told that they must rule out any other reason).

(b) The tribunal of fact are never obliged to draw an inference in any of the above cases: the facts simply establish that an inference may rather than must be drawn.

(c) The inference can never prove guilt on its own.

Identification evidence

14.1 Introduction

We have already looked at situations where the fact-finders may need to be alerted to the possible danger of relying on a particular source of evidence — see **Chapter 5**. Usually, this happens on a case-by-case, witness-by-witness, basis. But there is one whole category of evidence where it is thought that the risk of unreliability is much greater than normal, or at least greater than the inexperienced fact-finder would expect. This is identification evidence. Courts have tried to minimise the danger by requiring a warning to be given by the judge to the jury where a case turns on such disputed evidence. We shall look first at the rationale behind the concerns (**14.2**) and next at the methods now used to deal with them (**14.3–14.8**). Finally, we will look at how evidence is produced to prove identification in court and the procedures that must be followed (**14.9**).

14.2 Identification evidence and miscarriages of justice

Intuitively, most people consider that identification evidence is very reliable and accurate. Indeed, identification witnesses themselves often think so and come into the witness box convinced that they have identified the criminal correctly. That there are dangers in over-reliance on such evidence has been plain since at least the early 20th century and the case of Adolf Beck. Beck was twice convicted wrongly (in 1896 and 1904) of offences of fraud. In the 1870s, when Beck claimed to have been in South America, a 'John Smith' was convicted in England of several frauds. Each offence alleged that Smith had become intimate with a woman, persuaded her to put valuable jewellery into his possession, and then disappeared. In 1895, several more women were called as witnesses at a new trial. The offences seemed identical. Each woman identified the accused, this time Adolf Beck. The prosecution even called two police officers to testify that Adolf Beck and John Smith were the same man. Beck was convicted and sentenced to seven years' imprisonment. After his release, the offences started again. In 1904, Beck was again convicted on the word of several women, each of whom claimed to have been intimate with him. Whilst Beck was held in custody, awaiting sentence, John Smith was caught committing another offence. Smith's appearance matched the descriptions given by the women, which included the fact that their seducer was circumcised. Prison records from the 1870s indicated that 'John Smith' was circumcised. Beck was not circumcised. Beck was released, pardoned and received a substantial sum in compensation. Following this case, the Court of Criminal Appeal was set up and the first set of general instructions on the conduct of identification parades was issued.

However, miscarriages of justice continued to occur in cases based upon identification evidence. As Lord Devlin has pointed out:

In 1912 a man on a charge of murder was identified by no less than 17 witnesses, but fortunately was able to establish an irrefutable alibi. In 1928 Oscar Slater, after he had spent 19 years in prison . . . had his conviction for murder quashed; he had been identified by 14 witnesses. Nevertheless, cases continued to be left to the jury as if they raised only a simple issue between the identifier and the accused as to which was telling the truth . . . In 1974 two shattering cases of mistaken identity came to light within four weeks of each other. (Patrick Devlin, *The Judge*, 1981.)

14.3 The special need for caution — *Turnbull* warnings

In May 1974, Lord Devlin was invited to chair a committee to investigate the law and procedure on identification and his committee's report (*Report to the Secretary of State for the Home Department of the Departmental Committee on Evidence of Identification in Criminal Cases*) was published in April 1976. It made several recommendations for changes to the gathering of identification evidence and its treatment in the courtroom, all of which were intended to be effected by statute. However, as Lord Devlin has observed:

The Court of Appeal decided to forestall legislation by giving in July 1976 . . . a comprehensive judgment laying down a new approach . . .

That judgment was given in *R v Turnbull* [1977] QB 224 by Lord Widgery CJ. The 'new approach' is as follows (see pp 228–30 of the report):

(a) First, whenever the case against an accused depends wholly or substantially on the correctness of one or more identifications of the accused which the defence alleges to be mistaken, the judge should warn the jury of the special need for caution before convicting the accused in reliance on the correctness of the identification or identifications. In addition he should instruct them as to the reason for the need for such a warning and should make some reference to the possibility that a mistaken witness can be a convincing one and that a number of such witnesses can all be mistaken. Provided this is done in clear terms the judge need not use any particular form of words.

(b) Secondly, the judge should direct the jury to examine closely the circumstances in which the identification by each witness came to be made. How long did the witness have the accused under observation? At what distance? In what light? Was the observation impeded in any way, as for example by passing traffic or a press of people? Had the witness ever seen the accused before? How often? If only occasionally, had he any special reason for remembering the accused? How long elapsed between the original observation and the subsequent identification to the police?

(c) Was there any material discrepancy between the description of the accused given to the police by the witness when first seen by them and his actual appearance?

(d) If in any case, whether it is being dealt with summarily or on indictment, the prosecution have reason to believe that there is such a material discrepancy they should supply the accused or his legal advisers with particulars of the description the police were first given. In all cases if the accused asks to be given particulars of such descriptions, the prosecution should supply them. Finally, he should remind the jury of any specific weakness which had appeared in the identification evidence.

(e) Recognition may be more reliable than identification of a stranger; but even when the witness is purporting to recognise someone whom he knows, the jury should be reminded that mistakes in recognition of close relatives and friends are sometimes made.

(f) When the quality (of the identifying evidence) is good, as for example when the identification is made after a long period of observation, or in satisfactory conditions by a relative, a neighbour, a close friend, a workmate and the like, the jury can safely be left to assess the value of the identifying evidence even though there is no other evidence to support it: provided always, however, that an adequate warning has been given about the special need for caution.

(g) When, in the judgment of the trial judge, the quality of the identifying evidence is poor, as for example when it depends solely on a fleeting glance or on a longer observation made in difficult conditions, the situation is very different. The judge should then withdraw the case from the jury and direct an acquittal unless there is other evidence which goes to support the correctness of the identification. This may be corroboration in the sense lawyers use that word; but it need not be so if its effect is to make the jury sure that there has been no mistaken identification.

(h) The trial judge should identify to the jury the evidence which he adjudges is capable of supporting the evidence of identification. If there is any evidence or circumstances which the jury might think was supporting when it did not have this quality, the judge should say so.

(i) Care should be taken by the judge when directing the jury about the support for an identification which may be derived from the fact that they have rejected an alibi. False alibis may be put forward for many reasons . . . It is only when the jury is satisfied that the sole reason for the fabrication was to deceive them and there is no other explanation for its being put forward can fabrication provide any support for identification evidence. The jury should be reminded that proving the accused has told lies about where he was at the material time does not by itself prove that he was where the identifying witness says he was.

Note that identification evidence given by police officers has no special status. Typically, officers receive training in observation and they might be thought to possess greater ability to identify people than is possessed by ordinary members of the public. However, in *Reid v R* (1990) 90 Cr App R 121, the Privy Council stated that:

. . . experience has undoubtedly shown that police identification can be just as unreliable and is not therefore to be excepted from the now well established need for the appropriate warnings.

This remains the position, even where the police witness claims to have recognised the accused at the scene of crime, having known him previously (see *R v Bowden* [1993] Crim LR 379).

14.4 Form of a *Turnbull* warning

When a trial judge directs a jury about identification evidence, in the summing-up, there is no set form of words that is needed for the *Turnbull* warning. In *Mills v R* [1995] 1 WLR 511, the Privy Council stated that *Turnbull* was not a statute and did not require the incantation of a formula. A judge has:

a broad discretion to express himself in his own way when he directs a jury on identification. All that is required . . . is that he should comply with the sense and spirit of the guidance in . . . *Turnbull* . . .

Notwithstanding the discretion that a judge clearly has, there is a specimen direction (number 30) formulated by the Judicial Studies Board:

This is a trial where the case against the defendant depends wholly or to a large extent on the correctness of one or more identifications of him which the defence alleges to be mistaken. I must therefore warn you of the special need for caution before convicting the defendant in reliance on the evidence of identification. That is because it is possible for an honest witness to make a mistaken identification. There have been wrongful convictions in the past as a result of such mistakes. An apparently convincing witness can be mistaken. So can a number of apparently convincing witnesses.

You should therefore examine carefully the circumstances in which the identification by each witness was made. How long did he have the person he says was the defendant under observation? At what distance? In what light? Did anything interfere with the observation? Had the witness ever seen the person he observed before? If so, how often? If only occasionally, had he any special reason for remembering him? How long was it between the original observation and the identification to the police? Is there any marked difference between the description given by the witness to the police when he was first seen by them and the appearance of the defendant?

See further the JSB website, www.jsboard.co.uk/criminal.

14.5 Poor quality identification evidence — submissions of no case

You have seen, in **14.3** points (g) to (i), how the Court of Appeal in *R v Turnbull* [1977] QB 224 recognised that identification evidence may sometimes be of poor quality. The suggestion was that cases based on such weak evidence should be stopped on a submission of no case to answer unless there was some evidence which might support the accuracy of the identification.

At the conclusion of the prosecution evidence in a trial, the defence may make a submission of no case to answer. Generally, such submissions are governed by the principles set out in *R v Galbraith* [1981] 1 WLR 1039 but in cases where evidence of identification is disputed, the submission will be based upon *R v Turnbull*:

    (a) Where there is no identification evidence at all, the judge's decision is simple. The submission succeeds.

    (b) Where there is identification evidence but it is of poor quality and is unsupported by other evidence, again the judge should withdraw the case from the jury. First, the judge should assume the identification evidence to be honest (that is, he or she does not need to form a view about the credibility of the prosecution witness). Then if the judge considers that the identification evidence has a base which is so slender that it is unreliable and thus not sufficient to found a conviction, he or she should uphold the submission and order the defendant's acquittal on the charge. See, for example, *Daley v R* [1993] 4 All ER 86.

    (c) Where there is identification evidence of poor quality but which is potentially supported by other evidence, the judge will allow the case to go to the jury. The judge should tell the jury what other evidence is capable of supporting the accuracy of the identification. See **14.6**. According to *R v Akaidere* [1990] Crim LR 808, a judge should not tell a jury that the identification evidence is of poor quality and the case would have been withdrawn if there was no supporting evidence. The reason for this ban is that, whilst it is for the judge to decide if there is evidence *capable* of supporting the identification, it is a question of fact for the jury to decide whether it does support it. The jury might be inappropriately influenced in their decision if they knew of the judge's view.

We shall consider how identification evidence may be supported in **14.6**.

14.6 Support for poor quality identification evidence

One possible form of support was specifically considered in *R v Turnbull* [1977] QB 224 —the fact that the defendant had put forward a false alibi (see point (i), **14.3**). If a defendant's alibi is rejected as a lie, this fact can offer support but a careful direction is required (*R v Keane* (1977) 65 Cr App R 247). It does not follow that, because an alibi has been rejected by the jury as false, the defendant was wherever the identification witness says he was. The jury should consider if there is a reason why the defendant might have offered a false alibi, consistent with his innocence. An example might be where he was with a girlfriend and did not want his wife to find out about it, so offered a different, false, alibi. You will see the parallel with the general treatment of lies by the accused; *R v Lucas* [1981] QB 720, **13.3.1**.

In the absence of other sources of evidence to support a poor quality identification (for example, D's fingerprints on the murder weapon), the judge should consider whether several identification witnesses may support each other. If they have each been hampered in their observation (eg, passengers on a night bus passing an incident on the street), the judge may have to withdraw the case from the jury and direct an acquittal. If they have observed in satisfactory conditions (eg, several spectators at a sunny day-time football match observe an assault by a fellow spectator), then their evidence may be presented to the jury as capable of supporting each other's identification evidence. In that situation, the judge should also direct the jury that several honest witnesses can all be mistaken. See *R v Weeder* (1980) 71 Cr App R 228; also *R v Breslin* (1985) 80 Cr App R 226.

In some situations, several identification witnesses may offer mutual support even though they have each witnessed a different incident, where it is alleged that each incident involved the same offender.

14.7 Situations where a *Turnbull* warning may be unnecessary

As you know by now, the concern that lay behind the decision in *R v Turnbull* [1977] QB 224 was that an identification witness may be mistaken but be persuasive because he appears to be sincere and convincing. In fact, he is sincere and has probably convinced himself that his identification is accurate. But he may still be wrong. The *Turnbull* warning is intended to alert the jury to the danger of being misled. But what if *mistaken* identification is not an issue at the trial? This may arise in three ways.

(a) There may be no possibility of mistake. If so, there is no need for a *Turnbull* warning. One example is when the only person who could be the offender is the defendant. In *R v Slater* [1995] 1 Cr App R 584, an offence took place in a nightclub and the accused accepted that he had been there. The accused was 2 metres tall and the Court of Appeal noted that there was no evidence to suggest that anyone remotely similar in height to the accused was present in the nightclub where the offence took place; no *Turnbull* warning was needed. Conversely, in *R v Thornton* [1995] 1 Cr App R 578, an offence occurred at a wedding reception. The accused accepted that he was at the reception. There were a number of people present who were dressed similarly to the accused (black leather jacket, black trousers) and several people were allegedly involved in the offence. The Court of Appeal thought that a mistaken identification was clearly possible; a *Turnbull* warning should have been given.

(b) Where the defence allege that the identification witness is lying. In this situation, mistake is simply not a live issue for the jury to consider. The issue now is simply the veracity of the witness. Does the jury believe the identification witness or not? In *R v Courtnell* [1990] Crim LR 115, the Court of Appeal accepted that point but noted that if there was evidence that might support the contention of mistaken identification, the judge should direct the jury accordingly, even though the defence had not raised that issue at the trial. In *R v Courtnell*, there was no such evidence and the judge had not erred in omitting a *Turnbull* direction. Similarly, in *R v Cape* [1996] 1 Cr App R 191, the defendants were alleged to have been involved in a fight in a pub. The pub landlord, who knew the men, testified that they were so involved. The defendants admitted being in the pub at the time but denied involvement; they suggested the landlord was lying and motivated by a grudge. The issue for the jury was simply whether they accepted the evidence of the landlord as truthful; that did not call for a *Turnbull* warning.

In *Beckford v R* (1993) 97 Cr App R 409, the Privy Council reiterated the need to consider carefully all of the issues before the jury. Beckford and two co-accused were tried for murder. The sole witness to the crime identified all three men as being present. At trial, the accused all ran alibi defences and alleged that the witness was lying because either (i) he was a compulsive and inveterate liar or (ii) he was susceptible to mental aberrations (having previously been a patient in a mental hospital). The Privy Council considered that there were two questions for the jury to consider:

(i)   Is the witness honest? This was at the heart of the defence case. If the jury found he was not honest, they would disregard his evidence.

If the jury found him to be an honest witness, they would need to consider (and be directed on) a second question.

(ii) Could the witness be mistaken? If this was a possibility, on the evidence, it would require a *Turnbull* direction from the judge. The direction should then be given even if the defence did not rely on the possibility of mistake.

(c) Where the evidence does not identify a person. Where an eyewitness gives evidence only of *description* (for example, clothing or general characteristics), this is not identification evidence. In *R v Gayle* [1999] 2 Cr App R 130, the Court of Appeal noted that the danger of an honest witness being mistaken about distinctive clothing, or the general description of a person he or she has seen (eg, short or tall, black or white, direction of movement) is minimal. What the jury need to concentrate upon is the honesty of the witness.

Where the prosecution try to prove that a defendant was present at a particular place by calling witnesses who will say that they saw *a man* driving a car, and they can identify *the car*, then a full *Turnbull* warning is not needed. The prosecution will need to produce other evidence to prove that the defendant was driving the car at the material time. This was the view taken by the Court of Appeal in *R v Browning* (1991) 94 Cr App R 109. The explanation for the distinction between identification of a person and of a car was said to be that, whereas people may change their appearance frequently (eg, facial expression or bodily posture), cars do not change their shape, colour or size (unless of course they are altered deliberately). Nevertheless, a jury should still be directed about any difficulties regarding observation of the car (eg, if the witness was a driver who got a fleeting glance of the car whilst being overtaken).

14.8 Appeals and identification evidence

A failure to observe the *Turnbull* guidelines will often lead to a successful appeal: see *R v Hunjan* (1979) 68 Cr App R 99. Indeed, the Privy Council said, in *Reid v R* (1990) 90 Cr App R 121, that they had:

no hesitation in concluding that a significant failure to follow the identification guidelines as laid down in *Turnbull* . . . will cause a conviction to be quashed because it will have resulted in a substantial miscarriage of justice . . . If convictions are to be allowed upon uncorroborated [unsupported] identification evidence there must be strict insistence upon a judge giving a clear warning of the danger of a mistaken identification which the jury must consider before arriving at their verdict. It is only in the most exceptional circumstances that a conviction based on uncorroborated identification evidence will be sustained in the absence of such a warning.

An example of such 'exceptional circumstances' may be found in *Freemantle v R* [1994] 3 All ER 225. Here, the Privy Council said that if the identification evidence was of exceptionally good quality, this would be an exceptional circumstance. Amongst the factors which the Privy Council thought showed the exceptionally good quality of the identification evidence, was a dialogue between the accused, Freemantle, and one of the eyewitnesses, Campbell. Campbell shouted to the man he saw, 'Freemantle me see you'; the man's reply was regarded as an implied acknowledgement of the accuracy of that identification. See also *Scott v R* [1989] AC 1242.

14.9 Establishing a link between the accused and the crime

14.9.1 Ways to make a link

Suppose that a defendant (or suspect) denies being the offender, there are several ways to produce evidence which can show that he or she is the offender. For example:

- visual identification by an eyewitness;
- aural (voice) identification by an ear witness;
- prints left at the crime scene — these could be prints made by fingers, palm, foot or even ear;

- fibres left at the crime scene;

- DNA left at the crime scene;

- handwriting left at the crime scene;

- fingerprints, etc, or property from the crime scene which have been found to match ones found on the defendant or on his or her clothing, among his or her possessions or in his or her house.

We now need to consider what must be done in order to turn any of these pieces of information into admissible evidence that could be used in a trial. In all of these situations, there will be a witness as to the facts. This person must make a witness statement to say 'I heard something', 'I saw someone, 'I found this letter', 'I picked up this cigarette butt', and so on. A comparison must then be made between that information and the defendant (or suspect).

Comparison by an eye or ear witness is usually done by letting the witness see or hear the suspect in controlled conditions (for example, an identification parade). In order to insulate the witness from attack in cross-examination at trial, the witness should give a description of the person he or she saw or heard *before* comparing his or her recollection with the suspect's appearance or voice. See Code D, para 3.1.

Finders will need to send their discoveries elsewhere for testing. They should protect their discoveries by sealing them in plastic bags, to avoid possible contamination. Such bags must be labelled so that the expert making the comparison can show the connection between what he or she is testing and what was found. Defence counsel may object at trial either that a discovery has been contaminated by coming into contact with other material, or that there is no evidence to link the sample tested in a laboratory by an expert witness to what was found at the crime scene.

In the case of prints, fibres, DNA or handwriting, comparison must be made with a specimen obtained from the suspect. DNA and fingerprints may already be available to the police, following the suspect's conviction on an earlier occasion. Otherwise, a specimen must be obtained now. We will consider how that happens in **14.9.6**. Once we have the specimen, we need an expert to make the comparison. If there is a sufficient match, we will have our evidence of identity. The expert witness must provide an expert report, to be disclosed to the defence and used at trial. The probative value of that evidence will vary from case to case. A fingerprint or DNA match may be very probative but some fibres or types of glass, for example, may be in very common use and so have a low probative value. If they were rare, for example pieces of handblown mediaeval glass from a church window, the match would have a higher probative value. Even with a good match and uncommon material, we have only circumstantial evidence to link the suspect to the crime scene. This means that the match may be explained away at trial by the defence, or somehow shown to be less probative. For example, in the trial of several youths for the murder of Damilola Taylor at the Old Bailey in 2002, the prosecution alleged that the fatal injury to the victim was caused by a shard from a glass bottle. Fragments of the bottle were recovered at the crime scene. One of the accused youths possessed a pair of trainers on which was found a tiny piece of glass. Scientific tests showed it to match the type of glass which had been found at the crime scene. Thus, the police had evidence to make a link between the youth and the crime scene. At trial, the defence explained this apparently damaging match by showing that the youth had visited the crime scene a day or two after the death of Damilola Taylor. This was confirmed by police officers who were present at the time. The piece of glass could have got onto his trainer then, quite innocently. There are other ways to challenge expert evidence (on identification and other matters) which we will consider in **Chapter 15**.

14.9.2   Admissibility and exclusion of evidence

Quite apart from the risks which attach to identification evidence in general (to which the *Turnbull* direction relates), questions arise as to the ways in which identification evidence should be (a) gathered and (b) presented in court. Some forms of identification evidence, eg, dock identifications, are thought to carry such a risk of prejudice to the accused that the courts have frequently excluded such evidence. Exclusion is at the court's discretion either at common law or under the Police and Criminal Evidence Act 1984, s 78 (see **12.1.3**). In general the courts have sought to ensure that identification evidence is gathered in 'controlled circumstances' and to this end a code of practice (Code D) has been laid down by virtue of s 66 of the 1984 Act. Some aspects of the admissibility of identification evidence have already been dealt with in **Chapters 5** and **10** of this Manual.

Many Court of Appeal decisions illustrate that non-compliance with Code D may be an important factor in deciding whether to exclude the evidence pursuant to s 78 of the 1984 Act. See, for example, *R v Leckie* [1983] Crim LR 543; *R v Gall* (1990) 90 Cr App R 64 and *R v Conway* [1990] Crim LR 402.

However, breaches of Code D do not automatically lead to the exclusion of the identification evidence. See *R v Grannell* (1990) 90 Cr App R 149; *R v Quinn* [1990] Crim LR 581; *R v Penny* [1992] Crim LR 184; *R v Palmer* [2002] EWCA Crim 2645. For example, in *R v Forbes* [2001] AC 473, the House of Lords held that two street identifications by an eyewitness had been rightly allowed in as evidence at a trial, notwithstanding non-compliance with Code D.

Whether there is a breach of Code D or not, s 78 of the 1984 Act would need to be considered. For example, evidence of a street identification, in the absence of an identification parade, *might* be excluded. In the final analysis, the fairness of allowing the other identification evidence to be called will depend on a variety of factors which are usually taken into consideration under s 78.

14.9.3   Cases where the link between the accused and the crime is based upon an eyewitness

This topic is dealt with generally in Code of Practice D, issued under PACE 1984. Code D can be found in *Blackstone's Criminal Practice* Appendix 2, or the *Archbold Supplement*. Code D and the Annexes A–D are particularly important. In considering the use to be made of an eyewitness, we must start by distinguishing between two situations:

(i) Where an eyewitness identifies the accused as the offender in court, while giving evidence at the trial (see **14.9.3.1**); or

(ii) Where an eyewitness identifies the accused as the offender before the trial begins (see **14.9.3.2**).

14.9.3.1   In-court eyewitness identification (usually called dock identification)

Dock identification should not generally be allowed (*R v Howick* [1970] Crim LR 403). The reason for this ban is the lack of probative value of a dock identification. It is easy for a witness to 'identify' the alleged criminal when he or she is standing rather obviously in the dock and the exercise adds little or nothing to a previous act of identification. In the absence of a previous identification by that witness, to allow a dock identification would flout the basic principles that govern the production of identification evidence (through an identification parade, for example).

A dock identification may be permissible when a defendant refuses to attend a parade (*R v John* [1973] Crim LR 113, CA) or renders a parade impracticable, eg, by changing his appearance (*R v Mutch* [1973] 1 All ER 178, CA).

There is no logic in making a distinction between a dock identification in a Crown Court and in a magistrates' court. However, in road traffic offences it is usually necessary to prove that the defendant was the driver of the car at the time of the offence. Generally, there is no dispute that the accused was the driver but a failure to call any evidence on that issue is likely to result in an acquittal. In summary trials for road traffic offences, the custom has evolved where a witness (usually a police officer) is asked, 'Do you see the driver in court?' Because of the sheer number of such offences which are tried by magistrates, if there had to be an identification parade in every case where the accused did not expressly admit that he or she was the driver, 'the whole process of justice in a magistrates' court would be severely impaired' (*Barnes v Chief Constable of Durham* [1997] 2 Cr App R 505). Thus, it seems that in this type of case the onus is on the accused to raise the issue of disputed identification before the trial starts, and seek an identification procedure.

14.9.3.2   Out-of-court eyewitness identification

The obvious way to avoid the prejudice of a dock identification is to refer to an out of court identification made in less prejudicial circumstances. Code D lays down a regime for ensuring this (so far as is possible): see, in particular, Code D, para 3. All forms of out-of-court identification would seem to be admissible either as prior consistent statements (under the principle in *R v Christie* [1914] AC 545), under the rules in *R v Osbourne* [1973] QB 678 or under the CJA 2003, s 120(4) and (5) (see **6.2.4.2**). See also *R v Rogers* [1993] Crim LR 386 confirming the admissibility of a street identification.

When the *identity* of the *suspect is known* to the police *and* he or she is *available*, four forms of identification procedure may be used to confirm or refute identification. In a *video identification*, the witness is shown images of a suspect, together with images of at least eight other people who resemble the suspect. The images may be moving or still (see Code D, annex A). An *identification parade* puts the suspect into a line-up of at least eight other people who resemble the suspect as far as possible (see annex B). *Group identification* is less formal — the suspect is put into an informal group of people, perhaps walking through a shopping centre or in a queue at a bus station (see annex C). *Confrontation* involves a direct confrontation between witness and suspect. This will usually take place in a police station and the witness shall be asked, 'Is this the person?' (see annex D).

If the suspect does not dispute identification by a witness, no identification procedure is necessary unless the officer in charge of the investigation considers it would be useful (Code D, paras 3.12 and 3.13). If identification is disputed, an identification procedure shall be held if practicable unless, in all the circumstances, it would serve no useful purpose in determining the suspect's involvement in the offence (para 3.12). There will be no such useful purpose where it is not disputed that the suspect is already well-known to the eyewitness, or there is no reasonable possibility of the witness making an identification.

If an identification procedure is to be used, the officer in charge of the case will consult with the identification officer as to the suitability and practicability of holding either a video identification or an identification parade. (An identification officer is the officer responsible for the arrangement and conduct of identification procedures, usually an inspector: para 3.11). A video identification will normally be offered to the suspect unless it is not practicable or an identification parade or a group identification would be practicable and more suitable (paras 3.14 and 3.16). The suspect may refuse the offered procedure and may then make representations as to why a different procedure should be used. The identification officer shall then offer an alternative procedure if one is suitable and practicable. If the suspect refuses or fails to take part in any practicable identification procedure, arrangements may be made for covert video identification or covert group identification (para 3.21). As a last resort, if none of the other procedures are practicable, a confrontation may be arranged.

If an eyewitness makes an identification after an identification parade has ended, the suspect and his or her solicitor should be informed. The police should also consider whether to give the witness a second opportunity at a parade (Code D, annex B, para 20). Where two witnesses were put into the same room after taking part in a parade, and only one had identified the suspect, but later the second made a statement doing so, neither witness's evidence had to be excluded. See *R v Willoughby* [1999] 2 Cr App R 82, where the Court of Appeal held that merely 'firming-up' a tentative identification at a parade does not come within the ambit of what is now annex B para 20. As to the witness who had not previously identified the suspect, the Court observed that even if para 20 is breached, so long as the breach is relatively minor and innocent (eg, no coaching has occurred), the trial judge may decide not to exclude that evidence under s 78 of the 1984 Act.

When the *identity* of the *suspect is known* to the police but he or she is *not available*, the identification officer may arrange a video identification. The suspect will be 'unavailable' if not immediately available to participate in a procedure and will not become available within a reasonably short time. Failure or refusal to participate may be treated as not being available (see Code D, para 3.4 and 3.21).

When the *identity* of the *suspect* is *not known* to the police, then clearly the steps outlined above cannot be taken. To discover the identity of the suspect an eyewitness may be taken to a particular neighbourhood (usually shortly after the alleged offence) to make a street identification (if possible) or given an opportunity to look through police photographs. See Code D, paras 3.2 and 3.3.

14.9.4 Cases where the link between the accused and the crime is made by recognition of voice

An alleged recording of an accused's voice should be heard by the jury but expert evidence on it should also be presented (see *R v Bentum* (1989) 153 JP 538; *R v Robb* (1991) 93 Cr App R 161).

In *R v Deenik* [1992] Crim LR 578, a witness testified to recognising the accused's voice (as that of the person who had committed the offence) on overhearing the accused being interviewed. It was held that it was not necessary to exclude the evidence merely because the accused was unaware that the witness was listening to the interview. The Court of Appeal has said that where a witness identifies a suspect by hearing his or her voice, Code D has no application and there is no obligation to hold a voice identification parade. However, reference to Code D shows that a witness attending an identification parade may ask to hear any member speak (see Code D, annex B, para 18).

In any event, what the judge should do is to direct the jury using a suitably adapted form of *Turnbull* warning. Research suggests that identification by voice is less reliable than visual identification, so the warning should be in stronger terms. See further *R v Hersey* [1998] Crim LR 281; *R v Gummerson* [1999] Crim LR 680; *R v Roberts* [2000] Crim LR 183.

A tape of the perpetrator's voice may be played to the jury, if the accused has given evidence, so they may form their own judgement of the opinions of the experts. This was stated by the Court of Appeal in *R v Bentum* (1989) 153 JP 538 and approved by the Court of Appeal in Northern Ireland in *R v O'Doherty* [2003] 1 Cr App R 5. This is the position, notwithstanding that experts called for both prosecution and defence in *R v O'Doherty* had expressed the view that there are dangers in playing tapes to juries. The Northern Ireland Court of Appeal also said that where expert evidence is given of voice analysis, the evidence should normally deal with both auditory and acoustic analysis. Where a tape is played, the jury should be given a specific warning about the danger of relying upon their own untrained ears. The evidence of Dr Nolan, a Reader in Phonetics at the University of Cambridge, was effectively ignored in so far as he rejected the notion that there was any benefit in playing a tape to the jury. For example, 'jury members were already inevitably under psychological bias from the very fact that [the accused] was in the dock and had been confidently identified by a police officer of his acquaintance'. Dr Nolan made a comparison with identification parades, where the purpose of requiring at least eight other participants was to give a degree of protection to an innocent suspect. 'The jury were in effect given a line-up of one and asked "Is this the person or not[?]".' The Northern Ireland Court of Appeal rejected those concerns, and made a comparison with the case law on the playing of videotapes to a jury (see **11.9.5**). It might be that identical concerns could be raised about that, too.

14.9.5 Cases where the link between the accused and the crime is based upon security film/photographs etc

The jury can look at a CCTV film or a still photograph and form their own view as to whether the person shown is the accused sitting in the dock. See *Kajala v Noble* (1982) 75 Cr App R 149, DC, and *R v Dodson and Williams* [1984] 1 WLR 971. According to *R v Blenkinsop* [1995] 1 Cr App R 7 a full *Turnbull* warning would not be appropriate in such cases. However, it may be preferable to call a witness who knows the accused and recognises him on the film (in which case a *Turnbull* hearing would generally be appropriate).

R v Fowden [1982] Crim LR 588, *R v Grimer* [1982] Crim LR 674, *Taylor v Chief Constable of Cheshire* [1987] 1 All ER 225 and *R v Caldwell* (1994) 99 Cr App R 73 deal with the situation where witnesses (usually police officers) who know the accused are called upon to identify him as the person caught on film, etc. The propositions which emerge from these cases are:

(a) Where there are several witnesses, they should not be allowed to view the film etc together but should be asked to view the film individually and state whether they recognise the person on the film (see also Code D, annex A).

(b) At trial, attempts should be made not to reveal to the jury that the witness knows the accused through previous encounters in the course of investigations into other criminal offences.

(c) A *Turnbull* warning should be given to the jury.

All of these cases were considered and approved by the Court of Appeal in *Attorney-General's Reference (No 2 of 2002)* [2002] EWCA Crim 2373, [2003] Crim LR 192.

In *R v Stockwell* (1993) 97 Cr App R 260, the Court of Appeal accepted that the opinion evidence of a facial-mapping expert is admissible, particularly in cases where there is a possibility that the person caught on the film was disguised. However, one must take care that the opinion evidence of a facial-mapping expert stays within acceptable bounds. It is acceptable to call such an expert at trial to demonstrate to a jury particular characteristics or a combination thereof, with the aid of specialist enhancement techniques if appropriate.

It is not acceptable for such an expert to offer an estimate of probabilities or to state the degree of support provided by particular facial characteristics. These are subjective opinions and will be inadmissible until such time as a 'national database or agreed formula or some other such objective measure is established': see *R v Gray* [2003] EWCA Crim 1001.

In *R v Clarke* [1995] 2 Cr App R 425, the Court of Appeal held that evidence of facial mapping by way of video superimposition (of police photographs of the accused upon photographs of the offender taken by a security camera) was admissible as a species of real evidence to which no special rules applied.

In *R v Clare* [1995] 2 Cr App R 333, the Court of Appeal accepted that a police officer, who had viewed a security video of a crowd disturbance at a football match over 40 times (having the facility to stop the video and examine it in slow motion), had thereby become an expert on that video so as to justify calling him to give evidence interpreting the video and the role and identification of the person caught on the video. In *R v Thomas* (1999) LTL 22/11/99, the Court of Appeal held that there is no obligation on the prosecution to put the accused on an identification parade before people on whom neither the police nor the Crown ever intend to rely as identification witnesses. Before T was put on trial for four bank robberies, a police officer studied CCTV videos and single-frame shots of the robberies 'repeatedly'. The Court of Appeal said that the officer had 'acquired special knowledge that the [trial] court did not possess'; in effect, he had become an 'expert' and there was no purpose in seeing if he could pick out T on a parade.

In *R v McNamara* [1996] Crim LR 750 the Court of Appeal held that where a jury requested a view of the accused to compare with a man on a video, no inference could properly be drawn if the accused chose to absent himself from the dock.

Where a crime has been seen by an eyewitness as well as being recorded on a surveillance video, the witness may be allowed to view the video and to amend his/her witness statement in the light of what he or she sees on it (see *R v Roberts* [1998] Crim LR 682).

Where a security tape exists, and it shows an offence being committed, but does not show the accused who is now on trial, that tape is material evidence which must be disclosed to the defence. See *Sangster v R* [2002] UKPC 58.

14.9.6   Cases where the link between the accused and the crime is made by fingerprints or DNA profiles

The problem here is primarily how fingerprints or body samples can *properly* be obtained from the accused. The governing statutory provisions in this regard are to be found in the Police and Criminal Evidence Act 1984, ss 61 to 65 (as amended) and supplemented by Code D, para 4 (fingerprints) and para 6 (body samples).

14.9.6.1   Taking fingerprints

Expert evidence on fingerprints is likely to be excluded if there are less than eight matching ridge characteristics. If there are no exceptional circumstances, the prosecution should not attempt to introduce such evidence. A judge would also consider whether there were any dissimilar characteristics between the print and that taken from the accused, and the size, quality and clarity of the print relied upon. See for example, *R v Buckley* (1999) 163 JP 561.

Police and Criminal Evidence Act 1984, s 61:

(1)   *Except as provided by this section no person's fingerprints may be taken without the appropriate consent.*

(2)   *Consent to the taking of a person's fingerprints must be in writing if it is given at a time when he is at a police station.*

(3)   The fingerprints of a person detained at a police station may be taken without the appropriate consent if—

    (a)   he is detained in consequence of his arrest for a recordable offence; and

    (b)   he has not had his fingerprints taken in the course of the investigation of the offence by the police.

    . . .

(4)   The fingerprints of a person detained at a police station may be taken without the appropriate consent if—

    (a)   he has been charged with a recordable offence or informed that he will be reported for such an offence; and

    (b)   he has not had his fingerprints taken in the course of the investigation of the offence by the police.

    . . .

(6)   Any person's fingerprints may be taken without the appropriate consent if—

    (a)   he has been convicted of a recordable offence;

    (b)   he has been given a caution in respect of a recordable offence which, at the time of the caution, he has admitted; or

    (c)   he has been warned or reprimanded under section 65 of the Crime and Disorder Act 1998 (c 37) for a recordable offence.

(7)   In a case where by virtue of subsection (3), (4) or (6) above a person's fingerprints are taken without the appropriate consent—

    (a)   he shall be told the reason before his fingerprints are taken; and

    (b)   the reason shall be recorded as soon as is practicable after the fingerprints are taken.

[(7A) to (9) omitted]

The definition of 'recordable offence' includes *all* offences punishable by imprisonment. See the National Police Records (Recordable Offences) Regulations 1985, SI 1985/1941.

Section 65 of the 1984 Act has the following definitions:

'fingerprints' include palm prints;
'appropriate consent' mean—

    (a)   in relation to a person who has attained the age of 17 years, the consent of that person;

    (b)   in relation to a person who has not attained that age but has attained the age of 14 years, the consent of that person and his parent or guardian; and

    (c)   in relation to a person who has not attained the age of 14 years, the consent of his parent or guardian.

Expert evidence may also be given of comparisons of ear prints: *R v Dallagher* [2003] 1 Cr App R 11.

14.9.6.2   Body samples (DNA profiles)

The governing provisions are the Police and Criminal Evidence Act 1984, ss 62 and 63, as amended by the Criminal Justice and Public Order Act 1994. These are set out below. Section 62 deals with intimate samples and s 63 deals with non-intimate samples.

'*Intimate sample*' means (a) a sample of blood, semen or any other tissue fluid, urine or pubic hair; (b) a dental impression; (c) a swab taken from a person's body orifice other than the mouth; ('intimate search' means a search which consists of the physical examination of a person's body orifices other than the mouth).

'*Non-intimate sample*' means (a) a sample of hair other than pubic hair; (b) a sample taken from a nail or from under a nail; (c) a swab taken from any part of a person's body including the mouth but not any other body orifice; (d) saliva; (e) a footprint or a similar impression of any part of a person's body other than a part of his hand.

Section 62 of the 1984 Act provides:

(1)   . . . an intimate sample may be taken from a person in police detention only—

    (a)   if a police officer of at least the rank of inspector authorises it to be taken; and

    (b)   if the appropriate consent is given.

(1A) An intimate sample may be taken from a person who is not in police detention but from whom, in the course of the investigation of an offence, two or more non-intimate samples suitable for the same means of analysis have been taken which have proved insufficient—

    (a) if an officer of at least the rank of inspector authorises it to be taken; and

    (b) if the appropriate consent is given.

(2) An officer may only give an authorisation under subsection (1) or (1A) above if he has reasonable grounds—

    (a) for suspecting the involvement of the person from whom the sample is to be taken in a recordable offence; and

    (b) for believing that the same will tend to confirm or disprove his involvement.

[(3) to (9) contain various procedural rules about the taking of intimate samples.]

(10) Where the appropriate consent to the taking of an intimate sample from a person was refused without good cause, in any proceedings against that person for an offence—

    (a) the court, in determining whether . . . there is a case to answer; and

    (b) the court or jury, in determining whether that person is guilty of the offence charged,

    may draw such inferences from the refusal as appear proper.

For the definition of 'recordable offence' see the note following s 61 in **14.9.6.1.**

Section 63 of the 1984 Act provides:

(1) Except as provided by this section, a non-intimate sample may not be taken from a person without the appropriate consent.

(2) Consent to the taking of a non-intimate sample must be given in writing.

(2A) A non-intimate sample may be taken from a person without the appropriate consent if two conditions are satisfied.

(2B) The first is that the person is in police detention in consequence of his arrest for a recordable offence.

(2C) The second is that—

    (a) he has not had a non-intimate sample of the same type and from the same part of the body taken in the course of the investigation of the offence by the police, or

    (b) he has had such a sample taken but it proved insufficient.

(3) A non-intimate sample may be taken from a person without the appropriate consent if—

    (a) he . . . is being held in custody by the police on the authority of a court; and

    (b) an officer of at least the rank of inspector authorises it to be taken without the appropriate consent.

(3A) A non-intimate sample may be taken from a person (whether or not he is in police detention or held in custody by the police on the authority of a court) without the appropriate consent if—

    (a) he has been charged with a recordable offence or informed that he will be reported for such an offence; and

    (b) either he has not had a non-intimate sample taken from him in the course of the investigation of the offence by the police or he has had a non-intimate sample taken from him but either it was not suitable for the same means of analysis or, though so suitable, the sample proved insufficient.

(3B) A non-intimate sample may be taken from a person without the appropriate consent if he has been convicted of a recordable offence.

(3C) A non-intimate sample may also be taken from a person without the appropriate consent if he is a person to whom section 2 of the Criminal Evidence (Amendment) Act 1997 applies (persons detained following acquittal on grounds of insanity or finding of unfitness to plead).

(4) An officer may only give an authorisation under subsection (3) above if he has reasonable grounds—

    (a) for suspecting the involvement of the person from whom the sample is to be taken in a recordable offence; and

    (b) for believing that the sample will tend to confirm or disprove his involvement.

[(5) to (9A) contain various procedural rules about the taking of non-intimate samples. See also Code D, para 6.]

Section 63 (especially s 63(3A) and (3B)) brings the position with regard to obtaining *non-intimate* samples into line with the position relating to obtaining fingerprints (see above).

Thus a *non-intimate* sample can be taken from a person for the first time without the appropriate consent in a variety of circumstances, for example, whenever the person has been convicted of a recordable offence (s 63(3B)). Even where a non-intimate sample cannot be taken without the appropriate consent, the refusal to consent may form the basis for an inference of guilt at common law (see **13.4.3**). Section 63(3C) and s 63(9A) were inserted by the Criminal Evidence (Amendment) Act 1997.

Section 64 of the 1984 Act makes provision for the destruction of samples where suspects are eventually cleared of any offence — see Code D, annex F. Regarding the effect of breaches of these statutory rules, see *R v Nathaniel* [1995] 2 Cr App R 565, in which it was held that the trial judge should have applied PACE 1984, s 78, to exclude evidence obtained from a blood sample which should have been destroyed. Lord Taylor CJ said:

> To allow that blood sample to be used in evidence . . . when the sample had been retained in breach of statutory duty and in breach of undertakings to the accused must . . . have had an adverse effect on the fairness of the proceedings.

Subsequently, the House of Lords has drawn a distinction between, on the one hand, trying to use a DNA profile as evidence in a trial when it should have been destroyed (as was the position in *R v Nathaniel*) and using such a profile as part of a criminal investigation. The position is governed by different parts of s 64 — s 64(3B)(a) and (b), respectively. In *R v B (Attorney-General's Reference (No 3 of 1999))* [2001] 1 Cr App R 475, the House of Lords considered the use of a DNA profile from a man (B) acquitted of burglary. The profile had been placed on the national DNA database but, contrary to s 64(3B)(b), was not removed following his acquittal. Subsequently, the profile provided a match with DNA obtained from a rape victim. B was arrested and one of his hairs was removed, legally but without his consent. The hair provided another DNA match. At trial, the prosecution did not rely on the first DNA profile. B was convicted and appealed. The House of Lords held that the 1984 Act did not stipulate a consequence for a breach of s 64(3B)(b) and that the subsection did not legislate that evidence obtained as a result of the prohibited investigation was inadmissible. Section 64(3B)(b) had to be read in conjunction with s 78 of the 1984 Act. Section 64(3B)(b) prohibited the use of a sample liable to destruction for the purposes of any investigation of other offences. It would not prohibit the use of any evidence resulting from such investigation in any subsequent criminal proceedings. The House also considered article 8 of the European Convention on Human Rights and concluded that its interpretation of s 64(3B)(b) did not contravene the Convention.

14.9.6.3   Adducing evidence of DNA profiles

In *R v Doheny* [1997] 1 Cr App R 369, the Court of Appeal laid down the following guidelines as regards the adducing (in court) of DNA evidence:

(a) The scientist should adduce the evidence of the DNA comparisons between the crime stain and the defendant's sample together with his calculations of the random occurrence ratio.

(b) Whenever DNA evidence is to be adduced the Crown should serve on the defence details of how the calculations have been carried out which are sufficient to enable the defence to scrutinise the basis of the calculations.

(c) The Forensic Science Service should make available to a defence expert, if requested, the databases upon which the calculations have been based.

(d) Any issue of expert evidence should be identified and, if possible, resolved before trial. This area should be explored by the court in the pre-trial review.

(e) In giving evidence the expert will explain to the jury the nature of the matching DNA characteristics between the DNA in the crime stain and the DNA in the defendant's blood sample.

(f) The expert will, on the basis of empirical statistical data, give the jury the random occurrence ratio — the frequency with which the matching DNA characteristics are likely to be found in the population at large.

(g) Provided that the expert has the necessary data, it may then be appropriate for him to indicate how many people with the matching characteristics are likely to be found in the United Kingdom or a more limited relevant sub-group, for instance the Caucasian, sexually active males in the Manchester area.

(h) It is then for the jury to decide, having regard to all the relevant evidence, whether they are sure that it was the defendant who left the crime stain, or whether it is possible that it was left by someone else with the same matching DNA characteristics.

(i) The expert should not be asked his opinion on the likelihood that it was the defendant who left the crime stain, nor when giving evidence should he use terminology which may lead the jury to believe that he is expressing such an opinion.

(j) It is not appropriate for an expert to expound a statistical approach to evaluating the likelihood that the defendant left the crime stain, since unnecessary theory and complexity deflect the jury from their proper task.

(k) In the summing-up careful directions are required in respect of any issues of expert evidence, and guidance should be given to avoid confusion caused by areas of expert evidence where no real issue exists.

(l) The judge should explain to the jury the relevance of the random occurrence ratio in arriving at their verdict and draw attention to the extraneous evidence which provides the context which gives that ratio its significance, and to that which conflicts with the conclusion that the defendant was responsible for the crime stain.

(m) In relation to the random occurrence ratio, a direction along the following lines may be appropriate, tailored to the facts of the particular case: 'Members of the jury, if you accept the scientific evidence called by the Crown this indicates that there are probably only four or five white males in the United Kingdom from whom that semen stain could have come. The defendant is one of them. If that is the position, the decision you have to reach, on all the evidence, is whether you are sure that it was the defendant who left that stain or whether it is possible that it was one of that other small group of men who share the same DNA characteristics.'

Opinion evidence

15.1 General rule

You may recall an occasion when someone (a parent or teacher perhaps) said to you, 'When I want your opinion, I'll ask for it!' In the courtrooms of England and Wales, the approach is effectively the same. In civil and criminal cases, the opinions of witnesses are not generally admissible.

Opinions, and conclusions, are for the court to reach, based upon the information placed before it. If a conclusion on a point of law is required, the court will base its conclusion upon the legal arguments put before it by the advocates. Any factual conclusion will be based upon the evidence in the trial (or other form of hearing). Any witness should normally be confined to stating the facts.

When reaching conclusions of fact, the court should make its decisions for itself. So, a rule evolved that a witness should not be asked questions, or offer answers, which require the witness to venture an opinion on a fact in issue. To do so could appear to exert improper influence over the court. This is sometimes known as the 'ultimate issue' rule.

There is also a risk that the court might be unaware of the factual basis (or lack of it) on which the witness's opinion is founded. What the court really needs are the original facts, upon which the witness's opinion is based.

Finally, in situations where the court is quite capable of forming an opinion on the fact in issue, it would be a waste of time to allow a witness to state his or her opinion on that fact.

Any description of the rule against opinion evidence, even if it is supported with examples, fails to give a true impression of the impact of the rule upon the questioning of witnesses. An objection to a particular question is often made on the basis that the witness is being invited to state opinion. Sometimes the question itself is really nothing more than comment on the witness's evidence.

The general rule excluding opinion evidence is subject to two important exceptions. These arise in cases where the court lacks the witness's competence to form an opinion on a particular issue. That may arise through (a) lack of the necessary direct knowledge or (b) lack of the necessary expertise.

15.2 Witnesses of fact who offer their opinion

Statements of opinion by an eyewitness (E) to the facts in issue are often really a convenient way of stating several facts. Thus an assertion by E that the defendant was drunk is a convenient way of stating the various facts which E saw (or heard or smelt) which led him to form that opinion. Such a statement will generally be admissible as long as a proper appraisal of the facts does not call for any special expertise.

In civil cases this exception has been put into statutory form: the Civil Evidence Act 1972, s 3(2):

It is hereby declared that where a person is called as a witness in any civil proceedings, a statement of opinion by him on any relevant matter on which he is not qualified to give expert evidence, if made as a way of conveying relevant facts personally perceived by him, is admissible evidence of what he perceived.

If a degree of precision is required, then a witness's best guess or estimate by itself will probably not do. In a case concerning a road accident it will often be necessary to consider the speed at which the vehicles involved were travelling and E may be allowed to state his opinion on this issue. However, if the charge is driving over the speed limit or driving with an amount of alcohol in the blood which exceeds the maximum prescribed by law, precision is needed. See, for example, the Road Traffic Regulation Act 1984, s 89 (see **5.2.2**), which states that it is insufficient to use the opinion of just one witness to prove a speeding case.

15.3 Expert opinion evidence

15.3.1 General principle

There are many situations in which an issue the court is required to determine is so far removed from the court's experience that it needs the opinions of experts to help it determine the issue in question. When such need arises the opinion of an expert *is* admissible. This was recognised as long ago as *Folkes v Chadd* (1782) 3 Doug KB 157. The converse is also true: if an issue calls for expert evidence, the evidence of a non-expert should not be admitted: see *R v Inch* (1989) 91 Cr App R 51.

It is not possible to list all the matters in respect of which expert evidence is required; some matters (eg, medical and scientific) obviously call for the opinions of experts. However, the line between matters which do call for expert evidence and matters which do not is often extremely fine (especially in relation to psychiatric evidence) and the courts consider the question most carefully. In *R v Turner* [1975] QB 834, CA at p 841 Lawton LJ put the point very effectively in this way:

The fact that an expert witness has impressive scientific qualifications does not by that fact alone make his opinion on matters of human nature and behaviour *within the limits of normality* any more helpful than that of the jurors themselves; but there is a danger that they may think it does. (Emphasis added.)

As we saw above, expert evidence will usually be excluded if it merely offers an opinion on normal human behaviour. But this sometimes begs the question, 'What is normality?' In a development from the position in *R v Turner*, expert evidence may now be called not merely where the accused is alleged to be suffering from a recognised mental illness, but also if it could show that the accused is suffering from a personality disorder which would tend to affect the reliability of the confession or other evidence. See, for example, *R v Pinfold* [2004] 2 Cr App R 5.

There are particular difficulties in criminal cases when there *is* evidence of *abnormality* but the central issue in the case turns on the application of an objective test. By definition the 'reasonable man' cannot be assumed to be abnormal. In so far as an expert's evidence would *only* be relevant if such an assumption could be made then it would appear to be inadmissible. You should refer to practitioner works to review the (sometimes contradictory) case law on this subject. It has affected such issues as duress, recklessness and provocation.

Expert evidence is probably encountered most frequently in civil cases (and there are many rules of civil procedure which relate to expert evidence — see the **Civil Litigation Manual**). We saw earlier that witnesses of fact can express their opinion on an issue, even though it may be an 'ultimate issue' for the court to decide. The same is true for an expert witness. In civil cases, this is established by the Civil Evidence Act 1972, s 3(1) and (3):

(1) *Subject to any rules of court made in pursuance of this Act, where a person is called as a witness in any civil proceedings, his opinion on any relevant matter on which he is qualified to give expert evidence shall be admissible in evidence . . .*

(3) *In this section 'relevant matter' includes an issue in the proceedings in question.*

Sometimes, an expert may seem to trespass into ultimate issues in criminal cases, for example, *R v Stockwell* (1993) 97 Cr App R 260 — an early use of facial mapping evidence. There is no statutory equivalent of the CEA 1972 to permit experts in criminal cases to offer their opinions on ultimate issues but it seems to be a matter of the form that questions take now, rather than their substance. See further *Blackstone's Criminal Practice*, 2005.

15.3.2 Who is an expert?

Where a matter calls for expert evidence, only a suitably qualified expert can give it. Indeed the starting point in examining in chief an expert witness is to establish his or her expertise. But this does not necessarily mean that there must be formal qualifications. See, for example, *R v Stockwell* (1993) 97 Cr App R 260, where the 'expert' in facial mapping had 'no scientific qualifications, no specific training, no professional body and no database'. Other examples are *R v Silverlock* [1894] 2 QB 766 — a solicitor who had for many years studied handwriting as a hobby (handwriting expert); *Ajami v Comptroller of Customs* [1954] 1 WLR 1405 — a banker with 24 years' experience of Nigerian banking law (foreign law expert). (Matters of *foreign* law are generally treated as calling for expert evidence.) However, it will not be easy to satisfy a judge that a witness is an expert in a field if he lacks formal qualifications.

It has sometimes been said that an expert witness would be disqualified from giving evidence in a trial if he or she had an interest in the proceedings (see, for example, *Liverpool Roman Catholic Archdiocesan Trustees Inc v Goldberg (No 3)* [2001] 1 WLR 2337). Such a situation might arise where the expert is an employee of one of the litigants, or is related to one. It ought to be clear that the expert owes an overriding duty to the court, not to himself or herself or to a litigant (see, for example, CPR, r 35.3). Currently, the position is that a litigant who wishes to call an expert as a witness should disclose to the other litigant(s) and the court any interest that the expert has, or may seem to have. That interest will not automatically disqualify the expert, although disqualification may be required on the facts of the particular case. It has been said that it is 'the nature and extent of the interest or connection which matters, not the mere fact of the interest or connection' (see Nelson J in *Armchair Passenger Transport Ltd v Helical Bar plc* [2003] EWHC 367). Apparent bias is not enough to disqualify an expert from being called as a witness. The key questions are:

- Does the person have relevant expertise.

- Is he or she aware of the overriding duty as an expert to the court, and is willing and able to fulfil it?

If allowed to testify, the interest or connection may still be relevant to the weight of the evidence given by the expert. In conclusion, 'it is always desirable that an expert should have no actual or apparent interest in the outcome of the proceedings in which he gives evidence', according to Lord Phillips MR in *R (Factortame Ltd) v Secretary of State for Transport, Local Government and the Regions (No 8)* [2003] QB 381.

15.3.3   Status of expert evidence

Expert evidence should be treated like the evidence of any other witness. It is a misdirection to tell a jury that they must accept it. See, for example, the speech of Lord Diplock in *R v Lanfear* [1968] 2 QB 77. However, in *R v Anderson* [1972] 1 QB 304 it was held that it would equally be a misdirection to tell a jury that it could disregard expert evidence which had been given by only one witness and which, if accepted, dictated one answer. See also, to the same effect, *R v Bailey* (1978) 66 Cr App R 31.

In civil cases, it has been said that:

even though it is always for the judge rather than for the expert witness to determine matters of fact, the judge must do so on the basis of the evidence, including the expert evidence. The mere application [by a judge] of 'common sense' cannot conjure up a proper basis for inferring that an injury must have been caused in one way rather than another when the only relevant evidence is undisputed scientific evidence which says that either way is equally possible.

See Lord Rodger of Earlsferry in *Fairchild v Glenhaven Funeral Services Ltd* [2002] 3 All ER 305, HL. Similarly, where two or more experts have been called as witnesses:

'a coherent reasoned opinion expressed by a suitably qualified expert should be the subject of a coherent reasoned rebuttal'. This does not mean that the judgment should contain a passage which suggests that the judge has applied the same, or even a superior, degree of expertise to that displayed by the witness. He should simply provide an explanation as to why he has accepted the evidence of one expert and rejected that of another. It may be that the evidence of one or the other accorded more satisfactorily with facts found by the judge. It may be that the explanation of one was more inherently credible than that of the other. It may simply be that one was better qualified, or manifestly more objective, than the other. Whatever the explanation may be, it should be apparent from the judgment.

See Lord Phillips of Worth Matravers MR in *English v Emery Reimbold and Strick Ltd* [2002] 3 All ER 385.

The dilemma for judges (and other fact-finders) in relying on expert evidence is well illustrated in the case of Angela Cannings (*R v Cannings* [2004] 2 Cr App R 7), a mother convicted of the murders of two of her children on the basis of expert evidence as to sudden infant deaths. Quashing her convictions, the Court of Appeal observed that:

Not so long ago, experts were suggesting that new born babies should lie on their tummies. That was advice based on the best-informed analysis. Nowadays, the advice and exhortation is that babies should sleep on their backs . . . This advice is equally drawn from the best possible known sources. It is obvious that these two views cannot both simultaneously be right . . . [R]esearch in Australia [suggests] that the advice that babies should sleep on their backs had not achieved the improvement in the rate of cot deaths attributed to modern practice . . . Our point is to highlight the fact that even now contrasting views on what might be thought to have been settled once and for all are current.

15.3.4   Upon what can an expert base an opinion?

An expert's opinion will be based upon much more than the facts of the particular case he or she is considering. It will be based on the expert's experience and any information that he or she has obtained from extraneous sources such as textbooks, articles and journals.

Such information (often referred to as secondary facts) is not treated as hearsay but simply as part of the basis for the expert opinion. Obviously the facts of the particular case on which the opinion is given (the primary facts) should be proved by admissible evidence (whether or not by the expert).

For example, an expert valuer of antiques may be called to give opinion evidence of the value of certain Chinese vases. The opinion may be based on her own knowledge of previous sale prices of similar vases; it may also be based on secondary facts — reports of sales at foreign auction rooms, or books published for the antiques trade specialist. However, if the valuation is based on the 'primary fact' that these vases date from the era of the Ming dynasty in China and are in excellent condition, these primary facts must themselves be proved by admissible evidence. This might be done either by this witness testifying about what he or she observed when looking at the vases (maker's marks, absence of cracks, chips, etc) or by calling other witnesses who have examined the vases. Thus, our expert may need dual expertise — first, on current sale room prices for excellent quality Ming vases; secondly, how to identify an 'excellent quality Ming vase'. See generally *English Exporters (London) Ltd v Eldonwall Ltd* [1973] Ch 415 and *H v Schering Chemicals Ltd* [1983] 1 WLR 143. Compare *R v Bradshaw* (1986) Cr App R 79, in which 'as a concession to the defence' a psychiatrist was allowed to base his opinion as to the accused's mental state upon statements made out of court by the accused (ie, hearsay).

In *R v Jackson* [1996] 2 Cr App R 420 the Court of Appeal held that although strictly speaking an expert witness should not give an opinion based on scientific tests which had been made by assistants (in the expert's absence), maximum use should be made of written statements and formal admissions in proving such tests where it is not disputed that the tests were properly carried out.

A good example of the difference between primary and secondary facts is *R v Abadom* (1983) 76 Cr App R 48. A was charged with robbery. An expert gave opinion evidence that glass found on A's shoes came from a window which had been broken during the robbery. Samples of glass taken from the shoes and the window had the same refractive index. The expert stated that, according to statistics produced by the Home Office Research Establishment, the chances of the glass being from two distinct sources were minimal. A was convicted and appealed on the grounds that the statistics were hearsay. The Court of Appeal held that the statistics were secondary facts supporting the expert's opinion. So long as the primary facts (ie, that the samples compared were (a) glass taken from A's shoes and (b) glass from the robbery scene and they shared the same refractive index) were proved by admissible evidence, the expert could (indeed should) state why he arrived at his opinion on those facts.

Secondary facts cannot be introduced as evidence in the absence of an expert's opinion. For example, on a drink-driving charge a defendant who is not a medical expert cannot refer to a medical journal to support his defence. See *Dawson v Lunn* [1986] RTR 234. Note that the CJA 2003, s 127 allows proof of the primary facts through hearsay evidence in criminal cases.

15.3.5   Advance notice of expert evidence

15.3.5.1   Civil proceedings

The Civil Evidence Act 1972, s 2(3), made provision for rules of court to be made in relation to advance notice of expert evidence in civil cases. By CPR, r 35.13, a party who fails to disclose an expert's report may not use the report at the trial or call the expert to give evidence orally unless the court gives permission.

A party should be sure that he wishes to use the expert's report as evidence in his case *before* disclosing it to the other side. CPR, r 35.11, provides that *any* party to whom such a report is disclosed can put it in evidence. In general an expert's advice which is sought by a party for the purposes of pending or contemplated litigation would be protected from disclosure (at any stage of the proceedings) by legal professional privilege (see **Chapter 17** of this Manual) but r 35.11 makes it clear that the privilege is lost once the report has been disclosed under the advance notice procedure.

Even where a party relies on legal professional privilege in respect of an expert's opinion, it should be remembered that there is no property in a witness. A party who chooses not to use an expert's evidence can claim privilege in respect of the expert's opinion given to that party but he cannot muzzle the expert. Other parties to that litigation are entitled to instruct the expert and seek his opinion (subject to the procedural restrictions): see *Harmony Shipping Co SA v Saudi Europe Line Ltd* [1979] 1 WLR 1380, CA.

The amount of expert evidence which can be used in civil cases is affected by CPR, r 35.7(1), which provides:

Where two or more parties wish to submit expert evidence on a particular issue, the court may direct that the evidence on that issue is to be given by one expert only.

Unless the parties agree on the expert under this rule, the court may select an expert from a list submitted by the parties, or direct how the expert should be selected. Once selected, each instructing party may give instructions to the expert, sending a copy to the other instructing parties.

15.3.5.2 Criminal proceedings

The prosecution are obliged to disclose their expert evidence to the defence (see the *Criminal Litigation and Sentencing Manual*). The defence are also obliged to disclose such evidence. In the Crown Court, rules require any party proposing to adduce expert evidence to furnish the other parties with a written statement of the expert's finding or opinion. Such party then, *on request* in writing by any other party, must provide a copy of, or opportunity to examine, the record of any observation, test or calculation on which the finding or opinion is based. See the Criminal Procedure Rules, r 24.

A party may elect not to comply with the rules on disclosure if that party has reasonable grounds for believing that compliance might lead to intimidation or attempted intimidation of an expert witness or to interference with the course of justice. In those circumstances, the party must give notice of the grounds for non-compliance to the other parties. If the rules are not complied with in other circumstances, the expert evidence can only be used with the court's permission.

15.3.6 Opinion evidence and the hearsay rule

15.3.6.1 In civil proceedings

In civil proceedings, hearsay statements are rendered admissible by the Civil Evidence Act 1995, subject to ss 5 and 6(2) of the Act. 'Statement' is defined in s 13 of the Act for the purpose of civil proceedings as 'any representation of fact *or opinion* however made' (emphasis added). Accordingly, the fact that opinion evidence is presented as hearsay will not generally affect its admissibility in civil cases. This will apply to both expert opinion evidence (typically in the form of an expert report) and also to statements of opinion by witnesses of fact (where covered by CEA 1972, s 3(2)).

15.3.6.2   In criminal proceedings

By the Criminal Justice Act 1988, s 30:

(1)   An expert report shall be admissible as evidence in criminal proceedings, whether or not the person making it attends to give oral evidence in those proceedings.

(2)   If it is proposed that the person making the report shall not give oral evidence, the report shall only be admissible with the leave of the court.

(3)   For the purpose of determining whether to give leave the court shall have regard—

(a)   to the contents of the report;

(b)   to the reasons why it is proposed that the person making the report shall not give oral evidence;

(c)   to any risk, having regard in particular to whether it is likely to be possible to controvert statements in the report if the person making it does not attend to give oral evidence in the proceedings, that its admission or exclusion will result in unfairness to the accused or, if there is more than one, to any of them; and

(d)   to any other circumstances that appear to the court to be relevant.

(4)   An expert report, when admitted, shall be evidence of any fact or opinion of which the person making it could have given oral evidence.

In this section 'expert report' means a written report by a person dealing wholly or mainly with matters on which he is (or would if living be) qualified to give expert evidence.

(4A)   Where the proceedings mentioned in subsection (1) above are proceedings before a magistrates' court inquiring into an offence as examining justices this section shall have effect with the omission of—

(a)   in subsection (1) the words 'whether or not the person making it attends to give oral evidence in those proceedings', and

(b)   subsections (2) to (4).

This section applies to statements of fact *and* opinion in the expert report. The effect is clear. It creates a hearsay exception specifically directed at expert reports. When the expert attends as a witness the report is admissible without leave. However, where the expert is not available as a witness the court's leave to use the report is required.

There is no specific provision applicable to criminal cases to allow out-of-Court statements which are essentially shorthand for facts perceived (cp. the CEA 1972, s 3(2)). However, the CJA 2003, ss 114 and 115 allow out-of-court statements to be used in evidence, whether they are statements of fact or opinion.

Judgments as evidence of the facts on which they are based

16.1 Introduction

How might a case which has already been decided be relevant to a current case?

The judgment in the earlier case may have established a legal principle or precedent that is relevant to the legal issues in the current case.

Alternatively, the parties and the issues in the two cases may be the same. It may be necessary to refer to the judgment in the earlier case to prevent unnecessary repetition of litigation. In a civil case, we might refer to the concept of *res judicata*, and say that the earlier case establishes an issue estoppel (or a cause of action estoppel) between these litigants. Legal certainty requires an end to litigation. Likewise, in a criminal case, the accused can enter a special plea, either *autrefois acquit* or *autrefois convict*, to prevent successive proceedings for the same crime. This principle is often described in criminal cases as the rule against double jeopardy. For more information, you should consult the practitioner texts concerned with these topics.

A third possibility is that the facts that were proved in the earlier case may be relevant to the facts in issue in the current case.

16.2 General rule

The general rule is that such judgments are inadmissible if offered in later trials as evidence of the facts upon which they were based. This rule is often regarded as having been established in a civil case: *Hollington v F Hewthorn and Co Ltd* [1943] KB 587 (hence, the rule is often referred to as the rule in *Hollington v Hewthorn*). Mr Hollington brought a civil claim for damages for the death of his son, caused in a road accident. His cause of action was the allegedly negligent driving of the defendant's employee. The court held that it was not possible to call evidence of the employee's conviction for driving without due care and attention on that specific occasion in order to prove the facts on which that conviction was based. To succeed on the issue of negligence, Mr Hollington had to call evidence, starting from scratch. The driver's conviction did not weigh in the scales at all — it was simply inadmissible and so unusable as evidence.

One consequence of this judgment was that proceedings in the civil courts were often extended unnecessarily because (unless the facts were admitted by the convicted party) the same issues had to be proved all over again. The inconvenience of this general rule is obvious. A further unfortunate consequence was that in some civil trials, matters which had already been established beyond reasonable doubt (in a criminal trial) were not found to be established to the lower standard of proof, on the balance of probabilities. That inconsistency was a matter for serious concern (although, in fairness, we should observe that the evidence in the two trials might have been different).

An example of the sort of problem thrown up by this rule is found in *Hinds v Sparks* [1964] Crim LR 717. Hinds had been tried for and convicted of a robbery and had appealed unsuccessfully to the Court of Criminal Appeal. Later, a journalist, Sparks, published a statement asserting that Hinds had committed a robbery some years previously. Hinds sued Sparks for defamation. The law of defamation requires the defendant to prove the truth of his assertion. Sparks was unable to produce any evidence to support his assertion, other than the robbery conviction. Unfortunately, the rule in *Hollington v Hewthorn* made that evidence inadmissible to show Hinds had committed a robbery. Hinds won his claim.

There are now a number of exceptions to the rule in civil and criminal proceedings. With one exception, these relate to the admissibility of previous convictions. In only one example is the conviction conclusive evidence of the facts upon which it was based (see Civil Evidence Act 1968, s 13, **16.3.3** below). We shall look at the exceptions in civil cases, then criminal cases.

16.3 Use of a previous judgment as evidence of the facts in civil cases

16.3.1 Use of a criminal conviction as evidence of the facts upon which it was based in a subsequent civil case

The Civil Evidence Act 1968, s 11, reverses the actual decision in *Hollington v F Hewthorn and Co Ltd* [1943] KB 587 (ie, the conviction for driving without due care would now be admissible evidence in the civil trial to help Mr Hollington prove negligence). It therefore creates a major exception to the general rule. Section 11 puts the legal burden of proof on to the party (let's call him X) who denies that the person convicted of the offence in question did commit it. Section 11 does not say that the conviction is conclusive of the facts; it simply creates a rebuttable presumption.

Civil Evidence Act 1968, section 11

(1) *In any civil proceedings the fact that a person has been convicted of an offence by or before any court in the United Kingdom or by a court-martial there or elsewhere shall (subject to subsection (3) below) be admissible in evidence for the purpose of proving, where to do so is relevant to any issue in those proceedings, that he committed that offence, whether he was so convicted upon a plea of guilty or otherwise and whether or not he is a party to the civil proceedings; but no conviction other than a subsisting one shall be admissible in evidence by virtue of this section.*

(2) *In any civil proceedings in which by virtue of this section a person is proved to have been convicted of an offence by or before any court in the United Kingdom or by a court-martial there or elsewhere —*

   (a) *he shall be taken to have committed that offence unless the contrary is proved; and*

   (b) *without prejudice to the reception of any other admissible evidence for the purpose of identifying the facts on which the conviction was based, the contents of any document which is admissible as evidence of the conviction, and the contents of the information, complaint, indictment or charge-sheet on which the person in question was convicted, shall be admissible in evidence for that purpose.*

(3) Nothing in this section shall prejudice the operation of section 13 of this Act or any other enactment whereby a conviction or a finding of fact in any criminal proceedings is for the purposes of any other proceedings made conclusive evidence of any fact.

(4) Where in any civil proceedings the contents of any document are admissible in evidence by virtue of subsection (2) above, a copy of that document, or of the material part thereof, purporting to be certified or otherwise authenticated by or on behalf of the court or authority having custody of that document shall be admissible in evidence and shall be taken to be a true copy of that document or part unless the contrary is shown.

16.3.2 Challenging a conviction

Remember, X is the party against whom the presumption in s 11 will operate. How should X go about rebutting this presumption? This question has been considered by the courts on several occasions. The prevailing view is that it will not avail X simply to challenge the technical correctness of the conviction. X must prove either:

- that he or she (or whoever else was convicted) did not commit the crime; or
- that the crime was not committed at all.

The practical consequence of s 11 is that it is extremely difficult for a party to challenge successfully the presumption that the person convicted did in fact commit the offence in question. One need simply note the different standards of proof involved in securing the criminal conviction (beyond reasonable doubt) and in the civil trial (balance of probabilities). See *Stupple v Royal Insurance Co Ltd* [1971] 1 QB 50, *Taylor v Taylor* [1970] 1 WLR 1148 and *Wauchope v Mordechai* [1970] 1 WLR 317.

It has been said (in *Brinks Ltd v Abu Saleh (No 1)* [1995] 4 All ER 65 by Jacob J) that a convicted defendant must adduce fresh evidence which 'entirely changes the aspect of the case' in order to be permitted to contest a civil action based on the same facts. Others have since argued that this requirement to adduce fresh evidence which 'entirely changes the aspect of the case' is a very difficult one to surmount and, if it were applied generally, the effect would be to prevent a convicted defendant from ever contesting a civil claim. The matter was considered in *J v Oyston* [1999] 1 WLR 694.

The defendant [O] was convicted by a jury of raping J, and indecently assaulting her. Subsequently, J sued the defendant for damages. O now wished to call evidence about J (the claimant/complainant), which had not been produced at his criminal trial, although it had been put before the Court of Appeal when he appealed unsuccessfully against his conviction. J asserted that to allow O to call evidence which was intended to show that no crime had been committed would constitute an abuse of process and should not be allowed. Smedley J rejected that assertion. Smedley J ruled that it was entirely legitimate for O to seek to disprove allegations of rape and indecent assault, notwithstanding his convictions for both offences. In effect, J wanted to stop O from doing precisely that which s 11(2)(a) permitted him to do. That would be quite contrary to the intention of Parliament as enshrined in s 11 and as interpreted by Lord Diplock in *Hunter v Chief Constable of the West Midlands Police* [1982] AC 529. It may be difficult for a party successfully to rebut a presumption under s 11, but it must be a matter for that party to decide whether or not he or she wants to attempt it.

Conversely, it seems that where a *claimant* seeks to re-litigate a matter which has already been determined against him or her by a criminal court (that is, a convicted defendant seeks to challenge the correctness of the conviction by initiating a civil claim against the prosecuting authority), the claim is likely to be struck out as an abuse of process under

CPR, r 3.4(2)(b). See *Hunter v Chief Constable of the West Midlands Police* (and cf. Civil Evidence Act 1968, s 13, below).

Section 11 only applies to subsisting convictions. If a party in a civil claim wishes to use a conviction under s 11, the civil proceedings should be adjourned until any pending criminal appeal has been heard: see *Re Raphael* [1973] 1 WLR 998. A party seeking to rely on s 11 should state this clearly in the appropriate statement of case (see the **Drafting Manual**). This should include details of the conviction and the issue to which it is relevant. Section 11(4) allows a certified copy of the conviction, indictment etc to be used to prove the facts on which the conviction was based.

16.3.3   Use of convictions in defamation cases

A convicted criminal might try to use libel proceedings to reopen a criminal case which resulted in his conviction (in similar vein to Mr Hinds, **16.2**). Section 11 would not prevent this because it only creates a rebuttable presumption. Now, in this situation a defendant could try to persuade the judge that the claim should be struck out as an abuse of process (under CPR, r 3.4; cf *Hunter v Chief Constable of the West Midlands Police* [1982] AC 529, **16.3.2**). That application might or might not succeed. This specific situation was addressed by s 13 of the Civil Evidence Act 1968, which creates an irrebuttable presumption that the person convicted of the crime did in fact commit it.

Civil Evidence Act 1968, section 13

(1)   *In an action for libel or slander in which the question whether a person did or did not commit a criminal offence is relevant to an issue arising in the action, proof that, at the time when that issue falls to be determined, that person stands convicted of that offence shall be conclusive evidence that he committed that offence; and his conviction thereof shall be admissible in evidence accordingly.*

(2)   *In any such action as aforesaid in which by virtue of this section a person is proved to have been convicted of an offence the contents of any document which is admissible as evidence of the conviction, and the contents of the information, complaint, indictment or charge-sheet on which that person was convicted, shall, without prejudice to the reception of any other admissible evidence for the purpose of identifying the facts on which the conviction was based, be admissible in evidence for the purpose of identifying those facts.*

(3)   *For the purposes of this section a person shall be taken to stand convicted of an offence if but only if there subsists against him a conviction of that offence by or before a court in the United Kingdom or by a court-martial there or elsewhere.*

The effect of s 13 is that an action in defamation will be struck out if it is based on the defendant's assertion that the claimant committed an offence for which the claimant has been convicted. In other words, in defamation cases a person convicted of an offence is *conclusively* presumed to have committed it. Some care still needs to be taken, though — s 13 does not give publishers carte blanche to make *general* attacks on the character of convicts (see *Levene v Roxhan* [1970] 1 WLR 1322).

16.3.4   Use of a criminal acquittal as evidence of the facts upon which it was based in a subsequent civil case

An acquittal is not covered by any exception in the Civil Evidence Act 1968, so it appears that the rule in *Hollington v Hewthorn* still applies: the acquittal is inadmissible evidence if it will be used to show that the criminal defendant did not commit the offence. This may be justified by reference once more to the different standards of proof which apply in the two trials. See further *Blackstone's Civil Practice*, 2005.

16.3.5   Use of a civil judgment as evidence of the facts upon which it was based in a subsequent civil case

There is no *general* provision allowing for previous civil judgments to be used as evidence of the facts on which they were based. However, s 12 of the Civil Evidence Act 1968, allows a very limited range of civil judgments to be used as evidence of the facts on which they are based. See *Blackstone's Civil Practice*, 2005.

16.4   Use of a previous judgment as evidence of the facts in criminal cases

16.4.1   Use of a criminal conviction as evidence of the facts upon which it was based in a subsequent criminal case

Until relatively recently the common law rule excluding judgments as evidence of the facts on which they are based was of general application in criminal cases. For example, where A was charged with handling stolen goods, it was not permissible to prove that B was convicted of the theft of the goods in question to show that the goods were stolen. You may wonder why a rule established in a civil case (*Hollington v Hewthorn*) should hold sway in criminal cases, too. In fact, the rule in criminal cases pre-dates *Hollington v Hewthorn*. The example that you have just read is taken from *R v Turner* (1832) 1 Mood CC 347.

For convictions, the rule has been changed by the Police and Criminal Evidence Act 1984, s 74. A distinction needs to be drawn between (a) convictions of the accused and (b) convictions of persons other than the accused.

16.4.1.1   Convictions of the accused

Police and Criminal Evidence Act 1984, s 74(3), as amended by the CJA 2003, provides:

> *In any proceedings where evidence is admissible of the fact that the accused has committed an offence, if the accused is proved to have been convicted of the offence —*
> (a)   *by or before any court in the United Kingdom; or*
> (b)   *by a Service court outside the United Kingdom,*
> *he shall be taken to have committed that offence unless the contrary is proved.*

The general rule is that evidence that the accused has previously offended is inadmissible at his trial (see **Chapters 8**). This is so, regardless of whether or not the accused was actually convicted of the earlier offence. In exceptional situations, the fact that the accused has previously offended *may* be relevant and admissible (see CJA 2003, s 101). Where one of these exceptional situations applies, the prosecution can take advantage of s 74(3). This provision works in the same way as CEA 1968, s 11(2). It sets up a rebuttable presumption that the accused did indeed commit the previous offence.

Section 74(3) does *not* deal with questions of admissibility. All it says is that, where it is relevant and admissible to prove that D committed an offence, the act of adducing evidence that he has been convicted of it results in a rebuttable presumption. It will then be for D to try to prove, on a balance of probabilities, that he did not commit the offence.

So, remember what we are looking for. These are situations where it is relevant and admissible to show that the accused has previously *committed* an offence. In such situations, if the prosecution prove his conviction for the earlier offence, they can rely on s 74(3) to reverse the burden of proof on that fact. This still begs the question, How does the prosecution prove the conviction? See **16.4.1.3**.

16.4.1.2   Convictions of persons other than the accused

In 1972, the 11th Report of the Criminal Law Revision Committee had recommended the abolition of the rule in *Hollington v Hewthorn* in criminal proceedings. The Committee apparently thought that it was recommending simply that a conviction would be admissible in evidence to deal with the situation 'where it was necessary as a preliminary matter for it to be proved that a person other than the accused had been convicted of an offence' (see *R v O'Connor* (1986) 85 Cr App R 298, per Taylor J). This would ease the burden on the prosecution in the following situations, for example:

- In a trial for handling stolen goods, in order to prove that the goods were stolen the prosecution could prove the conviction of the thief.

- In trials for harbouring offenders, the prosecution could prove the conviction of the offender.

The Police and Criminal Evidence Act 1984, s 74(1) and (2) (as amended by CJA 2003, Sch 36), provide:

(1)   *In any proceedings the fact that a person other than the accused has been convicted of an offence by or before any court in the United Kingdom or by a Service court outside the United Kingdom shall be admissible in evidence for the purpose of proving that that person committed that offence, where evidence of his having done so is admissible, whether or not any other evidence of his having committed that offence is given.*

(2)   *In any proceedings in which by virtue of this section a person other than the accused is proved to have been convicted of an offence by or before any court in the United Kingdom or by a Service court outside the United Kingdom, he shall be taken to have committed that offence unless the contrary is proved.*

That seems quite straightforward. The effect of s 74(2) is very similar to the effect of the Civil Evidence Act 1968, s 11(2), in civil cases. That is, it puts the legal burden of proof on the party who denies that the convicted person committed the offence in question (of course the *standard* of proof in a criminal case will vary according to whether that party is the prosecution or the defence). Prior to the amendment of s 74(1) by the CJA 2003, the judicial interpretation of this provision had caused considerable practical difficulties, with several cases going to the Court of Appeal (see, for example, *R v Robertson* (1987) 85 Cr App R 304). In its amended form, s 74(1) does not say in what circumstances a conviction will be admissible to prove that a non-defendant has committed an offence, it simply says that, when such a matter may be put before the court (and see in particular, CJA 2003, s 100), evidence of a conviction for the offence is admissible to show its commission by that person.

It remains to be seen how the amended version of s 74(1) is treated by the courts. Previous case law on the original subsection indicated that it was 'a provision that should be sparingly used' (see *Robertson*). It should also be noted that the exclusionary discretion in PACE 1984, s 78 was often relied upon by defendants who were opposing use of the provision by the prosecution.

It should be noted that s 74(1) only provides a short cut for proving matters which otherwise may be proved by calling a witness. For example, in a case where one of several defendants has entered a guilty plea, the prosecution can then call the former co-defendant to testify for the Crown against the rest. In that event the remaining defendants can then cross-examine the former co-defendant, on both the facts and his credibility. The trial judge may also warn the jury to take care when assessing the evidence of the former co-defendant. By using s 74(1) instead, the opportunity of cross-examination and the need for a 'care' warning are both removed. It is arguable that this situation could deny the accused a fair trial, contrary to the European Convention on Human Rights, art 6. Perhaps this is why the Court of Appeal said (in *Robertson* and subsequent cases) that s 74(1) is to be used sparingly.

16.4.1.3   Proving a conviction

This is a two-limb process that can be done using PACE 1984, s 73(1) and (2).

One limb is that the prosecution must call a witness to produce the certificate of conviction. What qualifies as a certificate is explained in s 73(2). The other limb is that the prosecution must call a witness to say that the person named in the certificate is the accused in the dock. It could be the same witness for both limbs, usually a police officer.

(1)   *Where in any proceedings the fact that a person has in the United Kingdom been convicted or acquitted of an offence otherwise than by a Service court is admissible in evidence, it may be proved by producing a certificate of conviction or, as the case may be, of acquittal relating to that offence, and proving that the person named in the certificate as having been convicted or acquitted of the offence is the person whose conviction or acquittal of the offence is to be proved.*

(2)   *For the purposes of this section a certificate of conviction or of acquittal—*

    (a)   *shall, as regards a conviction or acquittal on indictment, consist of a certificate, signed by the proper officer of the court where the conviction or acquittal took place, giving the substance and effect (omitting the formal parts) of the indictment and of the conviction or acquittal; and*

    (b)   *shall, as regards a conviction or acquittal on a summary trial, consist of a copy of the conviction or of the dismissal of the information, signed by the proper officer of the court where the conviction or acquittal took place or by the proper officer of the court, if any, to which a memorandum of the conviction or acquittal was sent;*

    and a document purporting to be a duly signed certificate of conviction or acquittal under this section shall be taken to be such a certificate unless the contrary is proved.

16.4.1.4   What does the conviction prove?

Where a conviction is introduced into evidence in a trial, the judge must be careful to direct the jury as to:

- what issue in the trial it relates to; and
- what the effect of the conviction is.

First, it is important for judge and counsel to be clear on the exact issue to which the conviction is said to be relevant. If it is liable to be misused by the jury, the judge should probably exclude evidence of the conviction, using PACE 1984, s 78. Secondly, the conviction is *not* conclusive evidence that an offence was committed by anyone. That is shown by s 74(2), which creates a rebuttable presumption. It was confirmed in *R v Dixon* [2001] Crim LR 126 that if the defendant testifies that no such offence was committed, it is for the jury to decide whose account to believe.

By PACE 1984, s 75(1):

Where evidence that a person has been convicted of an offence is admissible by virtue of section 74 above, then without prejudice to the reception of any other admissible evidence for the purpose of identifying the facts on which the conviction was based—

    (a)   *the contents of any document which is admissible as evidence of the conviction; and*

    (b)   *the contents of the . . . indictment . . . on which the person in question was convicted, shall be admissible in evidence for that purpose.*

16.4.2   Use of a criminal acquittal as evidence of the facts upon which it was based in a subsequent criminal case

This situation is unaffected by PACE 1984. If the acquittal is that of the defendant, D, then generally it will be inadmissible as evidence in the current trial. However, facts involved in the offence of which D was acquitted may be relevant and the acquittal admissible (see *R v Z* [2000] 2 AC 483; *R v Hay* (1983) 77 Cr App R 70; *R v Terry* [2004] EWCA Crim 3252).

If the acquittal is of someone other than the accused, generally it is inadmissible. Again, it may be relevant to an issue in the current case. An example may occur if the credibility of a witness is challenged (and the witness has previously testified for the prosecution in a trial where he allegedly fabricated a confession) (see *R v Cooke* (1987) 84 Cr App R 286). The general principle is illustrated by the decision of the Privy Council in *Hui Chi-ming v R* [1992] 1 AC 34. A man was killed. D1 and D2 were charged with his murder. D1, the alleged killer, was tried first. The jury acquitted him of murder but convicted him of manslaughter. At D2's trial, as an accomplice to murder, the defence wanted to use evidence of D1's acquittal for murder. The trial judge ruled that it was inadmissible. The ruling was upheld by the Privy Council on appeal, because the verdict of the first jury was irrelevant, being only evidence of their opinion. You may feel that this produces exactly the same result as *Hollington v Hewthorn*, nearly 50 years earlier, and could also be criticised. It may make more sense if you bear in mind that there are often seemingly inconsistent verdicts involving different parties to a single crime. Also, an acquittal simply records a failure by the prosecution to prove their case beyond a reasonable doubt. It does not do the opposite and prove that D is innocent. Of course, in a case like that above, it would have been better for justice to have held a single trial of D1 and D2 before the same jury on the same evidence.

16.4.3   Use of a civil judgment as evidence of the facts upon which it was based in a subsequent criminal case

Due to the lower standard of proof in civil trials, any finding of fact would seem to be insufficiently probative to be admissible as evidence in a criminal trial.

Privilege and public policy

17.1 Introduction

Most of the rules of evidence involve analysis of the probative value of the evidence and lead to the exclusion of evidence that will not, for various reasons, be valuable in this way. However, there are occasional wider social, political or moral considerations (for example the exclusion of 'unfair' evidence under s 78 or improperly obtained confessions even though they are not prejudicial). However, generally the main concern of the rules of evidence in both civil and criminal cases is ensuring that the evidence that goes before the tribunal of fact will assist in proving the case. Even when policy reasons for excluding evidence arise, those policies (such as fairness or proportionality) are aspects of the interests of justice. In such cases competing aspects of the interests of justice have to be weighed against each other (such as unfair procedures vs accurate trial verdicts under PACE 1984, s 78).

The rules of evidence considered in this chapter reflect this concern to ensure that the interests of justice do not lead to admitting evidence that will cause a greater damage to society. With 'privileged' evidence, the concern for broader interests of justice outside the particular case have been taken to outweigh the interests of justice in the particular case. In the case of public policy exclusion the interests of justice are weighed against other social and moral questions (for example national security).

Both privilege and public policy arguments are most likely to arise during the disclosure/discovery procedures. This is so in civil cases (see the *Civil Litigation Manual* or *Blackstone's Civil Practice*, 2005, Chapter 48) and criminal cases (see the *Criminal Litigation and Sentencing Manual*, *Blackstone's Criminal Practice*, 2005 or *Archbold*, 2005).

17.2 Privilege

In broad terms the privileges which follow allow one (or in the case of 'without prejudice' correspondence either) party to prevent evidence from being put before the court on specific grounds. The types of privilege covered in this chapter are:

- The privilege against self-incrimination.
- Legal professional privilege
- 'Without prejudice' correspondence.

17.2.1 Privilege against self-incrimination

The privilege against self-incrimination influenced the development of the rules of evidence and procedure in a number of areas (particularly the exercise of the right to silence (**Chapter 13**) and the compellability of witnesses (**Chapter 4**)). The principle is also enshrined in article 6(1) of the European Convention on Human Rights.

The privilege has a more general application. No person is obliged to reveal a fact if doing so renders it reasonably likely that proceedings will be commenced that expose him or her to the risk of any criminal charge or sanction (*Blunt v Park Lane Hotel Ltd* [1942] 2 KB 253). In explaining the above test in *R v Boyes* (1861) 1 B & S 311 Cockburn J said that the risk of prosecution and punishment must be 'real and appreciable with reference to the ordinary operation of the law in the ordinary course of things; not a danger of an imaginary and unsubstantial character'.

The rule does not apply where the risk posed is a civil liability (Witnesses Act 1806) or criminal liability under foreign law (*King of Two Sicilies v Willcox* (1851) 1 Sim NS 301; Civil Evidence Act 1968, s 14) but can extend to penalties under EC law (*Rio Tinto Zinc Corporation v Westinghouse Electric Company* [1978] AC 547).

The privilege extends not only to the evidence that the person might give but to documents, items or information that the person is requested to provide during proceedings.

17.2.1.1 'Real and appreciable danger'

The evidence etc must *create* the risk of incrimination. If there is already strong evidence against the witness on the matter to which the privilege is said to relate, the rule of exclusion will not apply (*Khan v Khan* [1982] 2 All ER 60).

Furthermore if the risk can be avoided, the privilege will not apply. So in *AT&T Istel v Tully* [1993] AC 45, HL, an offer by the CPS not to prosecute the defendant in respect of any frauds revealed was held to be sufficient protection for the defendant and therefore the privilege did not apply.

Where the sanction or punishment that is faced is trivial, the court may also conclude that there is no real and appreciable danger (*Rank Film Distributors Ltd v Video Information Centre* [1982] AC 380).

17.2.1.2 To whom does the privilege apply?

In criminal cases the privilege only applies to the person asserting it. In other words, A could not exercise the privilege on the grounds that his answer would incriminate B (this is implicit from *R v Pitt* [1983] QB 25 where a witness was treated as compellable to give evidence against her spouse: this would not have been the case if she could have asserted a privilege against incriminating her spouse).

In civil cases the privilege does extend to spouses (Civil Evidence Act 1968, s 14(1)(b)) but no further.

Companies can be covered by the privilege (*Triplex Safety Glass Co Ltd v Lancegaye Safety Glass* [1939] 2 KB 395). However in such circumstances the privilege excuses an employee of the company from giving testimony (or disclosing evidence) that would incriminate the company; it does not excuse him or her from incriminating an employee of the company (*Rio Tinto Zinc v Westinghouse Electric*) other than himself.

17.2.1.3 Privileged evidence that is revealed

If a witness answers questions without claiming the privilege (before or after but during the proceedings) the evidence can be used against the witness in subsequent proceedings

(*R v Coote* (1873) LR 4 PC 599). However if the witness does claim privilege and is wrongly refused (and therefore forced to answer), the evidence must be excluded in the subsequent proceedings (*R v Garbett* (1847) 1 Den CC 236).

17.2.1.4 Statutory exceptions

The privilege is subject to numerous statutory exceptions. First of all the privilege does not protect the accused in criminal proceedings from answering questions in respect of those proceedings (*Criminal Evidence Act 1898, s 1(2)*).

In the following situations evidence that reveals criminal conduct may be admitted in specific types of proceedings (the type of proceedings being illustrated in each situation below). However in each situation, there are restrictions on the extent to which the information revealed can be used in subsequent criminal proceedings:

(a) *Theft Act 1968, s 31(1)*: in proceedings concerning the recovery or administration of property, the execution of any trust or an account for property or dealings with property, a person is not excused from answering questions simply because doing so would reveal he or she may have committed an offence under the Theft Act 1968. However, any statement or testimony made is not admissible in a subsequent prosecution under the Theft Act 1968. This protection also extends to the spouse of the witness. If the evidence poses a real risk of both a Theft Act and a non-Theft Act prosecution the court will apply the privilege against self-incrimination (*Renworth Ltd v Stephansen* [1996] 3 All ER 244) with the effect that the person is not obliged to answer the question.

(b) The same provision exists in the *Criminal Damage Act 1971, s 9* relating to the same types of civil actions, but the criminal offences to which it relates are criminal damage offences.

(c) *Children Act 1989, s 98*: in proceedings concerning the care, supervision or protection of children, a person cannot refuse to answer questions on the grounds either that that person or his or her spouse would be incriminated. Again such evidence will not be admissible in subsequent proceedings except perjury proceedings (s 98(2)). It has been suggested that this protection extends to oral or written statements made before trial (*Oxfordshire County Council v P* [1995] 2 All ER 225, *Cleveland County Council v F* [1995] 2 All ER 236). However in *Re G (A Minor)* [1996] 2 All ER 65, the Court of Appeal stated that the protection under s 98(2) should be restricted to evidence in the proceedings and not pre-trial statements. However the court recognised that the criminal courts were not bound by that view. In *A Chief Constable v A County Council* [2003] 1 FLR 579, the court took the view that statements made by parents to expert witnesses appointed by the court would be covered by s 98(2) privilege and therefore would not be admissible in subsequent criminal proceedings.

(d) *Criminal Justice Act 1987, s 2*: the Director of the Serious Fraud Office has broad powers to investigate persons in respect of offences of serious or complex fraud (ie those under Part 1 of that Act). Persons investigated can be required to answer questions or provide documentation. Such evidence can only be used at a later trial if the person is being prosecuted for the offence of providing false information under s 2 or subsequently makes a statement inconsistent with it (ie as a previous inconsistent statement: see **6.3.6**).

(e) *Insolvency Act 1986*: various statements that must be made under this Act could be incriminating. Section 433(1) of the Act provides that such statements may be used in evidence against the person who made them in subsequent proceedings. Section

433(2), however provides that in subsequent criminal proceedings such statements may only be admitted (or questions asked about them) if the person who made the statement has already admitted evidence relating to that statement. This restriction does not apply in relation to perjury and related proceedings or criminal proceedings under the Insolvency Act.

(f) Similar restrictions to those under the Insolvency Act apply in relation to investigations under the *Companies Act 1985, ss 434 and 447* and various other statutes in Sch 3 to the Youth Justice and Criminal Evidence Act 1999.

Insofar as any other statute appears to have revoked the privilege against self-incrimination without any restriction upon the extent to which statements made can be used in subsequent criminal proceedings, there is a potential breach of article 6(1) of the European Convention but this is not always so. In *Brown v Stott* [2001] 2 WLR 817, the Privy Council recognised that article 6 rights are subject to a limited qualification. Where there was a clear public interest in revoking the privilege, the statutory provision would not necessarily be held to be incompatible with article 6. In *Office of Fair Trading v X* [2003] 2 All ER (Comm) 183, the High Court upheld powers to search premises and to question persons present about items found during the search where the statutory framework for such searches included guarantees of a suspect's rights.

17.2.2   Legal professional privilege

Both civil and criminal litigation depends upon parties having access to effective legal advice. This in turn depends upon a party and his or her lawyer being able to communicate freely and without fear that the content of the discussion will be used by the other side. Furthermore, legal professional privilege is a function of article 6 of the European Convention on Human Rights (*S v Switzerland* (1991) 14 EHRR 670; *Foxley v United Kingdom* (2001) 31 EHRR 25).

There are two classes of legal professional privilege, which broadly are:

(a) Communications between a lawyer and his or her client (also known as 'lawyer-client privilege' or 'legal advice privilege').

(b) Communications between the lawyer or client on the one hand and third parties on the other where such communication relates to pending or contemplated litigation: *Waugh v British Railways Board* [1980] AC 521 (also known as 'litigation privilege').

Under both classes the privilege applies to communication with solicitors, barristers, foreign lawyers and in-house legal advisers (*Re Duncan* [1968] P 306; *Alfred Compton Amusement Machines Ltd v Customs & Excise Commissioners* [1974] AC 405).

17.2.2.1   Lawyer-client privilege

Communications between a lawyer and his or her client for the purposes of obtaining or giving legal advice are privileged whether or not litigation is contemplated (*Greenough v Gaskell* (1833) 1 My & K 98).

The privilege clearly covers any requests for advice from a client to a lawyer and any advice given by the lawyer to the client. However, unlike litigation privilege (**17.2.2.2**) this privilege does not attach to communications between a lawyer or a client and a third party to the lawyer-client relationship. Therefore in *Wheeler v Le Marchant* (1881) 17 Ch D 675, no lawyer-client privilege could be attached to communications between a solicitor and a surveyor, the purpose of which communication was to provide advice concerning land included in a will. Therefore factual information communicated to a solicitor for the purpose of advice will not be protected when provided by a third party even if the third party was responding to a request for that information by the solicitor for the purpose of giving advice. In *Three Rivers District Council v Bank of England (No 3)* [2003] QB 1556, the Court of Appeal ruled that even internal communications between employees of the Bank of England would not be covered by lawyer-client privilege even though some of those communications were to and from employees responsible for seeking legal advice from the Bank's solicitors. It was only the communication between employees at the Bank and the Bank's solicitors that were covered by the privilege. However, if a communication to which privilege attaches is passed on to a third party or internally within an organisation, privilege will not be lost: *USP Strategies v London General Holdings Ltd and others* The Times, 30 April 2004.

Lawyers do not restrict their advice and communication to explanation of the law. In *Belabel v Air India* [1988] Ch 317, Lord Taylor said at p 330:

> In most solicitor and client relationships, especially where a transaction involves protracted dealings, advice may be required [as] appropriate on matters great or small at various stages. There will be a continuum of communication and meetings between the solicitor and client . . . Where information is passed by the solicitor or client to the other as part of the continuum aimed at keeping both informed so that advice may be sought and given as required, privilege will attach . . . Moreover, legal advice is not confined to telling the client the law; it must include advice as to what should prudently and sensibly be done in the relevant legal context.

Even if between a solicitor and a client, only communications for the purposes of 'legal advice' are covered by this privilege. Therefore the purpose of any communication must be considered. In *Three Rivers District Council v Bank of England (No 4)* [2004] 3 WLR 1274, the House of Lords ruled that, in addition to advice on legal rights and obligations, this privilege could also attach to advice on the presentation of evidence at an inquiry or tribunal which is not a court of law as long as the advice is given in the 'legal context' to which Lord Taylor referred in *Belabel v Air India*. Their Lordships attached importance to the impact of such an inquiry on legal rights (Lord Scott at [43]) or the legal content of the inquiry (Lord Scott at [44] and Lord Carswell at [116]). Therefore communications between the Bank of England and its solicitors were privileged even if the purpose related solely to the presentation of evidence to the Bingham Inquiry investigating the collapse of BCCI. The inquiry was an ad hoc investigation initiated by the government.

However, lawyers do not restrict their advice to such matters. What if the purpose of the communication in question is mixed? In *Belabel v Air India* [1988] Ch 317, the Court of Appeal observed that whether communication was for the purposes of legal advice had to be interpreted broadly. In *Hellenic Mutual War Risks Association (Bermuda) Ltd v Harrison (The Sagheera)* [1997] 1 Lloyd's Rep 160, Rix J stated that documents would be privileged if the *dominant* purpose of the retainer (the employment of the lawyer) was the provision of legal advice. In *Three Rivers District Council v Bank of England (No 3)*, the Court of Appeal accepted without argument that 'purpose' in *Greenough v Gaskell* meant 'dominant purpose'. Therefore before lawyer-client privilege will attach to any communication, it must be established to have been predominantly about 'legal advice' in the broad sense of the phrase identified in *Three Rivers District Council v Bank of England (No 4)* (above).

The courts will not adopt a rigid or technical approach to determine whether one or more item is covered by lawyer-client privilege. As was noted above, in *Belabel* it was stated that the 'continuum' of communication rather than each individual communication is to be assessed when determining its purpose. However, in *United States of America v Philip Morris Inc* The Times, 16 April 2004, the Court of Appeal questioned the simple analysis of all communications under a solicitor's retainer and noted that *Belabel* had not created any rule that the 'continuum of communication' had to be entirely privileged or without privilege. In fact it was stated in *Belabel* that whether documents produced to note or record meetings would be covered by lawyer-client privilege would depend on whether they were 'part of that necessary exchange of information of which the object is the giving of legal advice as and when appropriate' (at p 332). The Court of Appeal in *USA v Morris* approved a decision of the judge at first instance not to award lawyer-client privilege to a series of communications but rather to order disclosure of all communications and to leave it to the respondent parties to claim privilege over any particular document when required. The effect of this judgment would appear to be to limit the extent of privilege to those documents which either requested or gave privileged advice or (in the words used in *Belabel*) were 'necessary exchange of information of which the object is the giving of legal advice'.

Where the communication was intended to be passed on to other parties, such communications will not be privileged (*Conlon v Conlon's Ltd* [1952] 2 All ER 462). In *R (Hoare) v South Durham Magistrates' Court* [2005] RTR 4, the Divisional Court held that a solicitor could be called to prove the identity of his client and the fact of a previous conviction (at which the solicitor was present) without offending lawyer-client privilege.

17.2.2.2   Third party or litigation privilege

The second class of legal professional privilege is aimed primarily at communications with potential experts or witnesses of fact although the rule is not restricted to persons in such classes. The object of this class is to extend privilege to communications with a third party to the lawyer-client relationship in certain limited circumstances.

Note that this class of privilege applies if there is communication between a third party and *either* the lawyer or the client.

This privilege will arise where the communication concerned pending or contemplated litigation. Where the communication takes place before any dispute had arisen it is highly unlikely that it will be privileged (*Wheeler v Le Marchant* (1881) 17 Ch D 675, CA). In *Re Highgrade Traders Ltd* [1984] BCLC 151, Oliver LJ at p 172 used the expression 'if litigation is reasonably in prospect' to define whether litigation was pending or contemplated and in *Mitsubishi Electric Australia Pty Ltd v Victorian WorkCover Authority* [2002] VSCA 59 an Australian court defined the test as 'a real prospect of litigation as distinct from a mere possibility'. This approach was approved in *United States of America v Philip Morris Inc* The Times, 16 April 2004, where it was noted that 'a mere possibility' of litigation being commenced would be inadequate.

In *Waugh v British Railways Board* [1980] AC 521, it was held that the dominant purpose had to be litigation. In that case the document in question was a report by an accident investigator that, had been prepared so that the defendants could assess their liability in a crash and so that they could take steps to prevent any such accident from happening again. The House of Lords held that the two purposes had been of equal weight so the document was not privileged. Quite what the dominant purpose of a document or communication is will depend on the facts of each case.

In *Re L (A Minor) (Police Investigation: Privilege)* [1997] AC 16, the House of Lords held that this type of privilege only applies in adversarial proceedings and therefore would not apply to advice concerning investigation and inquiries (but see *Three Rivers District Council v Bank of England (No 4)* [2004] 3 WLR 1274 (above), where it was accepted that communications in respect of a judicial enquiry formed by the government would be privileged). Furthermore, in *United States of America v Phillip Morris Inc* (above) it was stated that the prospect of a party being required to produce documents at the trial between two other parties did not amount to litigation for these purposes and therefore no privilege would attach to communication about such matters.

17.2.2.3   The effect of legal professional privilege

Communication falling under either class will not be admissible at trial unless the party who has the privilege waives it (see **17.2.2.4** below). The privilege renders the communications inadmissible and immune from discovery. However it does not prevent documents or items in the possession of the lawyer or third party from being admissible nor does it prevent the lawyer or third party from being called as a witness of fact on some matters (see **17.2.2.5** below). Furthermore, there are two exceptions to the rule that communications are privileged (see **17.2.2.6** below).

The privilege is that of the client not of the lawyer or third party (*Schneider v Leigh* [1955] 2 QB 195).

The communication will remain privileged after the proceedings to which they relate has ended and will also pass to successors in title (*Minet v Morgan* (1873) 8 Ch App 361).

17.2.2.4   Waiver of privilege

As the privilege is that of the client, only he or she can waive it. Where the alleged waiver was made in excess of the powers of the person doing so, privilege will not have been waived: *GE Capital v Sutton* (2004) 2 BCLC 662. Equally, waiver that is effected by compulsion will not cancel the privilege (*British American Tobacco (Investments) Ltd v United States of America* [2004] EWCA Civ 1064). The court will look carefully at the circumstances of the waiver to determine whether and exactly how much of the privilege has been waived (*Great Atlantic Insurance Co v Home Insurance Co* [1981] 1 WLR 529).

Where a client has purported to waive privilege in respect of one matter or communication but not in respect of others, the court may infer that other communications have been waived (*General Accident Fire & Life Assurance Corporation Ltd v Tanter* [1984] 1 WLR 100). In large documents, the court will apply the waiver to the whole document unless parts of it are deemed to be distinct and severable in their nature (*British Coal Corporation v Dennis Rye Ltd (No 2)* [1988] 3 All ER 816).

Particular difficulties arise when a party is forced to give evidence as to the nature of discussions with his or her lawyer. This is most likely to be the case where the accused remains silent as a result of legal advice when questioned by the police and the prosecution in a criminal case seek to rely on s 34 of the Criminal Justice and Public Order Act 1994 (see **13.4.1.1**). To explain that such silence was not motivated by a consciousness of guilt, the lawyer may have to give evidence. In *R v Bowden* [1999] 2 Cr App R 176, the Court of Appeal held that calling the lawyer in this way meant that the lawyer could be cross-examined as to the detail and reasons for the advice given and that it would be inappropriate for legal professional privilege to restrict this.

17.2.2.5   Limits on the scope of privilege

The privilege applies to the communications between lawyer and client not to facts that were perceived during the solicitor/client relationship such as the client's identity (*Studdy v Sanders* (1823) 2 Dow & Ry KB 347) or the fact of the client having attended the solicitor's office to receive advice (*R v Manchester Crown Court, ex p R* The Times, 15 February 1999).

Furthermore, documents or items do not become privileged simply because they are in the possession of a party's lawyer (*Dubai Bank v Galadari* [1989] 3 All ER 769). In *R v Peterborough Justice, ex p Hicks* [1977] 1 WLR 1371, the defendants were charged with forgery offences. The Court of Appeal refused to quash a warrant to search the party's solicitor's offices for allegedly forged documents stating that the solicitor had no better right to resist the warrant than the person upon whose behalf he or she held them. Therefore, whether the documents can be withheld depends on whether the client has some right other than legal professional privilege to keep them. This can be seen by contrasting the following two cases in which experts had received items of evidence for the purposes of advising a party and in which litigation privilege was alleged:

(a) In *R v King* [1983] 1 WLR 411, CA, it was held that a subpoena was properly issued to the prosecution requiring a handwriting expert, who had been retained by the defence, to produce documents containing the defendant's handwriting but which may have incriminated the accused.

(b) In *R v R* [1994] 4 All ER 260, CA, it was held that DNA samples that had been sent to an expert for his advice should not have been admitted. The DNA samples could not have been taken from the accused without his consent (**14.4.3**).

Note in the two cases the items of evidence were admissible to prove facts in their own right. Equally an expert whose expert opinion is privileged could be called by the other party to prove facts as opposed to opinions he or she has perceived (*Harmony Shipping Co SA v Saudi Europe Line Ltd* [1979] 1 WLR 1380, CA).

Facts related to a lawyer as part of his or her instructions will be privileged. However, if the lawyer perceives facts while acting for a client where those facts were not communicated to him or her by the client, those facts will not be privileged. In *Brown v Foster* (1857) 1 Hur & N 736, the plaintiff brought an action for malicious prosecution having been acquitted of embezzlement. In the course of the embezzlement trial, it was alleged that he had not made an entry in a ledger and the charge had been dismissed when it was revealed that an entry in a ledger had in fact been made. The defendant in the malicious prosecution proceedings was allowed to call the plaintiff's barrister in the embezzlement proceedings to say that the day before the ledger was admitted as evidence, there was no such entry. This was a fact perceived by the barrister rather than information received from the plaintiff under privileged instructions.

17.2.2.6   Exceptions to legal professional privilege

The privilege applies absolutely. There is no general power to override the privilege because of public interest considerations (*R v Derby Magistrates' Court, ex p B* [1995] 3 WLR 681). However the privilege is subject to two qualifications set out below which reflect public interest concerns:

(a) *Legal professional privilege does not apply to communications made in pursuance of a crime or fraud* (*R v Cox and Railton* (1884) 14 QBD 153). In *Crescent Farm (Sidcup) Sport Ltd v Sterling Offices Ltd* [1972] Ch 553, it was stated that fraud went beyond the tort of deceit and included 'all forms of dishonesty such as fraudulent breaches of contract, fraudulent conspiracies, trickery and sham contrivances' (per Goff J). Clearly a lawyer will regularly be exposed to the criminal past of a client and will even have to advise them that future conduct might be unlawful in some way. However in *Barclays Bank plc v Eustice* [1995] 4 All ER 411, CA, a distinction was drawn between legal advice as to the legal affect of what had happened and advice as to how to carry out a fraudulent unlawful purpose in the future. However the timing of the criminal conduct does not fully determine the matter. Advice as to the potential illegality of future conduct will still be privileged (*Butler v Board of Trade* [1971] Ch 680). The test is whether the communication was made in pursuance of the fraud or crime (*R v Snaresbrook Crown Court, ex p DPP* [1988] QB 532).

The issue for the court to determine is whether it was the purpose of the lawyer *or* the client to pursue a fraud or crime. *R v Central Criminal Court, ex p Francis & Francis*, HL, concerned the powers of search and seizure under s 10 of the Police and

Criminal Evidence Act 1984. The House stated that s 10 reflected the common law on legal professional privilege. The police, during a drugs investigation, had obtained orders requiring solicitors to produce documentation concerning the buying and selling of properties by a suspect and his family. The solicitors argued that the transactions and communications concerning them were privileged. However, the House concluded privilege would not apply if the intention of furthering a criminal purpose was that of the holder of the document or of any other party.

Merely instructing a lawyer to advance a case that may be proven to be untrue is not the furthering of a fraud or crime (*Snaresbrook Crown Court, ex p DPP*). However, where there is an agreement to pervert the course of justice that can be proven by evidence that is independent of the proof of the case in question, privilege will not attach to communication made in pursuance of that agreement (*R (Hallinan Blackburn Gittings and Nott) v Middlesex Guildhall Crown Court* [2005] 1 WLR 766). In *Kuwait Airways Corporation v Iraqi Airways Co* The Times, 25 April, 2005, the Court of Appeal held that if the alleged fraud was one of the issues in the case in question, there would have to be strong prima facie evidence of such fraud before privilege would be overruled.

(b) *Litigation privilege does not apply in non-adversarial proceedings.* In any proceedings concerning the upbringing of children, the welfare of the child is the court's paramount consideration (s 1(1) of the Children Act 1989). In *Oxfordshire County Council v M* [1994] 2 All ER 269, the Court of Appeal held that the welfare of the child required that communications with third parties should not be subject to privilege. In children cases such communications will generally address various aspects of the welfare of the child such as his or her physical, educational or emotional needs or harm the child may or may not have suffered. The court was also influenced by the fact that such third parties were appointed by the court in any event. The position was confirmed by the House of Lords in *Re L (A Minor) (Police Investigation: Privilege)* [1996] 2 WLR 395. There the House noted the investigative nature of children proceedings and the requirement of leave for third parties to be instructed. It was therefore held to be inappropriate for third party privilege to apply in cases resolved using inquisitorial procedures. In *Three Rivers District Council v Bank of England (No 4)* [2004] 3 WLR 1274, the House of Lords reiterated the restriction of litigation privilege to adversarial proceedings but noted that the inquisitorial nature of the CPR invited a reappraisal of litigation privilege.

Note that although most proceedings concerning the welfare of children will be those brought under the Children Act 1989, there are some proceedings in which this is not the case (such as wardship proceedings). Owing to the breadth of s 1(1) of the 1989 Act the welfare principle and its effect on third party privilege will be of equal application in such cases.

17.2.2.7   Proving evidence by other means

The privilege attaches only to the communications or documents set out above. The facts contained in the communications or documents are not covered by the privilege. Therefore if the fact can be proved by other means, other parties may attempt to do so. The extent to which the court must let them do so depends upon whether it is a criminal or civil case:

(a) *Criminal cases*: Once the information has been made available to the prosecution, the accused's privilege is lost. For example:

   (i)   A note from the accused to his barrister that was found on the floor had been properly used in cross-examination (*R v Tompkins* (1977) 67 Cr App R 181, CA).

(ii)   The written account from the accused to his solicitor was accidentally sent to the prosecution. It had properly been used by them at trail (*R v Cottrill* [1997] Crim LR 56, CA).

However the court will consider whether the evidence has been obtained unfairly and should therefore be excluded under s 78 of the Police and Criminal Evidence Act 1984 (*R v Cottrill* and *R v Willis* [2004] All ER (D) 287).

(b) *Civil cases*: The position is now governed by CPR, r 31.20, which provides:

> Where a party inadvertently allows a privileged document to be inspected, the party who has inspected the document may use it or its contents only with the permission of the court.

In deciding whether or not to grant permission, the court will have regard to pre-CPR case law concerning the granting of injunctions to restrain the use of such evidence. Injunctions were generally granted where the documents had been obtained by fraud (*Ashburton v Pape* [1913] 2 Ch D 469) or obvious error (*Goddard v Nationwide Building Society* [1987] QB 670, CA) but what if the mistake is not obvious? In *International Business Machines Corporation v Phoenix International (Computers) Ltd* [1995] 1 All ER 413 numerous documents were made available by the defendant to the plaintiff. These documents included documents that were clearly privileged in principle. However the plaintiff's solicitors took the view that privilege had been waived in respect of the documents and told the defendant's solicitors this. The defendant therefore applied for an injunction restraining such use and seeking their return. The court held that test was whether a reasonable solicitor would have realised that privilege had not been waived. In doing so the court would take into account the extent to which privilege was claimed in respect of other documents, the nature of the case, of the documents and the way in which discovery (disclosure) had taken place thus far. On that basis the documents in question were clearly privileged.

However the advent of the Civil Procedure Rules, has led to a stricter approach. In *USP Strategies v London General Holdings* The Times, 30 April, 2004, it was held that when a party obtains possession of communications to which an unwaived privilege attaches, the normal starting point is to order that the privileged material shall not be used and that any discretion to allow the use of such material should not be exercised merely to allow probative evidence to be admitted. However in extreme cases, the court could refuse to make an order restraining use of such evidence; in the public interest in the proper administration of justice (*ISTIL Group Inc v Zahoor* [2003] 2 All ER 252).

Note also that paragraph 608(f) of the Code of Conduct for the Bar restricts the extent to which a barrister may use a document which has come into his or her possession by 'some means other than the normal and proper channels'. If the barrister accidentally reads such a document and then realises that he or she should not have done so, he or she may withdraw if he or she:

- would be embarrassed in the discharge of his or her duties by knowing what was revealed in the document; and

- he or she can do so without jeopardising the client's interests.

17.2.3   'Without prejudice' communications

It was noted above (**17.2.2.1**) that where the communication was intended to be passed on to other parties, such communications will not be privileged (*Conlon v Conlon's Ltd* [1952]

2 All ER 462 (see also *Paragon Finance plc v Freshfields* [1999] 1 WLR 1183)). Generally communications between parties are not privileged (after all the main purpose of the privilege is to prevent other parties from knowing the strength of the party's case). However, this principle is subject to an exception where the parties are seeking to settle the case by negotiation so that parties need not fear that what they admit or concede when negotiating to settle a case will be seen by the tribunal of fact. This ground of excluding evidence resembles legal professional privilege but is different not least of all because the protection can only be waived by agreement between both parties.

Such communication is generally referred to as 'without prejudice' correspondence. As a matter of good practice those words should be clearly marked on any letters that are not intended to go before the judge however:

(a) the court is not bound to hold correspondence to be 'without prejudice' whenever the words are used (*Buckinghamshire County Council v Moran* [1990] Ch 623).

(b) the court is not bound to hold that correspondence without those words can never be 'without prejudice' (*Chocoladefabriken Lindt & Sprungli AG v Nestle Co Ltd* [1978] RPC 287).

(c) The real test is whether the correspondence is part of negotiations genuinely aimed at settlement (*South Shropshire District Council v Amos* [1986] 1 WLR 1271).

The rule prevents the correspondence from being admissible at trial (either on the matter or liability or on the issue of remedies). However, there are limited circumstances in which such correspondence will be admissible:

(a) If the negotiations reach settlement, the correspondence can be used as evidence of what was agreed (*Walker v Wilshire* (1889) 23 QBD 335; *Tomlin v Standard Telephones & Cables Ltd* [1969] 1 WLR 1378). It is not evidence on any other matter nor is the agreement between the claimant and the first defendant in any way admissible in respect of the dispute between the claimant and the second defendant on exactly the same matter (*Rush & Tompkins Ltd v Greater London Council* [1989] AC 1280, HL). The reaching of an agreement is not necessarily recognition of the truth of the allegations to which it relates and should not therefore be allowed to prove anything other than the fact of agreement. However where one of the parties who reached a settlement brings proceedings against a third party for a contribution to the damages in the main claim and the without prejudice correspondence refers to the degrees of contribution, the correspondence can be referred to (*Gnitrow Ltd v Cape plc* [2000] 1 WLR 2327).

(b) Where subsequent proceedings relate to wholly different subject matter and the correspondence reveals evidence in relation to that different subject matter then the correspondence will be admissible whether or not a settlement was reached (*Muller v Linsley & Mortimer* The Times, 8 December 1994).

(c) Where correspondence is marked 'without prejudice save as to costs' the court may, in limited circumstances, refer to the correspondence when determining costs issues. This detailed procedure is governed by CPR, Part 36 (see *Blackstone's Civil Practice*, 2005, Chapter 64) and in family proceedings by r 2.69 of the Family Proceedings Rules 1991, SI 1991/1247, and the case law deriving from *Calderbank v Calderbank* [1976] Fam 93. This will necessarily only apply where there was no settlement as the point of the analysis is to determine whether the party in question received a better order from the court than was offered by the other party and should therefore have the costs of the litigation paid by the other party.

(d) In proceedings relating to children, any admissions made by a parent concerning any harm that a child has suffered, whether made in an attempt to settle proceedings before trial of for other reasons will be admissible as evidence (*Re D (Minor)* [1993] 2 All ER 693).

17.3 Public policy exclusion

The rules we have examined in this chapter so far have concerned the inadmissibility of evidence because one or both parties has asserted a privilege in respect of it. These privileges exist because of a concern to maintain the integrity of the litigation process and the interests of justice above and beyond the needs of the particular case. However, there is also a rule of more general application that restricts the extent to which otherwise admissible evidence can be revealed to parties and admitted as evidence. The rationale for this rule is that there are other public policy reasons for keeping evidence out of court than its impact upon the interests of justice.

This area of law is also commonly known as public interest immunity (or PII).

17.3.1 The general rule

The test of public policy exclusion is simply a matter of balancing the interest of justice in disclosing the evidence in question, on the one hand, against the public policy for excluding it, on the other hand (*Conway v Rimmer* [1968] AC 910). The claim of public policy exclusion should be decided by the courts.

The mere fact that a government agency or the prosecution alleges that it is not in the public interest for evidence in their possession to be revealed does not determine whether or not it should be (*R v Ward* [1993] 1 WLR 619 and the Criminal Procedure and Investigations Act 1996, Part I). Further, if no party requests that the evidence be excluded on public policy grounds the court may (and should) consider whether to do so if necessary (*Duncan v Cammell Laird & Co Ltd* [1942] AC 624).

The public interest for these purposes is not determined by the class of document or source of information in question. Although such an approach had previously been adopted in relation to documents such as high level government papers, the House of Lords stated in *Burmah Oil Co v Bank of England* [1980] AC 1090 that 'class' claims should be evaluated and decided on their merits just like any other type of document. Therefore public interest immunity from disclosure or use will not automatically be granted in respect of a document merely because it is diplomatic correspondence or a confidential economic report, for example. In 1996 the Lord Chancellor issued a statement (1997 147 NLJ 62) that government departments would no longer seek exclusion simply on the grounds that the document fell into a particular class. Instead ministers will:

. . . focus directly on the damage that disclosure of sensitive documents would cause . . . Ministers will only claim immunity when they believe that disclosure . . . will cause real damage or harm to the public interest. Damage will normally have to be in the form of a direct and immediate threat to the safety of an individual or to the nation's economic interest or relations with a foreign state, though in some cases the anticipated damage might be indirect or longer term, such as damage to a regulatory process.

Therefore, a balancing exercise must be conducted in all cases. The fact that evidence from a particular class of source is more or less regularly excluded than that from other classes of source simply reflects the weight that is often attached to such sources when that balancing exercise is conducted rather than any absolute rule as to whether or not they should be excluded.

While in civil cases the interest of justice may vary from case to case, in criminal cases it has been said that where evidence may prove the accused's innocence or prevent a miscarriage of justice, the balance comes down heavily in favour of disclosure (*R v Keane* [1994] 1 WLR 746, CA). This does not prevent the court from having to consider the potential value of the evidence. The decision not to disclose material to the defence on the grounds of public interest immunity may undermine the right of the defendant to a fair trial in accordance with article 6 of the European Convention. The European Court has recognised that the withholding of some information about prosecution investigative procedures is permissible without breaching the right of the accused to a fair trail (*Klass v Federal Republic of Germany* (1978) 2 EHRR 214, 232). However in *Rowe and Davis v United Kingdom* (2000) 30 EHRR 1, the European Court of Human Rights stated that only such withholding of evidence as was strictly necessary would be consistent with a fair trail. In *R v H, R v C* [2003] UKHL 2847, the House of Lords considered the process for determining whether material in the possession of the prosecution could be withheld from the defence on the grounds of public interest immunity. As part of the identification of a seven-stage process for determining such disclosure issues (see **17.3.4.1** below), the House defined the test for public interest immunity in two stages:

1   Is there a real risk of serious prejudice to an important public interest (and, if so, what) if full disclosure of the material is ordered? If No, full disclosure should be ordered.
2   If the answer to . . . [2] is Yes, can the defendant's interest be protected without disclosure or disclosure be ordered to an extent or in a way which will give adequate protection to the public interest in question and also afford adequate protection to the interests of the defence?

17.3.2   The effect of public policy exclusion

Where evidence is excluded for reasons of public policy, no party can waive that right. Where no interested party has claimed that the evidence ought to be excluded on the grounds of public policy, that is simply a factor that the courts will consider in balancing the public policy against the interests of justice. In this sense the evidence is different to evidence excluded under one of the privileges set out in **17.2** above, as in privilege cases, the exclusion of the source of evidence depends upon a claim by someone that the evidence is privileged. Further, it is the fact or information that is excluded rather than the means of proving it (ie, the source or document itself) (*Rogers v Home Secretary* [1973] AC 388). Therefore, in contrast to evidence excluded on the grounds of a privilege, the information cannot be proved by some other route (for the contrast, see **17.2.2.7**).

17.3.3   Examples

The following cases are all examples for the exercise of the principle of public policy exclusion. The list is not comprehensive. For further cases see *Blackstone's Criminal Practice*, 2005, at F9.1 to F9.8, *Archbold*, 2005, 12–34 to 12–44. While 'class' claims no longer determine whether or not evidence will be admitted, the type of document or type of information contained in the document tends to raise similar concerns and issues.

17.3.3.1   National security, affairs of state and foreign policy interests

It was this type of claim of public policy exclusion that previously led to automatic exclusion by class of document. However in Sir Richard Scott V-C's *Report of the Inquiry into the Export of Defence Equipment and Dual-Use Goods to Iraq and Related Prosecutions* (House of Commons Paper 115, 95/96, at G18.86) the use of class claims even in relation to national security interests was criticised leading to the Lord Chancellor's statement (at **17.3.1** above). Therefore any statement even that national security evidence should be excluded as a matter of course has to be looked at critically. However the trend has been for such evidence to be excluded. For example:

(a) In *Duncan v Cammell Laird & Co Ltd* [1942] AC 624 the court refused to order the disclosure of plans for a submarine that sank during trials.

(b) In *Burmah Oil Co v Bank of England* [1980] AC 1090, the bank's refusal to produce confidential records of dealings with bank and other businesses was upheld. The refusal was at the request of the government on the grounds of national economic interests.

(c) In *Buttes Gas and Oil Co v Hammer (No 3)* [1981] 1 QB 223, information relating to a company's dealings with a foreign State would not be revealed where that company was in a border dispute with its neighbour. The public interest served by refusing to disclose the evidence was international comity.

17.3.3.2   Police information

Information that has been used during investigations will often be of potential benefit to the accused in criminal proceedings or to parties taking action against the police in respect of their policing. Examples include:

(a) In *Evans v Chief Constable of Surrey* [1988] QB 588, a report sent to the DPP by the police was held not to be disclosable in a civil action as it was held to be important to preserve the freedom of communication between the police and the DPP. Equally where the police have obtained evidence during a criminal investigation, the court must balance the confidentiality of such information obtained under the exercise of compulsory powers against the basic public interest in assuring a fair trial on full evidence in any subsequent civil proceedings: *Marcel v Commissioner of Police for the Metropolis* [1992] Ch 225, CA and *Taylor v Director of the Serious Fraud Office* [1999] 2 AC 177. In *Frankson v Home Office* [2003] EWCA Civ 655, the Court of Appeal rejected the argument that statements made to police officers under caution would necessarily be excluded in the public interest. There is therefore no general public interest in maintaining the confidentiality of statements made to prosecuting authorities that will outweigh the interest of a fair trial, although the court did leave open the possibility that an overriding public interest in non-disclosure could arise in specific cases.

(b) In *R v Horseferry Road Magistrates' Court, ex p Bennet (No 2)* [1994] 1 All ER 289, it was recognised that communications between prosecuting authorities in different countries could potentially be excluded although the evidence was admitted on that occasion as it showed that the accused had been unlawfully returned to the jurisdiction.

(c) In *R v Chief Constable of the West Midlands, ex p Wiley* [1995] 1 AC 274, it was held that whether or not statements made in the course of police complaints investigations should be excluded depended on the facts of each case.

(d) Where a criminal case appears to have been based upon informant evidence the courts have generally held that the identity of informants should not be disclosed although it may be ordered if it is necessary to establish the innocence of the accused (*Marks v Beyfus* (1890) 25 QBD 494). There is no general rule however that such evidence should not be disclosed, it is simply that generally the anonymity of the informant has been deemed to weigh heavily in the balance (*R v Keane* (above)). In *R v Agar* [1990] 2 All ER 442, the accused's case was that the informant and the police had cooperated in setting up the accused by inviting him to the informant's house and then planting evidence there. The Court of Appeal held that the defence should have been entitled to cross-examine the police officers as to whether the informant had told them that the accused was due to visit his house.

(e) A similar approach has been adopted in relation to persons who have allowed their houses to be used as police surveillance posts (*R v Rankine* [1986] QB 861). In *R v Johnson (Kenneth)* (1989) 88 Cr App R 131, the Court of Appeal stated that before the court can admit evidence from a surveillance, two matters should be proved (as a minimum):

(i) A police officer in charge of the observations (no lower in rank than sergeant) testifies that *before the observation took place* he or she spoke to the occupiers of the premises to be used about their attitude to the observation, including the risk of disclosure of the use of the premises.

(ii) A police officer of the rank of at least chief inspector testifies that *immediately before trial* he or she visited the place of the observation and spoke to the occupiers at that time about their attitude to the disclosure of its use as an observation post at trial.

Where the court rules that the identity of informants or the details of information held by the police must be revealed, the prosecution may decide not to proceed on the charges in question. In this way they can preserve their sources.

17.3.3.3   Other confidential information

The approach of the courts in such cases rather depends on the issues being litigated (ie the interests of justice) on the one hand and the source of information and the importance of confidentiality (the public interest in exclusion) on the other. The results have therefore varied considerably, for example:

(a) *D v National Society for the Prevention of Cruelty to Children* [1978] AC 171, in which exclusion was granted in respect of anonymous reports made to the NSPCC concerning child abuse to children.

(b) *Science Research Council v Nassé* [1980] AC 1028, in which public policy exclusion was unsuccessfully sought in respect of documents used to determine promotion applications for employees.

(c) *Lonhro Ltd v Shell Petroleum Company Ltd* [1980] 1 WLR 627, in which information given in confidence to a government inquiry concerning a matter of foreign policy was held to have been properly excluded.

(d) *Re M (A Minor) (Disclosure of Material)* [1990] 2 FLR 36, in which social services reports and case notes concerning a child in care were not disclosable. (However such immunity does not operate against a guardian appointed for the child by the court in Children Act 1989 proceedings. Such a guardian can be ordered by the court to have access to all social service records under s 42 and no immunity would prevent such disclosure.)

(e) *R v Hampshire County Council, ex p K* [1990] 2 All ER 129, in which Social Services Department records were held not to be disclosed unless the judge ordered so.

(f) *Lonhro plc v Fayed (No 4)* [1994] QB 775, in which a taxpayer's tax returns held by the Inland Revenue were held potentially to be subject to public interest immunity as they had been obtained from the taxpayer by compulsion.

17.3.3.4 Journalistic sources

The provisions of the Contempt of Court Act 1981, s 10, make general provision as to the circumstances in which a journalist may be required by court order to reveal sources of information. Section 10 provides:

No court may require a person to disclose, nor is any person guilty of contempt of court for refusing to disclose, the source of information contained in a publication for which he is responsible, unless it be established to the satisfaction of the court that disclosure is necessary in the interests of justice or national security or for the prevention of disorder or crime.

Therefore a journalist is not generally under an obligation unless the evidence is necessary for one of four purposes: the interests of justice, national security, prevention of crime or prevention of disorder. The effect is that journalistic sources are covered by public policy exclusion and must be weighed against the other reason for revealing the source, of which one is the interests of justice, a phrase that has been interpreted narrowly (*Secretary of State for Defence v Guardian Newspapers* [1985] 1 AC 339). In *X Ltd v Morgan-Grampian (Publishers) Ltd* [1991] 1 AC 1, the interests of justice were defined as the protection of important legal rights or the protection against serious legal wrongs. Disclosure must be necessary for those purposes; therefore important factors will include the significance of the evidence and the difficulty of obtaining the information from other sources.

The 'prevention of disorder or crime' ground has been interpreted to relate to crime in general not specific crimes (*Re an Inquiry under the Companies Securities (Insider Dealing) Act 1985* [1988] AC 660). Therefore the section cannot be used in this way to force a journalist to disclose sources so that they can be called as witnesses in the case unless this is in the 'interests of justice'.

17.3.4 Determining whether to exclude evidence

As noted at the start of this chapter, whether or not evidence will be disclosed is a question of procedure rather than the rules of evidence. You should therefore refer to the ***Criminal Procedure*** and the ***Civil Procedure Manuals*** for detail. However in outline the procedures are as follows.

17.3.4.1 Criminal cases

Public policy exclusion will generally arise as part of the disclosure proceedings relating to unused material (ie evidence the prosecution will not rely upon). Under ss 3, 7 of the Criminal Procedure and Investigations Act 1996, the prosecution are under an obligation to disclose material at the primary disclosure stage which might reasonably be considered to undermine the prosecution case or assist the defence case. The 1996 Act also provides the making of applications to the court to determine whether the evidence ought to be revealed. The extent to which the defence should be involved in such applications or should be informed depends on the degree of sensitivity of the material in question. There are three possibilities:

1. For the least sensitive class of material, the prosecution must inform the defence of the application (and the defence will be allowed to participate at the hearing) and of the class of material to which it relates at the very least.

2. For more sensitive material (where the prosecution allege that harm would be caused to a public interest by merely identifying the material in question), the prosecution must inform the defence of the application and the defence can make representations about the procedure to be adopted for determining the public interest immunity issue. However, the prosecution do not have to reveal the nature of the material and the defendant and his or her representatives are not permitted to attend.

3. For the most sensitive cases (those in which the public interest to be protected would be threatened merely by revealing the fact of an application), the prosecution may apply to the court without notifying the defence of the application at all.

As the decision not to disclose evidence to the defence threatens the right to a fair trial, the process for determining what evidence should be revealed should itself safeguard the right to a fair trial protected by article 6(1) of the European Convention of Human Rights. In *Rowe and Davis v United Kingdom* (2000) 30 EHRR 1, the European Court of Human Rights stated, at paragraph 61, 'any difficulties caused to the defence by a limitation on its rights must be sufficiently counterbalanced by the procedures followed by the judicial authorities'.

In *R v H* [2003] 1 WLR 411, the House of Lords considered the procedures under the Criminal Procedure and Investigations Act 1996 in the light of developing practice in the UK courts and European jurisprudence. The result of this consideration was a seven stage process to be adopted when the prosecution opposed the disclosure of evidence on the grounds of public interest. The court must:

1. Identify and consider the material that the prosecution seek to withhold.

2. Determine whether the material is such as may weaken the prosecution case or strengthen that of the defence. (Disclosure does not have to be ordered for evidence that does not do one or the other.)

3. Determine whether there is a real risk of serious prejudice to an important public interest if full disclosure of the material is ordered. (If no serious prejudice, disclosure should be ordered.)

4. Determine whether the defendant's interest can be protected without disclosure or limited disclosure can be ordered that will both give adequate protection to the public interest and also to the interests of the defence. The court may have to consider what measures can be taken to offer adequate protection for the defence short of full disclosure.

5. Consider whether measures proposed in answer to (4) represent the minimum derogation necessary to protect the public interest in question. (The court is under a duty to get as close as possible to full disclosure while offering adequate protection for the interest in question.)

6. Consider whether any order for limited disclosure under (4) or (5) above may render the trial process unfair to the defendant. (If the trial process is rendered unfair fuller disclosure should be ordered even if this leads the prosecution to discontinue the proceedings so as to avoid having to make disclosure.)

7. Keep the fairness of the trial process under constant review during the trial in light of the order for limited disclosure. (The House noted that it was important that the answer to (6) should not be treated as final.)

The House therefore recognised that not only is there an issue of whether or not evidence ought to be disclosed but also that the court ought to consider ways in which evidence could be partially disclosed. The balance between disclosure and public interest immunity can therefore be achieved not simply by ordering or refusing disclosure of evidence but also by altering the way in which evidence is disclosed. The House noted in particular possibilities such as formal admissions of some or all of the facts the defence seek to prove with the evidence, disclosure short of full disclosure by the preparation of summaries or extracts of evidence, or the provision of edited or anonymised documents.

The House also noted that occasionally a fair trial would require that the defendant was represented at disclosure hearings of the more sensitive types. In such cases, as noted above, the defendant and his or her representatives may not even be informed of the application. The House therefore approved the practice of appointing 'special counsel' to argue the defendant's case for disclosure at such hearings. However, special counsel would only be appointed in exceptional circumstances. Special counsel would not be acting for the defendant and therefore would not be under any obligation to report to him or her about matters revealed during the disclosure hearing. However, special counsel would be in a position to challenge the prosecution case from the a defence perspective so as to ensure that the adversarial nature of the trial process was safeguarded.

Where the person holding the information is not a party to the proceedings he or she may make an application to the court to rule the information should be excluded. Alternatively, such matters fall to be resolved when the third party is the subject of a witness summons requiring him to attend court to produce the document or information.

17.3.4.2   Civil cases

CPR, r 31.19(1) makes detailed provision for determining whether evidence should be revealed. Such applications may be made without notice and will not generally be served on the other party unless the court orders otherwise. Where the information is sought from a non-party to the proceedings the application is made under CPR, r 31.17 (see also *Blackstone's Civil Practice*, 2005, Chapter 48).

APPENDIX 1
SMALL GROUP QUESTIONS

This appendix sets out a series of 12 sessions that should help you in working through the subject matter of this Manual. For each session, any preparation that you must undertake will be identified. Usually this is simply the reading of the Manual. However occasionally you will be asked to look at other texts. There are numerous references in this appendix and in the Manual itself to *Blackstone's Criminal Practice, Blackstone's Civil Practice* and *Archbold*. Use of such practitioner works is an important aspect of practice as an advocate. While other works could have been referred to, references have been, where possible, limited to these for the sake of simplicity. You should use the 2005 editions of each (or the 2006 editions when available, although it is possible that specific references may change between versions).

As general guidance, you should remember that the focus of this Manual is on the practical application of the subject areas. This means that the questions below often require you to put yourself in the position of an advocate and to carry out particular activities that might be expected of a lawyer appearing at court. Furthermore, these are *evidence* case studies. Any fact asserted, even in these problem questions, should be treated as something that a party will have to prove. Do not accept what is said uncritically.

Session 1: proof and preliminaries

This session is intended to lay the foundations for the rest of the evidence course by introducing fundamental concepts. By understanding these concepts you will be in a better position to understand the detailed rules of evidence and the principles behind them.

Preparation

You should read **Chapter 1** of this Manual. While there are references to other Manuals and practitioner texts in this chapter, they are for deeper and further reference. You do not have to refer to them in preparing for this class.

Objectives

This session is designed to ensure that you have a sound understanding of:

(a) the basic terminology of the law of evidence;

(b) the facts that are open to proof or disproof under English law;

(c) the distinction between the concepts of relevance, admissibility and weight;

(d) the division of functions between the judge and jury; and

(e) the discretion to exclude evidence (apart from evidence obtained by illegal or unfair means).

Question 1: relevance

(a) Ian is charged with indecently assaulting John, a boy aged 13. The prosecution is able to prove that Ian is a homosexual.

Is this evidence relevant? Why?

(b) Kevin is charged with the rape of Linda. The prosecution is able to prove that Kevin is a heterosexual.

Is this evidence relevant? Why?

(c) Michael is charged with burglary. The prosecution is able to prove that he has ten previous convictions for burglary.

Is this evidence relevant? Why?

Question 2

Alan Smith has been charged with the theft of a bottle of claret from Walter's Wine Warehouse, Hackney. He intends to plead not guilty. The prosecution proposes to call, among others, Mrs Edwina Walter, the owner of the Warehouse, WPC Duncan, Mr Hughes and Inspector Jenkins.

The following are extracts from the witness statement made by Mrs Walter:

In late April 2002, I had an argument with a customer, Alan Smith, who claimed that I had shortchanged him. I denied this. He became very angry and started swearing. He insisted that I was mistaken and said that I would live to regret it . . . Mr Smith has been back in the Warehouse many times since then and I suspect that he has been up to no good . . . My takings have been considerably lower than normal in the three months of May, June and July 2002. At about 1.20 pm on 7 August 2002, I saw Mr Smith enter the Warehouse. He was wearing a baggy brown coat. He went to the far end of the shop where we keep our best claret. He bent down behind some wine crates, out of my line of vision, then got up and hurriedly left the shop. Later that day, WPC Duncan showed me a bottle of claret priced £17.50 which I identified as having come from the Warehouse. She also asked me for a till roll to see if it showed the sale of any item priced £17.50. It did not.

WPC Duncan, in her witness statement, says:

I was passing the Warehouse at about 1.25 pm on 7 August when a man wearing a large brown trenchcoat emerged. He looked startled to see me and rushed off. I followed him. He kept looking over his shoulder and then ran off. I ran after him. He turned into Cambridge Passage but by the time I got to the Passage, he had disappeared. I inspected some dustbins there and inside one of them I found a bottle of claret bearing a small price sticker bearing the words 'Walter's Wine Warehouse', and a price, £17.50 . . . At 4.15 pm I arrested and cautioned Alan Smith. He was still wearing the trenchcoat. I subsequently discovered inside the coat there was a false pocket, inexpertly stitched by hand, and measuring some 12 inches by 8 inches.

The statement of Mr Hughes, a suitably qualified expert, is to the effect that the bottle found by WPC Duncan bears fingerprints matching those taken from Alan Smith.

The statement of Inspector Jenkins relates to three interviews with Alan Smith at the police station. The third interview concludes as follows:

Q. Come on Al, don't waste any more of our time.
A. OK. OK. My hands are up. It was me. I took the bloody wine. That's what you thugs want to hear isn't it. Now lay off.

Alan Smith proposes to testify that he was, at the time of the alleged offence, with Mr Evans, whom he intends to call, at the Slug and Lettuce public house, Islington. He will say that

Mrs Walter is lying because he once caught her out short-changing him, and proposes to cross-examine her about that and about the fact that she is blind in one eye and shortsighted in the other. He will also say that he confessed to the crime because Inspector Jenkins, exasperated by his constant denials in all three interviews, had threatened to punch him where it would hurt: a confession seemed the only way to prevent this from happening.

(a) Of the facts which the parties are proposing to prove, which will be:
   (i)   facts in issue; and
   (ii) collateral facts; and
   (iii) preliminary facts?

(b) Which items of evidence are irrelevant (or not sufficiently relevant)?

(c) Which of the facts in issue
   (i) can be proved by direct evidence; and
   (ii) must be proved by circumstantial evidence?

(d) For each such fact in issue to be proved by circumstantial evidence, identify
   (i) the circumstantial evidence necessary to prove the fact in issue; and
   (ii) the generalisation or argument you would use to explain how those items of evidence combine to prove that fact in issue?

(e) Identify any items of real evidence that might be adduced in the case. What might they prove?

(f) Is it likely that there will be a need for a *voir dire* in this case? Why?

Session 2: burdens and standards of proof; presumptions

How does the court decide who wins or loses a case? The rules of evidence place a burden on one side or another to prove the case at trial. This session considers how this risk of losing the case is apportioned. It also considers the concept of presumptions, which are rules of evidence that change the way in which burdens of proof work at trial.

Preparation

Read **Chapters 2** and **3** of this Manual.

While reading the chapters you will have to conduct some research. It is suggested that you use either *Blackstone's Criminal Practice* or *Archbold* although you can conduct the research required in a law library or even online.

Objectives

By the conclusion of this session, you should be able:

(a) to analyse the facts in issue in both civil and criminal cases and indicate who bears the legal burden of proof and who bears the evidential burden on each fact in issue;

(b) to decide who has the right to begin adducing evidence in a trial;

(c) to identify the standard of proof appropriate to a burden;

(d) to understand and to use properly the terminology applicable to both burdens and standards of proof;

(e) to classify presumptions;

(f) to know when to apply a presumption to a given set of facts; and

(g) to know the effect which a presumption has on the incidence of the legal and evidential burdens.

Question 1

Identify:

- the facts in issue;
- the incidence of the evidential burden;
- the incidence of the legal burden; and
- the standard of proof

for each case set out below.

Case 1

Alan has been charged with possessing an offensive weapon, contrary to Prevention of Crime Act 1953, s 1. He is alleged to have had a chisel with him in a public street. He was found with the chisel at 2 am. He does not deny this but says he is a sculptor and while he was at a party, inspiration had struck him for a sculpture and he was on his way to his studio. He adds that he always carries a chisel in case he is attacked.

Prevention of Crime Act 1953, s 1(1), provides that:

Any person who without lawful authority or reasonable excuse, the proof whereof shall lie on him, has with him in any public place any offensive weapon shall be guilty of an offence.

Section 1(4) of the Act defines an offensive weapon as:

any article made or adapted for use for causing injury to the person, or intended by the person having it with him for such use by him.

Case 2

Arabian Ltd, the charters of a ship, are suing Bulk Traffic Co, the owners of the ship, for breach of contract. The ship blew up and sank during its voyage. No one is able to determine the cause of the explosion.

Bulk Traffic alleges that the contract was frustrated by the explosion. Arabian Ltd says that any frustration was self-induced and does not afford a defence to its action.

Case 3

Following a collision between his car and a lamp-post, Charles is accused of driving without due care and attention. He told the police officer who interviewed him at the hospital that he remembered nothing of the incident. Later, he told the police that his doctor told him that in all likelihood he simply blacked out (non-insane automatism).

Question 2

Explain the burdens and standard of proof in the following case.

In an action by A for breach of contract for the carriage of a consignment of television sets by lorry from London to Manchester, the contract provided that B, a lorry owner, was not liable for loss caused by fire provided that the lorry owner's servants were not negligent. The lorry and its load were destroyed by fire in a service area on the motorway. B claims that he is not liable for the loss. A asserts that B was facing bankruptcy and that the lorry was deliberately set on fire so that B could claim on his insurance from the insurers of the lorry. Alternatively A asserts that the fire was caused by the carelessness of the lorry driver.

Question 3

On 1 January 1995 Mr and Mrs Bush (aged 22 and 24 respectively), set off from Folkestone, England in their yacht, *Mermaid,* to cruise to Australia. On 16 August 1997 the *Mermaid* was discovered adrift in open seas off the island of Bali in the Indian Ocean. Mr and Mrs Bush were not aboard.

Neither set of parents has heard from the couple since they left Folkestone, although Mrs Bush sent her parents a picture postcard of Cape Town which was postmarked '1 April 1996'. Title to Mr and Mrs Bush's house is registered at the Land Registry in Mrs Bush's name alone. Mr Bush's parents now claim:

(a) that as neither Mr Bush junior nor his wife have been heard from, save for the postcard, since they left Folkestone, they should be given up as dead; and

(b) that their son and daughter-in-law made mutual wills in which all property went to whichever outlived the other; that their son's will bequeathed the house to his parents should he survive his wife; and that since their son probably outlived his wife, they should inherit the house.

Mr and Mrs Bush bring an action under the will to secure the inheritance. Assuming that trial takes place on 1 October 2003, will Mr and Mrs Bush senior be able to rely on any presumptions to prove their case? Will any presumptions operate against them?

Session 3: witnesses

This session concerns the rules that determine who is able to give evidence and who can be made to do so. Later sessions will address the rules concerning what a witness can say in evidence, this one simply addresses whether they will be in court at all.

Preparation

Read **Chapter 4**. Again *Blackstone's Criminal Practice* or *Archbold* may prove useful in answering these questions as may *Blackstone's Civil Practice*. Not all of the answers to the questions below can be found in this Manual: you are expected to conduct some independent research.

Objectives

By the conclusion of this session, you should be able:

(a) to identify when, during the course of a trial, the issue of competence is likely to arise;

(b) to know the procedure for determining the competence of a witness;

(c) to know whether any given witness is competent;

(d) to know whether any given witness is compellable;

(e) to know when a witness may give unsworn evidence; and

(f) to understand the procedural issues relating to witnesses.

Question 1

John is 11 and Bob is 16. Bob is severely mentally handicapped and has difficulties in communicating with people. It is alleged that both John and Bob were sexually abused by

Graham. Both are very nervous about giving evidence and claim that Graham's brother, Joshua, has been rude and offensive to them each time he sees them.

What steps should be taken in respect of John and Bob before they give evidence at Graham's trial on indictment for indecent assault?

Question 2

Ellen leaves her husband, Edgar, and goes to live with George and Gary, his 12-year-old son. Edgar and his brother, Harry, are jointly charged with:

- assault occasioning actual bodily harm on Gary;
- inflicting grievous bodily harm on George;
- attempting to kidnap Ellen.

Consider the following issues:

(a) Are Ellen and Gary competent and compellable witnesses for the prosecution?

(b) If they are compellable, how can their attendance be secured if they prove unwilling?

(c) Edgar and Harry both wish to call Harry's wife, Hilda to give evidence in their favour. Hilda has left Harry and is reluctant to testify for either Edgar or Harry. Can she be compelled to do so?

(d) Advise whether Harry can be called as a defence witness either on his own behalf or for Edgar. To what extent can he be compelled to do so?

Session 4: the examination of witnesses

Following on from the previous session, this session concerns various rules that regulate what questions may be asked of a witness and rules that regulate the extent to which the credibility of witnesses may be attacked.

Preparation

Read **Chapters 5** and **6**. Using *Blackstone's Criminal Practice* or *Archbold* may be of use for answering questions on criminal matters.

Objectives

By the conclusion of this session, you should be able to understand and apply the rules (and exceptions) relating to leading questions, refreshing memory, previous consistent or self-serving statements, unfavourable and hostile witnesses, cross-examination on documents, and previous inconsistent statements.

Question 1

Simon, aged 14, was the victim of a robbery on the way home from school. He arrived home looking upset. His mother said, 'Was it the boys from St Joseph's?' Simon nodded. She said, 'Was it that Adrian?' Simon said, 'Yes. He was with another boy I didn't know. They knocked me to the floor and took my Walkman.' The police were called and Adrian was subsequently arrested. In interview Adrian said that he had been present at the time of the robbery but had played no part in it. He said it had been carried out by his friend, Charlie.

Charlie was later arrested by PC Harmon. Simon positively identified Charlie as the other boy in a video identification conducted by Inspector Khan. In his police interview, Charlie said that he was not involved in the incident. The following day Charlie attended his solicitor with Dan, a friend, who was also present at the scene of the alleged robbery. A proof of evidence was taken from Dan by Charlie's solicitor in which Dan stated that Adrian carried out the robbery alone.

Adrian and Charlie were charged with robbery contrary to s 8 of the Theft Act 1968 and sent to the Crown Court for trial. The trial is held eight months after the alleged offence.

(a) Advise prosecution counsel on what steps to take in relation to the following issues:
    (i)   When giving evidence Simon has a very hazy recollection of events.
    (ii) Simon gives evidence of having identified the second boy at the video identification but is unable to remember his numerical position at the video identification.
    (iii) Whether Simon's mother can give evidence of Simon's initial complaint about the incident.

(b) Advise counsel for Charlie on what steps to take in relation to the following issues:
    (i)   PC Harmon states in evidence that as he was being arrested for his part in the robbery Charlie had said, 'So what if we did? He owed me some money anyway.' In cross-examination, Charlie's counsel inspects the officer's incident report book. The alleged admission appears to have been added after the main body of the notes had been completed. Charlie's counsel puts to the officer that he has made up his evidence which the officer denies.
    (ii) In cross-examination of Adrian by Charlie's counsel, it emerges that Adrian holds a grudge against Charlie.
    (iii) Dan gives evidence on behalf of Charlie. He says that Adrian was the only one involved in the robbery. Prosecution counsel puts to Dan in cross-examination that his evidence is a late invention concocted to help his friend out of trouble.
    (iv) Charlie's counsel fails to suggest to Simon that Charlie was not an active participant in the robbery.

Question 2

Read the following witness statements. Then read the trial transcript and as you do so, identify any procedural and evidential errors that occurred during the course of the hearing.

STATEMENT OF WITNESS

Statement of:	Stephen WELHAM
Age of witness:	Over 18
Occupation of witness:	Financial Services Manager
Address and telephone number:	187 St John's Avenue, Friern Barnet

This statement, consisting of two pages, each signed by me, is true to the best of my knowledge and belief and I make it knowing that, if it is tendered in evidence, I shall be liable to prosecution if I have wilfully stated in it anything which I know to be false or do not believe to be true.

Dated the 7th day of March 2005

Signed: S. Welham

Signature witnessed by: J. Osborn

On Wednesday 6 March 2005 I was returning from work at about 8 pm, and left the Underground at Highgate. It is a short walk round the corner to the bus stop for the bus home. I must have been thinking about work, because the next thing I knew a young fellow had stepped in front of me barring my path. He was in his early 20s, casually dressed with a waist-length dark cotton coat. He must have been about 5' 10'' and well-built. He asked if I had a fiver. I started to say it was none of his business, when I noticed another youth standing against the railings a couple of yards away looking on casually. The man in front pulled me forward with one hand. I tried to push him away, but suddenly felt a sharp pain in my shin, followed by a blow to the side of my face. I lost my balance and fell to the ground. He then ran off in the direction of Muswell Hill. The other man simply disappeared — he must have gone in the other direction.

I picked myself up and went back to the main road. I saw a police car waiting at the lights. I flagged it down and explained to the driver that I had just been attacked by two muggers, and that one of them had run off towards Muswell Hill. I was told to get into the car and the other officer asked for a description. We went down a side road and stopped alongside some parked cars. The officers jumped out, and when I looked out of the side window I saw them with the man who had hit me.

I have a 2 inch long bruise on my left shin and am rather tender where I was hit in front of my right ear.

Signed: S. Welham

Signature witnessed by: J. Osborn

STATEMENT OF WITNESS

Statement of:	John WOOD
Age of witness:	Over 18
Occupation of witness:	Joiner
Address and telephone number:	157 Granville Avenue, London N22

This statement consisting of one page, each signed by me, is true to the best of my knowledge and belief and I make it knowing that, if it is tendered in evidence, I shall be liable to prosecution if I have wilfully stated in it anything which I know to be false or do not believe to be true.

Dated the 7th day of March 2005

Signed: J. Wood

Signature witnessed by: J. Osborn

Yesterday evening Alan LYNCH and myself went out for a drink. We are both unemployed at the moment. When we got to Highgate we both realised we didn't have any money. We stood talking outside the pub for a couple of minutes, a bit fed up. A City gent came round the corner, and Alan bumped into him. Alan asked for a fiver; it was all a piece of fun. I saw a police car coming up Archway Road, so decided to make myself scarce.

Signed: J. Wood

Signature witnessed: J. Osborn

STATEMENT OF WITNESS

Statement of:	D Sgt William CRANSTOUN
Age of witness:	Over 18
Occupation of witness:	Detective Sergeant
Address and telephone number:	Muswell Hill Police Station

This statement consisting of two pages, each signed by me, is true to the best of my knowledge and belief and I make it knowing that, if it is tendered in evidence, I shall be liable to prosecution if I have wilfully stated in it anything which I know to be false or do not believe to be true.

Dated the 7th day of March 2005

Signed: W. Cranstoun

Signature witnessed by: J. Osborn

On 6 March 2005 at 20.00 acting on information received I went with D.C. Henson and Stephen WELHAM towards Muswell Hill via Queen's Wood Road. I noticed a young man who I now know to be Alan LYNCH walking along the pavement. He looked over his shoulder and then ducked behind a parked car. I pulled up, and D.C. HENSON and I got out. I introduced myself. Stephen WELHAM called out 'He is the one'. I asked LYNCH where he was going. LYNCH replied, 'I am meeting some friends in Hornsey'. I asked him whereabouts, to which he replied, The Nightingale'. I asked, 'Where do you live?' Lynch said 'Lymington Avenue'. D.C. HENSON said 'Wood Green?' LYNCH said 'Yes'. I said, 'But that's in the opposite direction'. LYNCH replied, 'Yeah, but I've not come from home'. I said, 'Where have you come from?' LYNCH said, 'I don't have to answer these questions, do I?' D.C. HENSON said, 'Why did you try to hide from us?' LYNCH said, 'I was doing up my shoelace'. I said, 'Have you been near Highgate Underground station this evening?' LYNCH replied, 'What's it to you?' I said, 'I have reason to believe you assaulted this gentleman', indicating Stephen WELHAM, 'and I am arresting you on suspicion of assault'. I then cautioned him, to which he said, 'You've got the wrong man. You are making a big mistake.' LYNCH was then taken to the police station.

Later, I saw LYNCH at the police station with D.C. HENSON. I reminded LYNCH of the caution. D.C. HENSON said, The man in the car was punched and kicked this evening near Highgate tube a couple of minutes before we stopped you. He has positively identified you. You tried to hide from us when you saw our car. Do you want to tell us about it?' LYNCH looked into the corner of the room for a couple of minutes, then said, 'All right, I might have asked for money. It was a bit of a lark. It wasn't nothing serious. Give us a break'. I asked if he wanted to make a written statement, to which LYNCH replied, 'No. Nothing in writing'.

On 6 March 2005 at 22.15 LYNCH was charged, the charge was read over, arid he was cautioned. LYNCH made no reply.

Acting on local knowledge, on 7 September in company with D.C. HENSON, I attended at 157 Granville Avenue N22 where I saw John WOOD. As a result of our conversation John WOOD made a statement under caution at Muswell Hill Police Station.

Signed: W. Cranstoun

Signature witnessed by: J. Osborne

D.C. Henson made a statement in the same terms, with necessary changes.

Alan Lynch of 298 Lymington Avenue, Wood Green, N22 will say:

I am aged 22 and live at home with my parents, a brother and a sister. I am a car mechanic, but lost my job four months ago for bad timekeeping. I have several previous convictions for petty offences going back a long time. My most recent conviction was for fighting outside a pub when I was 20. I was fined £75.

On Wednesday 6 March I was arrested by the police. I was on my way to meet some friends at the Nightingale pub in Hornsey. We had nothing planned. We often meet for a drink and a game of pool. I had been to see a friend's car in Mill Hill, and decided to get off the tube at Highgate and walk through the woods and then across to the pub. I would say it was about a 1.5-mile walk.

The bloke in Mill Hill is really a friend of a friend. I had agreed with Trevor Jones, one of my friends, to look over a car one of Trevor's friends was going to buy. The car was in Oakhampton Road but I didn't go into the house so don't know the full address. I had been given a tenner for doing it, so didn't want to say anything to the police.

As I was coming up to the woods my shoelace came undone. I stopped to do it up. Then a car pulled up, and next thing I knew there were two policemen asking me a lot of questions about where I was going, where I had been and where I lived. They accused me of thumping a bloke they had in the car, arrested me and took me to Muswell Hill Police Station.

When I was seen by the police at the station I did not admit I had hit anybody. I did not do it and I never said that I did to the police. I might have said that I had asked for money to look over the car, and that I hadn't done anything seriously wrong, but those comments were not about hitting anybody.

Trevor moved to Borehamwood a couple of years ago. I don't have his address, he just meets us every so often. I haven't seen him since I was arrested.

A. Lynch

POLICE V ALAN LYNCH
Trial Transcript

A   Clerk: The next case is Alan Lynch, sir, number 16 in the List. (*Lynch is brought into the court and enters the dock.*)
Clerk: Are you Alan Lynch?
Lynch: Yes.
Clerk: Alan Lynch, you are charged with assault occasioning actual bodily harm contrary to section 47 of the Offences Against the Person Act 1861 in that you, on the 6th day of March 2005, did assault one Stephen Welham thereby occasioning unto him actual bodily harm. Do you plead guilty or not guilty?
Lynch: Not guilty.

B   Clerk: You may sit down.
Prosecution Counsel: May it please you, sir, I appear on behalf of the prosecution and my learned friend Miss Lucy Davies appears for the defence. It is the prosecution's case that the defendant assaulted his victim outside the Three Tuns public house in Highgate, which as I am sure you are aware is somewhat notorious. However, this case is not one in which alcohol is a factor. It is more in the nature of a mugging. The prosecution's first witness is the victim, Mr Stephen Welham, who will tell you about the circumstances of the assault on his way home from work and the extent of his injuries. The second witness will be Mr John Wood, an identification witness. He will be

C   followed by Detective Sergeant Cranstoun, the arresting officer. I should at this stage mention that the arrest occurred a matter of just a few minutes after the incident. The fourth witness will be Detective Constable Henson, who was also present at the time of the arrest. Without further ado, and with your permission, sir, I will call Stephen Welham.

Usher: Mr Welham, please hold the Testament in your right hand and read the words on the card.

Welham: I swear by Almighty God that the evidence I shall give shall be the truth, the whole truth and nothing but the truth.

D   Pros: Is your full name Stephen Welham and do you live at 187 St John's Avenue, Barnet?

Welham: Yes.

Pros: Are you a financial services manager?

Welham: That's right.

Pros: And who is your employer?

Welham: Barclays International, in the City.

A   Pros: How do you get to work?

Welham: I catch the bus on Colney Hatch Lane down to Highgate tube on Archway Road, then change from the Northern Line at Tottenham Court Road on to the Central Line to Bank.

Pros: And the reverse on the way home?

Welham: Yes.

Pros: Do you remember your journey home on Wednesday 6th March 2005?

Welham: I think so — I'm not sure of the date.

Pros: Was there an occasion when your usual routine was broken?

B   Welham: Yes, a couple of months ago I was threatened in the street by him (*points to defendant in the dock*). — Do ch 'IDs not admitable

Pros: Could you tell us where this happened?

Welham: I was leaving the Underground and walking round the corner to catch the bus. As I turned the corner I was confronted by the defendant.

Pros: What did he do?

Welham: He demanded money. Ten pounds, as I remember. Of course I refused. He had an accomplice with him. He grabbed me by the throat and started kicking me and punching — he was really wild. I managed to push him away and they ran off.

C   Pros: Could you tell us what your injuries were?

Welham: I had a large bruise on my shin and the side of my face became puffed up.

Pros: Were you cut at all?   — Possibly leading

Welham: No.

Pros: How clearly did you see your attacker?

Welham: He was facing me the whole time. He was a young man in his early 20s wearing a dark cotton jacket. It was still light and I remember the lights in the Three Tuns were on. I had a good look at him.

Pros: What did you do after the attack?

D   Welham: I went back to the main road, where there was a police car. We went off towards Muswell Hill. We caught up with him and he was arrested.

Pros: When the police car stopped, what did you do?

Welham: I remained in it until I was asked to move into the front passenger seat.

Pros: When the police officers left the car, did you see what they did?

Welham: They arrested the defendant.

Pros: Did anyone say anything at that stage?

Welham: Yes, the police asked the defendant a lot of questions.

Pros: Did anyone else say anything?

E   Welham: The defendant gave them his name, and . . .

Pros: I had better stop you there. Did anyone apart from the police officers and the defendant say anything?

Welham: No.

Pros: Was anyone else present?

Welham: No. Only myself.

Pros: Did you say anything?

Welham: No. The policemen asked all the questions.

Pros: After the car stopped, did you identify anyone to the police officers?

F   Welham: Yes. When I looked out of the window I saw that they had caught my attacker, and I shouted something like 'That's him!'

Pros: Thank you Mr Welham. Please wait there in case there are any further questions.

Cross-examination

Def: Mr Welham, at what time do you finish work of an evening?

Welham: About 6 pm.

Def: Do you work overtime?

Welham: No. I am not in a grade that gets paid overtime.

Def: Do you ever work late?

G   Welham: Not normally. It depends on how much work we have on.

Def: How long does it take to get to Highgate from your office?

Welham: About 45 minutes.

Def: You seem unsure about the date of the alleged assault. How can you be sure it was the 6th of March?

A   Welham: I think I was working late that night.

Def: At what time did you arrive at Highgate?

Welham: About 8 p.m.

Def: That's after lighting-up time at that time of year?

Welham: I don't know.

Def: Do you remember if the street lights were on?

Welham: I didn't notice. It was quite light.

Def: Did you make a statement to the police after the incident?

Welham: Yes.

B   Def: Have you recently read that statement?

Welham: Why?   — *Avoid this phrase at all costs*

Def: I put it to you that you read your statement this morning before coming into court.

Welham: Well, I did, I wanted to get the facts straight.

Def: Do you drink, Mr Welham?

Welham: A little. Sometimes.

Def: Did you have a drink that evening?   — *Not in instructions – don't impugn. Is 'blah blah' OK, but 'were you drunk' NOT)*

Welham: No.

C   Def: I put it to you that the reason you were late that evening was that you had had a drink or two before leaving for home.

Welham: I have told you I was working late.

Def: You said you were confronted by your attacker, and after a brief exchange of words, he punched and kicked you, then ran off.

Welham: That's right.

Def: It would all have been over very quickly.

Welham: Yes, that must be right.

Def: He demanded ten pounds, Mr Welham?

D   Welham: Yes.

Def:But that is not right, is it?

Welham: Yes, I have already said he demanded money.

Def: You said ten pounds.

Welham: He demanded ten pounds.

Def: I put it to you, Mr Welham, that the man you saw did not demand ten pounds.

Welham: He demanded ten pounds.

Def: I put it to you, Mr Welham, that the man you saw did not demand ten pounds.

Welham: Yes, he did.

E   Def: I put it to you that when you described the attack to the police you did not mention a demand for ten pounds.

Welham: I did.

Def: It is true, is it not, that you told the police the day after the incident that the man who attacked you demanded five pounds not ten?

Welham: All right, it may have been five.

Def: May, or was, five pounds?

Welham: It was five pounds.

F   Def: After your attacker grabbed hold of you, would I be right in thinking you would have been watching his hands?

Welham: I don't recall — but I did get a good look at his face.

Def: It's only a natural reaction to look at what his hands were doing, isn't it?

Welham: I'm not sure.

Def: You have already told this court that you were repeatedly kicked and punched.

Welham: That's right.

Def: The assault you mentioned to the police wasn't at all wild, was it?

Welham: I don't know what you mean.

G   Def: I am referring to the statement you made to the police after the attack. The account of the attack contained in your statement is rather different from what you have told the court today, isn't it?

Welham: Not so far as I remember.

Def: Sir, perhaps the witness could be shown his statement. Mr Welham do you recognise this statement?

Welham: Yes.

Def: And is it your signature at the bottom?

A   Welham: Yes.

Def: And have you signed a declaration to say that the statement is true to the best of your knowledge and belief?

Welham: I did.

Def: Would you look at the second half of the first paragraph of the statement. (*Witness reads statement to himself.*)

Def: Do you now wish to tell the justices again about the nature of the attack?

Welham: No.

B   Def: Very well. About half-way down the first page, the ninth sentence begins, 'I tried to push him away'. Could you read that sentence?

Welham: I tried to push him away, but suddenly felt a sharp pain in my shin, followed by a . . . This is rather underhand.

Def: Could you please continue.

Welham: Followed by a blow to the side of my face. It is rather immaterial how many times he hit me. The fact is he hit me, and nothing can take that away.

Def: Will you accept that at the time of the incident you said you were only kicked once and punched once?

Welham: Of course, I have to.

Re-examination

Pros: Mr Welham, I have one or two further questions to ask you. You were working late on the evening in question.

Welham: Yes.

Pros: At about what time did you leave the office?

Welham: Let me see. It must have been about 7.15 pm.

Pros: Did you stop off anywhere either before catching the Underground or *en route?*

D   Welham: No.

Pros: Can you remind the Court how long it took to get to Highgate?

Welham: 45 minutes.

Pros: And the time of the attack?

Welham: 8 pm.

Pros: You were asked a number of questions by the defence about the lighting conditions and the period over which you saw your attacker. How well did you see him?

Welham: Very well. We were face to face for some time, and I got a very good look at him.

E   Pros: Mr Welham, you have already described him as a man in his early twenties wearing a dark cotton jacket. How tall was he?

Welham: About 5' 10''.

Pros: At the time of the attack, did you notice anyone else present?

Welham: There was an accomplice lounging against the railings.

Pros: Thank you, Mr Welham. Unless you have any questions, sir.

Chairman: Mr Welham, you go home via Highgate every day?

Welham: Yes

Chairman: Then you will appreciate that Muswell Hill Road slopes very steeply down towards Muswell Hill?

F   Welham: It does.

Chairman: Which way were you facing when you were attacked?

A   Welham: Towards Muswell Hill.

Chairman: So you were uphill of your attacker?

Welham: Yes.

Chairman: When you described your attacker as 5' 10'' did you take into account that you were uphill of him, and that he would therefore appear shorter than if you were at the same level as him?

Welham: I hadn't really thought about it. My impression was that he was about 5' 10''. Bearing in mind what you say, it may be that he was a little taller than that.

Chairman: I have no further questions.

B   Pros: Sir, may the witness be released?

Def: I have no objection.

Chairman: Very well, thank you Mr Welham.

(*J. Wood is called and sworn*).

Pros: Are you John Wood of 157 Granville Avenue, London N22?

Wood: I am.

Pros: Are you an unemployed joiner?

Wood: No. I got a job.

Pros: Who are you employed by, Mr Wood?

C   Wood: I've been taken on by me uncle.

Pros: Do you remember the events of the evening of 6th of March 2005?

Wood: No.

Pros: Do you remember an arrangement to visit a public house in Highgate?

Wood: Nope.

Pros: Have you ever visited a public house called the Three Tuns in Highgate? It's located at the corner of Archway Road and Muswell Hill Road. Do you know the public house I am referring to?

Wood: I don't live in Highgate.

D   Pros: It's not very far from Wood Green. Have you ever been to Highgate?

Wood: I may have passed through.

Pros: Have you every stopped off at the Three Tuns?

Wood: I can't remember.

Pros: Do you recognise anyone in court today?

Wood: No.

Pros: Mr Wood, please look around the room, and think carefully before answering. Is there anyone here that you know?

Wood: No.

E   Pros: I have no further questions of this witness.

Def: No cross-examination, sir.

(*D. S. Cranstoun is called and sworn.*)

Pros: Are you Detective Sergeant William Cranstoun, attached to Muswell Hill Police Station?

Cranstoun: I am.

Pros: Were you on patrol with Detective Henson on the evening of 6th of March 2005?

Cranstoun: I was.

(*At this point D. S. Cranstoun produces a notebook from his top pocket and* starts *flicking through it.*)

F   Cranstoun: Do you mind if I refer to my notes, your worship?

Pros: If I may help, sir

Chairman: Please do.

Pros: Could you help us, Sergeant, by telling the court when the notes were written up?

Cranstoun: Contemporaneously, while the events were fresh in my memory.

Pros: In the circumstances I would ask that the witness be permitted to refresh his memory.

G   Chairman: Yes, please continue.

Pros: I think you were given a description of a person who was alleged to have committed an assault?

A   Cranstoun: Yes, I was driving towards Muswell Hill along Queen's Wood Road.

Pros: Why did you choose that route?

Cranstoun: The main road to Muswell Hill is very long with only one turning off for some distance that leads anywhere. I guessed that the suspect would leave Muswell Hill Road as soon as he could, so I did the same.

Pros: As you were driving, did you notice anything suspicious?

Cranstoun: I noticed a young man walking along the pavement. He looked over his shoulder and then ducked behind a parked car.

Pros: Why was he looking over his shoulder?

B   Cranstoun: He must have been looking to see if he was being followed.

Pros: Then what did you do?

Cranstoun: I stopped the car and got out. Detective Constable Henson did likewise.

Pros: Did you speak to the gentleman in the street?

Cranstoun: Yes, sir.

Pros: What did you say?

Cranstoun: I introduced myself. Mr Welham called out, 'He is the one'. At that time I ascertained that the man we had stopped was the defendant, Alan Lynch.

Pros: What did you say?

C   Cranstoun: I asked the defendant where he was going. He replied, 'I am meeting some friends in Hornsey'. I asked him whereabouts, to which he replied, The Nightingale'.

Pros: Where is that?

Cranstoun: It is about 2 miles from there, cutting through the side roads, on the corner of Nightingale Road and Hornsey High Street.

Pros: What did you say after that?

D   Cranstoun: I asked, Where do you live?' The defendant said, 'Lymington Avenue'. Detective Constable Henson asked if that was in Wood Green. The defendant said, 'Yes'. I said, 'But that's in the opposite direction'. The defendant said, 'Yeah, but I've not come from home'. I said, 'Where have you come from?' The defendant said, 'I don't have to answer these questions, do I?' Detective Constable Henson said, 'Why did you try to hide from us?' The defendant said, 'I was doing up my shoelace'. I said 'Have you been near Highgate Underground station this evening?' The defendant replied, 'What's it to you?'

Pros: I think you then told the defendant that you were arresting him for the assault on Mr Welham, and gave him the caution.

Cranstoun: That is right.

Pros: Did the defendant say anything in reply to the caution?

E   Cranstoun: Yes. He said, 'You've got the wrong man. You are making a big mistake'.

Pros: Was the accused then taken to Muswell Hill Police Station?

Cranstoun: Yes, sir.

Pros: Did you speak to the defendant at the station?

Cranstoun: Yes, together with Detective Constable Henson. I started by reminding Lynch of the caution.

Pros: Did Detective Constable Henson remind the accused of the facts of the incident?

F   Cranstoun: He did. The defendant looked into space for a while, then said, let me see, 'All right, I might have asked for money. It was a bit of a lark. It wasn't nothing serious. Give us a break'.

Pros: I think you then asked the defendant if he wanted to make a written statement.

Cranstoun: But he refused.

Pros: I understand the defendant was then charged.

Cranstoun: Yes, sir.

Pros: At what time was that?

Cranstoun: 10.15 pm, sir.

Pros: Did he make any reply?

G   Cranstoun: No. None.

Pros: Thank you Sergeant.

Session 5: character evidence 1

This is the first of two sessions in which character evidence is considered. This session focuses on the admissibility of the defendant's good character and bad character in criminal proceedings under the Criminal Justice Act 2003, s 100(1) (c) and (d).

Preparation

Read **Chapter 7** and **Chapter 8**.

Objectives

This session is designed to assist you:

(a) understand the relevance of good character;

(b) understand the reasons for the prohibition of the cross-examination or adduction of evidence of the accused's bad character;

(c) understand the circumstances in which the defendant's bad character may become admissible under the Criminal Justice Act 2003; and

(d) understand the distinction between evidence of bad character relevant to a fact in issue and relevant to credibility

Question 1

Rajiv is tried for theft from his employer. What direction should be given in each of the following situations?

(a) He is of good character and gives evidence.

(b) He is of good character and does not give evidence.

(c) He is of good character and does not give evidence. However, the prosecution have proved a written statement he gave to the police in which he admitted that he took the money from his employer but that he did so at the request of his employer, who said he wanted to test how effective his security procedures were.

(d) He gives evidence. Although he does not have any previous convictions, it was put to him in cross-examination that he had been dismissed from his previous employment under suspicion of having taken money from the company.

Question 2

Mark is charged with causing grievous bodily harm with intent contrary to the Offences Against the Person Act 1861, s 18. The case is that on 23 December Mark was involved in an argument with a publican whom he hit with a billiard cue. Mark claims that it was an accident. The police have evidence that several weeks earlier Mark had confronted the publican because he suspected that he was having an affair with Mark's former girlfriend. He threatened that he would kill the publican if he had anything more to do with her. Advise the prosecution as to the admissibility of the evidence of the threats.

Question 3

David is charged with two counts of theft contrary to s 1 of the Theft Act 1968. The prosecution case in relation to the first count is that he stole various items of clothing from a department store by secreting them in a pocket he had sewn into his coat. He was detained as he tried to leave the store but managed to run away. He was later identified by two security guards at a video identification. On the second count, the prosecution case is that he stole 30 packets of razor blades from a supermarket using a foil-lined carrier bag so as not to trigger the alarm. Following his arrest, his home was searched and the police found two coats with false pockets sewn into them.

David pleads not guilty to both counts. His defence in relation to count one is mistaken identity. In relation to count two he states that he was intending to pay for the goods but had walked outside to get a trolley. At trial, one of the security officers who made the identification admitted that he had discussed the appearance of the suspect with his colleague prior to making his identification of David and admits that it may have influenced his identification. During the course of the trial David wears an Honourable Artillery Company tie that he bought in a jumble sale. He has never been a member of that, nor any other, regiment.

Advise the prosecution on the relevance and admissibility of the following:

(a) A previous conviction for perjury four years ago.

(b) Two previous convictions for theft within the last three years.

(c) A previous conviction for ABH a year ago in relation to which he pleaded not guilty and gave evidence at trial accusing the complainant of fabricating his evidence.

(d) The evidence of the first allegation of theft in relation to the second allegation of theft, and vice versa.

(e) Evidence that David was banned from a local superstore following an allegation of shoplifting for which proceedings were never brought.

Session 6: character evidence 2

This is the second of two sessions in which character evidence is considered. This session focuses on the admissibility of evidence in relation to the bad character of the accused under the Criminal Justice Act 2003, s 101(e), (f) and (g) or a witness other than the defendant in criminal proceedings.

Preparation

Read **Chapters 6.3.7, 7.3.2.1, 8.3.8, 8.3.9, 8.3.10** and **Chapter 9**.

Objectives

This session is designed to assist you:

(a) to understand and apply the rules relating to cross-examination as to credit and the rule of finality;

(b) to understand the restriction on the admissibility of evidence relating to the sexual history of the complainant in proceedings for a sexual offence;

(c) to understand the rules governing the admissibility evidence relating to a witness's bad character or the bad character of a co-accused;

(d) to understand the consequences of attacking another person's character;

(e) to understand the consequences of giving a false impression.

Question 1

Cecil is charged with the rape of Barbara at a party attended also by Dora, Edward and Francis. Cecil claims that Barbara consented to intercourse, being a prostitute of whom he is a regular client. Barbara, who has a previous conviction for soliciting, testifies that she was raped by Cecil. Among the prosecution witnesses to the circumstances immediately before and after the alleged rape are:

(a) Dora, two convictions for theft, one of which is spent;

(b) Edward, who has a history of mental illness; and

(c) Francis, who is an importer of obscene films.

Advise Cecil whether the complainant and the other prosecution witnesses may be cross-examined about the respective facts mentioned, and whether, if denied, those facts may be proved by the defence.

Question 2

Henry, James and Albert are jointly charged with burglary contrary to s 9(1)(b) of the Theft Act 1968. Henry and James both have a previous conviction for theft and two previous convictions for burglary. Albert has a previous conviction for obtaining social security benefit by false representations. The only evidence which connects them with the crime is that of Sam, who claims to have driven the getaway car and is now giving evidence for the prosecution. Sam has one previous conviction for burglary, two for assault occasioning actual bodily harm and one for obtaining property by deception.

(a) Henry's counsel wishes to cross-examine Sam about his previous convictions. Is he permitted to do so? If he does, will the prosecution be allowed to adduce evidence of Henry's previous convictions?

(b) James says in evidence that Sam is a liar. Can the prosecution adduce evidence of James's previous convictions?

(c) Albert says in evidence that Henry, James and Sam invited him to help with the break-in but he refused and did not take part. Can Henry's counsel adduce evidence of Albert's previous convictions?

(d) Albert wishes to cross-examine Henry and James about their previous convictions for burglary. Is he permitted to do so?

Question 3

Olive, Peter and Quentin are jointly charged with theft from their employer contrary to s 1 of the Theft Act 1968. Olive and Quentin plead not guilty but Peter pleaded guilty at the plea and directions hearing.

Olive has previous convictions for theft, drugs offences and some offences of violence. However, a number of those offences were committed when she was as young as 13 years of age. She is now 30. She has been in employment and out of trouble for the past 10 years. She says that only she and Quentin could have accessed the office in which the computer equipment was stored. She was approached by Peter, who had asked her to help him take some of the computer parts and that when she refused he said that he would approach Quentin.

In your brief you have a copy of Peter's interview in which he alleges that both Olive and Quentin helped him to steal the computer parts. Peter has three convictions for theft in the last two years. Quentin gave a no comment interview but his defence statement alleges that he took no part in the theft.

At the plea and directions hearing the prosecution indicated its intention to make an application to adduce evidence of Olive's previous convictions.

Advise Olive as to the likelihood of the prosecution succeeding in its application and, if the application is unsuccessful, the possibility of her bad character otherwise being adduced at trial.

Session 7: hearsay

This session is the first of two that concern the challenging concept of hearsay evidence. As you will see from the reading for this session it is strongly recommended that you adopt a methodical approach to hearsay and its exceptions. In line with that approach the focus of this class is to determine whether or not the evidence might be classed as hearsay, original or real evidence. It is **not** about whether or not the evidence will be admissible at trial. That issue will be dealt with in session 8.

Preparation

Read **Chapter 10**. You may find reference to *Blackstone's Criminal Practice*, *Archbold* and *Blackstone's Civil Practice* of use. This session addresses some revision points in addition to hearsay evidence. You will need to refresh your memory on previous consistent statements (**Chapter 6**) and character evidence (**Chapters 7, 8** and **9**).

Objectives

By the end of this session, you should be able to:

(a) Distinguish between hearsay evidence and original evidence.

(b) Distinguish between hearsay evidence and real evidence.

(c) Apply the above distinctions in analysing a case study.

(d) Identify when evidence may be hearsay by implication.

(e) Identify when evidence may be original evidence under the doctrine of 'negative hearsay'.

Question 1

Peter is charged with indecently assaulting Ruth, a 14-year-old girl. The prosecution case is that Peter fondled her breast while standing at a bus stop. Peter instructs his solicitor as follows:

I was standing at a bus stop awaiting a number 17 bus at about 9 pm one evening. There were two other people there. One of them was an elderly lady. The other was a teenage girl. I heard the elderly lady shout out 'This child tried to pick my pocket. Catch the thief!' The girl looked as though she was about to escape so I caught hold of her from behind. She cried out 'Stop touching me up, you dirty old man'.

Unfortunately while all this was happening, a bus arrived and for some reason the old lady got onto it. She was probably frightened.

The police arrived soon afterwards and I told them what had happened. However Ruth said 'He grabbed me to fondle me. He is making this all up. There was no woman here'.

The police arrested me and charged me with indecent assault. I was released on bail. On my way home I noticed a wallet lying on the pavement at the bus stop. In it there was some cash and a photograph. The photograph had 'Dear Mum I thought you might like this photo of you and our Jack' written on the back and is dated '12/8/01'. It shows an old lady and a young boy at the seaside. The picture resembled the woman I had seen.

It is true that I have a previous conviction for indecent exposure arising out of some high spirited antics after a football match. Unfortunately I have also recently lost my job. Some female colleagues said that I had made indecent suggestions to them while working there.

(a) Discuss the evidential matters raised in these instructions (there are some revision points here).

(b) What are the likely consequences (if any) if Peter chooses to give evidence of his version of events?

(c) Of the matters raised in the statement above, which could be proved by Ruth if she gave evidence for the prosecution?

Question 2

The following is an extract from a prosecution witness statement concerning a fight between Tina and Carol, who have been charged with affray. The statement was made by a prosecution witness, Vicky.

I know both Tina and Carol and have done for some time. We work together in a shoe shop. A couple of years ago, Carol started going out with a bloke named Danny.

Last May I met Carol to do some shopping before we went to work. Carol said she had had a row with Danny and that he had stormed out. He had come back the following day and they had made up.

As we were having lunch someone who appeared to be a friend of Carol's came and spoke to us. She said that she had been in the local pub the previous evening and she had seen Danny who was with a girl with dark hair about 5' 5'' tall. They had been chatting away in a very friendly manner. At one stage she had overheard the girl say, 'She won't find out if you don't tell her. We can go to my Dad's allotment'. Danny and the girl had then left. Danny had his arm around the girl.

I instantly knew that the girl was Tina. She is about 5' 5'', has black hair and her dad owns an allotment. I was due to work the afternoon shift. Carol must have known too because she said 'That bitch, Tina. She is going to get it for this!'

When we got to work, Tina was there and Carol went straight over to her and said 'What do you think you are doing you dirty slag?' Tina replied 'What are you talking about?' Carol said 'You know. If you don't leave Danny alone, I will sort you out'. Carol and I then turned away to go and get changed for work. As we were leaving I heard Tina say 'Don't you think you can mess with me. Don't blame me if you can't keep your bloke.' I then heard a loud smacking sound and Carol fell over. Some of the other staff members and customers came over to hold Tina back. The manager and I took Carol upstairs. The manager gave her first aid while I went to call an ambulance.

Identify any hearsay statements or original evidence in the statement, and give reasons.

Question 3: hearsay evidence of identifications

Robert Smith is being prosecuted for causing death by reckless driving and for failing to stop after an accident in Kensington, London. Robert says that on the night in question he was driving his car (registration number NFC 62P) in Bristol. Immediately after the accident, Mary saw a car disappearing and memorised the number, which she quickly wrote down with lipstick on the back of her hand. Later she showed her hand to a police officer, who wrote down the number in his notebook. Mary cannot remember the number any more but says she wrote the correct number on her hand, while the police officer says that he saw 'NFC 62P' written on her hand. May Mary's statement to the police officer be admitted?

Session 8: hearsay exceptions

This session builds on the previous one by finishing the analysis that is necessary whenever evidence is alleged to be hearsay. The questions in the previous sessions concerned whether the evidence was hearsay whereas in this session, the concern is whether the evidence is *admissible* despite being hearsay.

Preparation

Read **Chapter 11**.

Objectives

This session is designed to ensure that you can:

(a) demonstrate a sound understanding of the principles underlying the exceptions to the hearsay rule (other than the special provision relating to confessions which will be dealt with in **Chapter 12** of this Manual);

(b) identify the circumstances in which the exceptions may apply;

(c) identify which preliminary facts need to be proved and (when applicable) which procedural steps need to be taken; and

(d) raise and/or counter an objection to hearsay evidence.

Question 1

Arthur is charged with murdering his ex-lover Edith in June 1996. He has pleaded not guilty and has given notice of an alibi defence.

Advise the prosecution whether it will be possible to adduce the following items of evidence:

(i) Testimony by a police officer that as he was approaching the place where Edith was found dying from stab wounds he heard an unknown person shout, Hello Arthur, where are you rushing off to?'.

(ii) Testimony by a doctor that just before she died Edith said, 'I have a terrible pain in my back where Arthur stabbed me'.

(iii) Testimony by Oliver, a friend of Edith's, that several days before she was stabbed she told him that Arthur had threatened to kill her.

Question 2

Alvin is being prosecuted for causing death by dangerous driving. The prosecution case is that Alvin ran down Bert as he was crossing the road at a pelican crossing when the lights were on red to traffic. The prosecution alleges that Alvin was driving at excessive speed for the conditions (it was dark and raining), and that he failed to keep a proper look out.

Alvin's case is that he was driving at a reasonable speed and that Bert ran across the road in front of his car when the crossing lights were on green to traffic.

PC Trotter was on the scene soon after the accident and spoke to Charles who stated that the crossing lights were on red to traffic at the time of the accident and that another witness had told him (Charles) that Alvin was driving too fast. PC Trotter noted down Charles' statement. Unfortunately shortly after the accident Charles died of natural causes. It has not been possible to locate any other eyewitnesses.

Although he did not sustain any head injury Bert died in hospital several days after the accident. Whilst he was being taken to the hospital he told an ambulanceman that he had waited until the crossing lights changed in his favour before starting to walk across the road.

The prosecution proposes to call PC Trotter to prove the note and to call the ambulanceman to give evidence. Leaving aside any tactical considerations, prepare an objection to this evidence and, in each case, prepare an argument to support the overruling of the objection.

Session 9: confessions and illegally obtained evidence

The last of the exceptions to the rule against hearsay that will be covered is confession evidence. However this exception is subject to so many rules and restrictions that it merits consideration in its own right. Furthermore, confession evidence is also commonly rendered inadmissible under the broad discretion to exclude evidence on the grounds of fairness (s 78 of the Police and Criminal Evidence Act 1984) so this topic can usefully be considered at this point.

Preparation

Read **Chapter 12**. You should have access to *Blackstone's Criminal Practice* or *Archbold* while preparing for this session. You should be prepared to use these sources to conduct further research on these subjects and on the questions.

Objectives

By the end of this session, you should be able to:

(a) demonstrate a sound understanding of the principles governing the admissibility of confession evidence;

(b) apply those principles to specific factual situations;

(c) describe the procedural requirements when the admissibility of a confession is challenged;

(d) demonstrate a sound understanding of the basis upon which a judge might exclude evidence *other than* confessions on the ground that it is illegally or improperly obtained (including any procedural requirements); and

(e) raise and/or counter an objection to the admissibility of confessions and illegally or improperly obtained evidence.

Question 1

DI Alladice was investigating a gang believed to be involved in smuggling cannabis from Holland to the UK. Without obtaining proper authorisation, he planted a Listening device in a flat rented by Ben, a suspected member of the gang. The listening device recorded a conversation between Ben and an unknown visitor, in which Ben said, 'There's a load of cannabis coming into Harwich tomorrow. Charlie is using the Volvo for the job. He'll drop the stuff off with Dave in Birmingham.' The following day Alladice kept watch at the ferry terminal at Harwich. He arrested Charlie as Charlie disembarked in a Volvo car from the ferry. The car was searched, and bags of cannabis were found concealed in the doors. There were no fingerprints on the bags.

At the police station Charlie was cautioned. He asked for his solicitor, Mr Grabbit, but was told that he could not see him, as any delay would lead to the alerting of Charlie's accomplices. He was then interviewed for several hours by Alladice. Charlie denied all knowledge of the cannabis or the gang. At one stage he said to Alladice, 'I've never had anything to do with drugs in my life.' At last Alladice said, 'Look son, do yourself some good. We've bugged your house and we've got cast iron evidence against you. You're going to go down, but just remember that the judge will make it easier for you if you co-operate.' Charlie then said, 'All right. I agreed to bring the cannabis in and take it to Dave, but only because Ben threatened to beat me up if I didn't.' Charlie's flat was later searched, and three ecstasy tablets were found in a bathroom cabinet.

Charlie agreed to deliver the Volvo to Dave under covert police surveillance. Alladice replaced the cannabis in the car and also hid a revolver under the back seat, instructing Charlie to tell Dave that Ben thought he would need it to protect the consignment of cannabis. Charlie followed these instructions. Alladice arrested Dave after Dave had taken possession of the cannabis and the revolver.

Ben, Charlie and Dave have been charged with conspiracy to evade the prohibition on the importation of a controlled drug, and Dave is also charged with unlawful possession of a firearm.

Advise the prosecution on the evidential matters arising.

Question 2

Steve and Dave were arrested on suspicion of committing a burglary. Steve and Dave were taken to the local police station where they were interviewed separately.

Steve claims that he asked to see his solicitor but that his request was refused on the ground that waiting for his solicitor would cause unreasonable delay to the investigation. He further claims that it was only when the police told him that Dave had confessed (and had implicated Steve) that he decided to confess. Steve then made a taped statement in which he admitted his part in the burglary but claimed that it had been master-minded by Dave. In fact Dave had not made any confession and he maintained his silence throughout his interrogation. Both men now stand jointly charged with burglary. During the trial a *voir dire* is held to determine the admissibility of Steve's confession.

On the assumption that the trial judge accepts in substance Steve's account of what took place during his interrogation, prepare an argument to support the exclusion of his confession (be prepared to make oral argument in class):

(a) under Police and Criminal Evidence Act 1984. s 76(2), and

(b) under Police and Criminal Evidence Act 1984, s 78.

Session 10: lies and silence

This session concerns the evidential value of evasiveness by parties. Such behaviour can be circumstantial evidence of the guilt (or liability) of the party in question. Most of the rules are criminal although such evidence is admissible in civil cases at common law.

Preparation

Read **Chapter 13**. You will also need to have access to either *Blackstone's Criminal Practice*, *JSB Guidelines or Archbold* to conduct further research during your reading.

Objectives

By the conclusion of this session you should be able:

(a) to identify the general circumstances in which a party's evasive conduct can be put before the tribunal of fact as supporting an inference which is adverse to the party in question;

(b) as regards lies by the accused, to recognise which factors affect the probative value of the lies as circumstantial evidence against the accused and say how a judge should direct the jury on such evidence;

(c) as regards silence by the accused to recognise which factors affect:

    (i) the probative value of such evidence, and

    (ii) the public policy aspects of permitting such evidence to support any inference against the accused and state when silence can support an adverse inference against the accused;

(d) as regards a refusal to give body samples, to recognise that there are rules about the taking of such samples and state the evidential effect of a refusal without good cause to consent to the taking of such samples.

Question 1

Joe was charged jointly with Imran with theft contrary to s 1 of the Theft Act 1968. At trial Joe and Imran ran cut-throat defences, each man suggesting that the other had committed the theft.

When first questioned by the police about the offence, Joe had claimed that he had been ill on the date of the theft and had spent the day in bed at home. However, when the police proved this to be false, he claimed that he had spent the day fishing. He said that he had lied to the police originally because he had told his employer he was ill so that he could spend the day fishing. When Joe gave evidence he gave details of his alibi which he had not previously mentioned to the police. His testimony was evasive and contradictory and Imran's counsel was allowed to cross-examine him about his previous conviction for theft.

When interviewed by police Imran made no comment to all questions put to him. At trial he declined to give evidence.

How should the judge deal with these issues when summing up the case to the jury?

Question 2

Alan, aged 30, is charged with having unlawful sexual intercourse with Martha, aged 15. The alleged offence came to light in the following circumstances. Martha's mother found Martha in bed with a naked man who promptly leapt out of the bedroom window and ran off. Martha's mother then telephoned the police. About two minutes after the phone call a police officer arrested Alan (who was naked) approximately a half mile away from Martha's house. The officer then asked Alan to explain his presence in that place in that condition (naked). Alan refused to do this. Meanwhile Martha told her mother that she had met Alan at a fun fair two weeks previously and that he had been the man in bed with her when her mother came into her bedroom. When interviewed by the police Alan claimed that, although he knew Martha, he had not met her at the fun fair. The police have now discovered that Martha's friend Louise can confirm that Martha met Alan at the fun fair.

Consider what, if any, inferences of guilt may be drawn from Alan's conduct.

Session 11: identification

There are various ways in which it can be proved that the person committing an offence was the accused. This session concentrates on the rules and procedures relating to proof of identification by eye witnesses. It will be seen that in criminal cases there are various rules to ensure that identification evidence is used responsibly by tribunals of fact.

Preparation

Read **Chapter 14**. You will find that this session draws upon some of the other areas you have considered earlier in the course.

Objectives

This session is designed to ensure that, as regards corroboration, you are able to:

    (a) identify when corroboration or a corroboration warning or a general warning to exercise caution is required/desirable;

    (b) demonstrate an understanding of the legal definition of corroboration.

This session is designed to ensure that, as regards identification, you are able to:

    (a) identify the circumstances in which a judge might withdraw from the jury a case based on identification evidence;

    (b) identify the circumstances in which a *Turnbull* warning should be given and display knowledge of the usual terms and content of such a warning;

    (c) display a sound understanding of the basis upon which a judge might exclude an item of identification evidence (including an understanding of the key points of the Code of Practice on Identification issued pursuant to PACE 1984, s 66); and

    (d) raise and/or counter an objection to identification evidence (including knowledge of appropriate procedural matters).

Question 1

Mark was tried and convicted on a charge of unlawfully wounding John (contrary to Offences against the Person Act 1861, s 20). The assault occurred when a fight broke out outside a public house at closing time. John was the only eye-witness called by the prosecution. He was a regular at the pub but his assailant was a stranger. Mark's defence throughout the trial was mistaken identity. John had identified Mark as his assailant shortly after the alleged assault when the police took him to the local bus station where Mark was waiting. He was suffering from a hand injury which was consistent with his being involved in a fight but he explained that he had fallen over when he was running to try to catch a bus. He claimed that he had spent the evening at the cinema but he could not remember the name of the film or the price he had paid to get in.

The police officers who took John to the bus station gave evidence at trial of his confident identification of Mark on that occasion. However, John (whose general confidence had deteriorated since the assault), when called as a witness, was unable to state whom he identified at the bus station. Mark had requested an identity parade but the police decided it was impracticable to hold one.

In summing up on the identification issue the trial judge said:

> The defendant says that John has identified the wrong man. He says that he went to the cinema on that evening and that he had nothing to do with the events outside the pub. Of course, you should look with great care at the circumstances in which the identification was made. John did not know the defendant and he only had a short time to observe his attacker. Against this it is only fair to point out that only a short time had elapsed between the attack and John's clear identification of the defendant at the bus station. We have also heard how the defendant could remember nothing about the film he had just seen and there was the injury to his hand. Of course in the end, members of the jury, it is a matter for you to decide having heard the evidence of the prosecution witnesses and the defendant.

    (a) Draft an argument in support of an appeal against conviction on behalf of Mark. You should also prepare a counter-argument on behalf of the prosecution.

    (b) If Mark had admitted being present at the time of the assault but claimed that he had nonetheless been misidentified by John, would it have been unnecessary for the judge to give any *Turnbull* warning?

Question 2

Ed Hammond is charged with burglary and theft of a car. You represent him at trial. The prosecution case is that 10 Leaways Road was burgled at 9 pm on 5 June in which he stole various valuable items. The car was stolen for use in the robbery.

The prosecution intends to call Tina Thurlow, whose statement says she saw a man getting into a red Ford Escort with an M registration number plate at about 9.20 pm just outside the house. He was about 100 yards from her. She was standing across the street, which has good lighting. She saw the man emerge from the alley between 10 and 12 Leaways Road, quickly walk about 20 yards and get into a car and drive off (away from her). She subsequently identified Ed in an identification parade. The man she saw was wearing a black jacket, dark trousers and 'some sort of woolly hat', which she said she thought was odd because it was warm.

Tina has produced a plan of the street. The marked with an X indicates where she was standing.

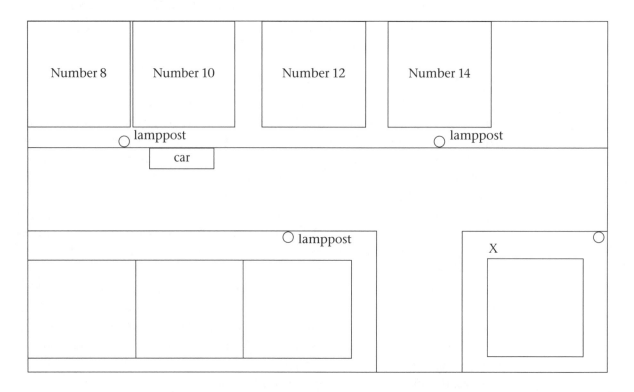

Tina's friend, Sally Sanderson, also witnessed the incident but was not invited to participate in an indentification procedure. However, she is able to identify the man as she recognised him having seen him around the neighbourhood. The prosecution intend to call Sally to give evidence and identify Ed Hammond at trial.

A police witness, PC Steel, says in his statement that he found the Ford Escort car stored in a garage belonging to a man named Alan Grayson. He searched the car and found a balaclava helmet in the footwell of the front passenger seat.

There is also a statement from Alan Grayson which states that he was phoned by Ed at about 10.30 on 5 June, who asked him to look after a car for him. He then arrived at about 11 pm and left the Ford Escort in Alan's garage. Before doing so he took a heavy bag out of the front passenger seat. Ed was wearing a black leather jacket and dark jeans at the time. Alan was not asked to identify Ed at a parade.

The car had been stolen a day previously. The unused material that the prosecution have revealed to the defence shows that Alan Grayson has numerous previous convictions including three for burglary (all of domestic premises) that all took place in the last eight years. It also reveals that the police attended Alan Grayson's property as a result of an anonymous phone call from a phone box, the message being 'If you're looking for the car what done a house in Leaways Road you should go to Grayson's place'.

Ed's instructions to you are that he was nowhere near 10 Leaways Road that night. He does know the road. It is generally well lit but there are lots of cars parked on it even late at night. There are also a lot of trees along the road. Your instructing solicitors instructs you that they have visited the street and think that the alleyway would have been in darkness and that there are two trees between the lamp posts on either side of number 10, one just outside number 10 and slightly to the right. Ed knows Alan. Alan does occasionally stores cars for Ed (who buys and sells cars). He also says that Alan does occasionally commit burglary.

(a) Prepare the cross-examination of Tina Thurlow concerning her identification evidence.

(b) What applications might you expect to make in respect of Tina, Sally and Alan's evidence?

Session 12: opinion, judgments, privilege and public policy

This session covers a few areas. Unlike many of the subjects covered in this Manual, these subjects apply as much in civil cases as in criminal cases.

Preparation

Read **Chapters 15** to **17**. You may find reference to *Blackstone's Civil Practice*, *Blackstone's Criminal Practice* and *Archbold* useful during your reading, especially where procedural issues are concerned. The **Civil Litigation Manual** may also prove useful.

Objectives

By the end of this session you should be able to:

(a) demonstrate a sound understanding of the principles underlying the general exclusionary rule in relation to evidence of opinion;

(b) identify when opinion evidence will be admissible despite the rule of exclusion;

(c) apply the special rules concerning the evidence of expert witnesses;

(d) demonstrate a sound understanding of the rule restricting the admissibility of proof of judgments in previous cases and its exceptions;

(e) demonstrate a sound understanding of the privilege against self-incrimination and legal professional privilege;

(f) demonstrate a sound understanding of the principle of public policy exclusion.

Question 1

You are appearing for Susan, who is suing Thomas for negligence, alleging that a bad fall she had had on a slippery patch on the floor of Thomas's shop, when she was 18 weeks pregnant, had caused a miscarriage five days later.

(a) After Susan has given evidence, you call her mother, Una, an experienced midwife, who testifies that Susan was extremely shocked and that her symptoms started the next day. Thomas's counsel objects (i) when Una states that such a heavy fall as Susan's bruises suggest must have caused the miscarriage and (ii) when she offers in support of her view an article in a medical journal, which she produces. How would you try to meet these objections?

(b) A shop assistant, Vera, who saw Susan fall, says it was a bad fall as the floor was so slippery and the fall must have affected the course of the pregnancy. Counsel for the defendant objects. Do you consider that you can successfully counter the objection?

(c) The defence calls Dr White, an obstetrician, who testifies that Susan's miscarriage would probably have occurred spontaneously, and that his experience totally contradicts the views expressed in the article cited by Una. He adds that Susan's evidence is quite untrustworthy because her grief at the loss of her baby must have affected her veracity and the reliability of her memory. Do you consider that you can successfully object to the admission of any of Dr White's evidence?

Question 2

Brian Laird and his brother Charles, together with three other men, have been jointly charged with conspiracy to obtain property by deception. It is alleged that all five men (who lived in the same block of flats) had obtained money from elderly house occupiers for whom they pretended to do substantial roofing work. Charles Laird will plead guilty but Brian and all the other co-accused will plead not guilty. Defence counsel are aware that at the trial, the prosecution, in reliance upon s 74(1) and (2) of the Police and Criminal Evidence Act 1984, will seek to admit in evidence Charles's conviction (of the offence charged).

(a) You are counsel for Brian Laird — what action will you take before the prosecution opens its case?

Make a note of the submissions you will make to the trial judge on the question whether this evidence should be excluded.

(b) You are counsel for the prosecution — make a note of the submissions you will make to the trial judge opposing the exclusion of this evidence.

Question 3

Consider the correspondence in the following cases:

(a) *Ackroyd v Smithson*: This correspondence concerns damages in respect of a motor car accident. The solicitors for the claimant are Adolphus & Ellis, those for the defendant are Carrington & Payne.

From Carrington & Payne
To Adolphus & Ellis

29 September 2005

Dear Sirs

Ackroyd v Smithson

Further to our telephone conversation of 28th September, we confirm that we have instructions to make an offer on behalf of our client of £17,500 by way of compensation for the physican injuries suffered by your client without prejudice as to liability. We also confirm that the special damages have been agreed at £377.25.

We look forward to hearing whether this offer is acceptable to your client.

Yours faithfully,

Carrington & Payne

Adolphus & Ellis
3 October 2005

From Carrington & Payne

Dear Sirs,

Re Ackroyd v Smithson

We thank you for your letter of 29th September.

We regret that we do not have instructions to accept the offer of £17,500. However, an offer of £20,000 would be favourably considered by our client.

Yours faithfully

Adolphus v Ellis

From Carrington & Payne
To Adolphus & Ellis

10 October 2005

Dear Sirs

Ackroyd v Smithson

We thank you for your letter of 3 October.

Our client is not prepared to offer more than £17,500.

Yours faithfully

Carrington & Payne

No further correspondence is sent and the matter proceeds to trial.

    (i)   Is any part of this correspondence admissible in relation to the issue of liability?

    (ii)   Is any part of this correspondence admissible if the claimant seeks at trial to adduce evidence to show that the special damages to which he is entitled are in excess of £377.25?

(b) *Ball v Herbert*. This is a case which involves a claim by the claimant for damages for trespass to land and for an injunction restraining the defendant from parking motor cars on a field, the property of the claimant, known as Muddock's Square. The solicitors for the claimant are Carrington & Kirwan, those for the defendant are Ellis & Blackburn.

From Carrington & Kirwan
To Ellis & Blackburn

2nd October 2005

Dear Sirs,

Re Ball v Herbert: Without Prejudice

We have now taken our client's instructions. The terms upon which he would be prepared to discontinue proceedings against you are as follows:

1. Mr Herbert will forthwith remove any motor vehicles remaining parked on Muddock's Square and will thereafter refrain completely from parking motor vehicles of any description there.

2. Mr Herbert will pay to Mr Ball £25 by way of damages for trespass to land.

3. Mr Herbert will pay to Mr Ball £50 as a contribution towards Mr Ball's costs in this matter.

Are these terms acceptable to your client?

Yours faithfully,

Carrington v Kirwan

From Ellis & Blackburn
To Carrington & Kirwan

10 October 2005

Dear Sirs,

RE BALL: **WITHOUT PREJUDICE**

We have taken our client's instructions and confirm that the terms set out in your letter of 2nd October, for which we thank you, are acceptable to him.

We understand that no cars or other vehicles remain parked in Muddock's Square.

We enclose herewith our cheque for £75 in respect of damages and costs.

Yours faithfully,

Ellis & Blackburn

Some months have passed without incident but now Mr Herbert has started to park vehicles once more on Muddock's Square.

Question 4

You are instructed for Country Farmers Ltd against Mammon Properties Ltd. Mammon Properties Ltd is the owner and occupier of land on which is constructed an irrigation work which, on 3 December 2004 flooded your lay client's farm. On 7 December 2004, your instructing solicitors intimated to Mammon Properties that their client would look to that company for compensation. Consider and advise whether the following documents can be obtained on discovery from the defendant:

(a) A report from surveyors, dated 1 January 2002, to Mammon Properties, advising that the irrigation work was prone to flooding and should be altered.

Doesn't concern pending litigation

Not larger client r/ship

Lit not dominant purpose

(b) A report from surveyors, dated 3 September 1990, to the Ministry of Defence tenants of the land before Mammon Properties. This report passed to Mammon Properties with the land.

(c) Advice from Mammon Properties Ltd's salaried solicitor as to the best method of evading liability for the nuisance by means of a tortious conspiracy with another of the company's servants.

Agreement to pervert the course of justice?

INDEX